ENCYCLOPAEDIA OF INDIAN GOVERNMENT: PROGRAMMES AND POLICIES

ENCYCLOPAEDIA
OF
INDIAN GOVERNMENT:
PROGRAMMES AND POLICIES

Vol. 19

Trade and Commerce

Edited by

Satish Tiwari

ANMOL PUBLICATIONS PVT. LTD.

NEW DELHI - 110 002 (INDIA)

ANMOL PUBLICATIONS PVT. LTD.
4374/4B, Ansari Road, Daryaganj
New Delhi - 110 002

Encyclopaedia of Indian Government: Programmes and Policies

First Edition, 2000
ISBN 81-261-0515-1 (Set)

PRINTED IN INDIA

Published by J.L. Kumar for Anmol Publications Pvt. Ltd., New Delhi - 110 002 and Printed at Mehra Offset Press, Delhi.

Contents

Preface

Encyclopaedia of Indian Government: Programmes and Policies contains authoritative information on about fifty departmental policies and their future developmental programmes.

Organised to be completed in 40 volumes, this gigantic work covers Agriculture; Atomic Energy; Chemicals and Fertilizers; Coal; Commerce; Communication; Culture; Defence; Education; Environment and Forests; External Affairs; Finance; Food & Consumer Affairs; Food Processing Industries; Health and Family Welfare; Home Affairs and Internal Security; Human Resources; Industry; Information and Broadcasting; Labour, Law, Justice and Company Affairs; Non-conventional Energy Sources; Ocean Development; Parliamentary Affairs; Personnel, Public Grievances and Pensions; Petroleum and Natural Gas; Planning and Programme Implementation; Planning and Statistics; Posts and Telegraphs; Power; Rural Development; Science and Technology; Social Justice and Empowerment; Space; States Affairs; Steel; Steel and Mines; Sugar and Edible Oils; Surface Transport; Textiles; Tourism; Urban Development; Water Resources; Women and Child development etc.

Based on the information derived from authoritative sources, this work contains authentic facts and figures. I am deeply beholden to all the scholars whose writings are cited or substantially made use of in the present work. I am also thankful to Anmol Publications Pvt. Ltd. for undertaking publication of this encyclopaedia. I am solely responsible for shortcomings in presentation of matter.

Encyclopaedic in nature, this will prove a dependable reference work for scholars and academics besides those appearing for different competitive examinations.

—**Satish Tiwari**

1

Introduction

The Ministry of Commerce is responsible for the national external trade and related matters such as export promotion measures, commercial relations with other countries, development and regulation of export oriented industries and commodities and state trading. The Ministry formulates and implements policies in the sphere of foreign trade, reflected in the Export-Import Policy of the country. In addition, the Ministry also undertakes promotional measures to promote exports.

Trade Policy liberalisation began in June, 1991 and focussed on liberalisation, openness, transparency and globalisation. The reform package focussed on outward orientation in the economy from import regulating -activity to export promotion activity, moving away from quantitative restrictions to tariff protection and improving competitiveness of the Indian industry to meet global market requirements.

Trade policy reforms have provided an export friendly environment conducive to accelerated export performance with simplified procedures. Trade reforms revised continuously since 1991 have helped to strengthen the export production base, remove procedural irritants, facilitate input availability besides focusing on quality and technological upgradation and improve competitive edge.

After a setback during 1991-92 when exports declined by 1.5% in dollar terms, revival of exports started during 199293. Indian exports registered an average growth of 20% in dollar terms during 1993-94 to 1995-96. However, this high growth could not be sustained and export growth rate declined to 5.3% in 1996-97 and to 1.5% during 1997-98. During April-December, 1998-99 India's exports were valued at US $ 24,287 million registering a decline of 2.88% in dollar terms, though in Rupee terms the growth was positive and high at 11.69%.

Export performance 15 influenced infer-alia by international market conditions, supportive infrastructure, credit availability and policy framework. Export promotion measures are continuously being taken through changes in policies and procedures for providing an export friendly environment, involvement of States in export promotion and also consultation with trade and industry.

Highlights of trade performance

India's exports during April-December, 1998-99 was US $ 24,286.87 million compared to the export level of US $ 25,006.48 million for the corresponding period of the previous year registering a decline of 2.88%.

Imports during April-December, 1998-99 was US $ 31,582.86 million, which is 7.12% higher than the level of US $ 29,484.77 million during the same period last year.

The trade deficit for April-December, 1998-99 was US $ 7,295.99 million, which is higher than the deficit at US $ 4,478.29 million during the same period lost year.

The principal commodities in respect of which India's exports registered an increase during April-November, 199899 in dollar terms are tea, guargum meals, rice, castor oil, coal, gems and jewellery, readymade garments, natural silk textiles, coir and coir manufactures, handicrafts, processed fruits and juices, floriculture products and mica.

Sectoral performance

Plantations

Export of plantations crops increased from Rs.2,464 crores in April-March, 1996-97 to Rs. 3,127 crore 5 in 1997-98 registering a growth of 26.9%. During April-November, 1998-99 these exports increased by 3 1.7% in Rupee terms. Export of coffee increased by 15.3% during the period while that of tea increased by 49.7%.

Agriculture and allied products

The export growth of this category of products has been negative at 4.9% decreasing from Rs. 16,317 crores in April-March, 1996-97 to Rs. 15,519 crores in April-March, 199798. During April-November, 1998-99, however, exports of agri and allied products increased from Rs.9,017 crores to Rs. 10,243 crores mainly due to improved export of rice.

The items registering significant increase during this period include: rice, spices, quargum meal, castor oil, shellac, processed fruits and juices, miscellaneous processed items, floriculture products. Items recording decrease in exports are pulses, tobacco, sesame and niger seed, groundnut, oil meals, sugar and molasses, meat and meat products and spirit and beverages.

Marine products

The exports of marine products were valued at Rs. 4,313 crores in April-March, 1997-98 which is 7.6% higher than the exports valued at Rs.4,008 crores during April-March, 1996-97. During April-November, 1998 these exports declined to Rs.2,973 crores from Rs.2, 990 crores achieved during April-November, 1997, showing a fall of 0.6%.

Ores and minerals

This category of items registered a decline of 4.8% during April-March, 1997-98 when exports fell from Rs. 4,162 crores achieved in 1996-97 to Rs.3,962 crores. During April-November, 1998, there was a decline of 10.8%, when exports declined from the level Rs. 2,447 crores in April November 1997 to Rs.2, 184 crores in April-November, 1998.

Leather and leather manufactures

The export of Leather and Leather Manufactures also registered a decline of 4% during 1997-98, the value of exports declining from Rs.5, 701 crores to Rs.5, 462 crores over the period. However, during April-November, 1998, these exports have registered a significant increase of 15.6%, increasing from a level of Rs.3, 694 crores in April-November, 1997 to Rs. 4, 270 crores in April-November, 1998. Most of the leather products are exported to developed countries like Germany, France, USA, UK, Italy, Japan and CIS countries.

Gems and jewellery

Gems and Jewellery sector is a major item of India's exports. This sector registered a 12.7% export growth during 199798, when exports increased from Rs. 16,872 crores in April-March, 1996-97 to Rs. 19,014 crores in April-March, 199798. During the current year, a higher growth of 33.5% has been witnessed, when exports increased to R5. 15,583 crores during April-November, 1998 from a level of Rs.] 1,673 crores achieved during the corresponding period last year.

Chemicals and allied products

Chemicals and allied products registered a positive growth in export of 14.7% during April-March, 1997-98 when its value increased to Rs. 16,702 crores from a level of Rs. 14,564 crores achieved during the corresponding period of the previous year. In April-November, 1998, export growth was only 2.3%, the value of exports increasing from Rs. 10,563 crores in April-November, 1997 to Rs. 10,809 crores in April-November, 1998.

Engineering goods

The export of engineering goods registered an 8.3% growth during the year 1997-98. The value of such exports increased to Rs.15, 585 crores as compared to Rs.14, 396 crores achieved during 1996-97. However, disappointingly, during April-November, 1998, engineering exports witnessed a decline of 3%, its value falling to Rs.9,835 crores from Rs. 10, 140 crores during April-November, 1997.

Textiles

Textiles, a major item in India's export basket witnessed a positive growth of 7.2% last year, when its export value increased from Rs.28,561 crores achieved during 1996-97 to Rs. 30,618 crores during 1997-98. Textile exports registered a positive growth of 7.9% during April-November, 1998 over the corresponding period of the previous year, with its value increasing from Rs.20,073 crores to Rs.21,653 crores. Readymade garments [24.9%], natural silk textiles [30.70%] and coir and coir manufactures [33.6%] were the high growth items under this category during April- November, 1998.

Handicrafts

Export of Handicrafts registered a high growth during both, last year and the current year. During 1997-98, it's export value increased to Rs. 1,927 crores from Rs. 1,689 crores during 1996-97, registering a growth of 14. 1 %. During the period April-November, 1998, the growth rate has been 36.3%, with its value increasing to Rs. 1,865 crores from a level of Rs. 1,368 crores achieved during April-November, 1997.

Export promotion measures

India's external trade sector was further liberalised with changes introduced in the new EXIM Policy 1997-2002. Interest rate on export credit was lowered from 12% to 9% w.e.f. 6th August, 1998. Bank guarantee has been dispensed with for certain categories of exports and reduction in transaction cost have been effected through decentralisation and simplification of procedures etc. DEPB rates for more than 2000 items have been announced and DEPB has been made a more effective instrument of export promotion by seeking to neturalise the incidence of special customs duty of 5%. License- on production programmes basis has been allowed with flexibility like change in description of export product. Advance licenses with actual user condition have been allowed based on positive value addition. Advance licenses to Export House/Trading House/Star Trading House/Super Star Trading House are now being issued automatically. The licensing functions have been decentralised extensively. Manufacturing units with an annual manufacturing turnover of Rs.300 crores and Rs. 1000 crores have been made eligible for Star Trading House status and Super Star Trading House status respectively. Hotel and Tourism sector have been made eligible for Export House/Trading House/Star Trading House/Super Star Trading House status.

The benefits of Export Promotion Capital Goods Scheme has been extended to a number of sub sectors of engineering sector. During the year 1998-99, standard input output norms for additional 156 items of the engineering products were fixed. Import of computer drawn designs/drawings has been made freely importable. A special task force to consider the credit needs of the seafood industries has been constituted. An interest subsidy scheme to subsidize a portion of interest on the bank loans obtained for the purpose of modernization/upgradation of the marine product industry has been introduced. Value addition norms and wastage norms for gold/platinum/silver jewellery and articles have been rationalised. Value addition will be' calculated after the deduction of the agency commission. Personal carriage of samples of jewellery upto US $ 1,00,000 has been allowed for export promotion tours. Personal carriage by foreign buyers from EPZs/EOUs has also been allowed. Legal Undertaking Limits for different categories of exporters, have been modified. Under the loan scheme, period for fulfillment of export obligation has been increased from 90 days to 120 days.

The Export Processing Zones [EPZs] set up as enclaves, separated from the Domestic Tariff Area by fiscal barriers, are intended to provide an internationally competitive duty free environment for export production at low cost. This enables the products of EPZs to be competitive, both quality-wise and price-wise in the international market. The seven EPZs at Kandla [Gujarat], Santa Cruz Mumbai, Falta [West Bengal], Noida (U.P), Cochin Kerala, Chennai (Tamilnadu) and Vishakhapatnam [Andhra Pradesh]. This contributed Rs. 4,817.3 crores during 1997-98 and Rs. .3,350.5 crores during the period of April-December, 1998.

These Zones provide basic infrastructure such as developed land for construction of factory sheds, standard design factory buildings providing ready-built sheds, roads, power, water supply and drainage. In addition, Customs clearances are arranged within the Zones at no extra charge. Provision is made for locating banking/post office facilities and offices of clearing agents in the Service Centre located in each of the Zones. EOUs on the other hand have to put up their own infrastructure. As on 3 1.10.1998, 527 units are in operation in Export Processing Zones.

The Policy and Procedures applicable to EPZ units are under constant review and improvements are brought out from time to time. The special package for revival of exports announced by the Commerce Minister in the Parliament on 5.8.1998 include the following specific measures for boosting export from EOU/EPZ units:

— Enhancement of corporate tax holiday from 5 to 10 years.

— Sub-contracting facility in the domestic tariff area.

— Export through courier.

The Export Oriented Units (EOUs) Scheme introduced in the year 1981 is complementary to the EPZ scheme. It adopts the same production regime but offers a wide option in locations with reference to factors like source of raw materials, ports of export, hinterland facilities, availability of technical skills, existence of an industrial base and the need for a larger area of land for the project. 1, 186 units a re at present in operation under the EOU Scheme.

Exports from EOU units, which stood at Rs.8,728.7 crores in 1996-97, rose to Rs.9,697 crores in 1997-98 representing a growth of over 11 %. During 1998-99 April-December), these exports were estimated as Rs.9,000 crores.

A centrally sponsored "Export Promotion Industrial Park" (FPIP) Scheme was introduced in 1993-94 with a view to involving the State Governments in the creation of infrastructure facilities for export oriented production. The Scheme provides that 75% of the capital expenditure incurred towards creation of.such facilities, ordinarily limited to Rs. 10 crores in each case, will be met from a central grant to the State Governments. In addition, a maintenance grant equivalent to 2% of export turnover of each unit established therein will also be made available to State Government for a period of 5 years from the date of commercial production of that unit. Central Government have so far approved 19 proposals for establishment of EPIPs in the States of Punjab, Haryana, Himachal Pradesh, Gujarat, Bihar, Jammu & Kashmir, Assam, Madhya Pradesh, West Bengal, Orissa, Meghalaya and Manipur. While the EPIP in Rajasthan at Sitapura (Distt. Jaipur) has been completed, the Park at Suraipur, Distt. Gautombudh Nagar Uttar Pradesh Hoodi, Distt., Bangalore (Karnataka) and Ambarnath, Distt. Thane (Maharashtra) are nearing completion. Other Parks are at various stages of implementation.

The Export House/Trading House/Star Trading House/Super Star Trading House Scheme allows the registered exporters certain additional benefits available to them under this policy. They are 6 Super Star Trading Houses, 37 Star Trading House, 366 Trading House and 1804 Export Houses in the country at present.

The Government has initiated several measures to encourage project exports. Bonds by RBI and FCGC have already been issued to our project exporters against their outstanding receivables from Iraq for their projects covered under the Inter. Governmental Deferred Payment Agreements. Market Development Assistance for reimbursement of 50% of cost of preparation and submission of bids, and for opening overseas offices and consultancy firms, continues to be provided

A "Consultancy Trust Fund" of US $ 0.5 million with the World Bank was set up to be utilised for engaging Indian consultants for World Bank financed projects. Further, in addition to suppliers' credit and buyers' credit, Exim Bank has also been extending lines of credit to various developing countries with a view to encouraging India's project exports

Steering group for research

Following the decisions taken in a meeting of the heads of their associates of select research institutes held in February, 1998 a number of 'lead' researchers were identified to continue and/or to undertake studies on the issues related to WTO. These include market access schedules and export potential in Services Agriculture and Industry sectors. The new issues to be taken for research are Trade and Environment, Electronic Commerce, Technical Barriers, etc.

The Research Programme Committee, a Standing Committee of the Ministry of Commerce, is looking after identification of research, sponsoring of such studies and considering proposals made by individual scholars.

Commercial relations

The 66 Commercial Offices functioning in Indian Missions/Post abroad provide the institutional framework and promote India's trade and economic exchanges abroad. In the wake of fast changing and expanding international scenario efforts are being undertaken in-this Ministry in consultation with the Ministry of External Affairs for restructuring and streamlining the Indian Commercial Wings with a view to equip them to discharge their functions efficiently and effectively.

In recognition of the fact that our geographical proximity, cultural affinity and economic synergies can be used to our mutual benefit, the seven countries of South Asia viz. Nepal, Pakistan, Bangladesh, Sri Lanka, Bhutan and Maldives have organised themselves into an association called the South Asian Association for Regional Cooperation (SAARC). The major achievement has been the operationalisation of the Agreement for Preferential Trading Arrangement (SAPTA). The ultimate objective, as mandated by the leaders of the SAARC member-countries is to establish a Free Trade Area in the region (SAFTA) by 2001 AD.

In consonance with India's 'Look East Policy' and after having become a Full Dialogue Partner with ASEAN, ASEAN India Working Group on Trade and Investment (ASEAN-India WGTI) has been established under the aegis of the ASEAN India Joint Cooperation Committee. This is likely to give a major thrust to cooperation with ASEAN in trade and investment . The first meeting of ASEAN-India WGTI was held on 25-26 May, 1998 in New Delhi. The meeting acknowledged the need for enhancing the interaction between the private sectors on both sides and evolving ways for information exchange by involving private sectors. The ASEAN also recognised the need for enhancing cooperation in core infrastructure projects in India.

Direction of trade

USA is India's largest trading partner accounting for nearly 20% of our exports and 10% of the imports, The share of non-traditional items and value added products have been increasing in our exports to USA while our imports comprised mostly of engineering products and chemical products.

SAARC Preferential Trading Arrangement (SAPTA)

SAPTA establishes a framework for the exchange of trade concessions among the member countries of SAARC. The final objective of the negotiations under SAPTA is the achievement of the South Asian Free Trade Area SAFTA. The, 10th SAARC Summit at Colombo took a concrete decision to transform this goal into a reality. Taking initiatives in this direction, India signed a Free Trade Agreement with Sri Lanka on December 28, 1998.

Directorate general of anti-dumping & allied duties

The Directorate General of Anti-Dumping and Allied

Duties was created on 13th April, 1998. The Directorate would investigate allegations of dumping and subsidies and recommend suitable duties to the Central Government. The number of cases recommended for imposition of Anti-dumping duties by the Designated Authority in the Ministry of Commerce increased to a total of 23 products by 30.9.1998. Recommendations have been made for imposition of provisional duties in another 3 cases, while 13 cases are under investigation including 6 review cases as on 30.9.1998 for imposition of duties or otherwise.

Quality control and pre-shipment inspection

The Export Inspection Council of India was set up by the Government of India under Section 3 of the Export (Quality Control and Inspection) Act, 1963, to provide for sound development of export trade through quality control and preshipment inspection.

During 1998-99, (upto 30.11.1998) export consignments worth Rs. 2,742.25 crores were certified under Consignment-Wise-Inspection (CWI) and In-Process Quality Control (IPQC) System.

ElAs have also been authorised by the Government of India to issue certificates of origin under the Generalised System Preferences (GSP) for export to Japan, EEC, USA, Canada and East European Countries. During 1998-99 (upto 30.11.1998) 3,33,904 GSP certificates have been issued by ElAs.

Government has 'also recognised 21 private inspection agencies and 8 other Government inspection agencies to supplement the work of quality certification under the Act. 15 Agencies have also been recognised for fumigation of export cargo. As a result of these efforts, there has been a significant improvement in the quality of goods exported from India.

Institutional support

The India Trade Promotion Organisation (ITPO) has a key role to play in promotion of trade by organising fairs and exhibitions in India and abroad and other related activities. It has been decided to support and encourage the activities of setting up of permanent trade fairs/ Exhibition Complexes at different important locations viz. Mumbai, Calcutta, Chennai, Bangalore and Hyderabad etc. with active involvement of the local/State Governments and trade and industry circles. ITPO also organises export development programmes for selected products in identified markets to improve awareness of India's export capability and generate business enquiries and export orders.

The Indian Institute of Packaging has been set up jointly by the Ministry of Commerce, Government of India and the packing and allied industries in the country. The year 199798 was marked by concerted efforts to popularise packaging as a subject, promotion of packaging consciousness, propagation of scientific knowledge and upgradation/modernisation of packing industry. In the process, eco-friendly packaging has gained considerable importance

The Indian Institute of Foreign Trade (IIFT) which was established in 1963 has been rendering useful service in the areas of human resource development for international business, trade and economics through need based training programmes, seminars and workshops, supported by continuous research on a variety of topical subjects in the field of foreign trade and international business.

National Centre for Trade Information (NCTI) has been designated as TRAINS (Trade Analysis and Information System) focal point in India for obtaining data from UNCTAD.

MMTC/STC/PEC

MMTC

The annual turnover of MMTC was Rs. 2,2 10 crores during April-October, 1998-99 compared to Rs.2,053 crores during the corresponding period of 1997-98. MMTCs turnover of canalised export during the current year (April-October, 1998) is lower in value terms at Rs. 510 crores as against Rs. 541 crores in the corresponding period of last year. Depressed market conditions of the Japanese steel industry coupled with the financial crisis in South Korea as well as similar situation for world ferro chrome industry are some of the factors inhibiting the performance in the current year.

The non-canalised exports decreased to Rs 53 crores during April-October of the current year as against Rs. 164 crores in the corresponding period of last year.

STC

The total turnover of STC during April-October, 1998-99 is estimated at Rs. 1,552 crores which is higher than the turnover of Rs. 1,282 crores achieved during the corresponding period of previous year.

The export turnover of the Corporation during April-October, 1998-99 amounted to Rs. 153 crores. During the year, exports of coffee, cashew, consumer goods and textiles showed improvement.

PEC

The Projects and Equipment Corporation of India Ltd. achieved total turnover of Rs. 44.8 crores during the year 1997-98 as compared to Rs.235.87 crores, for the year 1996-97. The turnover comprises of export sales worth Rs.224 crores and import sales of Rs. 225 crores. During 1997-98, PEC has continued to diversify in the non-engineering products.

The DGCI&S compile trade data and monitor the performance. It has made significant progress in the of Foreign Trade Statistics. Special efforts we reduce time log in the collection and dissemination of trade data and to release aggregate data on exports a within a very short time. A new value added p "India Trades" was launched and presentations made to trade and industry.

Official language and SC/ST Cell

To fulfill the statutory obligation and to implement various aspects of the Official Language Policy of the Government the Ministry has a Hindi Division. The Division continued its efforts to accelerate the implementation of various factes of the official language policy of the Government.

As per the policy of the Government of India, an SC/ST cell is functioning in the Ministry of Commerce under the charge of a liaison Officer.

2

Organisational Set-up

Department of commerce

The Department of Commerce in the Ministry of Commerce is headed by the Secretary. This Department is responsible for the country's external trade and all matters connected with it, such as commercial relations with other countries, state trading, export promotional measures and the development and regulation of certain export oriented industries and commodities. The Department of Commerce formulates policies in the sphere of foreign trade, in particular, the import and export policy of the country. The Secretary is assisted in the discharge of duties by a Special Secretary, Additional Secretaries and a number of other senior officers functioning as Divisional Heads.

Functional divisions

The Department of Commerce consists of eight principal functional Divisions as mentioned below:

— Administrative and General Division;

— Finance Division;

— Economic Division;

— Trade Policy Division;

— Foreign Trade Territorial Divisions;

— Export Products Divisions;

— Export Industries Division; and

— Export Services Division

— Autonomous bodies

— Commodity Boards

There are five statutory Commodity Boards under the Department of Commerce. These Boards are responsible for production, development and export of tea, coffee, rubber, spices and tobacco respectively. The names and addresses of these Commodity Boards are given in Appendix - II.

Export inspection council, New Delhi

The Export Inspection Council, a statutory body is responsible for the enforcement of quality control and compulsory preshipment inspection of various exportable commodities covered under the Export (Quality Control & Inspection) Act, 1963.

Indian institute of foreign trade, New Delhi

The Indian Institute of Foreign Trade, registered under the Societies Registration Act, is engaged in the following activities:

— Training of personnel in modern techniques of international trade;

— Organisation of research in problems of foreign trade;

— Organisation of marketing research, area surveys, commodity surveys, market surveys; and

— Dissemination of information arising from its activities relating to research and market studies.

Indian institute of packaging, Mumbai

The Indian Institute of Packaging is registered under the

Societies Registration Act. The main aims of the Institute are to undertake research of raw materials for the packaging industry, to organise training programmes on packaging technology, to stimulate consciousness of the need for good packaging etc.

Indian diamond institute

The Indian Diamond Institute IDI is registered under the Societies Registration Act. It was established in 1978 with the objective of strengthening and improving the availability of trained manpower for the gems & jewellery industry by conducting various Diploma/Post Graduate Diploma level courses in this field. Some of the important courses conducted by IDI for the gems & jewellery sector include:

— Diploma in Diamond processing;

— Diploma in Diamond Trade Management:

— Diploma in Gemology;

— PG Diploma in Diamond Technology; (A PG Diploma in Gemology; and

— PG Diploma in Jewellery Designing, Manufacturing & Appraising.

The institute is financed by the Government of India, Ministry of Commerce and the Gem and Jewellery Export Promotion Council. The Institute has been striving to augment its resources by undertaking consultancy and job works.

Export promotion councils

There ore at present eleven Export Promotion Councils under the administrative control of the Ministry of Commerce. These Councils are registered as non-profit organisations under the Companies Act/Societies Registration Act. The Export Promotion Councils perform both advisory and executive functions. These Councils are also the registering authorities under the Export and Import Policy, 1997-2002. These Councils have been assigned the role and functions under the said policy,

Federation of Indian export organisations, New Delhi

The Federation of Indian Export Organisations (FIEO), New Delhi, is an apex body of various export promotion organisations and institutions. It also functions as a primary servicing agency to provide integrated assistance to Government recognised Export Houses/Trading Houses and as a Central Co-ordinating Agency in respect of Export Promotional efforts in the field of consultancy services in the Country. FIEO is also involved in dissemination of awareness on modern information technology through internet & home page of EDI and El Commerce among the exporters.

Indian council of arbitration, New Delhi

The Indian Council of Arbitration, set up under the Registration Act, promotes arbitration as a means a commercial disputes and popularises the concept arbitration among the traders, particularly those engaged national trade. The Council, a non-profit service a organisation is a grantee institution of this Ministry. The main objectives of the Council are to promote the knowledge an arbitration and provide arbitration facilities for amicable and quick settlement of commercial disputes with a view maintaining the smooth flow of trade, particularly, our export trade on a sustained and enduring basis.

Marine products export development authority, Cochin

The Marine Products Export Development Authority, a statutory body, is responsible for development of the marine products industry with special reference to exports.

Agricultural and processed food products export development authority, New Delhi

The Agricultural and Processed Food Products Development Authority is also a statutory body which as the focal point for agricultural exports, particularly the marketing of processed foods in value added form

Public sector undertakings:

The following trading/service corporations are fun under the administrative control of the Ministry of Commerce

— State Trading Corporation of India Ltd. (Cashew Corporation of India Ltd. being merged as a Division in STC);

— Minerals and Metal Trading Corporation of India Ltd. and its subsidiary Mica Trading Corporation of India Ltd;

— Projects and Equipment Corporation of India Ltd,;

— Spices Trading Corporation of India Ltd.;

— Export Credit Guarantee Corporation of India Ltd.,

— India Trade Promotion Organisation.

Advisory bodies

Board of Trade

There is a Board of Trade under the Ministry of Commerce which was constituted on May 5, 1989 to provide a forum for ensuring continuous dialogue with trade and industry in respect of major developments in the field of International Trade. The Chairman of the Board of Trade is the Commerce Minister and Director General of Foreign Trade is the Member Secretary. The membership of the Board includes the Governor, Reserve Bank of India; Secretaries of the Ministries of Commerce, Industry, Finance and Textiles; Special Secretary, Prime Minister's Office; President of FICCI, ASSOCHAM, CII,

FIEO, FASSI; representatives of Trade and Industry and a few specialists.

Export promotion board

There is an Export Promotion Board under the Chairmanship of the Cabinet Secretary to provide policy and infrastructural support through greater coordination among concerned Ministries for boosting the growth of exports. Secretary, Ministry of Commerce; Secretary, Ministry of Finance; Secretary, Department of Revenue; Secretary, Department of Industrial Policy & Promotion; Secretary, Ministry of Textiles; Secretary, Department of Agriculture & Cooperation; Secretary, Ministry of Civil Aviation; Secretary, Ministry of Surface Transport; Secretary, Deptt. of Electronics are members of the Board. This Board was constituted on 1st August, 1997.

The representations received from various Chambers of Commerce, organisations and exporters are examined by the various divisions at the Ministry and emerging issues are taken up with the concerned Ministries. In case of disagreement, the matter is placed before the Export Promotion Board for final decision The Export Promotion Board has taken important decisions regarding the electronics, textile and garments, plastic and gems & jewellery, telecommunications, infrastructure, toys and engineering exports sectors etc.

Attached and subordinate offices

This Directorate is headed by the Director General of Foreign Trade and is responsible for execution of the Exim Policy announced by the Government from time to time for promotion of exports. In addition, work relating to issue of licences and monitoring of export obligations etc. is also looked after by this organisation. The Directorate has its Headquarters at New Delhi and there are 31 regional offices in the field formations. The subordinate offices are located at the following stations:

Ahmedabad	Amritsar	Bangalore
Baroda	Bhopal	Calcutta
Chandigarh	Chennai	Coimbatore
Cuttack	Ernakulam	Guwahati
Hyderabad	Jaipur	Kanpur
Ludhiana	Maduri	Moradabad
Mumbai	CLA, New Delhi	Panipat
Panaji	Patna	Pondicherry
Pune	Rajkot	Shillong
Srinagar (Functioning at Jammu)	Surat	Varanasi
	Visakhapatnam	

Directorate general of anti-dumping & allied duties:

Directorate General of Anti-Dumping & Allied Duties was inaugrated in April 1998 with a view to institutionalizing the system of investigation of dumping as well as subsidies cases. The Directorate is headed by an Additional Secretary in the Ministry of Commerce and also has a Facilitation Cell which advises all interested parties of information required, procedures and time frames involved besides assisting the industry with regard to technical issues.

Directorate general of commercial intelligence and statistics, Calcutta:

This Directorate is the primary Government agency for the collection, compilation and the publication of the foreign, inland and ancillary trade statistics and dissemination of various types of commercial information. The Directorate brings out a number of publications, particularly on trade statistics, which are utilised in framing economic policies, formulating trade agreements with foreign countries and monitoring these agreements. These publications are also used by the trading public and research scholars. It maintains a commercial library which is used by the exporters, importers, research scholars and others.

Export processing zones:

Ministry of Commerce has set up seven Export Processing Zones at various location as below:

— Kandla Free Trade Zone, Gandhidham;

— Santacruz Electronics Export Processing Zone, Mumbai;

— Falta Export Processing Zone, Falta (West Bengal);

— Madras Export Processing Zone, Chennai;

— Cochin Export Processing Zone, Cochin;

— NOIDA Export Processing Zone, NOIDA, (U.P); and

— Visakhapatnam Export Processing Zone, Visakhapatnam

The above Export Processing Zones are responsible for the administration of Free Trade Zones and in setting up 100% Export-Oriented multi-product industrial units.

Office of the custodian of enemy property, Mumbai and branch office at Calcutta:

The office of the Custodian of Enemy Property is located at Mumbai with a Branch office at Calcutta. As the enemy propries are scattered through out the country, the work relating to their day to day preservation and management is being done through 'the Revenue Departments of various State Governments. Both movable and immovable properties of Pakistani nationals are vested in the Custodian.

The enemy properties in India are being administered by the Custodian of Enemy Property for India, Mumbai, who is entrusted with the custody, management and administration of enemy properties arising out of Indo-Pak Conflicts of 1965 and 1971 in accordance with the provisions of the Enemy Property Act, 1968, as amended in 1977. Enemy Properties comprising both movable and immovable properties of Pakistani nationals were valued at Rs.23.21 crores in 1971 and are vested with the Custodian in the form of:

— land, buildings etc. scattered throughout the country

— securities, shares, debentures etc,

— bank balances; and

— provident fund balances and gratuity.

A cash balance of Rs.46,08,562/- is held in the personal ledger account with Central Bank of India by the Office of Custodian of Enemy Property, Mumbai. As per the provision of the Enemy Property Act, 1968, the CEP is authorised to levy fees equal to two percent on the gross income from the properties vested in the CEP. Till November, 1998 an amount of Rs. 1,34,17,446/-- in the form of levied fees has been credited to Government of India under Section 17 of the Enemy Property Act, 1968.

The Custodian is also entrusted with the work relating to settlement of claims for ex-gratia payment to Indian nationals & companies whose properties were seized by Pakistan during and after the Indo-Pakistan conflict of September, 1965. Under the Ex-Gratia Scheme, 25% of the verified value of the claim, subject to a maximum of Rs.25 lakhs is paid to those Indians Nationals/Companies who had lost their properties in Pakistan during the Indo-Pak Conflict of 1965.

Pay and accounts office.

The Pay and Accounts Office common to both-the Ministry of Commerce and Ministry of Textiles, is responsible for the payment of claims, accounting of transactions and other related matters through the four Departmental Pay & Accounts Offices in Delhi, two in Mumbai, two in Calcutta and one in Chennai. These Departmental. Pay and Account Offices are controlled by the Principal Accounts Office at Delhi with the Chief Controller of Accounts as the Head of the Department of the Accounts Wing.

3

India's Foreign Trade

During the current year, as per provisional estimates exports amounted to Rs. 1,0 1, 850 crores in April to December, 1998 as compared to Rs. 91,192 crores during April to December, 1997 registering a growth of 11 .7% in Rupee terms. Imports have registered an increase of 23.2% in Rupee terms having increased to Rs. 1,32,447 crores in April to December, 1998 from Rs. 1,07,523 crores during April to December, 1997. The trade deficit during April to December, 1998 is estimated at Rs. 30,597 crores. The details of foreign trade in Rupee terms and dollar terms for the period April -December, 1998-99 are given in Table I(a) and I(b) respectively

Trends in India's foreign trade

Commodity trends

During April to November, 1998, the principal commodities which registered significant increase in exports over the corresponding period of the previous year include tea, guargum meal, rice, leather manufactures excluding footwear, castor oil, coal, gems and jewellery readymade garments, natural silk textiles, coir and coir manufactures, floriculture products, mica and handicrafts. Commodities that witnessed the moderate growth up to 15% include spices, coffee, tobacco (manufactured), cashew, fruits and vegetables, processed fruits and juices, miscellaneous processed items, shellac, basic chemicals, pharmaceuticals & cosmetics, man-made textiles, madeups, etc., plastic and linoleum, rubber glass and other products, jute manufactures and sports goods.

Exports of other cereals, pulses, unmanufactured tobacco, sesame and niger seeds. ground nut, oil meal, marine products, sugar and molasses, meat and meat products, spirit and beverage, iron ore, processed minerals, other ores and minerals, leather footwear, residual chemicals and allied products, engineering goods, electronic goods, project goods, cotton yarn, fabrics, made-ups, etc., wool and woollen manufactures, carpets, cotton raw including waste and petroleum products declined during the period.

Export commodities

The export performance of principal commodities/groups during 1997-98 and April to November, 1998 are reviewed in the following paragraphs.

Plantations

Plantation crops primarily comprise tea and coffee. Exports of plantation crops increased during April to November, 1998 by 3 1.8% in Rupee terms. Exports of coffee increased by 15.3% during this period to Rs. 1, 225 crores from 1 062 crores during the same period of last year. Exports of tea increased from Rs. 971 crores during April to November, 1997 to Rs. 1,454 crores during April to November, 1998 registering a positive growth of 49.7%.

Agriculture and allied products

This group comprises a wide variety of agricultural products covering cereals, pulses, tobacco, spices, nuts and seeds, oilmeals, guargum meals, castor oil, shellac, sugar and molasses, processed food, meat and meat products, etc. Share of items under the group

'Agricultural and allied products' was 11.3% in total exports during April to November, 1998. During April to November, 1998, the exports of agricultural and allied products showed an increase of 13.8% from Rs. 8,919 crores during April to November, 1997 to Rs. 10, 151 crores during April to November, 1998.

The items which have indicated significant increase during this period as compared to the correspondence period of the previous year are rice, guargum meal, castor oil, miscellaneous processed items. The items which recorded decline in exports are other cereals, tobacco (unmanufactured), sesame and niger seed, ground nut, oil meals, sugar and molasses, meat and meat products, spirit and beverage & pulses.

Marine products

The exports of marine products are Rs. 2,973 crores during April to November, 1998 as against Rs. 2,990 crores during April to November, 1997 indicating a decrease of 0.6 %.

Ores and minerals

Ores and minerals are traditional items of exports. Their contribution in the total exports is about 2.4% during April to November, 1998. The main item of exports in this category ore iron ore, manganese ore, chrome ore, aluminum, mica and coal. During April to November, 1998, the exports of ores & minerals were valued at Rs. 2,183 crores registering a decline of 10.8% over the same period of last year. Iron ore and processed minerals have shown a sharp decline during this period and mica has registered a positive growth of 20% during April to November, 1998 as compared to the corresponding period of the previous year.

Leather and leather manufactures

The value of exports of leather and leather manufactures

has increased from Rs. 3,694 crores during April to November, 1997 to Rs. 4,269 crores during April to November, 1998, showing a positive growth of 15.6%. Leather goods account for 4. 1 % share in the total exports during April to November, 1998, 'Footwear' exports constitutes 29% of the exports of leather and leather products and exports of leather footwear declined by 19.4% during April to November, 1998 as compared with corresponding period of the previous year. Most of the leather products are exported to developed countries like Germany, France, U.S.A., U.K., Italy, Japan including CIS countries.

Gems and jewellery

Gems and Jewellery is a major export item accounting for about 17.3% of our total exports during April to November, 1998. The exports of gems and jewellery during April to November, 1998 amounted to Rs. 15,583 crores as compared to Rs. 17,672 crores; during the corresponding period of lost year, showing a positive growth rate of 33.5%.

Chemicals and allied products

Chemicals and allied products have a positive growth of 1.8% during April to November, 1998 over the same period of the previous year in Rupee terms. The plastic and linoleum products in the international market are very competitive and stringent environmental and public health controls need to be maintained. Quality Control in terms of packaging standards, delivery schedules require further attention if a continuous increase is to be maintained.

Engineering goods

The share of engineering goods contributes 10.9% to the total exports during April to November, 1998. The main items under the group 'Engineering Goods' are ferro alloys, nonferrous metals, machine tools, machinery and instruments, transport equipment, residual engineering items, etc. Exports off engineering goods amounted to Rs. 9,834 crores during April cc to November, 1998 as against Rs. 10,139 crores during April to November, 1997 showing a decline of 3%. Other products covered under this group are capital goods and consumer durables.

Electronic and computer software

In the event of technological advancement and breakthrough in industrial infrastructure, electronics and computer software industry has been identified as a thrust sector for export. The non-traditional sector consists broadly of consumer electronics, control instrumentation and industrial electronics, computer systems, communication equipment, components and software.

Electronic goods excluding software has a share of 1.4% of India's exports during the period April to November, 1998. Exports of electronic goods excluding software during April to November, 1998 are valued at Rs. 1,220 crores as compared to Rs. 1,886 crores during April to November, 1997 showing a decline of 35.3%.

Textiles

Textiles including carpets, handicrafts and raw cotton are the major traditional export items accounting for nearly 27.7% share in the total exports during April to November, 1998. Total value of Indian textiles exports during April to November, 1998 increased to Rs. 21,588 crores, from Rs. 20,039 crores during the corresponding period of previous year showing a positive growth rate of 7.7%. Coir & coir manufactures recorded the highest growth in this sector of about 33.3% followed by natural silk textiles (30.1%) and readymade garments (24.9%) and lute manufactures (8.3%) and man-made textile made-ups, etc. (0.7%). Cotton yarn fabrics made-ups, etc. and wool and woollen manufactures recorded negative growths of 10% and 12.3 % respectively. Handicrafts recorded a positive growth of 36.3% during April to November, 1998 compared to the corresponding period of the previous year. Raw cotton including waste and carpets showed a decline of 78.6% and 8.3% respectively during April to November, 1998.

Handicrafts

The main items of exports of handicrafts are various types of handmade carpets and works of art, such as metal artware, textiles (hand printed), woodwares and zari goods. Exports of carpets declined during April to November, 1998 to Rs. 1,278 crores from Rs. 1,394 crores, during April to November, 1997 indicating a negative growth of 8.3%. During April to November, 1998, handicrafts exports increased to Rs. 1 865 crores from Rs. 1 368 crores during the corresponding period of the lost year showing a positive growth of 36.3%.

Trends in India's imports

The trends in India's principal imports during the year 1997-98 as compared to 1996-97, total imports amounted to Rs. 1, 17,948 crores during April to November, 1998 as compared to Rs. 92,989 crores during the same period of the lost year showing a positive growth rate of 26.8% in Rupee terms.

Imports of items under bulk category comprising inter-alia, POL, fertilizers, edible oils, sugar, newsprint, paper board and manufactures etc. registered an increase to Rs. 37,708 crores during April to November, 1998 from Rs. 36,61 3 crores during April to November, 1997 reflecting a growth of 3%. The imports of sugar increased to Rs. 768 crores during April to November, 1998 showing an increase of 477.4%. The other major items which witnessed an increase are wheat (62%), edible oil (132.8%), fertilizer crude (46.8%), sulphur and unroasted pyrites (12.7%) and paper board and manufactures (9.6%).

Items which recorded negative growth are cereal preparations (68.9%), fertilizer manufactured (12.6%), petroleum crude and products (1 0.9%), newsprint (6.5%), metalliferous ores and scrap (4%), nonferrous metals (9.4%), pulp and waste paper (10%), iron and steel (0.5%) and crude rubber including synthetic (2.3%).

In other items, major growth has been recorded during April to November, 1998 over the same period of the last year in such items as project goods, (99%), nonmetal mineral manufactures (59.4%), other raw minerals (38.3%), pearls, precious, semiprecious stones (24.4%), dyeing and tanning materials (20.8%), raw hides and skins (27.3%), textiles yarn, fabric, etc. (31.5%), professional instruments, etc. (32.8%), electronic goods including computer software (23.6%) and leather (9%).

High decline has been recorded in such items as pulses (62.7%), wool raw (24.8%), transport equipment (17.3%), silk raw (2.9%) and synthetic and regenerated fibres (28.8%) and fruits & nuts (1 6.2%).

Imports of major products are reviewed in the following paragraphs.

Crude oil and petroleum products

The imports of petroleum crude and products during April to November, 1998 were valued at Rs. 18,431 crores as against Rs. 20,686 crores during April to November, 1997 showing a decline of 10.9%.

Fertilizers

The total imports of fertilizers have declined from Rs. 3,281 crores during April to November, 1997 to Rs. 3,163 crores during April to November, 1998 showing a negative growth of (3.6%). This includes crude fertilizers as well as those of manufactured and sulphur and unroasted pyrites.

Pearls, precious and semiprecious stones

The diamond industry in the country draws heavily on imports of rough precious and semiprecious stones. Imports of pearls and precious and semiprecious stones amounted to Rs. 9,813 crores during April to November, 1998 as compared to Rs. 7,8[illegible]0 crores during the corresponding period of the previous year showing a positive growth of 24.4%.

Capital goods

Imports of Capital goods largely represented by machinery, including transport equipments, project goods and professional instruments have shown an increase from Rs. 16,449 crores during April to November, 1997 to Rs. 20,404 crores during April to November, 1998 showing a growth of 24%. In this category, project goods have shown a higher growth of (99%) followed by professional instruments (32.8%), electrical machinery (47.7%) and non-electrical machinery (3.7%) during April to November, 1998 as compared to corresponding period of the previous year. Decline has been registered in transport equipment (1 7.3%).

Chemicals and chemical materials

Organic and inorganic chemical materials and medicinal & pharmaceuticals products constituted the major components of imports under this category. The imports of organic and inorganic chemicals rose to Rs. 7,660 crores during April to November, 1998 from Rs. 6,982 crores during April to November, 1997, showing a positive growth of 9.7%.

The medicinal and pharmaceutical products have registered an increase from Rs. 898 crores during April to November, 1997 to Rs. 986 crores during the period April to November, 1998 showing a positive growth of 9.8%.

Direction of India's foreign trade

The trends of India's export to and import from different regions are given in table-IV & V respectively. The exports figures in respect of regions and sub-regions shown in table IV do not include export of crude oil from Mumbai high and petroleum products to respective countries of consignment, but these are included in the aggregate of exports. During April to November, 1998, Asia and Oceania accounted for 34.8% of India's total exports, West Europe (27.4%), America (25.6%), Africa (6.4%) and East Europe (3.1 %).

During April to November, 1998, Asia and Oceania was the largest supplier of goods and accounted for 45.2% of our imports, followed by West Europe 32.2%, America 11 %, Africa 8.5% and East Europe 2%.

A comparison of respective shares of sources of our imports reveals that regions whose shares have increased during April to November, 1998 compared to the corresponding period of the last year include West Europe from 29.9% to 32.2%, Africa from 7% to 8.5%. Imports have declined from Asia and Oceania i.e. from 48. 1 % to 45.2%, America 11.9% to 11% and East Europe from 3. 1 % to 2%.

4

Quality Control and Preshipment Inspection

Export inspection council

The Export Inspection Council of India was set up by the Government of India under Section 3 of the Export (Quality Control and Inspection) Act, 1963 to provide for the sound development of export trade on a long term basis by ensuring export worthiness of the exported items through pre-shipment inspection and quality control.

The Export Inspection Council (EIC) consists of a Chairman appointed by the Central Government, 4 ex-office members and 15 members nominated by the Central Government. The EIC is an apex body for controlling the activities relating to the quality control and pre-shipment inspection of all the notified commodities meant for export. The main functions of the EIC as assigned in the Act are:

(i) To advise the Central Government regarding measures for enforcement of quality control and inspection in relation to commodities intended for export and to draw up programmes therefore; and

(ii) To make arrangement for pre-shipment inspection of notified commodities for export.

With a view to inculcating quality consciousness among the manufacturers and to motivate them to upgrade their infrastructure for effective quality assurance and to adopt quality discipline, the EIC has been engaged in quality development and export promotional activities by way of arranging training on various quality control techniques to the personnel at all levels in the industry. In addition, the EIC also arranged seminars and workshops designed to educate the manufacturers and exporters on maintaining quality including packaging.

During the year under report upto 30th November, 1998, 15 seminars/workshops/training programmes in different disciplines were arranged by the Export Inspection Agencies at different places to propagate the adoption of quality assurance systems. Extension services were also rendered to the Fish Processing Units for meeting the requirements of European Union (EU) directives.

The Export (Quality Control and Inspection) Act, 1963, inter-alia, empowers the Government to notify the commodities which shall be subjected to quality control or inspection or both prior to export; specify the type of quality control or inspection which will be applied to such commodities; establish, adopt or recognise one or more standard specifications for a notified commodity and prohibit the export of notified commodities unless it is accompanied by a certificate of export worthiness from the Inspection Agencies recognised under the Act.

997 items under product group heads of engineering, chemicals and allied products, food and agricultural products, jute and jute products, coir and coir products, footwear and footwear components, cashew, fish and fishery products, egg products, etc., are under the aegis of Compulsory Quality Control Inspection System.

With a view to create higher demand for Indian goods in the overseas markets, the quality standards of the notified items are periodically reviewed and upgraded. The Export Inspection Council continues to strive for upgradation of Quality System in the individual manufacturing units. A notification on fish and fishery products which makes the Indian fishery industry primarily responsible to ensure that fishery products meet the health requirements as per the international standards and European Union (EU) standards was published on 21.8.1995.

All the fish and fishery product processing units 'who wish to export to EU countries are being inspected by an inter-departmental Inspection Panel and Supervisory Audit Team and only such units which fully conform to the prescribed standards of food hygiene and safety are being authorised by EIC to export to EU. As on 30th November, 1998, 7 Freezer Vessels and 49 Processing Units could qualify for -approval to process fishery products for export to the EU.

Machinery for quality control and inspection

Export inspection agencies

For carrying out pre-shipment inspection of export goods, the Government of India under Section 7 of the Act, has established five Export Inspection Agencies (EIAs) one each with headquarters at Mumbai, Calcutta, Cochin, Delhi and Chennai, which function under the administrative and technical control of the Export Inspection Council. In addition to their headquarter offices, the EIAs have a network of 47 sub-offices located at important industrial centres and ports of shipment. These EIAs have facilities of well equipped laboratories for testing quality of export products.

During the year 1997-98, export Consignment Worth Rs. 6,453.11 crores were certified under Consignment-Wise Inspection (CWI) and In-Process

Quality Control (IPQC) System together. During the year 1998-99 (upto 30.11.1998), the value of consignment certified come to Rs. 2,742.25 crores.

At the request of the overseas buyers or the Indian exporters, the EIAs also undertake inspection for such items which have not so for been brought under the ambit of the Act. EIAs have also been authorised by the Government of India to issue certificates of origin under the Generalised System of Preferences (GSP) for exports to Japan, EEC USA, Canada and East European countries. During the year 1997-98, 4,78,273 GSP certificates were issued by the EIAs. During the year 1998-99 (upto 30.11.1998) 3,33,904 GSP certificates have so far been issued by EIAs.

Other recognised agencies

Government has also recognised 21 private inspection agencies and 8 Government inspection agencies to supplement the work of quality certification under the Act. 15 Agencies have also been recognised for fumigation of export cargo.

Quality standards for exports

For all commodities notified under the Act, quality standards are prescribed by the Government. While in a large of cases, buyers' requirements have been recognised as the basis for inspection, for products involving safety or health hazards, minimum standards have been prescribed Commodities for which minimum standards have been prescribed are not allowed for export unless the minimum standards are achieved, though the foreign buyer may be inclined to accept the product below such minimum standards, In a phased manner, minimum standards are being prescribed for the rest of the notified products. The standards are reviewed periodically in consultation with trade and industry and also keeping in view the latest technological changes and the changing needs of the overseas buyers. Efforts are being made to explore the possibilities of partnership with reputed international inspection agencies for both process and product inspection as well as training programmes for upgrading the standards in Indian Marine Processing Units.

Systems of inspection

Three systems of inspection are in operation at present. They are:-

(i) Consignment-Wise Inspection (CWI)

(ii) In-Process Quality Control (IPQC)

(iii) Self-Certification (SC)

(i) Consignment-Wise Inspection

Under Consignment-Wise Inspection, each export consignment of a notified commodity is inspected and tested by the recognised inspection agencies by selecting consignments on the basis of statistical sampling plan to check conformity of the products with the prescribed standards.

In-Process Quality Control (IPQC)

The IPQC system lays emphasis on the responsibility of manufacturers and processors in ensuring consistent quality of the product during each stage of production by exercising various levels of controls namely. raw material and bough-out components control, process control, product control, meteorological control and packaging control, The certificates of inspection in favour of the products for which a unit has been approved under the scheme are issued either by the EIAs or by the Unit itself. These units are then kept under surveillance by the EIAs and random spot checks of the consignments are carried out by the EIAs from time to time.

Self - Certification (SC)

Under the Self-Certification system, the manufacturing units fulfilling the stringent norms prescribed for design and development, raw material and bought-out components, process control, product control, metrological control, packaging, after sales service, quality audit, house keeping and maintenance etc. are authorised by the Central Government to issue certificates of inspection for their own products themselves. There were 7 units approved under Self-Certification as on 31.3.1998. During 1998-99 (upto 30.11 1998) there are 9 units under Self-Certification Scheme.

With a view to enable the manufacturers and exporters to take up the responsibility of ensuring quality of export products rather than depending upon EIA inspection, the machinery for enforcement of Compulsory Quality Control and Pre-shipment inspection has been simplified and streamlined by taking the following steps:

(i) Super Star Trading Houses, Star Trading Houses, Trading Houses and Export Houses have been exempted in respect of all commodities notified under the Export (Quality Control and Inspection) Act, 1963.

(ii) Units approved by the EIAs under the system of IPQC have been authorised to issue statutory certificates by themselves instead of the EIAs.

(iii) Industrial units set up in EPZ, FTZ and 100% EOUs have been exempted from the purview of compulsory Pre-shipment inspection.

(iv) Items notified under the Export (Quality Control and inspection) Act, 1963, have also been exempted provided, the exporters have a firm letter from the overseas buyers stating that they do not want pre-shipment inspection from any official Indian Inspection Agency, which should be filed by the exporters before the Customs Authorities of the Port of shipments. However, the above exemption is not applicable to the exports of fish and fishery products and egg products.

Pilot test house

In order to meet the increasing demand for prompt, efficient, accurate and comprehensive testing of engineering products, particularly from the small scale sector, the EIC has set up a Pilot Test House (PTH) at Mumbai. The PTH consists of different sectional laboratories covering a comprehensive range of testing mechanical and electrical engineering products including material analysis. Apart from carrying out testing of samples drawn by the EIAs from export consignments, PTH also offers several technical support facilities to the industry, viz., assessment of the quality parameters of products, assistance in obtaining approval under the IPQC system, providing common facilities for testing, R & D projects for quality upgradation and tailor-made training programmes for industry.

An advisory Committee with Director (I&QC) and representatives from the Bureau of Indian Standards, Notional Test House, Indian Institute of Technology, Mumbai, Engineering EPC, M/s Tata Engineering & locomotives Company Ltd. and Crompton Greaves Co. was constituted for advising PTH on policy, planning, expansion and action programmes for improving its efficiency so as to provide prompt service to the industry. The PTH is providing regular extension service to the industry for improvement of the quality of export products.

During the period from 1.4,1998 to 30.11,1998 2,419 samples were tested and the total income was Rs.

12,09,651. About 675 samples are likely to be tested during the period from 1.12.1998 to 31.03.1999 accruing an additional income of about Rs. 4,84,181.

Procedure for handling of quality complaints

Procedures have been evolved for assessment, evaluation and settlement of complaints on quality, received from foreign buyers, by the Regional Sub-Committees on Quality Complaints set up at Ahmedabad, Bangalore, Calcutta, Chennai, Cochin, Delhi, Hyderabad, Kanpur, Ludhiana and Mumbai.

During the year under report, EIC has compiled a mannual titled "Quality Assurance and Monitoring System Mannual on Export of Fresh, Frozen and Processed Fish & Fishery Products". EIC has also prepared a mannual on Egg products titled "Quality Assurance and Monitoring System Manual on Export of Egg Products"

During the year under report, EIC has obtained third party inspection work from Public Health Departments of Government of Rajasthan for EIA Delhi. EIC has also obtained third party inspection work for EIA Delhi and EIA Calcutta from Bharat Coking Coal Ltd. and Coal India Ltd.

5

Export Processing Zones

The Export Processing Zones (EPZs) set up as enclaves, separated from the Domestic Tariff Area by fiscal barriers, are intended to provide an internationally competitive duty free environment for export production at low cost. This enables the products of EPZs to be competitive, both quality-wise and price-wise, in the international market. India has seven EPZs at Kandla (Gujarat), Santacruz (Mumbai), Falta (West Bengal), NOIDA (U.P.), Cochin (Kerala), Chennai (Tamil Nodu) and Visakhapatnam (Andhra Pradesh). The Santacruz Electronics Export Processing Zone (SEEPZ) is meant exclusively for export of electronics and gem and jewellery items whereas the other zones are multi-product Zones.

Export oriented zones

The Export Oriented Units (EOUs) Scheme introduced in early 1981, is complementary to the EPZ Scheme. It adopts the some production regime but offers a wide option in locations with reference to factors like source of raw materials, ports of export, hinterland facilities, avail ability of technological skills, existence of an industrial base and the need for a larger area of land for the project. 1,186 units are in operation under the scheme at present.

Infrastructure

Each of the Zones provides basic infrastructure such as developed land for construction of factory sheds, standard design factory buildings providing ready-built sheds, roads, power, water supply and drainage. In addition, Customs clearance is arranged within the Zones at no extra charge. Provision is made for locating banking/post office facilities and offices of clearing agents in the Service Centre located in each of the Zones. EOUs on the other hand have to put up their own infrastructure. At present 527 units are in operation in Export Processing Zones as on 31.10.1998.

Product coverage

While the EPZ operating units broadly fall under the product groups of electronics, engineering items, chemicals and allied products, gem and jewellery; textiles, garments, plastics and rubber products. EOUs are mainly concentrated in textiles and yarn, food processing, electronics, chemicals, plastics, granites and minerals/ ores. Majority of the units are located in Tamil Nadu Andhra Pradesh, Karnataka, Maharashtra and Gujarat.

Export performance

Exports from EOU/EPZ units which stood at Rs. 13,067.64 crores in 1996-97 rose to Rs. 14,514.30 crores in 1997-98 representing a growth of over 11%. Details of exports from EPZs/EOUs during the last three years are indicated below:

(Rs. in crores)

Year	EPZs	EOUs	Total
1995-96	3235.63	7009.00	10244.63
1996-97	4338.92	8728.72	13067.64
1997-98	4817.30	9697.00	14514.30
1998-99	3350.50	9000.00	12350.00

Export promotion measur.

The policy and procedures applicable to EPZ units are under constant review and improvements are brought about from time to time. The special package for revival of exports announced by Commerce Minister in the Parliament on 5.8.1998, include the following specific measures for boosting exports from EOU/EPZ units:

1. Enhancement of corporate tax holiday from 5 years to 10 years;
2. Subcontracting facility in the domestic tariff area; and
3. Exports through courier.

Private/joint sector EPzs

Government has permitted development of EPZs by private, state or joint sector. The Inter-Ministerial Committee on private EPZs has already cleared three proposals for setting up of private EPZs in Bombay, Surat and Kancheepuram. In addition, establishment of an EPZ at Greater NOIDA by Government of U.P has also been cleared.

Export Promotion Industrial Park (EPIP) scheme

A centrally sponsored 'Export Promotion Industrial Park' (EPIP) Scheme has been introduced in 1993-94 with a view to involving the State Governments in the creation of infrastructural facilities for export oriented production.

The scheme provides that 75% of the capital expenditure incurred towards creation of such facilities, ordinarily limited to Rs. 10 crores in each case, will be met from a central grant to the State Governments. In addition, a maintenance grant equivalent to 2% of export turnover of each unit established therein will also be made available to State Governments for a period of 5 years from the date of commercial production of that unit.

The Central Government has so far approved 19 proposals for establishment of EPIPs in the **States** of Punjab, Haryana, Himachal Pradesh, Rajasthan, Karnataka, Kerala, Maharashtra, Tamil Nadu, Andhra Pradesh, Uttar Pradesh, Gujarat, Bihar, Jammu & Kashmir, Assam, Madhya Pradesh, West Bengal, Orissa, Meghalaya and Manipur. While the EPIP in Rajasthan at Sitapura (District Jaipur) has since been completed, the Park at Suraipur, District Gautambudh Nagar (Uttar Pradesh), Hoodi, District Bangalore (Karnataka) and Ambarnath District Thane (Maharashtra) are nearing completion. Other Parks are at various stages of implementation.

Export houses, trading houses & super star trading houses

The objective of the scheme of Export Houses, Trading Houses, Star Trading Houses and Super Star Trading Houses is to give recognition to the established exporters and large Export Houses to build up the marketing infrastructure and expertise required for export promotion.

The Registered Exporters having a record of Export performance over a number of years are granted the status of Export Houses/Trading Houses/Star Trading Houses/Super Star Trading Houses subject to the fulfilment of minimum annual average export performance in terms of FOB value or net foreign exchange earnings on physical exports prescribed in the EXIM Policy.

The Export Houses, Trading Houses, Star Trading Houses and Super Star Trading Houses' Scheme allows the Registered Exporters certain additional benefits available to them under the policy.

6

India Trade Promotion Organisation

India Trade Promotion Organisation (ITPO) is the premier trade promotion agency of the country and provides a broad spectrum of services to trade and industry so as to catalyse the growth of international trade and modernisation of different industrial segments. At ITPO, the promotion of trade is an exacting mission translating into search for new frontiers and new-horizons in the world of commercial interaction both at macro and micro level. ITPO's programmes are carried out in close contact with the Indian industry whose promotional needs it seeks to serve. Its mission is to successfully organise trade fairs/exhibitions in India and abroad, buyer-seller meets, trade promotion and product development programmes apart from information dissemination on products and markets.

Fairs in India

ITPO's exhibitions at Pragati Maidan, New Delhi and in other parts of the country effectively mirror the latest developments in various sectors of industry and cater to both export and import requirements. International events that have over the years developed and institutionalised include International' Shoe Fair, Shoe Comp, India International Trade Fair, Consumexh, Delhi Book Fair and Mystiquie India. The other fairs/

exhibitions to be organised by ITPO upto March, 1999 are National Children Fair '98, Winter Show '98, Print Pack '99 TexStyles India '99 and Food Expo '99 in Pragati Maidan; India International Leather Fair '99 at Chennai and International Leather Goods Fair '99 at Calcutta. The fairs organised/to be organised by other institutions in Pragati Maidan include India Engineering Trade Fair, International jewellery and Watch Exhibition, 5th International Mining Machinery Exhibition, Garmentech, IT India '98, 3rd International Petrotech, India International Garments Fair, India Handicrafts and Gifts Fair, Spring '99 and Carpet Fair '99.

Fairs abroad

During 1997-98, ITPO had organised participation in 44 events abroad, of which twenty one fairs were organised on subsidised basis and twenty three fairs on self-financing basis. The participants who participated in these events had reported business booked to the tune of Rs. 47,100.58 lakhs and business under negotiation amounting to Rs. 1,36,205.71 lakhs.

During 1998-99, ITPO's programme of participation in fairs/exhibitions abroad consist of 42 events out of which 18 are on subsidised basis and 24 are on self-financing basis. During April '98 to September '98, ITPO had organised participation in 21 fairs/exhibitions abroad which include 7 general international fairs, 12 specialised commodity fairs and 2 exclusive Indian exhibitions in Cairo [Egypt] and Baku [Azerbaijan]. Out of 21 events, 9 have been organised in Europe, 6 in South East Asia, 4 in American countries and 2 in WANA region. The participants in these events have reported business booked to the tune of Rs. 9,385.27 lakhs and business under negotiation amounting to Rs. 71,839.85 lakhs. ITPO, on behalf of Government of India, organised India's participation at Expo '98, Lisbon (Portugal), May

22 to September 30, 1998. The theme of the Expo '98 was 'OCEAN' Heritage to the mankind.

During April '98 to September '98, two buyer-seller meets were organised in japan, one for home furnishings and another for garments and fashion accessories which have resulted in export orders valued at US $ 6.28 million and enquiries of us $ 14.72 million. Two more buyer-seller meets, one for textiles and garments in Philippines and another for engineering products in Sao Paulo (Brazil) are planned for the balance part of the year. A total of 3 Contact Promotion Programs (CPP) are scheduled during October '98 to March '99 for home furnishings in Spain and Portugal and auto parts in Singapore, Philippines and Sri Lanka

Trade development and merchandising

ITPO also organises a number of export development programmes for selected products in identified markets, to improve awareness of India's export capability and generate business enquiries and export orders. The products and markets are identified on the basis of market research/study conducted by ITPO's foreign offices and Indian Missions abroad.

Visit of a large number of buying delegations from Japan, Europe, USA, Middle East, Africa, South East Asia, Latin America, etc. have been coordinated. In each case the buyers are put in direct touch with Indian companies for products of their interest.

ITPO is also bringing out catalogues covering various export products from India, for increasing awareness among overseas buyers. Such catalogues have so for been brought out on Automotive & Ancillary Industry, Electronics Industry, Handicrafts Industry and Granite & Marble Industry.

ITPO also organises display of Indian products catalogues in overseas market as part of its developmental activities. During April -September '98, ITPO organised 2 product catalogue shows in Egypt (Cairo) and Baku (Azerbaijan). In the coming months of this year, ITPO is proposing to organise two more product catalogue shows in Baghdad (Iraq) and Lima (Peru).

Product Promotion Programme (PPP) is another developmental activity of ITPO for promotion of product in specific markets on behalf of selected Indian companies, by establishing contacts with overseas importers. During October '98 to March '99, ITPO is planning to organise PPP for leather products in USA and Canada, home furnishings, carpet and floor coverings in Australia and New Zealand and for computer softwares and services in USA and Canada. Two market surveys on identifying trade and investment opportunities would be conducted in the coming months in Peru and South Africa/Zimbabwe.

Publication

The weekly Indian Export Bulletin is the main channel of dissemination of trade information to the members of India Trade Promotion Organisation, 4000 copies of which are printed and mailed every week.

Financial highlight

During the year 1997-98, the total income of the company was Rs. 90.57 crores including an operational income of Rs. 72.96 crores. The total expenditure during the year 1997-98 was Rs. 72.36 crores. The excess of income over expenditure has been Rs. 18.21 crores during 1997-98. The reserves and surplus of ITPO as on 31.3.1998 were to the tune of Rs. 135.90 crores. This includes Capital reserves of Rs. 49.66 crores fully utilised.

Other activities

The organisation chalked out a comprehensive Corporate Plan for the year 1998-2003 for making Pragati Maidan an exhibition venue of international standard. This includes modernisation of exhibition halls, development of multi-modular transport facilities, setting up of food plazas, upgradation of information technology and human resources development. In order to train the man-power, management development programmes, computer training programmes, seminars and short term workshops were conducted. More emphasis was laid on increasing use of Hindi in organisation. The organisation continued to enhance the trade information services for meeting the needs of trade and industry with the establishment of internet connectivity. The trade information available on various web sites was disseminated among the concerned quarters including domestic fairs department, TDMD and publicity department.

Indian institute of packaging, Mumbai

The Indian Institute of Packaging (IIP), Mumbai, a Research and Development, training and educational organisation set up in 1996, under the Ministry of Commerce, has been entrusted with the responsibility of bringing about improvements in the standards of packing in the country particularly for exports. IIP has been registered under the Societies' Registration Act, 1860.

It has on its roll 1000 members representing industries of a heterogeneous nature. It undertakes technical consultancy, testing services on packaging developments, training and educational programmes, promotional awards contests, information services, international affiliations with APF/WPO etc. and other important activities. The Institute has its regional branches at Calcutta, Chennai and New Delhi.

The packaging scenario all over the world is vast changing and in this context the domestic industries are expected to adopt the changes rapidly. The Institute gaining inspiration from the vast developments and anticipated future needs has centered its activities with a view to propagate scientific packaging and upgradation of technology and endeavour its resources towards environmental causes as well. The activities and other programmes of the Institute during the year upto November, 1998 and anticipated activities upto March 1999 are summarised below:—

Testing and U.N. certification

Nearly 5500 samples were tested and U.N certification was done for 750 items by the Institute at its facilities at Mumbai, Calcutta, Delhi and Chennai. Four certificates were issued by the Eastern Regional Centre as per Australian wool Corporation/New Zealand specifications for testing of wool samples for exports. It is envisaged that approximately 2000 samples will be tested and 200 UN Certificates will be issued in the remaining period.

Research and development

Due to the demand for eco-friendly packaging and eco regulations, more and more Companies are adopting modern techniques and eco-friendly packaging systems. The institute undertook the following major packaging development projects during the year:—

(i) All India Study on Packaging of Processed Food on behalf of Ministry of Food Processing Industries, New Delhi.

(ii) Development of Packaging for a Component of X-Ray Machine on behalf of G.E., Elpro Medical Systems Ltd., Pune.

(iii) Packaging of Cheque Processing Equipment of behalf of Infotech Limited, Mumbai.

Besides this, the following packaging developmental studies are under progress:—

(i) Studies on post harvest movement of fresh fruits and vegetables on behalf of Agricultural and Processed Food Products Export Development Authority, New Delhi

(ii) Packaging of Sports Goods for Sports Goods Export Development Council, New Delhi

(iii) Designing and Developing packaging system for window air-conditioners for M/s. Voltas limited, Thane.

A total of 8 consultancy and advisory visits were undertaken by the experts of the Institute during the period. Nearly, 20 organisations also availed themselves of the Institutes advisory services whereby specialists from the Institute visited the industrial units in need of immediate advice and examined their problems for immediate remedial measures. Another 5 projects and 15 advisory visits are likely to be completed upto March, 1999.

Technical feasibility study and services

The following projects were undertaken during the period:—

(i) CFB Box Manufacturers.

(ii) Co-extruded Multi-layer films for packaging of edible oil.

(iii) Distribution, logistic, damage and other aspects related to packaging of refrigerators and washing machines.

Training programmes/seminars

The Institute continued to pass on its expertise to the industry personnel by way of conducting Seminars and

Training Programmes at all the four centres of the Institute. Under the Intensive training Course at Mumbai and Calcutta, during the year as Many as 47 participants including 14 overseas participants from developing countries under India's International Assistance Scheme such as the Colombo Plan, the SCAAP and the ITEC were benefited. The Institute also conducted various seminars and short term training programmes Such 05 Executive Development Programmes, Workshops on Packaging techniques, in-plant training programmes and collaboration programmes.

As many as 16 Executive Development Programmes were conducted by the Head Office and three regional centres of IIP. The programmes were spread over various industry/commercial centres all over India. The number of centres covered are 10 and a total of 625 industry delegates benefited from such programmes.

Education

The 14th batch of the Two-year Post Graduate Programme commenced in August, 1998 with 35 students.

Distance education programme

For the 3rd batch of Distance Education Programme, 72 participants have registered. The 4th batch will commence from January, 1999.

Information services

The Institute's bi-monthly magazine viz. 'Packaging India' which is a standard publication on techno-commercial information in packaging sector was regularly published. The Library of the Institute continued to provide excellent services to the students and the industry circle.

Internet

The Institute had installed Internet multi-media system at its Head Office and three regional centres. The system is also being used for publishing IIP activities as well as packaging activities of the members.

Exhibitions

The Institute has organised INDPACK '98 exhibition at Pune from 29th October to 1st November, 1998. There were 61 exhibitors spread over an area of 1700 sq. mtrs.

Conference on packaging

A Conference on "Packaging of Consumer and Industrial Products" was organised by the Institute on the 30-31st October, 1998 at Pune to coincide with the INDPACK '98 exhibition. 65 delegates from the Packaging, allied and user industries participated.

Perspective

The endeavours of the Institute to strengthen and expand its activities will no doubt be continued. The programmes will be pro-active and will be aimed at reaching the industries spread far and wide in the country.

— To facilitate further the educational programmes, additional Hostel facilities are planned.

— The women Entrepreneurship Programme proposed, will help generate a new era in the packaging field.

— The planning for building-up the infrastructure in the laboratories will facilitate upgradation and improved services in the quality schemes.

— Proposed expansion of Regional Centres and new Centres of IIP, will help to reach more industries and export community

Indian institute of foreign trade

The Indian Institute of Foreign Trade (IIFT) established in May 1963 by the Government of India, has been rendering useful service in the areas of human resource development for international business, trade and economics through need based training programmes, seminars and workshops, interfaced with and supported by continuous research on a variety of topical subjects in the field of foreign trade and international business

Foundational programmes

The Institute organised the following foundational pro grammes during the years 1997-98 and 1998-99 (Upto December, 1998).

(a) Masters Programme in International Business (MPIB): Shri Rama Krishna Hegde, Hon'ble Commerce Minister, Government of India had awarded certificates to 92 successful students of 12th Masters Programme in International Business (1996-98) at the Annual Convocation held on July 15, 1998.

The 13th Masters Programme in International Business (1998-2000) with the class size of 84 was inaugurated on 15th July, 1998 by Shri Subodh Bhargava, Chairman, Eicher Group of Companies.

(b) Executive Masters in International Trade (EMIT): Fifth EMIT Programme, scheduled for January December, 1998, was inaugurated by Shri Binay Kumar, Chairman-cum-Managing Director, Benaras House, New Delhi on 19th January, 1998. Thirty-eight senior and middle level executives representing various sectors of trade & industry and service institutions were admitted to the Programme.

(c) Post Graduate Diploma Programme in International Trade (PGDP): Thirty-second PGDP in International Trade with twenty eight participants was conducted during 6th October, 1997 to 3 April, 1998, Diplomas were awarded by Shri Romakrishna Hegde, Hon'ble Commerce Minister, Government of India to the 20 successful participants of the Programme in the Annual Convocation held on 15th July, 1998.

Management development programmes

Regular part-time management

The Institute organised the following Regular Management Development Programmes during the year 1997-98:—

Certificate course in export marketing (evening)

The four-month Certificate Course in Export Marketing was held twice during the period January-December, 1998. The first Programme was held during March 1-June 30, 1998 in which 53 participants had participated. The second Programme was conducted during. August 3-November, 30,1998 in which 60 participants had participated.

Certificate course in international business language (evening)

The Programme "Certificate Course in International Business Language" was organised during January-June, 1998.

Ninety nine students were admitted to the Course for teaching six languages, namely Arabic, French, German, Japanese, Russian and Spanish. Successful participants were awarded certificates at the Annual Convocation held on 15th July, 1998.

Certificate course on international trade logistics (evening)

The four-month Certificate Course on International trade logistics was conducted during 1 September-31 December, 1997 in which 25 executives had participated. Successful participants were awarded certificates at the

Annual Convocation held on 15th July, 1998. Currently another programme is in progress from 1 September, 1998 in which 25 participants have been participating. This programme will come to an end on 31 December, 1998. In addition to this, the Institute conducted 11 full time Management Development Programmes and 20 Sponsored Management Development Programmes during the period.

Marketing and functional research

The Institute attaches considerable importance to its research and consultancy activities as these add value to Institute's large number of training programmes and help the faculty develop analytical skills. During December, 1997-November, 1998 the Institute had completed 13 Research Projects and currently 12 projects are in progress. All these research studies have covered a very diverse set of problems relating to foreign trade management. The studies in progress are also very large amounting to 12 and again cover a world spectrum of problems relating to foreign trade. The client-base of the Institute has also considerably expanded. In addition to the Ministry of Commerce, the Institute is working for FIEO, CII, WTO.

Publications

The Institute has brought out the following journals, bulletins, newsletters, occasional papers and publications during the year 1998-99:-

(i) Non-Conventional Technology Based Services, Capabilities and Export Opportunities - September, 1998.

(ii) Monograph No.1: Trade Related Joint Ventures between India and Bangladesh -July 1998.

Foreign trade library

Foreign Trade Library of the Institute is one of the largest of its kind (specialising in International Business) not only in India but also in this part of the world, It has 74,621 volumes of books, reports, periodicals and documents on Business Administration, International Marketing and allied subjects and serves as a clearing house of commercial economic information for the faculty, participants of training programmes conducted by the Institute, research scholars and representatives of trade and industry.

Recently, WTO Documentation Centre has come into operation in the Foreign Trade Library. The objective of the Centre is to provide materials on issues relating to WTO and its implications for India for the benefit of policy makers, research scholars and academicians. The Centre brings out "WTO News Collection (monthly)". "WTO Documentation List (monthly)" and "Additions to WTO Centre" on a regular basis

National Centre for Trade Information (NCTI)

National Centre for Trade Information (NCTI) has been registered as a company under Section 25 of the Indian Companies Act, 1956, w.e.f. 31.3.1995. The company has a Board of Directors for administration of its affairs, which include representatives from National Informatics Centre, India Trade Promotion Organisation, Apex Chamber of Commerce/Industry/Trade, Export Promotion Councils and Commodity Boards etc.

ITPO and NIC are co-promoters of the company and have contributed a sum of Rs. 4.00 crores (Rs. 2 crores each) as corpus fund in the equity contribution of NCTI. NCTI has been provided with fully furnished space by ITPO and Satellite Earth Station and hardware against the contribution of Rs. 75 lakhs in kind each by ITPO and NIC. The company has started functioning w.e.f. March, 1996.

Membership

At the end of November, 1998, NCTI has 2021 members on its rolls.

Selective Dissemination of Information (SDI) service

The service inter-alia provides for Electronic trade Opportunities (ETOs) to a subscribing member by indicating a Chapter Number of Harmonised System Code of Classification.

Memorandum of Understanding (MoU)

NCTI signed 9 Memorandum of Understandings (MoU) with different organisations in different countries during the period. In addition, NCTI during May , 1997 signed an MoU with Trade Compass, USA for jointly developing and operating an Internet based website.

Weekly tabloid-trade point India

NCTI brought out 52 issues of Trade Point India. This weekly contains Electronic Trading Opportunities (ETOs) received on Global Trade point Network (GTP Net), particulars of overseas importers received from Indian Missions abroad and articles and information on International trade thereby facilitating India's exports, imports and joint collaborations.

Electronic Trading Opportunities (ETOs)

One of the most successful programmes launched by NCTI is the facility of ETOs. A database has been created besides publishing the same in the weekly tabloid, Trade Point India. A database of ETOs received during the year contains 24,675 demands from all over the world.

Trade fairs and exhibitions

NCTI participated in the Jute India, Exhibition held during the month of October, 1997, at Pragati Maidan, New Delhi NCTI also participated, in IIFT '98 held from November 14-27, 1998.

Symposiums/seminars/conferences

During the year NCTI organised Symposiums on:

(i) Electronic Commerce & Trade Point at New Delhi.

(ii) Brain Storming Session on Trade Information and Value Added Services in association with PHDCCI at New Delhi; and

(iii) NCTI and Trade Point in association with AIAI, Mumbai at Pune, Mumbai and Bangalore

Trade Analysis and Information System (TRAINS)

NCTI was designated by Ministry of Commerce to be Focal Point for Trade Analysis and Information System (TRAINS) of UNCTAD, a PC based information system on international trading conditions.

On-line connectivity

NCTI established on-line connectivity with FT-Profile of the Financial Times, London, Vans.Com of Vanscom Investor Service, Mumbai, Bisnet of FICCI, New Delhi, Greenbus all the Netherlands, WTCA Database of World Trade Association, New York and IDSS - Investment Decision Support System, a database on Indian Companies/Industries/ Economy.

Web-page

NCTI created a Web-Page on hosting at NIC's Web-Serve Similarly, a new Internet site was launched through a private Internet Service Provider with a view to making the site dynamic and inter-active.

Trade connect

NCTI launched a new Quarterly Publication, entitled "Trade Connect" for overseas circulation. The quarterly publications are being sent to the Indian Missions abroad for circulation amongst overseas trade promotion bodies.

Publicity

NCTI sent 82,000 specific designed mailers to select members of Trade and Industry in India in addition to 10,000 overseas mailers to overseas Importers. Export Promotion Organisations, Chambers to Commerce & Industry were also approached to incorporate in their publications the activities for circulating the same to their members through their newsletters and periodicals. Workships, symposiums, seminars and conferences etc. were also organised at major cities in India besides advertisements in financial dailies/magazines.

Database of NCTI

Ten different databases were created by NCTI which include database on importers, Trade fairs and exhibitions, Indian Missions Abroad, Overseas Missions in India.

Virtual trade point

(i) Virtual Trade Point, Calcutta being implemented with Bengal National Chamber of Commerce and Industry (BNCCI), is now expected to go on stream by December, 1998 end or January, 1999.

(ii) For VTP Mumbai space at Nariman Point proposed by AIAI is found suitable.

(iii) Association with Visversvaraya Industrial Trade Centre (VITC) Karnataka for VTP, Bangalore has been finalised. Suitable premises has been identified

Report on leather & leather goods and sports goods

NCTI submitted a detailed report on 20th November, 1998 to Ministry of Commerce on Leather & Leather Goods and Sports Goods Global Imports (1992-1996), Exports from India (1990-1996)- Statistical Analysis and Trends for Top 15 Countries for onward transmission to Leather Export Promotion Council.

7

Plantations and Agriculture

Tea

Tea plays an important role in the National Economy. It earns a substantial amount of foreign exchange to the country from its exports and also contributes to the National Exchequer by way of cess, sales tax, agricultural and corporate income tax etc. Tea Industry provides employment to about 1 million people in plantations directly, besides providing employment to another 1 million persons indirectly.

Production

The production of Tea in India during 1997-98 was estimated at 838.02 M. Kgs. During the current year (April to November, 1998) the production was estimated at 740.79 M. Kgs. vis-a-vis 708.45 M. Kgs. during the corresponding period of the previous financial year. It is expected that the total production during 1998-99 may be around 840 M. K.Kgs.

Export

The export of tea from India during 1997-98 was estimated at 211,76 M. Kgs. valued at Rs. 11953.91 crores with a unit price of Rs. 92.27 per Kg. During the current year for the period April, 1998 to November, 1998 the export was estimated at 141.95 M. Kgs. valued at Rs. 1,470.69 crores with a unit price of Rs. 103.61 Per Kg. The corresponding figures for the some period during the lost financial year were 146.81 M. Kgs. valued at Rs. 1,297.00 crores with a unit price of Rs. 88.35 per kg. This indicates a decline in export volume to the extent of 4.86 M. Kgs. and improvement in export earnings to the tune of Rs. 173.69 crates, On the basis of the trend in export of tea from India so for, it is estimated that the total export during 1998-99 may touch a figure of 220 M. Kgs. The export earnings from tea during 1998-99 may be around Rs. 2,104 crores. The expected export of 220 M, Kgs. during 1998-99 depends on substantial improvement in exports to CIS countries as also to U.K., Poland, U.A.E, Iron, Iraq and Pakistan during the remaining part of the year 1998-99.

Export import policy

While there is no restriction on the export of tea, import of tea is restricted. Tea is allowed for import only against a license except in the case of SAARC countries where the import has been mode free vide Notification issued by the Directorate General of Foreign Trade on 1st August, 1998. The rote of basic import duty on, import of any type of tea is 10% plus additional customs duty, special import duty etc. However, import of tea is allowed duty free for the purpose of re-export in value added form either through EOU/EPZ units or under Duty Exemption Scheme subject to specific value addition norms.

Prices

The average prices of tea sold at Indian auctions registered a spurt during the second half of 1997. The average auction prices rose from a level of Rs. 67.78 per kg. in July 1997 to Rs. 91.98 per kg in January 1998, As the rise in prices at auctions continued at unprecedented level, Ministry of Commerce acted quickly through the Tea Board invoking provisions of the Tea Market

(Control) Order to curb speculative tendencies. Tightening of auction norms and steps taken to bring substantial volumes of Tea to auctions ensured that supply was regular. This had the desired effect and the price rise was controlled.

Tea development

In order to increase Tea production, various Tea development schemes have been implemented by the Tea Board. These schemes are as under :

1. Plantation Development Scheme
2. Tea processing and Packaging Development Scheme
3. Tea Development Scheme for North Eastern States for the control of Jhum Cultivation
4. New Area Development Scheme
5. Small Grower Development Scheme
6. Marketing Development and Export Promotion Scheme
7. Research and Development Schemes
8. Human Resource Development Scheme

Tea research

Tea research activities of the Board cover different spheres like augmentation in production and productivity, quality improvement and innovative approaches thereon, review of regulations and formulation of new standards and specifications, giving technical inputs to the tea industry covering technical information particularly on export, working of various committees, and allied activities of the Board etc.

During 1998-99 all the ongoing research activities will continue. A number of new research schemes and a few pilot schemes at different Institutes are also proposed to be launched during 1998-99. Both TRA and UPASI-TRI in the North East and South India respectively will have increased financial support from the Board for their ongoing activities including Advisory Services. Both TRA and UPASI-TRI will be financially supported by the Board for specific activities like training, establishing quality control laboratory in South India etc.

Grant-in-aids from the Board under sponsored programmes will continue to different organisations like Assam Agricultural University, Himachal Pradesh Krishi Viswa Vidyalaya, CSIR Complex, Polampur. Grants are also given for carrying out fundamental research programmes in Biotechnology at Bose Institute, Calcutta. Similarly, for health benefit aspects of research on tea, capital support is given to TRA programme launched at Indian Institute of Chemical Biology under CSIR, Calcutta. Financial support is also provided for carrying out specific R&D works of short duration in highly demanding fields. Similar support is also provided by the Tea Board for holding various Conferences and Workshops.

Tea Board is having its own Darjeeling Tea Research Centre at Kurseong to provide technical support to the tea industry in Darjeeling Hills. This Centre is engaged in Biochemical, Soil and Tea Physiology Research Works on local agro climatic conditions

Tea Board is having a small unit of Notional Tea Research Foundation for mobilizing a corpus fund to promote specific scientific research out of this fund. Various committees of N.T.R.F. are engaged in launching various research schemes and the Board monitors the progress of such research schemes from time to time. All such activities will be further strengthened in 1998-99, Programmes supported under NTRF range from various applied research to fundamental research; carried out at different Tea Research Institutes as well as other institutes and universities in agricultural fields. NTRF is also having a separate entity on the Board's premises in Head Office.

Tea promotion

Tea Promotion activities of the Tea Board are carried out by the Headquarters mainly through its five overseas offices located at London, Hamburg, New York, Dubai and Moscow. Tea sampling/services for public relations work are conducted in four Units at Parliament House, Udyog Bhawan, North Block and Yojana Bhawan in Delhi and also at Mumbai, Chennai Secretariat and Tirupati.

The Export Promotion activities are aimed to popularise Indian tea at the trade and consumer level with Special Promotion Programmes to promote Indian teas in value-added form like packet tea, tea bags and instant tea. The medium of publicity includes press advertising, sampling/store demonstrations, participation in fairs/ exhibitions, educational programmes, lending support to importers and exporters for marketing of Indian brands of Tea etc.

Tea Board has also introduced a New Plan (Subsidy) Scheme viz., Market Development and Export Promotion Scheme, which would cover market research services, uninational campaigns for India tea in selected markets, brand promotion support to Indian Companies for launching their brands in the international markets, generic campaign for tea in new markets and setting up of an Umbrella Unit in India to meet requirements of product and packaging standards in international markets. During the year '1997-98, assistance under the scheme was provided to Darjeeling Tea Planters Association for conducting the first phase of a Darjeeling

"Logo Promotion and Presentation Programme" in Germany and Europe. Chairman, Tea Board led a delegation of Darjeeling Tea Planters' Association to West Europe during June, 1998 which covered Amsterdam, Zurich, Paris Hamburg for promotion of Darjeeling tea.

Promotional activities covering exchange of visits to from major tea importing countries also took place. A delegation led by Additional Secretary (Plantations), Ministry Commerce visited Sri Lanka during August, 1998 for bilateral talks in connection with promotion of tea, Important decisions such as setting up of the SAARC Tea Council, Joint Marketing of Tea By India and Sri Lanka etc. were taken during the meeting. Another delegation led by Additional Secretary (Plantation) and Chairman Tea Board also visited New York in October, 1998 to participate in the US Tea Convention, promotion of Indian Tea in USA and to explore the possibility of opening of a new office of the Tea Board in the West Coast.

Tea Board, through its overseas offices, participated in a large number of International Fairs/ Exhibitions mostly specialised events for Food and Drink as well as general Consumer events, for promotion of Indian teas in important countries coming under the jurisdiction of these offices. Tea Board, through its foreign offices also, conducted during the year 1998-99 specific promotional campaigns for supporting identifiable Indian tea brands as well as by providing promotional support to importers of such brands in important markets such as in WANA countries, CIS, UK, West Europe and Japan.

During December, 1998, India and Russia signed an agreement for import of Tea from India from January, 1999 till December, 2005 at approximate annual volume of 100,000 MT.

Welfare

The Board continued to undertake various welfare measures for the benefit of the tea plantation workers. These include:-

(i) Grant of Education Stipend to the wards of tea garden workers for prosecuting studies above the primary stage.

(ii) Financial assistance to various institutions and organisations under General Welfare Scheme for the benefit of tea garden workers and their families.

Stipend

Stipends are granted for the Secondary/Higher Secondary Education, General and Technical Courses including Post -Graduate Courses and Vocational Education. In case of physically handicapped and mentally retarded students stipend is granted right from the primary stage. Under the stipend scheme, actual tuition fees and 2/3rd hostel charges are paid to the children of persons directly employed in the registered tea estates and governed by the Plantation Labour Act. However, with the introduction of free education up to the Higher Secondary level, the payment of stipend is restricted to only hostel charges.

Rubber

The Rubber Board was constituted in 1955 mainly to promote production of natural rubber in the country. The strategy adopted for improving production (a) replanting of old and uneconomic plantations with high yielding rubber (b) expansion of area under rubber for newplanting and (c) productivity improvement of existing plantations through improved agro-management practices. During 1997-98, the target for replanting was 5,250 ha, and for newplanting 9,700 ha., against which the achievement was 4,942 ha. and 9,127 ha. respectively

The target for 1998-99 is 5,500 ha. under replanting and 11,000 ha. under newplanting. The achievement under replanting has been 3,700 ha. and under new planting 6,500 ha. The planting tempo has drastically come down owing to the steep fall in rubber price, average price of RSS-4 grade rubber was 5,122 in 1996. It came down to Rs. 3,988 in 1997. In 1998 the price has further fallen down.

India produced 583,830 tonnes of natural rubber during 1997-98 against the production of 549,425 tonnes during 1996-97. The target of production during 1998-99 is 610,000 tonnes of which the achievement till September 1998 has been 266,000 tonnes.

Short-term productivity enhancement techniques such as discriminatory fertiliser usage, soil moisture conservation, systematic plant protection, scientific crop exploitation and processing etc. were popularised, based on which the average productivity of rubber plantation was 1,545 kg per ha. This is the highest average productivity among major rubber producing countries in the world. Over 9 lakh small rubber growers eke out their living from rubber plantation. The plantations give employment to about 3.5 lakh workers in the rural villages.

Marketing system, price and quality control

Rubber is predominantly produced in Kerala, viz. the Southern most State in India which accounts for 94% of the production. It is taken to nearly 6,000 rubber manufacturers in different parts of the country by over 10,000 rubber dealers. Quality of Indian sheet rubber is good and compares favourably with correponding grades in the international market. Quality improvement programmes are undertaken to supply raw rubber as per consumers' specifications. Price of rubber in India is Rs. 33.00 per kg for RSS - 4 whereas current international price for the corresponding grade is Rs. 30.00 per kg, as at the end of October, 1998

Role of the board in promoting exports and consumption

Rubber export even though permitted under the present Exim policy does not take place to any significant extent owing to the demand recession in the world market and the world price ruling below the Indian price. During 1997-98, 1,415 tonnes of natural rubber was exported. During April to July, 1998, its export was 764 tonnes.

Export of rubber products is monitored by CAPEXCIL. However the Rubber Board promotes rubber products export through guidance for marketing and improvement in quality. Technological research is undertaken on improving the properties of rubber and quality of the final product to meet consumer requirements. Entrepreneurs are provided support to set up rubber processing, rubber wood processing and rubber products manufacturing units in the small scale sector. Supply of project reports, analytical service for quality screening, guidance for factory erection, trouble - shooting and improvement of product quality, running training courses in rubber production, crop processing and rubber goods manufacture etc. were also undertaken.

Development activities, extension, labour welfare programmes.

For expansion of rubber area and modernisation of the existing plantations, a Rubber Plantation Development Scheme is in operation. During the lost five years 1993-94 to 1998-99, fresh rubber plantations covered 38,500 ha. Productivity improvement through replantation of uneconomic holdings with high yielding planting material covered 26,000 hectares during the same period.

Short - term productivity enhancement techniques such as discriminatory fertiliser usage, soil moisture conservation Systematic plant protection, scientific crop-exploitation and processing etc. were popularised.

Welfare measures undertaken for plantation labour include granting educational stipend to children of rubber plantation workers, enlisting workers to the Group Insurance-cum-Deposit Scheme, providing them assistance for house construction and setting up sanitary facilities and medical reimbursement etc. An amount of Rs. 112.32 lakhs was spent on labour welfare measures. The target for 1998-99 is Rs. 110 lakhs of which expenditure till the end of September 1998 was Rs. 49.91 lakhs. The budget allocation will be fully utilised by the end of March 1999.

Breakthrough in research

Evolving high yielding clones and improving technological properties of raw rubber are priorities in research work. The Rubber Board has already evolved a high yielding clone RRII 105, the productivity of which is well over 2,000 kg per hectare. Breeding and selection work has identified several new clones. Test tapping of the newly developed clones during the 4th year of planting showed 53 clones to be superior to RRII 105 in yield. The yield increase ranges from 4 to 50 %. Irrigation trials showed better yield for irrigated plots in Dapchari with yield increase ranging from 300, to 500 kgs per ha. Silt pits in planted area to the extent of 150 to 200 pits with saw dust is noticed.

Epoxidised natural rubber was found to impart better technological properties to silica filled vulcanizates of natural rubber, SBR and nitrile rubber. Studies on evaluation of rubberised bitumen for pavement application indicated rubberised stretches perform better especially in heavy traffic areas.

Pollution control

Treatment of effluent discharge from raw rubber processing factories was promoted. Service rendered include designing effluent treatment plants, preparing drawings and estimates and providing technical knowhow for setting up treatment plants. In a short time, 27 effluent treatment plants were designed, each to suit local requirements. A few of them have won awards from the Pollution Control Board of Kerala. The Pollution Control Board has approved Rubber Board as Consultants for effluent treatment plants of rubber processing factories. A Scheme for providing financial and technical assistance for setting up biogas units for production of cooking gas from the effluent was formulated and implemented, under which 294 biogas plants have been set up. Water coming out of such biogas plants was within the safe limit for irrigation, after the hydraulic retention time of 30-40 days Effluent arising out of sheet rubber processing was anaerobically treated to produce methane gas, which is also used as domestic fuel and fuel in smoke houses for drying rubber sheets.

Welfare programmes undertaken for SC/STs

Group Rubber Plantations are raised in areas of concentration of SC/ST growers. Entire expenditure on planting and maintenance of the plantation upto the immaturity period is met by the Board and the concerned State Government on attaining maturity, the plantations are handed over to the tribal growers after teaching them the crop exploitation techniques and crop processing. More than 5,000 tribal families have been benefitted by this. Of this, over 500 families were benefitted during the current year.

SC/ST growers are given special assistance for raising rubber plantations as follows:-

(a) Capital subsidy.

(b) Supply of high quality planting materials at concessional rate.

(c) Fertiliser subsidy at 50% cost limited to Rs. 1 000 during the first three year period of raising plantations.

(d) Cash assistance for boundary protection.

(e) Assistance for group rubber farming in tribal/SC concentration areas where entire cultivation and maintenance expenditure upto maturity stage is met by the Rubber Board and the concerned State Government

(f) Training in rubber tapping and crop processing.

Women welfare

Women of the tribal and low income community are assisted to take up income generating activities such as poultry and piggery. They are supplied weaving equipments and smokeless chullahs. Altogether over 1600 families have been given the assistance.

The demand for Natural Rubber is expedited to grow from 600,000 tonnes in 1998-99 to 746,000 tonnes by 2000-01 . It calls for improvement in production through fresh planting and replanting of old rubber areas for improvement in productivity. The expected NR production by 2000 AD is 730,000 tonnes. The existing service on promoting products, export, labour welfare, assistance for SC/ST growers, quality improvement in crop processing and product manufacture, effluent treatment etc. will be continued.

Coffee

Coffee is one of the most important agricultural products traded world-wide and is extremely important to many developing countries. Infact, coffee is usually the second biggest traded commodity after petroleum as far as developing world is concerned. In India too, coffee has been traditionally grown from the past 400 years and is an extremely important foreign exchange earner as far as the commodities are concerned. Though coffee cultivation is taken up by many states in the country, it is mainly confined to 3 southern states of India viz. Karnataka, Kerala and Tamil Nadu. As on date, the total area under coffee in the country is around 3.05 lakh ha. out of which the 3 traditional coffee growing States viz. Karnataka, Kerala and Tamil Nadu contribute around 2.85 lakh ha. and the balance only form the share of other coffee growing states (non-traditional areas). Though coffee is a plantation crop over 98% of the coffee grows in the country are small holders having less than 10 ha. Actually the small holders contribute 65 % share of the area and 60% of the production share whereas the large growers (10 ha. and above) possess 35% of the plantation area and contribute 40 % of the production. The average productivity in the small grower sector is about 750 kg per ha. whereas it is 1000 kg per ha. in the case of large holdings.

Production and export

The overall productivity of coffee has risen from the level of 760 kg per ha. during 1997-98 to about 890 kg per ha. during 1997-98. The average production has increased from 1.70 lakh tonnes during 1991 period to 2.28 lakh tonnes during 1997-98. The final crop estimates for the year 1998-99 is placed of 2.30 lakh tonnes comprising Arabica 96,865 tonnes and Roubsta 1,33,135 tonnes.

The export target fixed as per the 9th plan projects of the Coffee board for the year 1998-99 is 1,70,000 tonnes. Against this, till date i.e. 14.12.1998, the achievement is 1,40,944 tonnes realising Rs. 1,184.34 crores. It is expected that the exports will far exceed in performance compared to previous years considering the present trend.

Quality control

In the post liberalisation phase, the functions of the Quality Control Division have assumed new dimension to cater to the fast emerging market requirements both in domestic and International sectors. To augment changing needs of the Coffee Industry, the Quality Control Division is being geared up through the implementation of the Government approved project viz. Quality Evaluation and Upgradation Programme.

In accordance with the main objective i.e. total quality management, action Was initiated to create quality awareness among different segments of coffee industry through different media, The relevant literature on quality management was circulated through well organised extension/research network. Meetings, group gatherings, exhibitions and seminars were conducted in different places of coffee growing areas.

The training on visual and organoleptic evaluation of Indian Coffee was imported to 88 persons belonging to different sections of coffee industry along with 62 technical officers of Extension Wing of the Board.

The Coffee samples received from growers, curers, traders and exporters were evaluated for their physical and cup qualify standards. A total of 1,144 samples inclusive of those received from the research department were evaluated for various Physical parameters and the samples were also subjected to organoleptic evaluation and other intrinsic qualities.

Inspection of curing works was also conducted before issuing Curing licences.

During January 1998, the Quality Control Division in co-ordination with Speciality Coffee Association of America organised a field tour and cupping sessions were conducted to promote the concept of Speciality Coffee.

Promotion

During the year under report, the Coffee Board participated in the selected International Exhibitions and Trade Fairs by exhibiting charts, blow-ups and promotional literature in different foreign languages highlighting the high quality and excellent aroma of Indian Coffee for the benefit of importers and roasters of different countries.

Special advertisements on the excellence of Indian Coffee were released in important coffee trade journals and magazines in such of those countries which have the potential markets for quality Indian Coffee.

During the period under review, the Coffee Board participated in the following international trade fairs:-

1. Ethnic 98- Food Drinks Exhibition, Burmingham, UK,
2. 50th International Trade Fair of Trieste, Italy,
3. International Fancy Food and Confection Show, New York and
4. 27th Annual Convention and Trade Show, Reno, Nevada.

Besides this, the Coffee Board also participated in important exhibitions within the country as detailed below:-

1. UPASI Industrial Exhibition, Coonoor.
2. Agro Food Tech, Mumbai.
3. Agro Tech-98, Chandigarh.

The Board also arranged service of coffee on many occasions upon received requests from various reputed organisations in addition to service of pure coffee at the Board's pavilion in the exhibitions.

Projecting and planning

Board submitted an elaborate development plan programme to support the various segments of the coffee industry in the country for the 9th Plan period for a total outlay of Rs. 105 crores. Out of the 41 schemes proposed by the Board categorised under 10 major programmes, the Planning Commission has given approval for 40 schemes. Though the final area of the 9th Plan allocation for the Board is yet to be known, the Government of India sanctioned a tentative allocation of Rs. 23 crores for both the years 1997-98 and 1998-99 (the first two years of the 9th Plan). The following are the major programmes the allocation proposed for 9th Plan, an allocation approved by the Government for the year 1998-99.

Research department

The Research Programmes of the Board were carried out under four major groups namely (a) Crop improvement (Botany and Tissue Culture); (b) Crop Management (Agronomy, Agricultural Chemistry and Plant Physiology); (c) Crop Protection (Plant Pathology and Entomology/Nematology and (d) Post Harvest Technology. The achievements during 1997-98 under each of the major groups are highlighted below:-

Crop Improvement

— Among the 12 crosses of Cauvery / Catimor genotypes established for evaluation, S.4631 Cauvery Crosses performed well in terms of plant height, number of primaries, bush spread as compared to S.4641

— Out of 18 HDT Crosses (Tall), S.4629 showed better plant height, bush spread, stem girth and number of primaries.

— Multilocational evaluation of SLN.6 crosses revealed that S.4375 was superior to S.4369.

— Under Large Scale multiplication programme under the Tissue Culture Project, Callus generation from Leaf explants of SLN.9 (S 2792, S.2794 and S.2800) were achieved,

— Cauvery Cultures (S.4347, S.4348, S.4350) were established from selected mother plants from the nucleus plot at CCRI.

— About 3100 plantlets regenerated from leaf, stem, anther, integument and endosperm of S.4350, CxR, Cauvery, Robusta, S.2803 and S.2800 were plated for hardening.

— Protocol for extraction of high quality DNA from leaf tissues of coffee is standardised mythology for study DNA polymorphism through RAPD profiles was also standardised for under taking DNA finger printing.

— About 7000 CxR Sucker Cuttings were made available to the growers

— The S.880 Ugandan Robusta recorded highest yield of 1281 Kg/ha., as against Costa Rican selection S.3399 (920 Kg/ha.), and S.879 Java selection (908 Kg/ha.).

Crop management

— Development of Efficient Water Management models in Coffee. In the experiment on Water requirement of Cauvery Coffee, the daily irrigation treatment with (1.00 CPE) Water (13) was found to produce significantly high number of bearing nodes when compared to daily irrigation with 0.75 CPE water.

— In another irrigation experiment carried out Regional, Coffee Research Station, R.V.Nagar on Cauvery coffee, application of 4 litres per plant per day with drip/pitcher/bamboo tubes gave significant high yield (2184-2984 Kg/ha.), when compared to unirrigated control (1450 Kg/ha.), during the first year.

— Studies on fertigation in robusta coffee at CCRI revealed that fertigation treatment with water soluble fertilisers (13:13:13: NPK) at the rate of 60:45:60 Kg NPK/ha., resulted in significantly higher yield (755 Kg/ha.) when compared to Control (ground application of 90:60:90 Kg NPK/ha.).

— A new battery operated low volume herbicide sprayer 'SAMURAI CDA' was evaluated and was found to be more efficient than hand operated 'Knap Sack' sprayer in terms of Weed Killing, labour and water saving and overall economics of Weedicide sprays.

— Application of 120:120:120 Kg NPK/ha., in two splits (pre and post monsoon) recorded highest yields at R.V.Nagar, Minimuluru and Koraput as per the initial studies.

— The ph of Bordeaux mixture when maintained in the range of 9 to 10 resulted in maximum efficacy.

— A total of 11,200 soil samples were tested and examined for ph, NPK and micro-nutrients for advisory purpose and a total of 400 leaf samples, 150 agro-chemicals and 15 water samples were tested.

Crop production

— Studies on Leaf Rust—Out of six leaf rust races attempted for isolation, only three races namely Race II, XII and XXIV were isolated. Record of Rust incidence on 12 arabica cultivars indicated that Kents, S.795, Cauvery, SLN. 10 and SLN. 6 had higher incidence of Leaf Rust during September to November compared to SLN. 11, SLN. 8 and SLN. 5.

— Studies on Black Rot—Bordeaux mixture in combination with Muriate of Potash (350 g/200 L) was found to be better than Bordeaux mixture alone in protecting the plants from Black Rot.

— Studies on Brown Root Rot - Robusta Plants with initial symptoms of brown root rot when treated twice a year with Trichoderma Viride, a bio-control agent showed recovery.

— Studies on the new stem disease - Research studies are in progress to identify the Casual Organism and suggest remedial measures to arrest further spread of the disease.

—Studies on White Stem Bore - In a laboratory trial, Endosulfan 35 EC and Lindane 20 EC showed efficacy against the adult stem Borer for 83 days, Chlorpyrifos 20 EC for 76 days, Nimbecidine for 33 days, Lindane 6.5 WP for 80 days and Cashew oil for 23 days. Field and Laboratory studies using synthetic Pheromone showed that Pheromone technique was effective in trapping and monitoring white stem borer adult female.

— Studies of Coffee berry Borer -The spread of the pest to uninfested areas has been arrested to a great extent. Cephalonomia Stephanoderis, the exotic parasitoid of berry borer was bred and about one lakh parasitoids were released in kodagu (Karnataka) and Waynad (Kerala). Beauveria bassiana sprays continued to record higher infectivity adult berry borer in field trials.

— Biological and Chemical Control of Mealy Bugs -A parasitoid breeding facility was started at CDF, Gonicoppal (Coorg district of Karnataka). About 1,40,000 parasitoids were released in 57 estates.

Post harvest technology

— Grading of Fruits —The size distribution of fruits in robusta cultivars have shown that the varieties CxR and diallelic crosses have better fruit size than old robusta and S.274.

— Drying of Coffee—Drying of coffee on tiled and concrete surfaces was comparatively faster by a day than drying on HDPE net spread on raised bamboo frame.

— Studies on different Processing methods—Pre-fermentation of arabica reduces washing time by 30-35% and the water used was found to be correspondingly less Quality of arabica processed by natural fermentation (24 hours), and soaking was found to be better than samples processed by alkali wash and natural fermentation. In robusta, coffee obtained by alkali method and semi dry process are comparable in quality and better than samples processed by dry method.

— Preliminary data on the analysis of effluents in different tanks revealed that the modified NEERI method recommended by the KSPCB can be applied for treating coffee effluent to certain standards.

— The data on moisture content of parchment and cherry revealed that they could be stored upto the end of May at estate level, in gunny and polythene knitted bags.

Development programmes

Starting from 6th Plan upto 9th Plan, the Coffee Board was involved in financing the small grower sector directly and was lending both short-term and long-term loan schemes. Consequent to the liberalisation and stoppage of marketing activities, the Board was faced with lot of difficulties in recovering the development loan dues from the grower sector as the coffee was no more being pooled with the Board and most of these loans were extended to the growers under liberalised terms and conditions. This led to the stoppage of direct loaning activities by the Board to the grower sector during the end of 8th Plan period. However, to provide the much needed financial support to the small grower sector particularly the tiny grower sector, Board proposed a comprehensive Coffee Development Plan in which 25% of the loan amount to take up critical activities viz., replantation, water augmentation, quality upgradation measures like construction of drying yards, storage houses etc., is proposed to be given as one time grant for the small grower sector coming under the category of ha and below. The balance 75% of the loan amount was to be availed from the financial institutions as loan component. For Coffee development in non-traditional areas viz. North East Region, Andhra Pradesh and Orissa also, the Coffee Board has proposed a comprehensive Coffee development plan in which 50% of the credit component will be given as an one time grant and the balance amount is to be availed from concerned State Government and tribals themselves. Board has already started operating these Schemes from the year 1998-99 onwards.

Future prospects of the coffee industry

Consequent to the liberalisation and giving up of the direct marketing activities, the Board has shifted its focus to other critical areas viz. research and development, transfer of technology through extension, providing market related information to the industry, supporting quality upgradation programmes, promotion of speciality coffees, generic promotion activities to enlarge the domestic coffee market, training of different segments of the industry for production improvement quality improvement on market related aspects. The primary, objectives of the Board for the 9th Plan are:

1. Increase the production level to 3 lakh tonnes by the of 9th Plan
2. Increase the export market to 2 lakh tonnes by the end of 9th Plan.

3. Enlarge the domestic market to 1 lakh tonnes by the end of 9th Plan.
4. Bridge the yield gap between Small Grower Sector (750 Kg. per ha.) and the Large Grower Sector (1000 Kg. per ha.).
5. Support the tribal sector in North East Region and other non-traditional areas for coffee development.
6. Promotion of speciality Coffees and Organic Coffees.
7. Arrange interaction between the foreign coffee buyers and the Indian Grower/Trader Sector.

Export of agricultural products

Exports of agricultural products are dependant on a number of factors such as domestic production and consumption exportable surpluses, consumer preferences, varieties traded, quality, domestic and international prices and availability of infrastructure facilities for storage, post harvest handling etc. Having regard to the social and economic importance of the agricultural sector, the export strategy of the Government is based on the premise that foreign earnings from this sector should be enhanced thereby leading to higher income to farmers. While doing so care is to be taken to make agricultural products available at reasonable prices to the domestic consumers.

The exports of Agri products which were valued at Rs. 7,760 crores at the beginning of the 8th Plan have risen to over Rs. 15,000 crores in 1996-97, the end of 8th Plan. The Agri products exported can be divided into three broad categories i.e. exports of raw products, semi processed products and export exclusive and value added products. The raw products exported are of low value and high volume; semi-processed products exported are of intermediate value and limited volume; and export exclusive and value added products are of high value and low volume. The major agricultural products exported from India are:

basmati and non-basmati rice, spices, cashew, tobacco, cereals, oil cakes and extractions, fresh fruits and vegetables, processed foods and vegetables, meat and meat products, sugar, shellac, niger seed, guargum, HPS groundnuts, etc

Rice

Rice constitutes bulk of the total foodgrains export basket. The international trade is dominated by Thailand, USA and Vietnam. Rice is freely exportable from the country without any quantity and price restrictions. However the export contracts are required to be registered with APEDA. Non-basmati rice is mainly exported to Bangladesh, Indonesia, Iran, Philippines and countries in sub-Sahara Africa. The major basmati rice export markets are Saudi Arabia, Kuwait, UAE, UK and USA.

Wheat and wheat products

Exports of wheat and wheat products are permitted subject to quantitative ceilings and MEP as notified by the DGFT from time to time. During the year 1998-99, export of wheat was banned due to shortage in the country. However, a quantity of one lakh tonnes has been released for wheat product exports. Besides this, exports of 45,000 MT of wheat have been permitted to neighbouring countries and 25,000 MT have been permitted for export to Iraq under its 'Oil for Food' programme.

Pulses

Pulses production in the country has been stagnating around 11 to 14 Million Tonnes as against domestic demand for around 20 Million Tonnes. To augment availability of Pulses in the country, pulses have been placed, under OGL. Due to gap in domestic demand and supply, India is a net importer of pulses. Exim Policy allows export of pulses under licence. The export of pulses in consumer packs with effect from 1.12.1997 has been permitted. The major buyers of Indian pulses are UAE, Sri Lanka and Kuwait-

Coarse grains

Jowar, Bajra, Maize, Ragi, small Millet and Barley constitute coarse grains. Exim Policy allows export of coarse grains subject to quantitative ceilings as notified by the Directorate General of Foreign Trade from time to time. For the year 1998-99, an export ceiling of 1 lakh MT was released.

Oil seeds and oil meals

Soyabean meal accounts for more than 70% of the export turnover from this sector. The export of oil meals picked up in 1996-97 and were valued at Rs. 3,486 crores. The exports during 1997-98 have been 5,825,162 MT amounting to Rs. 3,403.64 crones.

Tobacco

In India, about 6 million farmers and farm hands are engaged in cultivation of tobacco and industry directly or indirectly. Recognising the need for enhanced exports of tobacco and to regulate production for controlling recurring instances of imbalances in supply and demand, the Tobacco Board was set up by the Government of India on the 1st January, 1976 under the Tobacco Board Act, 1975.

Domestic production

The Tobacco Board is mainly responsible for regulating production, curing and marketing of Virginia tobacco to achieve the larger objective of ensuring remunerative returns to the tobacco growers. The Board determines the area to be cultivated having regard to the demand for the same in the domestic market and its potential for exports.

FCV Tobacco is mainly cultivated in Andhra Pradesh and Karnataka, and in some parts of Maharashtra and Orissa. The quantities authorised for production of Virginia tobacco as per crop size fixed by Tobacco Board for the year 199798 in Karnataka and Andhra Pradesh are 32.00 Million Kgs and 110.00 Million Kgs respectively.

Exports

In addition to export promotion, Tobacco Board has also initiated measures for improving quality and yield of FCV tobacco and for improving curing and storing facilities.

Welfare of SC/ STs

Tobacco Board has been assisting farmers from SC/ST communities to improve yields and quality of FCV tobacco by covering them under various developmental extension schemes. The assistance included:—

(i) Supply of 'Sulphate of Potash' fertilizer with a subsidy of 25% of the cost limited to Rs. 400/- to Rs. 700/- per hectare.

(ii) Cash subsidy of Rs. 400/- per hectare for pest and disease control.

(iii) Supply of sprinkler irrigation sets at 90% subsidy i.e. Rs. 18,000/- per set.

(iv) Subsidising a portion of transportation cost of coal used for tobacco curing in Karnataka.

(v) Cash subsidy of Rs. 2000/- per barns for construction of barley curing barns in barley areas.

(vi) Supply of tarpaulins at 25% subsidy to ensure proper storage of tobacco.

(vii) Supply of briquettes and furnace sets at 25% cost subsidy.

During 1997-98 an amount of Rs. 10.56 lakhs was spent under these measures and Rs. 14.64 lakhs is proposed to be spent in 1998-99.

Spices

India has a long history of producing and exporting spices, The world trade in spices is estimated around 4.5 lakh MTs of which India's share is 50.8% in quantity terms. Molar spices in the international trade are pepper, capsicum, seed spices, cinnamon and cassia.

Domestic production

The total production of spices in the country is estimate around 26 lakh Mts. (1996-97). The area under cultivation is estimated to be about 23 lakh hectares (1996-97). While almost all States produce spices, the important states accounting for sizeable area and production are Kerala, Karnataka Tamil Nadu, Andhra Pradesh, Rajasthan and Maharashtra.

The spices board

Spices Board Act, 1986 assigns to the Spices Board the responsibility of export development of 52 spices. Some of the major spices among them are pepper, chilli, ginger, turmeric, cardamom, coriander, cumin, fennel, fenugreek, celery, vanilla and saffron. The Board is implementing a number of schemes aimed at export development of spices such as quality evaluation and upgradation with a view to meet international standards and promotion of export of value added spices. The Board has well established quality evaluation and upgradation laboratory at Cochin which is engaged in surveying the quality of spices procured from different producing and marketing centres. It offers training of quality upgradation to growers and exporters and undertakes physical, chemical and biological analysis of the samples brought by the exporters.

Exports

Exports of spices is freely allowed under the present Exim Policy. As against the total estimated production of 26 lakh tonnes, the normal export of spices has been in the range of 2 lakh Mts to 2.5 lakh Mts. Pepper is the most important spice exported from India. Cardamom, chillies, ginger, turmeric, seed spices, curry powders and spice oils and oleoresins are the other main spices/spice products exported from India

Export promotion

The Spices Board has a number of schemes of assistance to spice exporters such as Brand Promotion, Logo Promotion, grant of "Spice House Certificate etc."

Suspension/abolition of cess on export of spices

Cess on export of spices has since been rationalised. Cess on export of all spices is levied at the rate of 0.5% ad valorem. This has been done to make the spices internationally competitive.

Apart from these schemes, Spices Board is also offering air freight/courier charges for sending samples abroad, assistance for upgradation of technology in spice processing, packaging developments.

Developmental activities

As per the Spices Board Act, the Board is responsible for the development of cardamom including its export promotion activities. Various programmes implemented by the Spices Board for the development of cardamom, including Production and Supply of Planting Material

Cardamom Replanting Scheme; Irrigation, land Development and Afforestation Programmes; Extension Advisory Scheme; and Tribal Development Programme.

Board is also assisting tribal growers of cardamom by implementing various developmental programmes with enhanced financial assistance. Similarly, in case of large cardamom also, assistance is given through these schemes.

Apart from that, Indian Cardamom Research Institute under the Spices Board carries out need based research programmes for the crop improvement work in cardamom as also post-harvest techniques.

Cashew

India has emerged as the largest producer, processor and exporter of cashew kernels in the world. Brazil, Tanzania, Mozambique and Kenya are the other major exporters.

Domestic production

The production of raw cashew nuts in the country is not adequate to meet the requirements of the processing capacity installed in the country. The cashew processors have, therefore, to import raw cashewnuts to meet their needs. During 1997-98, about 2.24 lakh tons of raw nuts worth Rs. 744 crores were imported.

Exports

Cashew kernels processed out of raw cashewnuts are exported to more than 30 countries. Very small quantities of, roasted/salted cashewnuts in consumer packs of 1 kg or less are also exported. Principal destinations of exports are the USA, Netherlands, Japan, U.K, Australia, Singapore, France, UAE and Germany.

Cashewnut shell liquid (NSL) is also exported to a small extent earning about Rs. 6.74 crores during 1997-98. The Cashew Export Promotion Council looks after the promotional activities related to exports. The activities undertaken by the Council include participation in fairs, trade delegations, arranging buyer-seller meets, regular publications etc.

Developmental programmes

The quality upgradation laboratory and technical consultancy wing set up by the council with the Plan funds released by the Ministry of Commerce, was inaugurated in September, 1997. This laboratory is equipped with state-of-the-art machinery and equipments.

As a horticulture item, central assistance for enhancing domestic production and productivity of raw cashewnuts is provided by the Ministry of Agriculture and Central Sector programme for integrated Development of Cashewnuts in India is being implemented by that Ministry. Under this programme, measures such as area expansion with clonal planting material, improvement of cashew by gestate propagation and maintenance of scion banks, adoption of intensive pest control measures are adopted, besides pilot demonstration for popularisation of clonal cultivation and preparations from cashew apple. A Training Centre to impart training to the technical personnel deputed by the Cashew processors, managers, supervisors, workers and other employees of the processor exports has been established at Quilon during the year 1997-98.

Horticulture and floriculture products, fruits and vegetables, processed fruits and juices and other miscellaneous products

The Agricultural and Processed Food Products Export Development Authority (APEDA) is engaged in the export promotion and development of fruits and vegetables and their products, meat & meat products, rice, wheat, floriculture & floriculture products, processed fruits and juices and several other miscellaneous agricultural products. Some of the major product groups are discussed below:

Floriculture and seeds

Floriculture and seeds have been identified as thrust area for export. APEDA implemented a UNDP project for enhancing production and exports of floriculture products. Under this project, workshops were held at Delhi, Bangalore & Pune and at Guwahati and Shillong in the North Eastern region to share information and experience with the industry/exporters and to create awareness on the potential for commercial production of floriculture products. Production manuals for Gladiolus, Antharium Eustoma Russellannum and Perennial statice have been prepared and disseminated to prospective growers and others concerned. This sector has shown a steady increase in exports from Rs. 55 crores in 1994-95 to Rs. 139 crores in 1997-98.

Fresh fruits and vegetables

India is the second largest producer of fruits and vegetables in the world. There has been significant increase in the export of fresh fruits and vegetables during the past few years. Exports increased from Rs. 433 crores in 1994-95 to Rs. 588 crores in 1997-98. The major fruits exported are mangoes, grapes, bananas, citrus fruits. Some new fruits introduced by Indian exporters in international markets are strawberries, pomegranates, lychees and custard apples. In order to improve quality of fruits and vegetables, draft pre-harvest manuals on Mandarin and Lychees have been prepared for dissemination to farmers and producers. APEDA has initiated a programme for an integrated training of horticulture producers for some identified fruits such as grapes, mangoes, lychees, kinnows in the selected regions. Farmers have been provided training in

Integrated post harvest management practices for better handling of the produce to ensure export of quality products.

Processed fruits and vegetables

Export of processed fruits and vegetables is another thrust area for encouraging export of value added products. A number of large national and multinational companies have now entered into the processed food industries with a thrust on exports. Some of the new products which have been introduced in the market are tomato paste in bulk aseptic packs, button mushrooms, freeze dried and Instant Quick Frozen fruits and vegetables and gherkins. Exports of processed fruits and vegetables increased more than two fold from Rs. 348 crores in 1994-95 to Rs. 762 crores in 1997-98. APEDA in its quality upgradation programme has covered 12 Mango pulp processing units in Andhra Pradesh for certification under the HACCP Quality Management Pool

Meat and meat products

While buffalo meat is exported both in fresh and frozen forms, the sheep and goat meat is generally exported in fresh form, Beef (i.e. meat of cow and its progeny) is banned for export.

The major markets for our meat and meat products are Malaysia, UAE, Kuwait, Mauritius, Lebanon, Jordan, Turkey, Saudi Arabia, Oman and Philippines. There has been a steady growth in the export of meat and meat products during the last ten years despite temporary/total ban imposed by some importing countries due to alleged unhygienic conditions of Indian slaughter houses as also prevalence of Rinderpest/Foot and Mouth Diseases in certain parts of India. During the period 1991-92 to 1997-98, exports have grown by 240%. However, there has been a decline of 6.4% in these exports during April-September, 98 as compared to the corresponding period of last year. From a level of Rs. 392.62 crores in April-September 1997, these have fallen to the level of Rs. 367.32 crores during period of current year mainly on account of substantial decline in exports to Malaysia and Philippines who have been confronted with a serious financial crisis for quite sometime.

In view of mounting concerns regarding quality of Indian meat from importing countries, a number of steps have been taken to improve the quality of Indian meat such as specifying internationally acceptable standards for Raw meat (Chilled and Frozen) and Processed Meat Products as well as animal casings, upgrading of slaughter houses and increased efforts for control of animal diseases.

New products introduced by APEDA

APEDA is a promotional agency and does not undertake direct exports of any products on its own account, However, it has made efforts to promote new products and open up new markets. Through the efforts of APEDA many new products from India have been introduced in the last three years. These include grapes, mangoes, pomegranates, cut- flowers, tomato prepared/ preserved, conned button mushrooms, freeze dried mushrooms and other vegetables, gherkins preserved/ fresh. As a result of these efforts, there have been enhanced exports of fruits such as pomegranates and cut-flowers.

Schemes of APEDA

Government is providing financial assistance to eligible exporters for establishment of various facilities for export of Scheduled Products of APEDA. These are:-

— Scheme for Development of Infrastructure and services. Scheme for Export Promotion and Market Development. Scheme for Packaging Development.

— Scheme for Assistance to Promote Quality and Quality Control.

— Scheme for upgradation of meat plants.

— Scheme for organisation building and human resource development and training,

— Scheme for generating relevant research through research institutions for common benefit of trade and industry.

— Scheme for setting up of Wholesale/ Marketing-cum-Auction Centres for flowers at Delhi, Mumbai, Bangalore, Chennai and Pune.

— Scheme for survey, feasibility studies, consultancy and data base.

Air freight subsidy scheme on selected fresh fruits and fresh vegetables and floricultural products.

Development efforts of APEDA

(i) Programme for setting up of VHT facilities with aid from Japan:

For export of fruits and vegetables, quality control is extremely stringent in Japan and the products are required to be treated with Vapour Heat Treatment measures before export.

Under this scheme, a pilot plant has been set up at New Delhi with technical know-how and assistance from Japan. Based on the experience gained from this experiment more plants are proposed to be set up subsequently in other areas such as Maharashtra, etc. The effectiveness of the process has been tested and the test reports sent to the Government of Japan for meeting their import requirements. The commercial scale adoption of the system is yet to be worked out.

(ii) Establishment of Integrated Cold Storage Cargo Handling facility at Major Airports:

An integrated cold storage and cargo handling facility has been set up of the IGI Airport, New Delhi and has been operational since January 1998. A similar facility has also been set up at Bangalore Airport. Such facilities are also being established at Chennai, Hyderabad and Thiruvananthapuram Airports.

SHELLAC

The Shellac Export Promotion Council looks after the export of lac in various forms like Shellac, both hand-made and machine made, dewaxed shellac, seedlac, aleuritic acid, bleached lac and shellac wax.

The exports of shellac are subject to registration with TRIFED and production of quality certificate from Shellac Export Promotion Council. The major importing countries of Indian Shellac are USA, Indonesia, Germany, Arab Republic of Egypt, UK, Italy and Canada. The decline in exports during the lost two years has been mainly on account of fall in prices in the international markets and a stiff price competition faced from Thailand and Myanmar.

Policy initiatives to increase exports

Since Agricultural exports offer the greatest potential for increasing the farm income, tackling unemployment and earning foreign exchange, the Government has been providing a thrust to agricultural exports by building upon conducive policy environment. A number of policy changes have been introduced to make agricultural exports more viable. Some of the measures undertaken include raising of investment limits of small scale sector to Rs. 3 crores and excluding rice milling from the list of items reserved for small sector.

8

Small and Tiny Enterprises

The primary objective of the Government's policy for Small and Tiny Enterprises would be to impart more vitality and growth impetus to the sector to enable it to contribute its mite fully to the economy particularly in terms of out put, employment and exports. In this context, it is heartening to note that at the end of the 7th Plan period the small scale sector accounted for mearly 35 per cent of the gross value of the out put in the manufacturing sector and over 40 per cent of the total exports from the country.

It also provided employment opportunties to around 12 million people. To ensure the growth of the Small and Tiny sector the Government proposes to review and modify all Statutes, regulations and procedures wherever necessary, to ensure that their operations do not militate against the interest of small and village enterprises.

As mentioned earlier in this paper, manufacturing units with an investment and plant and machinery up to * 75 lakhs and units which are willing to undertake an export obligation to the extent of 30 per cent of their annual production by 3rd year with an investment of Rs. up to 75 lakhs are eligigle for small scale registration. The investment limit in respect of Tiny Enterprises has been increased from Rs. 2 lakhs to Rs. 5 lakhs. With the objective of providing support to the service sector in view of its potential for generating employment, it has been decided that in future all industry related service and business enterprises irrespective of their location would be recognised as small scale industries and their investment ceiling would correspond to those of Tiny Enterprises.

Units in the small scale sector (other than Tiny Enterprises) would be entitled to benefits like preference in land allocation, power connection, access to facilities for skill/technology upradation. Tiny enterprises would in addition to these benefits will also be eligble for additional support including easier access to institutional finance, priority in the Government purchase programme and relaxation from certain provisions of labour laws.

Inadequate access to credit-both short—term and long—term remains a perennial problem facing the small scale sector. Emphasis would henceforth shift from subsidiese/cheap credit, except for specified target groups, and efforts would be made to ensure both adequate flow of credit on a normative basis, and the quality of its delivery, for viable operations of this sector. A special monitoring agency would be set up to oversee that the genuine credit needs of the small scale sector are fully met. To provide access to the capital market and to encourage modernisation and technlogical upgradation, it has been decided to allow equity participation by other industrial undertakings in the SSI, not exceeding 24 per cent of the total shareholding. this would also provide a powerful boost to ancillarisation and subcontracting, leading to expansion of employment opportunities.

Regulatory provisions relating to the management of private limited companies are being liberalised. A Limited Partnership Act will be introduced to enhance the supply of risk capital to the small scale sector. Such an Act would limit the financial liability of the new and non-active partners/entrepreneurs to the capital invested.

A beginning has been made towards solving the problems of delayed payments to small industries by setting up of factoring services through Small Industries Development Bank of India (SIDBI). Network of such services would be set up throughout the country and operated through commercial banks. A suitable legislation will be introduced to ensure prompt payment of small industries' bills.

To facilitate location of industries in rural/backward areas and to promote stringer linkages between agriculture and industry, a new Scheme of Integrated Infrastructural Develpoment (including Technological Back-up Services) for Small Scale Industries would be implemented with the active participation of State Government and Financial Institutions. A beginning in this direction will be made this year itself.

A Technology Development Cell (TDC) would be set up in the Small Industries Development Organisation (SIDO) which would provide technology inputs to improve productivity and competitiveness of the products of the small scale sector. The TDC would coordinate the activities of the Tool Rooms, Process-cum-Product Development Centres (PPDCs), existing as well as to be established under SIDO, and would also interact with the other industrial research and development organisations to achieve its objectives.

Adequacy and equitable distribution of indigenous and imported raw material would be ensured to the small scale sector, particularly the tiny sub-sector. Policies would be so designed that they do not militate against entry of new units. Based on the capacity needs, Tiny/ Small Scale Units would be given priority in allocation of indigenous raw materials.

A proper and adequate arrangement for delivery of

total package of incentives and services at the District level will be evolved and implemented.

Inspite of the vast domestic market, marketing remains a problem area for Small and Tiny Enterprises. Mass consumption labour intensive products are predominantly being marketed by the organised sector. The Tiny/Small Scale Sector will be enabled to access existing support mechanism. Market promotion would be undertaken through cooperative/public sector institutions, other specialised/professional marketing agencies and consortia approach, backed up by such incentives as considered necessary.

National Small Industries Corporation (NSIC) would concentrate on marketing of mass consumption items under common brand name and organic links between NSCI and State Small Industries Development Corporations (SSIDCs) would be established.

Government recognises the need to widen and deepen complementarity in production programmes of large/medium and small industrial sectors. Parts, components, sub assemblies, etc. required by large public/private sector undertakings would be encouraged for production in a techno-economically viable manner through small scale ancillary units. Industry associations would be encouraged to establish subcontracting exchanges, in addition to strengthening the existing ones under the SIDO. Emphasis would also be laid on promotion of a viable and competitive component market.

Though the small scale sector is making significant contribution to total exports both direct and indirect, a large potential remains untapped. SIDO has been recognised as the nodal agency to support the small scale industries in export promotion. An Export Development Centre would be set up in SIDO to serve the small scale industries through its network of field offices to further augment export activities of this sector.

A greater degree of awareness to produce goods and services conforming to national and international standards would be created among the small scale sector.

Industry Associations would be encouraged and supported to establish quality counselling and common testing facilities. Technology Information Centres to provide updated knowledge on technology and markets would be established.

Where non-conformity with quality and standards involves risk to human life and public health, compulsory quality control would be enforced.

Are-oriented programme of modernisation and technological upgradation aimed at improving productivity, efficiency and cost effectiveness in the small scale sector would be pursued. Specific industries in large concentrations/clusters would be identified for studies in conjunction with SIDBI and other banks. Such studies will establish commercial viability of modernisation prescriptions, and financial support would be provided for modernisation of these industries on a priority basis.

Indian Institutes of Technology (IITs) and selected Regional/other Engineering Colleges will serve as Technological Information, design and Development Centres in their respective command areas.

Government will continue to support first generation entrepreneurs thrugh training and other measures. Large number of EDP trainers and motivators will be trained to significantly expand the Entrepreneurship Development Programmes (EDP). Industry Associations would also be encouraged to participate in this venture effectively.

EDP would be built into the curricula of vocational and other degree level courses. Women entrepreneurs will receive support through special training programmes. Definition of "Women Enterprises" would be simplified. The present stipulation regarding employment of majority of women workers would be dispensed with and units in which women entrepreneurs have majority shareholding and management control, would be defined as "Women Enterprises".

Additional employment opportunities would be generated through training of multi-disciplinary barefoot managers to suit special requirements of the small scale sector.

The persistent complaint of small scale units of being subjected to a large number of Acts and Laws, being required to maintain a number of registers and submit returns, and face an army of inspectors, would be attended to within a specified time frame of three months.

Procedures would be simplified, bureaucratic controls effectively reduced, unnecessary interference eliminated an paper work cut down to the minimumto enable the entrepreneur to concentrate on production and marketing function.

The Government has also announced a number of steps for promoting Handloom sector, handicrafts sector and other village industries.

A number of organisations are engaged in exploration and development of mineral resources in India. These include Geolgical survey of India (GSI), Indian Bureau of Mines (IBM) and a number of public sector undertakings under the administrative control of the Ministry of Mines.

Geological Survey of India functions as the premier national organisation for earth science, entrusted with the task of scientific survey and research for locating mineral resources (except oil, natural gas and atomic minerals), systematic generation and continous updating of geoscience information through ground, airborne and marine survey, the entire gamut of activities being related to multifarious developmental needs of the country. The survey operates within the ambit of its charter 1873 and priorities laid down by the Government.

The other important functions of the organisation cover management of natural hazards like earthquake, floods, landslides, volcanism etc., providing geotechnical advice to all the major civil engineering, communication and urban development projects, geoenvironmental resource appraisal, upgradation of geoscientific expertise through training. The results of GSI investigations are documented in the form of scientific and technical reports, professional papers, maps, inventories and various types of publications.

The survey with its central headquarters at Calcutta, functions through six geographically based regions, three activity based Wings (Marine, Coal and Airborne Survey) and one training Institute. In each of the region/wings towards * greater collaboration and setting up of consultancy and commercial endeavours in the third world countries.

The Indian Bureau of Mines (IBM) is the national organisation under Ministry of Mines and engaged in promotion, conservation and scientific development of mineral resources of the country other than coal, petroleum and natural gas, atomic minerals and minor minerals. It performs regulatory functions, namely enforcement of Mines and Minerals (Regulation & Development Rules and the provision of Environmental Protection Act.

It also undertakes scientific techno-economic, research-orientid studies in various aspects such as geological, mining ore beneficiation and environment. IBM provides technical consultancy services to the mining industry for geological appraisal of mineral resources and preparation of feasibility reports of mining projects including beneficiation plants. It prepares mineral maps and countrywide inventory of minerals resources of leasehold and freehold areas.

IBM also functions as data bank for mines and minerals and publishes statistical periodicals and brings out technical publications/monogrphs on individual mineral commodities and bulletins on different connected subjects. it advises the Central and state governments on all aspects of mineral industry, trade and legislation. It imparts training to technical and non-technical officials of IBM and also persons from mineral industry and other agencies in India and abroad. IBM is organised into six functional agencies in India and abroad. IBM is organised into six functional divisions. It has its headquarters at Nagpur and 11 regional offices and well equipped ore-dressing laboratories and Pilot Plant at Nagpur, besides, twc regional ore-dressing laboratories at Ajmer and Bangalore. IBM also has a big Central Library with about 61,000 books.

Public sector

Minral Exploration Corporation Limited (MECL) was created in 1972 with the main objective of bridging the gap between the disc overy of mineral prospect and its eventual exploitation. Its identified major functions are to plan, promote, organise and implement programme for the exploration of mineral resources and to perform such functions as Central Government may from time to time, assign to the company in connection with exploration of the mineral resources in and outside the country.

The Corporation has its headquarters at Nagpur. MECL has fulfilled its main objective by establishing over 55,000 million tonnes of reserves of higher confidence for veriety of minerals. The drilling capacity of 72,000 m per annum at the time of inception in 1972 has increased to 4.25 lakh metre of drilling and mining capacity has increased from 1200 mtr in 1972 to 9000 m in the last year of Seventh Five Year Plan. During 1993-94, the turnover of the company was Rs. 40.73 crore.

Bharat Aluminium Company Limited (BALCO) was incorporated on 27 November 1965 as the first primary aluminium producing undertaking in the public sector. The Company is operating Korba Aluminium Complex in Bilaspur district of Madhya Pradesh and Bidhanbag Unit in Asanosl in west Bengal. It has a capacity to produce one lakh tonnes of aluminium metal/products. During the past few years, the Company's production of saleable metal/products has been about 92,000 tonnes per annum. Its net profit has been going up steadily and during 1994-95, it earned a net profit of Rs. 90.51 crore (provisional). The new projects of the Company include installation of a new Cold Rolling Mill having an installed capacity to produce 40,000 TPA of thin quality sheets/coils. The Comapny is also in the process of modernisation of their smelter plant at Korba for increased productivity and reduction of power consumption, which is a major factor in input costs.

National Aluminium Company Limited (NALCO) was incorporated on 7 January 1981 with the objective to produce alumina and aluminium. Its registerd office is at Bhubaneswar. It operates a bauxite mine to raise 24 lakh tonnes per annum of bauxite from the Parnchpatnali (Koraput) deposits, an eight lakh tonnes per annum alumina refinery at Damanjodi (Koraput), a 2,18,000 tonnes per annum aluminium smelter at Angul

(Dhenkanal) and six 120 MW captive power plants at Angul to feed the smelter. Aluminium Pechiney of France was the technical consultants for the project and had supplied the technical know-how and basic engineering package.

NALCO received ISO 9002 Certification from IROS for Alumina Refinery on 21 November 1994 and ISO 9002 Certification for quality system for Smelter Plan in March 1995 from RWTUV. Highest production of calcined alumina of 81,000 MT during January 1995 exceeding the rated capacity. NALCO produced 1,78,072 tonnes of aluminium and earned net profit of Rs. 294.62 (provisional) during the same period.

Hindustan inc Limited (HZL) was incorporated on 10 January 1966 to take over operations of the earstwhile Metal Corporation of India Limited and to develop mining and smelting capacities to substantially meet the domestic demand of zinc and lead metals. With headquarters at Udaipur, HZL's operations are spread over in the states of Rajasthan, Andhra Pradesh, Orissa and Bihar consisting of five mines with a total lead-zinc ore production capacity of 3.04 million tpa and four smelters with combined installed capacity of 1,49,000 tpa zinc and 65,000 tpa lead besides a rock phosphate and tungsten mine. The company offers a wide range of zinc and lead metai grades to its customers, besides a range of by-products.

The production of zinc metal by the company during the last four years has ranged between 84,600 tpa and 1,19,810 tpa. The lead production during the same period has ranged between 30,300 tpa and 34,500 tpa. The sales turnover of the company during 1994-95 was Rs. 97,274 lakh and its net profit (after tax) during the same period was Rs. 7,643 lakh.

HZL signed a Memorandum of Understanding with M/s. Niugini Mining Limited.Australia, to identify gold resources in India and later on if resources are found viable, to set up a joint venture. It has also signed an MoU with M/s. BHP Minerals, Austrails, for exploration and development of base and procious metals in Rajasthan. Besides, HZL and BRGM, France, have reached an agreement with Vietnam Rare and Precious Metal Corporation (VMC) for setting up of joint venture for exploration and development of Pac Lang Gold Prospect in Vietnam.

Hindustan Copper Limited (HCL) is the sole producer of primary copper metal in the country. It was incorporated on 7 November 1967, to take over from the National Mineral Development Corporation, projects, schemes and studies pertaining to exploration, exploitation, mining and smelting of copper. In 1972, the erstwhile Indian Copper Corporation Limit, a company incorporated in England was nationalised and merged with HCl. The main projects of the company are: (i) Khetri Copper Complex (KCC) in Rajasthan comprising Khetri, Kolihan, Chandmari and Dariba mines (since closed), concentrators at Dariba (since closed) and Khetri, Metallurgical and fertilizer plants at Khetri; (ii) Indian Copper Complex (ICC) at Ghatsila in Bihar comprising Mosaboni, Fathargora, Kendadih and Rakha Mines, three concentrators at Mosaboni, Moubhandar (since closed) and Rakha and metallurgical plants for copper and by-product recovery at Moubhandari (iii) Malanjkhand Copper Project (MCP) at Malanjkhand in Madhya Pradesh comprising an open pit mine, concentrator and leach copper plant; and (iv) Taloja Copper Project (TCP) at Taloja in Maharashtra for conversion of cathodes both imported and part of our own into continuous cast copper wirerods as value added product.

The company produces primary copper products in the form of cathodes, wirebars, wirerods and is also engaged in manufacturing of single super phosphate, sulphuric acid, gold, silver, selenium, tellurium, palladium, copper sulphate and nickel sulphate as by-products.

The current operation plants of the company are to produce and market about 70,000 Mt copper in different forms out of which 45,000 MT of refined copper is produced from indigenous ore resources. With the changed economic scenario in the country, HCL has initiated process of restructuring of companies to remain competitive. During 1994-95, the turnover of the company was Rs. 932.95 and its production of refined copper was 46,134 MT.

Bharat Gold Mines Limited operates the world famous century old Kolar Gold Mines in Karnataka State. The company was nationalised in 1956 and was incorporated as a public sector company under the Department of Mines, Government of India in March 1972. Though the gold mining is the principal activity of the company, as a corporate stategy, it has diversified into the field of mine construction and contract works, manufacture of mining machinery and components of equipment.

The company has three major activities namely: (i) Gold mining: Two mines in Kolar Gold Fields, Karntaka-Mysore Champion Amalgamated mine and Nundydroog mine, and three mines in Andhra Pradesh, Yeppamana mine, (Anantapur); Chigargunta mine; and Old Bisanatham mine, (Chittoor); (ii) Mine Project and Construction Division-Taking up mine construction and development works for other mining (coal and metal mines) industries all over India, and (iii) Workshop Diversification-The workshops manufacture mining machineries and components of certain equipment and undertake jobbing works, like machining and fabrication for major industries in the country.

The company's registered office is at Koar Gold Fields and its liaison office is at New Delhi. In 1994-95, the company produced 650.28 kg of gold.

The continued financial losses over the decade has resulted in the company being declared as a sick industry and consequently referred to Board for Industrial and Financial Reconstruction (BIFR) who have appointed ICICI as Operating Agency to formulate a rehabilitation package envisaging increase in gold production from the existing shallow mines to ensure economic viability, exploration and exploitation of gold from the BGML lease-hold areas in collaboration with a suitable joint venture partner and to recover gold from old mill tailings accumulated over the years by constructing a suitable gold recovery plant by BGML.

Sikkim Mining Corporation was established as joint venture of Sikkim State and Government of India in 1960 by proclamation of erstwhile "Sikkim Darbar". the objective of the Corporation is to mine multimental ore for production of copper, lead and zinc concentrates. The Corporation has only one mine (Bhotang Mine) Situated at Rangpo (East Sikkim). During 1994-95, the Corporation produced 270 mt tonnes of copper concentrate, 85 mt of lead concentrate and 568 mt of zinc concentrate. Zinc concentrate is being sold to M/s. Hindustan Zinc Ltd. since April 1994. Hindustan Copper Limited has stopped taking copper concentrate, M/s. HAMCO Mining and Smelting Limited, Calcutta, has lifted 3,500 tonnes of lead, 200 tonnes of copper and 200 tonnes of zono concentrates on trial basis in the year 1994-95.

The National Mineral Policy, 1993, announced on 5 March 1993, in brief, had dispensed with the reservation of all the minerals reserved for exclusive exploitation by public sector and also for the first time, sought to invite foreign investment in the mining sector. The amendments to the Mines and Minerals (Regulation & Development) Act, 1957 seek to further elaborate the principles enunciated in the National Mineral Policy by, among others, devolving more powers to the state governments, providing greater stability of tenure in mining leases and by accelerating inflow of private capital, both domestic and foreign, as also the state-of-the-art technology into the mineral sector.

The amended Act has deleted 15 minerals hitherto listed in the First Schedule of the MM (R&D) Act, 1957 requiring prior approval of the Central Government before the state government could grant a prospecting licence of a mining lease. The minerals so deleted are apatite and phosphatic ores, barytes, dolomite, gypsum, kyanite, magnesite, molybdenum, nickel, platimum and other precious metals, sillimanite, silver, sulphur and its ores, tin, tungsten and vanadium ore. With this deletion (excepting the atomic minerals and fuel minerals), there would only be 11 minerals left for which the state government would require prior approval of the Central Government. These are asbestos, bauxite, chrome ore, copper ore, gold, iron ore, lead, limestone (except where it is used in kilns for the manufacute of lime as building materials) manganese ore, precious stones and zinc. the amended Act has removed any restriction on equity holding by foreign nationals in a mining company.

As of now, any company registered or incorporated in India can apply for a prospecting licence of a mining lease from the concerned state government. For the first time, a minimum period of lease of 20 years, has been made mandatory. The maximum period for grant of lease has been increased to 30 years.

Further renewals are possible with approval of the Central Government. The period for which prospecting licence can be granted has been increased to three years and these licences can be renewed at the discretion of the state governments so that the total period does not exceed five years. The amended Act also provides that no appeal or revision will lie to the Central Government against orders passed by the state governments with regard to minor minerals. State governments have also been empowered to terminate leases of minor minerals without prior approval of the Central Government. The amended Act also introduces a new section, whch gives powers to carry out searches to check unauthorised mining.

The Act, was amended to increase the period before which a lease can lapse from one year to two years. In addition, the amendment also provides that notifications issued by state governments under their minor minerals concession rules must be placed before the State Legislature and also empowers the Central Government to modify leases not in conformity with the Act to bring them in line with the provisions of the MMR&D Act, 1957.

The history of modern iron and steel industry in India began in 1870 when the Bengal Iron Works Company set up its plants at Kulti in West Bengal. However, the first effort at large scale production got underway when the Tata Iron Steel Company (TISCO) was set up at Jamshedpur in 1907. This was followed by the establishment of Indian Iron and Steel Company (IISCO) at Burnpur in 1919.

The first unit in public sector now known as Visvesvaraya Iron and Steel Limited (VISL) started functioning at Bhadravati in 1923. After Independence, though development of steel industry was considered during the First Plan, it was only during the Second Plan period that efforts were made to set up three integrated steel plants each with 10 lakh ingot tonnes capacity at Bhilai, Durgapur and Rourkela. An expansion programme to double the capacity of the two private sector steel plants, namely, TISCO and IISCO to 20 lakh tonnes ad 10 lakh tonnes respectively was also taken up.

The three plants in the public sector came into existance in stages between 1956 and 1959 and the expansion of the private sector plants was completed in 1959. During the Third Five Year Plan, emphasis was laid on the expansion of the three public sector plants and preparation of plans to set up three more steel plants at Salem (Tamil Nadu). Vijaynagar (Karnataka) and Visakhapatnam (Andhra Pradesh) to create additional steel production capacity in the Fifth Plan.

Steel Authority of India Limited (SAIL) is a wholly-owned government undertaking. It is responsible for the management of steel plants at Bhilai, Durgapur and Rourkela, Bokaro and Burnpur and also the Alloy Steel Plant at Durgapur an the Salem Steel Plant. The management of IISCO was taken over the Government on 14 July 1976 with a view to improving its working. The company is now a wholly-owned subsidiary of SAIL. SAIL took over Maharashtra Elektrosmelt Limited, a mini steel plant producing ferro-manaanese and steel in January 1986. Visvesvaraya Iron and Steel Limited, a unit controlled by the Karnataka Government was taken over by SAIL in August 1989.

Authorised capital of SAIL and paid up capital, as on 31 March 1995 are Rs. 5,000 crore and Rs. 3,985.89 crore respectively. The turnover during 1994-95 was Rs. 13,688.54 crore (excluding IISCO). Production of crude steel, saleable steel and pig iron from steel plants under SAIL (excluding IISCO) during 1993-94 and 1994-95.

Apart from the integrated steel plants, steel is also produced by electric arc furnace units which are popularly known as mini steel plants, from steel scrap/ sponge iron. While integrated steel plants mainly produce mild steel in bulk quantities, the mini steel plants produce mild seel as well as alloy steels including stainless steels. From this sector, crude steel production during 1994-95 was 2.9 million tonnes (provisional).

The New Industrial Policy announced in July 1991 has removed iron and steel from the list of industries reserved for the public sector, and also exmpted it from the requirements of compulsory licensing. Enterpreneurs are, therefore, free to set up steel plants of any capacity, subject to certain locational restrictions.

Iron and steel has also been placed in the list of high priority industries where, subject to certain conditions, automatic approvals are available for foreign equity upto 51 per cent, and for technology agreements upto specified limits. There has been a very positive response from the entrepreneurs. A capacity of about 7.5 million tonnes for producing various categories of steel involving an investment of about Rs. 13,142 crore is in various stages of implementation.

Rashtriya Ispat Nigam Limited was incorporated as a public sector company in February 1982 to implement construction of the first shorebased Integrated Steel Plant in th country located at Visakhapatnam, Andhra Pradesh. The project has been completed in two stages: first stage was completed by March 1992 and the second and final stage by July 1992.

Visakhapatnam Steel Plant (VSP) is the most sophisticated modern integrated steel plant in the country. Some of the most modern technologies adopted in the plant are: seven metre tall coke ovens, dry quenching of coke with auxiliary power generation facilities, 3200 CuM blas furnaces, conveyor charging and bell-less top charging for blast furnaces, cent per cent continuous casting of liquid steel and sophisticated high speed rolling mills. VSP's manpower, considering its size is lowest in the Indian steel industry. Though the production in Visakhapatnam Steel Plant commenced in the year 1991-92, 1993-94 was the first full year of integrated operation.

Visakhapatnam Steel Plant has achieved high levels of techno-economic and operating performances during 1994-95 creating records in the Indian steel industry and surpassing the DPR Norms. On the marketing front, VSP ended the year with a turnover of about Rs. 2,266 crore, which is 19 per cent higher than that of the previous year. Domestic sales of steel showed substantial increase with sales volume registering 1.2 million tonnes, a 43 per cent growth over 1993-94. Exports accounted for 4.65 lakh tonnes of iron and steel with a total realisation of Rs. 471 crore in foreign exchange. By-product sales registered a turnover of Rs. 147 crore which is 65 per cent higher than what was achieved in the previous year. VSP made a cash profit of Rs. 55 crore (provisional), for the first time, as against a cash los of Rs. 233 crore made in 1993-94.

At present, rubber goods industry comprises of 32 tyre units, 220 medium scale units, 5,500 small scale units and an equal number of units in the tiny sector. It offers direct and indirect employment to over seven lakh people. There is an investment of about Rs. 3,500 crore and a turnover of over Rs. 7,000 crore in this industry. The major rubber goods produced by the industry are tyres and tubes of all kinds, surgical gloves, prophylactics, conveyor and vee belts, instruments, hose pipes, sport goods etc. Tyres and tubes constitute the most important segment of this industry. Of the total investment, over Rs. 2,000 crore have been in the tyre and tubes industry. This industry has been identified as of extreme focus for export purposes.

The export of tyres and tubes which was Rs. 593 crore in 1993-94 is expected to reach Rs. 750 crore in 1994-95 and Rs. 1,000 crore by 1995-96. The exports of rubber goods other than tyres and tubes are also steadily growing.

Over the years, engineering industries in the country have registered a phenomenal growth to generate a strong base in a wide-range of heavy and light engineering industries covering a broad spectrum of capital goods and consumer durable products. Bulk of capital goods required for power projects, fertilizer plants, cement plants, steel plants. mining equipment and petro-chemical plants are being met from indigenous production. Construction machinery and equipment for irrigation project, diesel engines, pumps and tractors for agriculture, vehicles, etc., transport are also being met from within the country. Engineering industries have also demonstrated their capacity to manufacture large size plants and equipment for virous sectors such as power generation, fertilizers and cement.

Machine Tool industry is the backbone of entire engineering sector. This industry which till few years back was confined to the manufacture of conventional machine holding has now geared itself to meet the growing challenge of a diverse requirement from the user sector.

Heavy electrical industry comprises equipment used for the generation, transmission, distribution and utilisation of power. It includes items such as generators, boilers, tubines, transformers, switchgears etc. The indigenous industry is equipped to meet the entire domestic requirement. The established capacity in the country for manufacture of thermal and hydro-power generating equipment is around 4,500 mw and 1,345 mw respectively. Most of these capacities are in the public sector, in companies such as BHEL. The entire industry has been delicensed under the New Indusrial Policy announced by the Government of India. Also under the new Policy, these items qualify for automatic approval as regard to foreign collaborations.

Stream and hydro turbines are manufactured both in the public and private sector. The total capacity is over 7,000 mw. The public sector undertaking BHEL has the largest capacity. Steam turbines upto 500 mw unit rating are being manufactured by BHEL. It also manufactures gas turbines.

Boliers of both the categories, namely, for industrial and power applications are being produced in the country. For power boilers, BHEL is capable of making boilers for super thermal power plants. M/s. ABL Durgapur, is a major unit manufacturing power boilers. There are 19 manufactures of industrial boilers in the country. The production of fludised bed boilers using biomass, agricultural waste, inferior grades of coal etc., has also started both for process application as well as for generating power.

There are 33 units in the organised sector manufacturing power and distribution transformers. The technology and design of power transformers manufactured in the country are comparable with the international standards. Manufacturing facilities for dry type distribution transformers have been established in th country. The technology and manufacturing facilities for amorphous core transformers and aluminium foil wound transformers are being established.

In the context of power system development in evolving a National Grid by end of current Plan period, conceted efforts are on for strengthening the transmission system by execution of 400 KV lines, introducing HVDC back-to-back tie lines, phased conversion of AC lines into DC lines and implementing load despatch and communication links besides system improvement measures by installing adequate reactive compensation system and PF correction capacitor banks.

AC transmission in 800 KV class has been adopted as the standard for the next higher level. Indigenous industry is technology sufficient in transmission system upto 400 KV reactive compensation system upto 220 KV and is in the process of indigenisation of HVDC technology and development of 800 KV class equipments. A total switchover to all Alluminium Alloy Conductors (AAAC), realising its techno-economic benefits, would give a boost to this sector.

The electrical industry covers a wide range of products which includes white goods (refrigerators, washing machines, air-conditiones, etc.), house-hold, electrical appliances, electrical fans, storage batteries, dry cells, power cables, telecommunication cables, electrical motors and electric lamps. The installed capacity is considered adequate to meet the domestic demand as well as exports. Under the new industrial policy, the entire industry has been delicensed. Many of the electrical items like electric motors, jelly filled cables, optic fibre cables and pumping sets also qualify for 51 per cent foreign equity and automatic foreign collaboration under the new industrial policy.

In the field of telecommunication, capacity has also been created for manufacture of optical fibre cables. Hindustan Cables Limited, a Government of India undertaking, and the Madhya Pradesh State Electronic

Development Corporation, an undertaking of the Government of Madhya Pradesh, have been permitted to establish capacities for the manufacture of OFC to the extent of 40,000 and 20,000 fibre km per annum respectively.

Keeping in view the safety and quality aspects of household electric appliances, Government have introduced compulsory ISI marking in respect of electrical immersion heaters, electrical iron, electrical stove and plugs and sockets.

Various steps have been initiated to ensure adequate testing facilities and availability of quality raw materials and components to the manufactures in order to help them conform to the requirements of the said scheme. There has been a greater consumer awareness about the quality and safetyof these goods.

The need for energy conservation has ensured greater focus in the manufacture of energy efficient electrical lamps. The industry is receiving adequate encouragement from the Government. A number of foreign collaborations have already been apporoved for manufacture of energy efficial lamps.

In the storage battery industry, some new units are coming up. The process of upgradation of technology in this industry is continuously benefiting the customers. The industry has started providing batteries to Maruti Premier 113 NE and Contessa Classic apart from light commercial vehicles.

The crane industry has a good potential for growth in the coming year in view of increased port and container handling activities and other projects like steel plant modernisation. Considerable investment is this area has been made by the indigenous crane manufactures. By and large the indigenous manufactures are capable of meeting the demand. The industry is delicensed.

At present there are eight units in the country engaged in the manufacture of lifts and escalators. The present installed capacity of these units is of the order of 3000 Nos per annum. A new range of lifts known as Sky Climbers has been/is under manufacture indigenously. These lifts are used for maintenance of TPS boilers/ bridges etc., and are being produced for the first time.

As elsewhere in the world, there is an increasing shift in India to have large power houses particularly Super Thermal Power Stations. Consequently, while there would be fewer but larger power generating stations, the demand for transmission line towers for transmission of energy would grow substantially. There are at present 25 manufacturing units reporting production to Ministry of Industry. There is sufficient capacity available in the country for manufacture of different types of transmission line towers. The industry is delicensed subject to locational angle.

Paper is a vital and core industry for any country and per capita paper consumption can be taken as a measure of growth and progress in areas related to industrial, cultural and educational activities. Per capita consumption in India is less than three kg as against more than 300 kg in highly developed countries.

The origin of the paper industry could be traced back to 1812 when first paper mill was set up at Serampur, West Bengal. At present there are more than 350 mills in the country with an annual installed capacity of around 37 lakh tonnes. A significant aspect of the paper industry is strong presence of smaller paper mills with an installed capacity of 33,000 tonnes per annum or less. They account for nearly 50 per cent of the total installed capacity and contribute about 50 per cent to the production of paper and paper board in the country.

Capacity utilisation of the paper industry has declined from 96.35 per cent in 1952 to about 60 per cent in 1994. Various reliefs and concessions have been extended in recent years to help the industry to improve its capacity utilisation and financial viability. These include liberalisation facility for import of raw materials, low excise on use of minimum 75 per cent non-conventional raw materials *viz.* bagasse, jute, wheat/rice straw, waste paper, etc., delicensing the manufacture of certain varieties of paper etc.

At present, the country is self-sufficient in respect of common varieties of writing and printing paper and paper board and only certain special varieties of papers are being imported. The import of paper has been brought under OGL and customs duty on import of paper has been reduced from 65 to 20 per cent in this year. The demand of paper and paper board up to the end of the Eighth Plan is likely to be met by some new mills, revival of the some of the closed mills, modernisation and expansion of some of the existing units. In order to encourage use ofnon-conventional raw material, paper units based on use of minimum 75 per cent pulp derived from bagasse, agricultural residues and other non-conventional raw materials have been exempted from industrial licensing subject to locational policy.

Until 1981, National Newsprint and Paper Mills recently known as *nepa* Limited which commenced in 1955 was the only unit in the country manufacturing newsprint. As on 1 January 1995, there are 22 newsprint mills in the country with an annual installed capacity of 5.50 lakh tonnes. However, one newsprint mills *viz.* rayalseema Paper Mills Ltd having an annual installed capacity of 20,000 TPA is lying closed.

Demand for newsprint is met by indigenous

production supplemented by imports. Import of newsprint which was decanalised earlier, has been decontrolled with effect from 1 May 1995. Now, import of newsprint is under OGL. The customs duty on the import of newsprint has been abolished with effect from 25 July 1991 in respect of standard newsprint and with effect from 1 march 1992 in respect of glazed newsprint. The production of newsprint for 1994-95 was about 4.02 lakh tonnes.

Cement, an important infrastructure core industry, is one of the most advanced industries in the country. Till about a decade ago, the country was deficient in cement and it had to resort to import in order to fill the gap in supply. After the complete de-control of price and distribution on 1 March 1989 and introduction of other policy reforms, the cement industry has made rapid strides both in capacity/production and in production and process technology. At present there are 107 large plants with an installed capacity of about 79 million tonnes. In addition, there are about 250-300 mini cement plants with an estimated capacity of seven million tonnes. The total operative installed capacity is estimated to be around 86 million tonnes. In 1993-94, production of cement was 57.96 million tonnes against a target of 60 million tonnes. The Production target fixed for 1994-95 was 62 million tonnes. With a production of 62.35 million tonnes, the industry was able to achieve the target. The growth rate recorded during the year was 7.6 per cent. During the year the capacity utilitisation has also increased from 80 per cent in 1993-94 to 86 per cent.

India is producing different varieties of cement the ordinary portland cement (OPC), portland pozzolana cement (PPC), portland blaster furnace slag cement (PBFS), oil well cement, white cement, etc. These different varieties of cement are produced strictly under BIS specifications and the quality is comparable to the best of the world.

Apart from meeting the entire domestic demand for cement, the industry is also exporting a large quantity. The export of clinker and cement has increased from 0.36 million tonnes in 1990-91 to 1.18 million tonnes in 1992-93 and 2.85 million tonnes in 1993-94. The export in 1994-95 was to the tune of 3.38 million tonnes.

Utilising a part of the funds provided by the World Bank to the cement industry and the grant from DANIDA, Denmark, a Human Resource Development Project is being implemented for providing demand driven training to the operators, line managers and supervisors to enhance their skills for handling latest equipments.

Four regional training centres have been set up and equipped with various classroom equipments, special equipments, computers, books, manuals and other training aids at ACC, Jamul (M.P.), Dalmia Cement, Dalmiapuram (T.N.), J.K. Cement, Nimbahera (Rajasthan) anmd Gujarat Ambuja, Ambuja Nagar (Gujarat). A large number of personnel of the cement industry and part-time trainers have already been trained in these RTCS. Fourteen training packages have already been developed abroad and 18 more are presently being developed.

Another innovative pilot project for bulk transportation and distribution of cement is being implemented with World Bank assistance at Kalamboli, New Bombay. Department of Industrial Policy and Promotion and the Associated Cement Companies Ltd. (ACC) are participating directly in the project. Under this project, special high.

The drugs and pharmaceuticals industry in India, during the last 40 years has shown tremendous progress if one takes into consideration the growth rate as seen in other developing countries. Today, India is in a position to meet 70 per cent of its requirement of bulk drugs and almost all its requirement of formulations. The industry continued to maintain the steady growth in terms of production as well as range of products in 1993-94 alslo. During 1994-95, the production of bulk drugs and formulations is estimated to be of the order of Rs. 1,518 crore and Rs. 7,935 crore respectively, showing a growth rate of 15 per cent over the previous year's production. In the case of individual drugs where decrease in production has taken place, it is noted that factors like decline in demand and obsolescence have a significant impact.

The pharmaceutical industry in india has the capability of producing a wide range of bulk drugs, covering a large spectrum of technologies and almost all formulations. In fact, the country is almost fully self-reliant in terms of formulation technology. In the case of bulk drugs, the technologies include those for sulpha drugs, vitamins, hormones and a number of new synthetic drugs like Flumequine, Pefloxacin, Ramipiril Ketorolac, Lisinopirl etc.

Among the bulk drugs which are critical to the country's health needs, the two most important ones are Penicillin and Rifampicin. The basic stage production of Penicillin and Rifampicin has been steadily growing and almost half of the country's demand for these two important drugs is met by indigenous production.

Two public sector undertakings, namely, Hindustan Antibiotics Limited (HAL) and Indian Drugs and Pharmaceuticals Limited (IDPL), account for almost 90 per cent of the Penicillin production in the Country. In addition to one private sector unit, which had commenced production of Penicillin in the last years, three more Penicillin manufacturing units in the private sector, with an investment of about Rs. 500 crore, are expected to commence commercial production in 1995. The indigenous production of Penicillin is thus expected to almost double from the existing level to meet the country's demand in the coming years.

In addition to the two manufactures of inermediates of Rifampicin from the basic stage, which today meets about 50 per cent of the indigenous demand of this important anti-TB and anti-leprosy drug, industrial license has been issued to another unit to produce this drug from the basic stage.

In view of the experience gained over the years, the Government had felt the need to modify the existing Drug Policy, 1986 so as to bring it in consonance with the Industrial Policy, 1991 and the present EXIM Policy as also to simplify and streamline the existing pricing system. The salient features of the Modifications in Drug Policy, 1986 announced on the 15 September 1994 are: (i) Abolition of Industrial Licencing for all bulk drugs, their intermediates and formulations thereof except in case of five bulk drugs reserved for manufacture in the public sector and bulk drugs produced by the use of recombinant DNA technology as well as those requiring in-vivo use of nucleic acid as the active principles; (ii) Foreign investment upto 51 per cent will be automatically permitted in the case of all bulk drugs, their intermediates and formulations; (iii) automatic approval, as per the industrial policy, for foreign technology agreements shall be given in the case of all bulk drugs, their intermediates and formulations, except those produced by the use of recombinant DNA techology; (iv) Measures to give further impetus to R&D in the During Sector are as follows: (a) A new drug which has not been produced elsewhere, if developed through indigenous R&D would be put outside price control for a period of 10 years from the date of commercial production in favour of the Company who undertook the R&D; (b) The Department of Chemicals and Petrochemicals would set up an Inter-Ministerial group to decide, within a set time frame, on measures to give further impetus to R&D in the Drug Sector, and (c) The Ministry of Health and Family Welfare would further streamline the required procedures and steps for the quick-evaluation and clearance of new durg applications, specially those developed through indigenous R&D; (v) The system of price control would be operated through a single list of price controlled drugs, selected on the basis of transparent and objective criteria as laid down in the Modifications in Drug Policy, 1986" and formulations based thereon with a MAPE of 100 per cent; (vi) In case of basic manufacture, higher by four per cent over the existing rates which are 14 per cent on net worth or 22 per cent on capital employed; (vii) To achieve uniformity in prices of widely used formulations, it has been decided that there should be ceiling on prices for commonlymarketed standard pack sizes of price controlled formulations and that it would be obligatory for all, including small scale units, to follow the prices so fixed; (viii) An independent body of experts, to be called the National Pharmaceutical Pricing Authority, will be entrusted with the task of price-fixation/revision and other related medicines which are taken out of price control. In case, the prices of these medicines rise unreasonably, the Government would take appropriate measures, incluing reclamping of price control. (x) A National Drug Authority would be set up by an Act of the Parliament, to be steered by the Ministry of Health and Family Welfare, to look after the quality control aspects, rational use of drugs and related matters; and (xi) To provide better focus to all matters relating to development and promotion of indigenous and other system of medicines, a separate Department would be created by the Ministry of Health and Family Welfare.

The Drugs (Prices Control) Order (DPCO), 1995 has been notified by the Government on 6 January 1995. This Order has now come into force in place of the DPCO, 1987. The new DPCo has taken into account the modifications in the Drug Policy, 1986 announced by the Government in September 1994 in regared to the price control on drugs and has been issued in exercise of the powers conferred on the Central Government in September 1994 in regard to the price control on drugs and has been issued in exercise of the powers conferred on the Central Government by Section 3 of the Essential Commodities Act, 1955.

Seventy six drugs have been identified for being kept in the First Schedule of the DPCO which lists the drugs to be kept under price control. Unlike the DPCO, 1987 now there is a single list of drugs under price control with a Maximum Allowable Post Manufacturing Expenses (MAPE) of 100 per cent. Twenty two drugs, so far outside price control have been brought in the price controlled category. Some of these were having a heavy annual turnover exceeding Rs. 10 crore. Eighty three drugs have been decontrolled. Many of these were having an insignificant annual turnover with a declining usage or negligible growth.

With price control on the 76 drugs mentioned in Schedule-I of the DPCO almost 50 per cent of the retail pharmaceutical market would be under price control. The associations of drugs manufacturers have been cautioned to advise all their members to exercise restraint and self discipline in regard to medicines going out of price control and to ensure that their prices are not raised unreasonably, so that Government is not constrained to excercise its powers to bring back these medicines under price control.

It is envisaged that the list of drug to be kept under

price control will be reviewed periodically, based on the data to be collected in this regard. Substantial changes have been brought about so as to make the reporting system by way of forms and information required to be submitted periodically by the Industry to the Government, less cumbersome.

An important provision introduced is the stipulation of time limits of two months for deciding applications for price revision of formulations and four months for price fixation/revision of applications regarding bulk drugs. There is also a stipulation in the DPCO enjoining the Government to notify on an annual basis the norms relating to conversion costs, packing material costs and packing charges.

The new DPCO also provides for fixing of ceiling prices for commonly used packs of formulations based on price controlled drugs and these prices would be applicable to all manufactures and also the single ingredient formultions sold under generic name. The small scale sector will not be required to come for price fixation for these packs and they will be required to only adhere to the discipline of observing the ceiling prices. In regard to the other packs they would continue to enjoy, as before, exemption from price control on formulations.

A provision has also been added in the DPCO to allow for exemption from price control to a new bulk drug, which has not been produced elsewhere if developed through indigenous R&D. Further a provision has also been built to allow the of use funds collected in the Drug Equilisation Account for the purpose of promoting higher education and research in pharmaceutical sciences and technology and purposes incidental thereto.

The DPCO 1995 lays down a more transparent procedure for the working of the price control mechanism, which would be in the ultimate interest of the consumers as well as the manufacturers.

About 250 units in the organised sector, five of these in the public sector (IDPL, HAL, SSPL, BCPL and BIL) and six in the joint sector, and about 5,000 units in the small scale sector are engaged in the production of drugs. Of these, more than 100 are engaged in the production of bulk drugs.

Indian Drugs and Pharmaceuticals Limited (IDPL) incorporated under the Companies Act, 1956 on 5 April 1961, is a premier undertaking. The company has five plants including two wholly-owned subsidiaries; one each located at Rishikesh (Uttar Pradesh), Hyderabad (Andhra Pradesh), Gurgaon (Haryana), Madras (Tamil Nadu) and Muzaffarpur (Bihar). IDPL is a major producer of antibiotics like Pencillin-G, Tetracycline, Oxytetracycline from the basic stages. It is a leading producer of Vitamins again from the basic stages. In Madras Plant (subsidiary), the company produces sufgical instruments and formulations.

The company has a fully equipped Research Centre at the Synthetic Drug Plant in Hyderabad. IDPL has also set-up three subsidiary companies in collaboration with the respective state governments for production of quality pharmaceutical formulations. Rajasthan Drugs and Pharmaceuticals Limited (RDPL), Jaipur (Rajasthan); Uttar Pradesh Drugs and Pharmaceuticals Limited (UPDPL), Lucknow (Uttar Pradesh) and Orissa Drugs and Chemicals Limited (ODCL), Bhubaneswar (Orissa).

Hindustan Antibiotics Limited (HAL) incorporated on 1 March 1954, was the first public sector undertaking in the field of pharmaceuticals. The company set-up primarily with the objective of manufacturing Penicillin and other antibiotics. It also produces streptomycin, gentamycin, haymycin and aurofungin, besides formulations.

The company has recently entered into MOU for a joint venture tie-up with MAX-GB Limited for upgradation of the Pencillin-G production facilities. HAL has three subsidiary companies promoted in collaboration with the respective state government-Karnataka Antibiotics and Pharmaceuticals Limited (KAPL), Bangalore (Karnataka); Maharashtra Antibiotics and Pharmaceuticals Limited (MAPL), Nagpuir (Maharashtra) and Manipur State Drugs and Pharmaceuticals Limited (MSDPL), Imphal (Manipur).

There are three public sector undertakings engaged in the manufacture of drugs and formulations located at Calcutta (West Bengal). These were private sector comapnies, poineers again in their own field, but had been ailing over the year for various reasons. The management of these companies were taken over by the Central Government in terms of the Industries (Development & Regulation) Act, 1951 and subsequently they were nationalised and new public sector companies were formed. Bengal Immunity Limited (BIL), Bengal Chemicals and Pharmaceuticals Limited (BCPL) and Smith Stanistreet Pharmaceuticals Limited (SSPL) are these three public sector undertakings with their main manufacturing activities concentrated in the State of West Bengal. BIl is one of the largest producers of SERA and vaccines toxoids.

It also produces other pharmaceutical formulations. BCPL with four manufacturing units, is the largest producer of anti-snake verum in India. It also produces chemicals like sulphuric acid, alum, chrome salts and home products like soaps, hair oil, perfumes etc. BCPL also produces herbal products. SSPL is engaged in the manufacture of pharmaceutical formulations.

The textile sector plays a vital role in the overall economy of the country. Textile exports account for over 30 per cent of the total exports from the country. The burgeoning growth in exports from the textile sector in the recent years has been one of the most striking features of India's economic development. The textile sector occupies a very prominent place in terms of employment generation.

The sectors like handloom, handicrafts, powerloom, sericulture and readymade * potential. The total employment in textile sector has risen from about 39 million during 1990-91 at about 47 million during 1994-95. The industry has witnessed a phenomenal growth during the last four decades. The spindleage increased from 11 million in 1951 to over 29.10 million and rotors from 45,000 in 1989 to 1,46,000 in 1994. The loomage, however has declined in the organised sector. Out of 1,227 cotton/man-made fibre textile mills, 187 mills are in public sector, 124 and 915 are in cooperative and private sectors respectively. Capacity utilisation in spinning sector of textile mills has increased from 69 per cent in 1985-86 to 84 per cent in 1993-94. However, the capacity utilisation in composite sector has declined from 62 per cent in 1985-86 to 54 per cent in 1993-94.

Research associations

Ahmadabad Textile Industry's Research Association, Ahmadabad, Bombay Textile Research Association, Bombay, South IndiaTextile Research Association, Coimbatore and Northern India Textile Research Association, Ghaziabad are four cotton textile research associations registered under the Societies Registration Act, 1860, and functioning under the adminstrative control of Ministry of Textile. The main objective of these institutions is to carry out research and render consultancy services (*i.e.* Quality Management Service-

ISO 9000) to industry on various aspects of textile technology with a view to reducing the cost and improving the quality and durability of fabrics, reducing pollution, conserving energy and utilising waste, adopting new technology and improving the technologies in the decentralised handloom sector.

Silk and Art Silk Mills' Research Association (SASMIRA), Bombay is a textile research association registered under the Societies Registration Act 1860 (XXI of 1860) of Maharashtra State. Its headquarters are located at Bombay. The SASMIRA's principal activities included research and development, provision of technical services, testing and training facilities in the fields of silk and art-silk. Man-Made Textile Research Association (MANTRA) established in 1981, occupies a status of the leading R&D and educational institution in India today. as one of the National Textile Research Laboratory, MANTRA caters to multifarious needs of textile and allied industry at large. Though activities of MANTRA are primarily aimed at planned and healthy growth of decentalised textile industry of south Gujarat, its impact beyond south Gujarat is also significant.

Indian Jute Industries' Research Association (IJIRA), Calcutta, registered under the West Bengal Societies Registration Act, 1961, is an autonomous cooperative research organisation under the administrative control of the Ministry of Textiles, Government of India.

The objective of IJIRA is to promote research and other scientific work connected with the jute trade and industries allied with or accessory thereto, to establish and maintain laboratories and foster education of persons engaged in or likely to be engaged in the said trade and industry, to encourage discoveries, to examine and publish information regarding the nature and merits of inventions, improvements, materials and designs connected with the said trades or industries.

The Jute Industry in the country is traditionally export oriented. India ranks number one in raw jute and jute goods production and number two in export of jute goods in the world. Jute packaging materials are facing tough challenges from other low priced synthetic substitutes. As a measure to use jute in non-packaging sectors, Government has undertaken a number of steps for diversification.

The most significant aspect of the diversification programme is the UNDP assisted National Jute Programme under which an assistance of the order of US dollar 230 lakh from UNDP is being utilised by providing matching input from Government of India. A large number of projects covering the areas of raw jute production, R&D, product development, human resource development, and marketing are under imnplementation. To fulfil these objectives, the National Centre for Jute Diversification is being set up.

In the silk sector, Government has made an allocation of Rs. 901 crore for development of sericulture during Eighth Plan. The employment generation during this period is targeted at 10.50 lakh persons which would bring the accumulated employment under the sericulture sector to 65 lakh persons by 1997. The employment in silk sector during 1994-95 is anticipated to be 61 lakh persons as against 50 lakh persons in 1993-94. During 1994-95, the silk sector has exceeded its export target of Rs. 837.31 crore by 12.8 per cent.

The handloom industry is an important sector which provides employment to about 12 million people and contributes over 20 per cent of total cloth production. Production of handloom cloth also increased from 4,295 million sq mtr. during 1990-91 to 6,028 million sq. mtr. during 1994-95 showing an annual increase of about 10.1 per cent. In order to further increase production and generate additional employment opportunities in the handloom sector during 1992-93, a scheme was introduced to develop 3,000 handloom development centres and 500 quality dyeing units which will benefit 30 lakh weavers till September 1995.

Already 122 Handloom Development Centres and 45 Quality Dyeing Centres have been set up. An Integrated Village Handloom Development Scheme, project package scheme and National Silk Yarn Bank scheme have been launched between 1991-95 with an outlay of Rs. 63 crore and Rs. 20 crore respectively for the Eighth Plan period. A project on development of handloom products using jute fibre titled 'Development and Transfer for Technology for use of Jute Fibre in Handloom Textiles' was sanctioned by the Government during 1993-94 with an outlay of about Rs. 10.30 crore. Beside, a scheme for setting up jute handloom development centres has been introduced in January 1995.

Export of cotton handloom textiles amounted to Rs. 1,229 crore (US dollar 392 million) in April-December 1994 against Rs. 911 crore (US dollar 291 million) achieved in April-December 1993, thereby registering an increase of 34.8 per cent both in rupee and dollar terms.

In the decentralised powerloom sector which contributes over 70 per cent of the total cloth production, new scheme to set up computer aid designing centres (CADs) in the area of powerloom concentration has been inroduced. The aim of such centres is to upgrade the existing quality and design of cloth production by the decentralised powerloom sector so as to enable the powerloom fabric to compete in the international market in an effective fashion. Two such centres have been established at Sholapur (Maharashtra) and Coimbatore (Tamil Nadu). Remaining five centres are under process of being set up.

Textile exports, including handicraft, jute and coir, presently account for about 37 per cent of India's total exports as against of 35 per cent during the previous year. There has been a significant increase in exports from the textile sector * including jute, coir and handicrafts have grown from the level of Rs. 9,932 crore during 1990-91 to Rs. 31,644 crore during 1994-95.

The Final Act of the Uruguay Round of GATT negotiations has been signed by 111 countries at the Minsterial Conference in Marrakesh on 15 April 1994. The agreement on textile and clothing which forms a part of the Final Act, signalled the end of the Multi-Fibre Agreement (MFA) era, in which discriminatory restraints were put by the developed countries on the exports of textiles by developing countries like India. The World Trade Organisation has consequently come into existence w.e.f. 1 January 1995. During the next 10 years the multi-fibre agreement would be phased out and in the different stages the quotas will be removed. The agreement is expected to boost textile exports in the coming years.

In order to provide systematic training to our fashion designers and help them compete in the international market in an effective manner, in addition to the existing National Institute of Fashion Technology (NIFT) centre at New Delhi, five more new NIF centres have been opened at Bombay, Hyderabad, Calcutta, Madras and Gandhi Nagar.

Handicrafts constitute an important segment of the decentralised sector of our economy and provides employment to over six million artisans, roughly 1/5th of the total household industries scatteed throughout the country especially in rural and semi-urban areas.

The Office of the Development Commissioner for Handicrafts implements Plan schemes covering various areas like training, design, development, technology upgradation, market promotion, exhibition and publicity exports etc. Export of handicrafts including hand-knitted carpets during 1994-95 was recorded at Rs. 4,458 crore as compared to Rs. 3,360 crore during 1993-94. The employment in the handicraft sector has increased increased to 64.2 lakh persons during 1994-95.

Special programmes have been launched to promote embroidery, *zari* and *zardosi* costume jewellery and imitation jewellery for both in the domestic and international market as a measure to generate more employment opportunity for crafts people. Besides, a UNDP assisted programme has been undertaken to promote wood based handicrafts for exports. *Kaleen* label has been introduced by Carpet Export Promotion Council (CEPC) to be fixed on the carpets for export as a hall-mark of commitmemt towards complete eradication of child labour from the Indian carpet industry and contribution towards welfare of children and carpet weavers. A country-wide census has been launched for the first time to collect information about the handicrafts artisans. This will help in building up the data base for this sector.

The manufacture of all types of automobile vehicles is delicensed. There has been a significant growth in the production of automotive vehicles during 1994-95 as compared to that in 1993-94 has been 1,94,999 as against 1,41,436 in 1993-94. Production of cars has gone up from 2,09,695 in 1993-94 to 2,64,007 in 1994-95. * The production of three-wheelers has gone up from 91,608 in 1993-94 to 1,27,532 in 1994-95. During 1994-95, the production of tractors was 1,62,900 as compared to 1,36,581 in 1993-94.

Sixty one units in the organised sector are manufacturing soap with an installed capacity of 6,60,772 tonnes per year. Production of soap in this sector was of the order of 3,40,366 tonnes during 1993-94 and 3,35,125 tonnes during 1994-95. There are 26 units in organised sector for manufacturing of synthetic detergents with an installed capacity of 6,05,000 tonnes per annum. Production of detergents was 3,07,738 tonnes during 193-94 and 3,09,738 tonnes during 1994-95.

Leather is a highly labour-oriented industry in India and has been identified as one of the major thrust areas for export. The export performance of leather sector has been improving considerably over the last 3-4 years. The value of export of leather and leather products went up from Rs. 3,693 crore during 1992-93 to Rs. 4,139.3 crore in 1993-94. In the year 1994-95, the export from this sector was to the tune of Rs. 5,000 crore (provisionally), showing a growth rate of nearly 18 per cent over the last year. Footwear in the leather sector has been identified as an area of extreme focus for exports and in 1993-94 leather footwear and footwear components valued at Rs. 1,481.3 crore have been exported.

A National Leather Development Programme (NLDP) with UNDP assistance of the order of US dollar 15.05 million and Government inputs of Rs. 28.43 crore is currently being implemented by the Government for integrated development of the leather industry through the selected institutions/agencies in the country. The duration of the programme is four years and it has started its operations in June 1992 in accordance with the Work Plan. The Programme covers, *inter-alia,* areas such as human resources development, improving support services, pollution control and enhancement of exports.

The Programme has already been able to establish linkages with some of the most reputed international organisations, such as AFPIC and MCT, Melbourne, in the areas of education and training. The Indian institutions have been able to upgrade the training systems for design and manufacture of footwear, garments and asserted leather products. The leather sector units in the country can directly seek assistance by the selected institutions on software.

The areas earmarked for assistance are human resource development, product development, development of supporting industries (components, machinery), marketing etc. A market research unit which has been established at Council for Leather Exports, Madras has commenced services. Resource Centre and Publication of bi-monthly *"World Leather Times"* has been started.

Chemical indusdry plays a pivotal role in the Indian economy. The Industry in India is well established and has witnessed rapid growth in the organic and inorganic sectors. The rate of growth of the chemical sector has consistently been higher than the average growth rate of the Indian industry. During the last decade (1981-82 to 1991), the industry has been averaging a growth rate of about 10 per cent per annum.

The present annual turnover in the chemical sector in India is estimated to be around Rs. 35,000-Rs. 40,000 crore which is likely to be doubled by the end of the century. In order to promote this highly technology oriented industry, a number of incentives have been given to promote development activities. With the liberalisation policy of the Indian economy, major reforms have been taken up in the Indian chemical industry.

Except for a small list of hazardous chemicals, all chemical items can be manufactured in India without requiring any industrial licensing. Even where licensing exists, the procedures have been streamlined.

Entrepreneurs are, therefore, now free to set up chemical industries, by intimating to the Government through the Industrial Entrepreneurs Memorandum.

Development of organic chemical industry in India had started in April 1950, based on ethyl alcohol, manufactured from fermentation and distillation of sugarcane molasses and benezene available as a coke-oven by-product. At present, a substantial part of the industry is based on feedstock derived from petroleum. Basic organic chemicals like phenol, methanol, formaldehyde, acetone and acetic acid are manufactured in the country in substantial quantities. Major inorganic chemicals like soda ash, carbon black, calcium carbide, red phosphorous and potassium chlorates are all manufactured in the country and a position of near self-dufficiency has been achieved in all these chemicals. Alcohol producing industry was started in 1940 mainly to utilise molasses produced from fugar factories. With the growth of alcohol-based chemical industry in 1950's, production of alcohol has assumed importance in its own right.

Oil crisis has revived interest in the use of renewable feedstock like alcohol. It is mainly in India that a wide-range of organic chemical products are manufactured on a commercial scale with alcohol as the feedstock. The major downstream products made from ethyl alcohol (industrial alcohol) are acetic acid, acetic anhydride, acetone, butanol ethylacetate, polythene, styrene, PVC and synthetic rubber.

In keeping with the policy of economic liberalisation the price and movement control on molasses and alcohol have been removed with effect from 10 June 1993. This would ensure maximum utilisation of capacity in both the alcohol manufacturing sector and the sector utilising alcohol for downstream products like acetic acid, acetic anhydride etc.

Moreover, this is likely to improve the viablity of the sugar units who may be able to pay better prices for sugarcane to farmers. State governments are being persuaded for implementation of the policy of decontrol in their states.

In order to check undue increase in prices of industrial alcohol, customs duty on import of denatured alcohol has been reduced to 10 per cent with effect from 20 October 1993. Customs duty on molasses also has been reduced to 10 per cent with effect from 1 April 1995.

Dyestuff industry provides important inputs to many consuming industries contributing to the national economy. It is capable of meeting most of the local demands. In the organised sector, the industry is self-sufficient in terms of most of the inputs. There are around 50 units in the organised sector having a total installed capacity of 36,700 tonnes per annum against which the production achieved during 1993-94 was 31,100 tonnes.

The production for various classes of dyestuffs in 1994-95 is estimated to 31,600 tonnes. A large quantity of dyes and dye-intermediates is being exported and valuable foreign exchange being earned in this sector.

The industry contributes about 10 per cent of the total exports. The exports in the chemical sector have gone up from a level of around Rs. 1,600 crore in the year 1990-91 to around Rs. 3,600 crore in 1993-94, registering an increase of about 120 per cent.

Pesticides including insecticides, fungicides, weedicides, etc., are used extensively in agriculture and public health. The pesticide industry in india has made impressive progress and more than 60 technical grade pesticides are being successfully manufactured in the country. At present, more than 125 units are engaged in the manufacture of these technical grade pesticides and over 500 units are making pesticides formulations. As a result of the increased production of pesticides in the country, import of technical grade pesticides has come down considerably.

The estimated production of technical pesticides during 1994-95 is over 85,800 mt from an annual installed capacity of 1.25 lakh mt. As compared to this, the production during 1993-94 was around 85,600 mt.

In order to use the idle capacity available with pesticide units, the country has been able to enter the competitive field of export of pesticides. During 1992-93, the country has exported pesticides valued at Rs. 168.7 crore. This has increased to Rs. 261.24 crore during 1993-94. The courtry has started producing some new pesticides but continue to import their intermediates in the absence of technology for producing them.

Efforts are being made to acquire the right technology to manufacture intermediates for pesticides like Butachlor, Enosulfan etc. Till 1987-88, country was not able to export chemicals in larger quantities because of high cost of production of chemicals in India as compared to international prices. However, due to upgradation of technology and support given by the Government for exports, the Indian chemical industry have shown an impressive performance in the field of exports. During 1992-93, the export of chemical touched Rs. 3,475.5 crore.

There are two public sector units, namely, Hindustan Organic Chemicals Limited (HOCL) and Hindustan Insecticies Limited (HIL) in the chemical sector HOCL was incorporated in December, 1960 at Rasayani, Raigad district, Maharashtra, with the main objective of manufacturing chemical intermediates required for the manufacture of drugs, dyestuffs, rubber chemicals and laminates etc.

The company has two units: one each at Rasayani (Maharashtra) and Cochin (Kerala). Rasayani Unit produces organic grup of heavy chemical and intermediates such as nitrobenzene, hydrogen, aniline, sulphuric acid, acetic acid etc. Cochin unit produces phenol, acetone and propylene.

The company has floated a subsidiary company called Hindustan Fluocarbons Limited for setting up polytetraflurethylene (PTFE) plant in Medak district of Andhra Pradesh. HIL, incorporated in 1954, has at present three units at Delhi, Udyogamandal (Kerala) and Rasayani (Maharashtra). The company als has a subsidiary Hyderabad and a factory at Kovur. HIL is engaged in the manufacture of DDT, BHC, malathion, endosulfan and butachlor, the five major pesticides used in the country. Monocrotophcs Plant has also been commissional last year and is in operation.

Attainment of industrialisation over the last 48 years has been striking feature of Indian economic development process which was launched as a conscious and deliberate policy in the early fifties. In pursuance of this policy, large investment has been made in building up capacity over a wide spectrum of industries. Industrial production has made rapid strides in terms of variety, quality and quantity.

There has been a substantial diversification of industrial base during this period with the consequent ability to produce a very broad range of industrial goods. Self-reliance has been achieved in basic and capital good. Indigenous capabilities have now been established to the point of virtual self-sufficiency so that further expansion in various sectors such as mining, irrigation, power chemicals, transport and communication can be based primarily on indigenous equipment.

Process of industrialisation has also fostered entrepreneurship and development of a wide variety of technical, managerial and operative skills. Today, the country is in a position to provide consultancy services as well as managers, technicians and skilled workers for setting up industrial projects aborad.

The Industrial Policy Resolution of 1948 marked the beginning of the evolution of Indian Industrial Policy. The resolution not only defined the broad contours of the policy, it delineated the role of the State in the industrial development both as an entrepreneur and as an authority.

Successive policy resolutions also reiterated this basic tilt in favour of the public sector. The Industrial Policy Resolution of 1956 gave the public sector a strategic role in the economy. It categorised industries which would be the exclusive responsibility of state or would progressively come under state control and others. Earmarking the pre-eminent position to the public sector, it envisaged private sector co-existing with the State and thus attempted to give the policy framework flexibility.

The Industrial Policy initiatives undertaken by Government since July 1991 have been designed to build on the past industrial achievements and to accelerate the process of making Indian industry internatinally competitive. It recognises the strength and maturity of the industry and attempts to provide the competitive stimulus for higher growth. The thrust of these initiatives has been to increase domestic and external competition through extensive application of market mechanism and facilitating forging of dynamic relationships with foreign investors and suppliers of technology. The process of reform has been continuous.

As on 31 March 1993 there were 245 central public sector undertakings, comprising of eight in the construction sector, 72 in services and remaining 165 in the manufacturing. The number of CPSUs as indicated above exclude nine companies, six insurance companies and three financial institutions with Central Government investment but without direct responsibility of management.

The total capital employed in the 245 CPSUs increased from Rs. 1,179.91 billion in 1991-92 to Rs. 1,399.33 billion in 1992-93. The overall rate of return on capital employed in the PSUs also increased from 2.0 per cent in 1991-92 to 2.43 per cent in 1992-93.

The number of small scale units as at the end of 31 March 1994 were 2.38 million comprising of 1.77 million registered units and 0.61 un-registered. The overall production in the small scale sector during 1993-94 has been estimated to have reached Rs. 2,416.5 billion. The total value of exports of these units has been Rs. 177.85 billion in 1992-93.

Industrialization

India has made rapid strides in industrialization, and today is one of the ten most industrialized nations of the world. But industrialization, as in the rest of the world, has brought with it unwanted and unanticipated consequences. These include unplanned urbanization, pollution and risk of accidents. Industrialization moreover not only affects the immediate environment, but has consequences for a larger region whose resources get intimately tied to new industrial development.

Yet as the country continues to industrialize and new plants come up, some of the underlying issues remain. Dirty industries continue moving South. Hazardous chemicals are dumped or brought for reprocessing to developing countries. Often, in developed countries, different values are attached to human life in the North and in the South. Different standards are applied, and processes and factories being discarded in developed countries get relocated in the developing ones.

The Bhopal disaster, when methyl isocyanate crept into the houses of sleeping residents on the morning of 3 December, 1984, killing over 3,000 people and maiming countless others for life, brought many of these issues into sharp focus. It was a tragic testimony of just how much could go wrong. The hazardous side of industry became painfully apparent to countless people in India and abroad. It questioned location policies, safety requirements of industries, the responsibilities of North-based multinational corporations, the preparedness for dealing with disasters, citizens' right to know about the industrial process and the risks involved.

Near the industries, water and air pollution problems are very serious. Water pollution not only affects surface water but also groundwater. It is estimated that 70 per cent of India's surface water is seriously polluted and 80 per cent of the population does not have access to safe drinking water. For instance in Patancheru in Andhra Pradesh, over 60 factories—most of them chemical units—discharge their toxic wastes into freshwater streams. In Bichhri in Rajasthan, chemical effluents from textile and chemical industries pollute the waters of rivers and wells.

The health impact of such cases is serious and the incidence of cancer, lung and skin diseases, and deformities is high in these areas. While they are restricted in extent, air pollution levels are high in industrial areas. For instance the average levels of particulate matter in the four metropolitan cities exceeds 360 mg/m while the WHO standard is 150 mg/m.

Another concern relates to occupational health incertain industries. Asbestosis, byssinosis and pneumonoconiosis are some of the occupational diseases reported. Silicosis has been reported in mines and other industries.

Several central and state statues, such as the Industrial Development Act, the Labour Acts, the Factories Act and the Municipal Acts have environmental provisions in them. However it was the enactment of the Water (Prevention and Control of Pollution) Act, 1974, and the Air (Prevention and Control of Pollution) Act, 1981, which made these environmental factors the principal object of legislation. The Bhopal tragedy caused a surge in environmental legislation and an umbrella Environment (Protection) Act was passed in 1986. This covers hazardous activities in addition to pollution.

Under the Environment (Protection) Act, 1986, the Central Government is responsible for laying down procedures and safeguards for handling hazardous substances. Rules have been made for the manufactures, storage and import of hazardous chemicals, their management and handling, as well as for the manufacture, use, import and storage of micro-organisms and genetically engineered organisms. Radioactive waste disposal is controlled through a regulatory board managed by the Bhabha Atomic Research Centre. The Government has also established a Central Crises Group Alert System with a control room at New Delhi to deal with major chemical accidents in the country.

Many industries and large projects need environmental clearance. The State Pollution Control Boards monitor industrial areas. The Government of India has made it mandatory to assess the environmental impact of new large undertaking in the country. The impact assessment covers not only air, water and soil polluiton, but also damage to historical monuments, wildlife, forests, and to natural resources in general.

Unique to India is the recently enacted Mandatory Public Liability Insurance which makes it imperative for units dealing with hazardous substances to take insurance cover against damage to health or property of the community in the vicinity of the industry.

Industrial location policy is a crucial element in determining the impact of industry on the environment. Unplanned industrial growth has in some cases led to industrail conglomerates and urban sprawl. This has often led to prime agricultural and forest land being diverted for urban and industrial use. Near forests, urban areas have led to deforestation. For certain industries, a two-stage clearance procedure has been adopted by the Ministry of Environment and Forests, considering the site specific nature.

While legislation today has enabled authorities to step in, this alone cannot lead to improved environment in and around industries. For this to happen public awareness, as well as awareness and concern among the decision-makers is required. Where people have been consicous they have protested and not let polluting industries spoil their environment. Where industries have been conscious they have got together and taken initiatives for effluent treatment. A typical example of joint efforts by industry in the safe disposal of effluents is the Baroda Effluent Channel in Gujarat, managed by the Gujarat Industrial Development Corporation.

There is urgent need to create widespread awareness. Towards this end the Ministry of Environment and Forests has made a beginning by introducing a scheme for an Ecomark to lable environment-friendly products. NGOs too have several programmes to create environmental consciouness. School programmes to involve students in environmental quality monitoring have begun.

But finally environmental factors will only be taken into account where alternatives are availabel. Today with Indai opening up its economy to greater internationl participation in the industrialization of the country, it si important to ensure that the best and cleansest technologies are available for htis growth, so that industrialization occurs with the minimum of negative consequences.

In a wide spectrum of industry and agriculture and the entire gamut of services, there has been great progress in the country during the post-Independence era. The growth in several sectors have indeed been spectacular and in several others it has been modest while in a few others outright dismal. On Monday, 10 November 1996, the foundation stone for the automobile plant of the Hyundai Motor Company of South Korea, was laid at Irungattukottai, some 40 km from Chennai. The plant involves an outlay of $ 700 million (around Rs. 2500 crore) in the first phase; and another $ 400 million (around Rs. 1440 crore) in the second phase.

A production capacity of around 100,000 passenger cars in the 1300 cc-1500 cc range is envisaged. The first car is expected to roll out of the assembly line by October 1998. Most importantly, HMC promises a 70 per cent indigenous content from the first car. Which means prospects for dozens of additonal collaboration arrangements and investments for the production of components. At full production, the turnover of HMC will be in the region of Rs. 6000 crore.

This is the third mega investment in the automobile sector involving outlays exceeding Rs. 1500 crore each. The other two relate to the Mahinndra-Ford India Ltd. project to produce passenger cars of similar capacity and in same medium segment; and by Ashok Leyland Ltd., planning to invest on facilities to expand capacity to 100,000 commercial vehicles.

In recent months total investments promised in Tamil Nadu exceed Rs. 5000 crore–an outlay that perhaps exceed all investments made on new projects in the first instance all through the past 50 years.

In all these areas, and in a wide spectrum of industry and agriculture and the entire gamut of services, there has been great progress through the years of Independent India. The growth in several sectors have indeed been spectacular and in several others, it had been modest; and in a few others outright dismal. The bench-making has been done both in regard to the potential offered by India and by developments in several other countries which started on industrialisation much later than we did. South Korea offers a ready example.

In looking at growth, over the last five decades, we can segment these into five distinct phase that roughly correspond with decennial slots.

In accordance with the prevailing thinking, the First Five year Plan stated that the objective of industrial planning was to make good the deficiencies in production of key industrial items and to initiated development, which would enable cumulative expansion of such basic production.

There was better appreciation in the First Plan of the need for coordination of industrial planning with the formulation of other economic policies, such as customs and excise tariff structure, import and export policy, investment and technology policy and monetary and financial policy. The Second Plan and later plans have been encreasingly concerned with the allocation of public resources and much less with indications and policies to direct the whole economy indesired directions.

The Industrial Policy Statement of 1973, inter alia,

identified high-priority industries where investment from large industrial houses and foreign companies would be permitted. The Industrial Policy Statement of 1980 focussed attention on the need for promoting competition in domestice market, technological upgradation and modernisation. The policy laid the foundation for an increasingly competitive export base and for encouraging foreign investment in high priority technology areas. This found expression in the Sixth Five Year Plan, which emphasised the need for productivity to be the central concern in all economic and production activities.

Nevertheless the sector continued to provide the thrust for the development of heavy industries. In critical areas such as power, railways, coal, petroleum, steel and fertilisers, the public sector has been intensely involved in setting the pace of development.

Apart from public investments in basic industry and infrastructure, the expansion of the private sector in line with Plan objectives and priorities were greatly facilitated by financial institutions. An elaborate network of specialised development banking institutions with the Industrial Development Bank of India at the apex was established to help finance industrial investment in the private sector. These institutions, numbering over 50, have become the major source of long-term finance for the corporate sector.

As the statement on Industrial Policy, 1991 says, "These policies created a climate for rapid industrial growth in the country. Thus on the eve of the Seventh Five year Plan, a broad-based infractructure had been built up. Basic industries had been established. A high degree of self-reliance in a large number of items–raw materials, intermediates, finished goods—had been achieved. New growth centres of industrial activity had emerged, as had a new generation of entrepreneurs. A large number of engineers, technicians and skilled workers has been trained."

The Sixth Plan had achieved augmentation of new capacity more or less in consonance with the targets in alarge number of insdustries including, among others, aluminium, zinc, lead thermoplastics, yarn, petrochemical intermediates, electrical equipment, cement and consumer durables. However shortfall in production had taken place in some basic industries, such as steel, cement, non-ferrous metals, fertilisers and certain other industries, including textiles, jute manufactures, sugar, drugs and pharmaceuticals, commercial vehicles and railway wagons. Production targets were exceed in a few industries like machine toos, passenger cars, motor cycles and scooters, consumer electronics and communication equipment. Domestic imbalances resulting from shortfalls in production hasd to be corrected through imports of essential commodities, like steel, cement, fertilisers and sugar.

A technological thrust was given during the Plan period in certain industries in the engineering sector. The first 500 MW thermal generating unit was commissioned and the manufacture of 500 MW turbo generators and boilers had commenced. There has been a systematic upgradation of production technology for other equipment, needed by the power sector. The manufacture of equipment for 1350 tonnes per day fertiliser units and blast furnaces of 3200 cubic metres capacity for steel plants was being undertaken in the country. A strong base had been laid for the rapid development of the electronics sector.

The Seventh Plan recognised the need to consolidate on these strengths and to take initiatives to prepare Indian industry to respond effectively to the emerging challenges.

A number of policy and procedural changes which were introduced in 1985-86 aimed at increasing productivity, reducing costs and improving quality. Production capacity restrictions on the industries were gradually reduced and broad banding, which enabled a manufacturer to choose and produce any product mix which suited him in the context of the prevailing market conditions was introduced. In 1986, as against a policy of re-endorsement of existing capacity, the scheme of minimum economic scale of production was introduced with Letters of Intent prescribing a minimum economic size for a single unit. The accent was on opening the domestic market to increased competition and readying the industry to stand on its own in the face of international competition. The public sector was freed from a number of constraints and given a large measure of autonomy. The technological and managerial modernisation of industry was pursued as the key instrument for increasing productivity and improving competitiveness in the world.

As a result of the policies pursued since Independence, the long term trend of industrial growth for over forty years since 1950 is a trend annual growth of just over 6 per cent. This, says rakesh MOhan in an essay in Bimal Jalan's book on Indian Economy, "is quite an achievement, given the magnitude of distortions built into the system." He divides the growth record into three distinct periods: 7.7 per cent annual growth over the first three plan periods (1950-1965), four per cent annual growth over the holiday (1966-69) and the Fourth and Fifth Plan periods (1969-79), and finally the recovery to about 7.7 per cent growth over the Sixth and Seventh periods.

The period 1966-1980, says Mohan is effectively the dark period for Indian economy. This period encompassed a number of exogenous shocks: the devastating three-year drought of 1965-68, the aftermath of increased defence espenditures resulting from 1962 was with China and two wars with Pakistan, the oil price shocks of 1973 and 1979, and the downturn in the availability of foreign resources. During this period, the Indian economy was constantly struggling to adjust.

As a result of policy changes, the composition of Indian industry had undergone great transformation. At Independence, the consumer goods industry accounted for almost half of all industrial production. In 1991 such industries accounted for only about 20 per cent. In contrast, capital goods production was less than 4 per cent of total industrial production. In 1991, it had gone up to 24 per cent. Similarly basic goods share had increased from 20 per cent to 40 per cent.

As per the quick estimates of the Index of Industrial Production, the overall growth of industrial production during April-June 1996 was 8.5 per cent over the corresponding period of 1995 with the following sectoral contributions. As per the use based classificaton of industries, the overall growth has been broad based. After being relatively sluggish in the last two years, Intermediate Goods have recorded a growth of 11.9% in April-June 1996.

Industrial performance based on the production of 172 industries which together have a weight of 88% of IIP indicate a growth of 9.98 per cent in April-June, 1996. There has been deceleration in the growth of certain core sectors such as electricity, crude petroleum, steel, fertilizers, ferro alloys, jute manufacturers etc.

The first five months of the current financial year witnessed a sharp drop in the growth rate of infrastructure industries to 3.5% from 7.8% for the corresponding period of 1995-96. Amongst the industries that declined are: crude petroleum at (-)10.4% from 7.2%, electricity at 2.4% from 8.2% and saleable steel at 4.6% from 8.5%.

The performance of six Infrastructure Industries which is a critical indicator of the overall health.

The Office of Economic Adviser (OEA) also collects advance information on the production of 24 selected industries which have a weight of around 50% in the IIP. According to the information available, these industries have recorded a growth of 5.8% during April-July, 1996.

As per the information provided by CMIE, the corporate sector recorded a robust 22% growth in sales during 1995-96. This was particularly impressive because it comes after an unsually high increase of 23% recorded during 1994-95. The growth was reasonably well spread over major industry groups. In particular, the automobiles group, the chemicals sector and machinery industry performed exceptionally well.

About a quarter of the companies surveyed recorded sales growth rates less than 10%. At the same time, a little over a quarter of the companies recorded growth rates of more than 50%. Growth was mostly concentrated amongst companies with a size of Rs.75 crore to Rs.100 crore in terms of sales.

Interest payment by the corporate sector increased at a faster pace (nearly 24%) compared to the growth in sales. High interest cost during the year adversely affected most companies except the very large ones. However, the higher interest cost did not dampened sales growth in 1995-96.

According to the report of the RPG Foundation, the performance of non-finance companies was the highest during 1995-96 when compared to the other years in the 90s. Despite the liquidity crunch, the companies fared well mainly due to high and relatively inelastic demand for industrial goods, increased velocity of circulation of money, better inventory management and a decline in the incremental capital output ratio of the corporate sector. Thus despite paying a higher interest of at least 3% points more, there was a marginal improvemeant in the average rate of capital employed and the net profitability of the corporate sector.

Advance indications of the corporate performance for the first half of 1996-97 are now becoming available. These indicate a slow down in sales growth to around 9 per cent compared to over 24 per cent in the previous year. With inflation at around 5 per cent, real sales growth is around 4-5 per cent. Inventory levels are also increasing and with that interest burden. The liquidity crunch witnessed in 1995-96 and resultant high interest rates are affecting corporate investment in the current year.

In a period of weak sales growth, one normally excepts a high inventory holdings. However, continued high interest rates in last few years has resulted in better inventory management and the inventory levels have been declining continuously. These were around 20 per cent of sales in 1995-96. Even a significant increase in inventory holdings will not make much difference to the production levels.

NCAER regularly conducts a Survey of Industrial Confidence. According to the latest information available the business confidence index for August has sharply declined indicating that second half of 1996-97 may be even worse than the first half. Psychologically the corporate sector is now excepting a slow down in industrial activity and the inertia of this deceleration may result in a slow down greater than what economic fundamental may indicate.

Power sector

Power generation during 1995-96 at 380.1 billion kwh recorded a growth of 8.3 per cent over 1994-95. Total generation of power during April-November, 1996 at 257.2 billion kwh, compared to 248.7 billion kwh during April-November, 1995 recorded a growth of 3.4 per cent. While thermal and nuclear generation went up by 6.5 per cent and 4.1 per cent respectively, hydro generation declined by 7.7 per cent. Owing to the low Plant Load Factor (PLF) of thermal plants, heavy Transmission and Distribution (T&D) losses and other operational and technical inefficiencies, full benefits are not being derived even from existing capacities.

Thermal plants at present account for 74 per cent of total power generation and hydro electricity plants 24 per cent, with the balance 2 per cent being generated by nuclear plants. The installed capacity of power generation as on March 31, 1996 was 83,288 MW. During the first 4 years of the 8th plan (1992-97) capacity addition has been 14,799 MW as against the 8th Plan target of 30,858 MW. About 12 per cent of the total capacity addition during the first four years has been accounted for by hydro and the remaining by thermal units.

Nearly half of the addition to capacity occurred in the Central Sector. 4.25 per cent was accounted for by the State Sector and the rest in the Private Sector. While the Central Sector has achieved 57.0 per cent of the 8th Plan, the State and Private Sectors achieved 42.3 per cent and 41.9 per per cent respectively. During the period (April-November) of the current year (1996-97) there has been a capacity addition of 53.460 MW of which 105.60 MW is in the private sector.

Several reasons have been identified for slippages in capacity creation in the Central and State sector. These include paucity of funds, delay in placement of order for main plant and equipment, delay in supply of equipment by suppliers, procedural delays in land acquisition, non-resolution of inter-state disputes, problems due to disturbed site conditions at some of the projects, unresolved issues in fuel linkages, suspension of work due to contract failures and resettlement and rehabilitation problems. Another important reason for slippages, particularly in State sector projects has been that the States saw the announcement of policy for private participation as an opportunity to cut back on their involvement in generation projects. As a result many projects that were scheduled for commissioning through the State sector resources have not been provided adequate funds for timely completion.

The PLF is an important indicator of operational efficiency of thermal power plants. The average PLF in the Central PSUs in 1995-96 and in April-November, 1996 was appreciably higher than that achieved by the State Electricity boards (SEBs). The low capacity utilisation of thermal power plants of the SEBs is largely due to deficiencies in management and operation, lack of proper maintenance and non-availabilty of coal of appropriate quality. There were wide inter-state variations in the average PLF of thermal plants and the average PLF in the case of Eastern and North Eastern regions continued to be much lower than the all India average during. 1996-97.

An action plan has been drawn up to improve the performace of the power sector in a phased manner. This involves short-term, medium-term and long-term measures and covers both the physical and financial aspects of generation, transmission and distribution of power. Short-term measures include overhaul and maintenance (O & M) of boileers and optimal operation of the regional grids. Significant improvements in the PLF of thermal power stations can be effected through medium-term measures like proper maintenance planning. In the long-term, the availability factor of the older thermal power plants can be improved by appropriate renovation and modernisation (R & M) programmes.

In the power sector, SEBs are responsible for distribution to all end users other than a small segment under the purview of privae distribution companies. As a result, in principle, all the electricity generated is to be sold to SEBs. But the financial condition of SEBs, though it differs from one state to the other, is fragile in most cases. The magnitude of losses incurred by SEBs over the period 1990-91 to 1994-95.

The industry and agriculture sectors continued to be the two most important categories of consumers in terms of their relative shares, with SEB electricity charges set at much below the unit cost for the agricultural sector and above the unit cost for the industrial sector. In none of the SEBs does unit revenue realisation from the agricultural sector cover even a reasonable fraction of the unit average cost for the SEB, and this is leading to heavy financial losses.

The commercial losses of SEBs which, in absolute terms, were a little over Rs. 4,000 crore in 1991-92, have shot up over a five year period to Rs. 10,941 crore in 1996-97 (RE). The hidden subsidy for the agriculture and domestic sectors has increased from Rs. 7,248 crore in 1991-92 to Rs. 19,227 crore in 1996-97 (RE) and is projected to further go upt to Rs. 21,580 crore in 1997-98. Introduction of proposed national minimum agricultural tariff of 50 paise/kwh, even if implemented, will leave uncovered a substantial proportion of the subsidy provided to the sector.

In addition the SEBs have continued to suffer from

high T & D losses, which stood at 21.8 per cent in 1992-93, have come down marginally to 20.9 per cent in 1994-95. These figures are very high when compared with the international average of less than 10 per cent for the advanced countries of the world. A reduction in T & D losses by 1 per cent would result in saving of capacity of about 800 MW at present day consumption. These T & D losses are due to the sparsely distributed loads over large rural area, substancial amount of energy sold at low voltage level. under-investment in the power distribution systems, inadequated billing and high pilferage. Inherent losses in conductors and equipment can be brought down through system improvement schemes and the pilferage and theft of energy can be reduced through appropriate administrative measures.

Restoration of the financial health of SEBs and improvement in their operational performance continue to remain the most crucial issues in the power sector. In terms of Section 59 of the Electricity (Supply) Act, 1948, SEBs are required to earn a minimum rate of return (ROR) of 3 per cent on their net fixed assest in service, after providing for depreciation and interest charges. This provision was to become operative from the accounting year of 1985. However the SEBs are yet to comply with this statutory stipulation. Whereas in 1992-93, the number of SEBs with a positive ROR were 11, there were only 6 such SEBs in 1994-95. Similarly, as against 5 SEBs with negative ROR in 1992-93, the number of such SEBs have increased to 9 in 1994-95.

There were only 3 SEBs with a ROR Return of more than 3 per cent in 1994-95. The managerial and financial inefficiencies in the state sector utilities have in turn adversely affected future capacity addition and system improvement programme. On the one hand, the SEBs do not have enough resources to finance future programmes and, on the other, their ability to raise investible funds from alternate sources in limited due to their poor financial and commerical performance.

Diagnostic studies aimed at reform and restructuring of the State power sector with a view to improving its physical and financial performance have been initiated in several States namely Haryana, Uttar Pradesh, Rajasthan, Gujarat and Andhra Pradesh. Similar studies are being considered in Kerala and Karnataka. the State of Orissa has provided the framework for reform envisaged through the enactment of a reform legislation, namely "The Orissa Reform Act, 1995" made effective from 1.495. A few other states are also considering similar steps.

The net budgetary support to the Central PSUs under the Ministry of Power as a proportion of the approved plan outlay has been declining steadily over the years. It stood at about Rs. 719.5 crore in 1996-97 and this amounted to only 10.6 per cent of total plan outlay. Owing to the decline in budgetary support, the central PSUs have to mobilise resources through internal and extra budgetary resources (IEBR). During 1995-96, the PSUs wer able to mobilise resources amounting to Rs. 3,593.8 crore as against the approved allocation of Rs. 4,326.9 crore under IEBR. Against the total plan outlay of Rs. 6,923.5 crore for the year 1995-96, the actual utilisation (Provisional) is of the order of Rs. 5,760.3 crore. During 1996-97, the IEBR component constitutes Rs. 4,565.5 crore (67 per cent) of the total approved plan outlay of Rs. 6,790.3 crore.

In view of the paucity of resources with Central/ State PSUs as well as the SEBs and the need to bridge the gap between the rapidly growing demand for the supply of electricity, there is a policy to encourage greater investment by private enterprises in the power sector. This policy, which has the objective of mobilising additional resources for capacity addition in power generation and distribution had been formulated in 1991, and is currently under implementation. The policy to invite private participation in the power sector also covers areas of transmission and distribution besides generation. The response to the policy has been expressed in putting up more than 124 power projects (requiring clearance of the Central Electricity Authority) for a total capacity of 67281 MW and involving and investment of about Rs. 2,46,472 crore. In addition, there are several projects (MOU/LOI projects costing up to Rs. 100 crore and Projects awarded through competitive bidding and costing up to Rs. 1000 crore) which are being set up by the private sector with the approval of the concerned State Government itself

In order to make the policy more attractive, the tariff notification has been amended twice to offer an assorment of incentives to investors. The Government has revised the hydro tariff guidelines to boost private investment in hydro-electric projects. To bring about private investment in the renovation, modernisation and upgradation of old power plants, the Government has finalised the policy and the guidelines have been issued. The Govenment has also taken steps to encourage captive/co-generation plants by industries. In order to encourage short gestation period projects, the Government has decided to permit setting up of power projects based on heavy fuel oils such as napha, heavy petroleum stock (HPS), low sulphur heavy stock (LSHS), heavy furnace oil (HFO), furnace oil (FO) and natural gas, wherever available, as primary fuel.

Under the current structure, the Independent Power Producers (IPPs) generally sell powers to SEBs which distribute power. Since most SEBs are financially distressed, the security package for an IPP is crucial to the success of a power project.

As an initial measure to attract private capital into the power sector, the Government of India had agreed to extend counter-guarantees to State-guarantees for the SEB's payment obligations to generating companies in respect eight fast track private power projects. This was a confidence building measure necessary for the initial batch of projects. Though these guarantees increase the comfort-levels of lenders in the initial phases, extensive use of these measures can lead to large contingent liabilities that would over-expose the concerned governments. Other options for securing the revenue stream of IPPs include Escrow Accounts, Guarantees from Multilateral Development Banks and Direct sale to high tension customers. The status of these eight fast track IPPs for which counter-guarantees have been or will be extended. Most of these projects are expecting financial and technical closure soon.

To facilitate the setting up of large sized thermal/ hydel power plants in the country, and to derive economies of scale, projects having a capacity of 1000 MW or above and supplying power to more than one stae are being considered as Mega projects. The SEBs and the State Government have been advised to introduce a more competitive element in the process of selection of selection of developers and award of projects. A notification was issued in October, 1995 enhancing concurrence of the Central Electricity Authority from Rs. 100 crore to Rs. 400 crore in the case of generating companies. The limit has been further enchanced to Rs. 1000 crore in September, 1996.

Capative power generation units in industry are used to supplement the power drawn from the grid and as a stand-by in case of power cuts. As of now, the country has an installed captive generation capacity of more than 10,000 MW. The policies relating to captive generation have also been liberalised. A 50 per cent thershold level has been prescribed for the industry's own consumption from the capative unit, and capacity in excess of this level can be sold to the grid.

In view of the widening gap between demand and supply and the huge capital cost involved in the installation of new power plants, a movement has been launched to make consumers aware of the need to save energy. Moreover, the Government is vigorously promoting energy accounting and monitoring systems. Energy audits have been carried out in a number of industrial units to identigy energy saving opportunities and eliminate wastage and to ensure that industries adopt the recommendations ofthese energy audits. Steps have been taken to improve the efficiency of domestic electrical appliances and agricultural pump sets and to promote the usage of fuel efficient engines and motors in both agricultural and transport sectors. Efforts are also being made to encourage co-generation of electricity in such industries as sugar, paper, cement, pertrochemicals and fertilisers.

The Government is working on a three-pronged strategy to overcome the existing structural constraints, technical inefficiencies and financial constraints. These include short and long-term measures to meet the power supply situation, encourage greater doses of private capital in power generation and facilitate reforms and restructuring in the state utilities. The Chief Ministers of different States met on 16th October, 1996 and 3rd December, 1996 to discuss and deliberate upon issues pertaining to the power sector. In the course of these deliberations a national consensus evolved for improving the performance of the power sector in a time bound manner and a Common Minimum National Action Plan for Power was adopted.

North-eastern Electric Power Corporation Limited (NEEPCO) was constituted in 1976 under the Companies Act to harness the power potential of the north-eastern region through planned development of power generation projects. The Corporation is responsible for operation and maintenance of the 150 mw Kopili-Hydro Electric Project which was commissioned in June/July 1988. The Corporation is presently executing the following projects: (i) Doyang Hydro-Electric Project (75 mw), Nagaland; (ii) Ranganadi Hydro electric Project (405 mw), Arunachal Pradesh; (iii) Assam Gas Based Project (291 mw), Assam; (iv) Kopali Ist stage extension Project (100 mw), Assam; and (v) Agartala Gas Turbine Project (84 mw), Tripura.

Tehri Hydro development Corporation limited (THDC) was incorporated as a joint venture public sector undertaking under the Companies Act, 1956 on 12 July 1988 for execution of Tehri Hydro Power Complex at Tehri (Garhwal) in Uttar Pradesh. The Corporation with equity participation of Government of India and Uttar Pradesh in the ratio of 75:25 (for power component of Tehri Complex) will also execute other hydro-electric projects with the consent of the state government. It has an authorised share capital of rs. 1,200 crore.

Tehri Hydro Power Complex with a generation capacity of 2400 mw comprises: (a) Tehri Dam and Hydro Powder Plant, 1000 mw (4 × 250 mw); (b) Tehri Pumped Storage Plant 1000 mw (4 × 250 mw); (c) Koteshwar Dam 400 mw (4 × 100 mw) and (d) Associated Transmission System (800 kv/400 kv) for evacuation of power. The project will generate 6,322 million units of energy per year and will provide additional irrigation facilities to 2.7 lakh hectare, besides stabilising existing irrigation facility in 6.04 lakh hectare of land.

Natpha Jhakri Power Corporation (NJPC) was incorporated on 24 May 1988 to plan, promote, organise, execute, operate and maintain hydro-electric power projects in the Satluj rover basin in Himachal Pradesh. The authorised share capital of NJPC is Rs. 1,000 crore and equity loan ratio is 1:1. Satluj river, which originates from lake Mansarover has so far been harnessed. The Nathpa Jhakri HEP is the first project taken up by the Corporation as a joint venture of Government of India and Government of Himachal Pradesh both sharing the cost of the project in the ratio of 3:1 respectively. The Nathpa Jhakri Hydro-electric project with an installed capacity of 1,500 mw is being executed by NJPC with partial assistance of 437 million US dollar from World Bank. The project is located in Kinnaur and Shimla districts of Himachal Pradesh and envisages to harness the hydro power potential in the upper reaches of river Satluj in the form of a run-of-over scheme.

Four major contracts in respect of the civil works pertaining to the Dam & Desilting Complex, the Head Race Tunnel and Surge Shaft, the Power House complex have been awarded in June - September, 1993 to three International Consortia each of whom has an Indian construction company as its partner. The work on these contracts has picked up momentum.

Damodar Valley Corporation (DVC), the first multi-purpose river valley project of the Government of India, was set up on 7 July 1948 under DVC Act (XIV of 1948) for the unified development of Damodar Valley region spread over the states of Bihar and West Bengal. DVC's objectives include flood control and irrigation, power generation and distribution, soil conservation, social and economic well-being of the people of Damodar Valley region. DVC's main projects include four dams at Maithon, Panchet, Tilaiya and Konar, four thermal power statin at Bokaro 'A', Bokaro 'B', Chandrapura and Durgapur and three hydel stations at Maithon, Panchet and Tilaiya and also one gas turbine station at Maithon.

DVC has practically become synonymous with power generation and distribution by supplying power to coal, mines, steelplants, railways and other big industries, besides state electricity boards of Bihar and West Bengal. Installed capacity of DVC in 1994-95 was 2,146 mw comprising of 1,920 mw thermal, 144 mw hydel and 82.5 mw bygas turbine. Total length of transmission lines of DVC runs over 5,000 circuit km. During the last financial year DVC generated 6,912 mw of power.

Bhakra Beas Management Board administers, maintains and operates the largest multi-purpose river valley project in the country to meet the irrigation and power needs of northern region which consitutes the granary of the nation and contributes over 90 per cent of foodgrains for the Public Distribution System. The installed capacity of power plants is 2,705 mw and the Board manages the operation of about 574 ckt km of 40 kv lines and 2,998 ckt km of 220 kv lines. The achievements during the last five years reflect complete harmony/congruence of individual and organisation goals' thereby creating synergy and a result oriented approach.

The National Power training Institute (formerly Power Engineers Training Society) was formed in 1980 as an autonomous body. The Institute is responsible for coordinating training programmes of the various state electricity boards, power stations, etc., and supplementing these with its own traiing activities. It has four regional power training institutes at Neyveli, Durgapur, Badarpur (New Delhi) and Nagpur. These institutes conduct regular induction courses, in-service refresher and short-term courses, on=job and on-plant training programmes for power engineers, operators and technicians of thermal power stations, state electricity boards, etc. A simulator installed at the training institute at Badarpur (New Delhi) Provides training to engineers and operators of 210 mw thermal units.

Central Power Research Institute (CPRI), which was set up in 1960 as a subordinate office under the erstwhile Central Water and Power Comission (Power Wing), was reorganised as a society under the Karnataka Societies Act, 1960 w.e.f. January 1978. CPRI functions as national laboratory for applied research in the field of electric power engineering. While CPRI has its units located at Bhopal, Hyderabad, Koradi, Muradnagar and Thiruvananthhapuram, the main complex of its laboratories is at Bangalore. The Institute is an apex body for research and development in the power sector and conducts tests of electrical apparatus in accordance with national/intermational standards so as to meet fully the research and testing needs of electrical, transmission and distribution equipment. It also serves as a national testing and certification authority for transmission and distribution equipment. The Institute possesses highly sophisticated laboratories comparable to those in development countries.

Energy Management Centre (EMC) was established by the Government of India in April 1989 to act as a focal point for exchange of experience among energy institutes within India and as a centre for information, research and training activities in the energy field based on cooperation between India and the European Communities. The activities of EMC are : (i) to develop a national energy database by collecting and analysing data on energy supply, demand and infromation on prices; (ii) identify barriers for improving energy efficiency and propose appropriate incentives and other measures to overcome them.

These would include recommendations for assistance with capital investment, taxes duties and other financial incentives; (iii) to review laws and regulations that have an impact on energy consumption and propose modifications and formulate suitable policies and actions; (iv) to suggest introduction of standards, labels and setting of consumption targets; (v) to organise public infromation and promotional and promotional campaign on an on-going basis; and (vi) to organise specific promotional campaigns for the main energy consuming sectors (industry, transport, agriculture, commercial and government buildings). The Centre also provides technical assistance in the field of energy efficiency and fuel sectors; promotes energy audits enterprises and provides recommendations to improve energy efficiency and fuel substitution; and * initiates follow-up actions where needed; and organises training for energy managers and equipment operators.

The investment in Research and Development. (R & D) has increased from a paltry Rs. 20 crore in the First Five Year Plan. Presently there are 214 universities, 400 national laboratories and 1300 in-house R & D centres in the industrial sector. Several Science & Technology departments have been set up in the areas of environment, non-conventional energy resources, bio-technology, ocean development, industrial research, space, atomic energy, defence, health, agriculture and electronics.

Identification and promotion of priority areas in R & D is done by Science an Engineering Research Council (SERC) set up under the Department of Science & Technology (DST). DST supports 12 autonomous research insitutions as well, for furthering research work in several discipline. Technology Information, Forecasting and Assessment Council (TIFAC) has been set up for generating technology forecasting and technology assessment documents and enabling a technology information system that is interactive and nationally accessible.

Industrial research in several diverse fields of scientific activity is being undertaken through a network of 40 laboratories and 81 field stations set up by the Council for Scientific and Industrial Research (CSIR). In the field of bio-technology, more than 24 specialised R & D centres have been developed for pursuing state-of-the-art research. Identical efforts for promoting new avenues of research are being undertaken in the field of ocean development as well.

The Union Budget for 1996-97 has taken various measures to promote R & D facilities. A matching one time grant has been awarded to CSIR and the Indian Council of Agricultural Research (ICAR) for modernisation of laboratories and institutes. The Technology Development and Application Fund created in 1995-96 has been proposed to be strengthened by Rs. 30 crore. A Five Year Tax Holiday under Section 80-IA of the Income Tax Act has been allowed to companies exclusively create for participation in R & D activities. The existing procedure for awarding weighted deduction under Section 35(2AA) of the Income Tax Act on sums paid for scientific research to a National Laboratory or a University or an IIT has been amended, by deleting the condition of approval by an outside body. In order to encourage R & D efforts, goods developed and patented in India and concurrently in specified countries have been exempted from levy of excise duty for a period of 3 years. The exemption procedure for customs duty on import of equipment and consumables for R & D institutions has been rationalised as well.

9

Sectoral Development

Sectoral deployment

In the pre-nationalisation days, large and medium industry and wholesale trade accounted for over 78 per cent of the bank credit. By March 1994, share of these sectors (excluding credit for public food procurement) had declined to about 42.7 per cent. Correspondingly, share of priority sectors, food procurement agencies, etc, has shown significant improvement.

Advances to priority sectors

Extension of credit to small borrowers in the hitherto neglected sectors of the economy has been one of the major tasks assigned to the public sector banks in the post-nationalisation period. To achieve this objective, banks have drawn up schemes to extend credit to small borrowers in sectors like agriculture, small scale industry, road and water transport, retail trade and small business which traditionally had very little share in the credit extended by banks. Taking into account the need to provide resource requirements to weaker sections, for specific needs, consumption credit (with certain limits) has been included in priority sector advances. Number of borrowal accounts with public sector banks for these categories of borrowers increased from 3.28 lakh between June 1969 and March 1994.

Credit to weaker sections

With a view to increase credit flow to small and poor borrowers, commercial banks were advised by the Reserve Bank of India to provide at least 10 per cent of their net bank credit of 25 per cent of their priority sector advances to weaker sections comprising of small and marginal farmers, landless labourers, tenant farmers and share-croppers, artisans, village and cottage industries, Scheme of Urban Micro Enterprises (SUME) and beneficiaries of Inteegrated Rural Development Programme, some scheduled castes and scheduled tribes and beneficiaries of Differential Rate of Interest (DRI) scheme. As at the end of March 1993, the amount of outstanding advances extended by public sector to weaker sections was Rs. 12,779 crore and accounted for 9.1 per cent of their net bank credit and 24.0 per cent of priority sector advances.

Credit flow to agriculture

Banks were intially given a target extending 15 per cent of the total advances as direct finance to the agriculture sector to be achieved by March 1985. This target was subsequently raised to 18 per cent to be achieved by March 1990. in terms of the guidelines issued by Reserve Bank of India in October 1993, both direct and indirect advances for agriculture will be taken together for assessing the target of 18 per cent provided lendings for indirect agriculture should not exceed one fourth of the total agriculture lending target of 18 per cent of the net bank credit. As on March 1994, public sector banks extended 13.1 per cent of the total advances to the agriculture sector.

Advances to SC/ST borrowers

People belonging to the scheduled castes and scheduled tribes have been recognised as the most vulnerable sections. Bank have been asked to make special efforts to assist them with adequate credit to enable them to undertake self-employment ventures toacquire income generating capital assets so as to improve their stantard of living. At the end of march 1994 the total outstanding amount of loan extended to scheduled castes/scheduled tribes by poublic sector banks was Rs. 4,737 crore involving 97.5 lakh borrowal accounts.

Development of Backward Areas

— Tax concession for promoting industrialisation was introduced for the first time in 1949 in the form of tax holiday for the first 5 years of production of new industrial units. This concession was avaliable as deduction from taxable profit computed at the rate of 6% of capital employed. This incentive was continued till 1980 when, to remove capital bias inherent in it, was reformulated as 80-I to provide for a deduction as percentage of profit rather than capital employed. This provision was modified and renumbered as Section 80-I w.e.f. 1.4.1991. Under this provision any new industrial undertaking or hotel came into business between 1.4.1991 and 1.4.1995 was entitled to a deduction of 25% from the profits (30% for companies for 10 years).

— In 1968 Planning Commission set up two Working Groups to evolve a criteria for identification 245 out of 396 districts were identified as backward. Government of India also introduced Investment Subsidy Scheme for identified backward areas. This scheme was, however, discontinued in 1988. States also introduced the Investment Subsidy schemes and these are still in vogue. In 1974, tax concessions in the form of relief in income tax to new units were introduced in Eighth Schedule of Income-tax Act as section 80HH, which was later replaced by notification in 1986. This listed the backward areas.

— In 1987 National Institute of Public Finance and Policy conducted a study to evaluate the fiscal concessions for backward areas. This study concluded that while the fiscal incentives for the backward development did successfully promote industrial dispersal, the criteria of identifying backward areas in a state with reference to its development indicators rather than any All India norm favoured developed states.

— The NIPFP study as well as the Economic Administrative Reform Commission recommended deletion of Section 80-HH of Income-tax Act which had indicated the backward areas.

— Accepting the recommendations of the study the Finance Act, 1993 modified the tax incentive scheme. Full tax holiday was introduced for the initial 5 years of production in case of industrial units starting production between 1.4.1993 and 31.3.1998 and set up a backward state or union territories specified in new 8th Schedule. These states were selected because all their districts were earlier classified as backward in notification issued in 1986.

— Following the introduction of the Bill, various representations were received and it was indicated that these concessions were extended to backward districts which would be identified by a Study Group. This has been reiterated by the Finance Minister recently.

— Current approach to industrialisation is based on providing industrial infrastructure. Both the NIPFP Study and the Study by World Bank indicated that location decision can only be marginally influenced. The factor which would be crucial in the location decisions could be the availability of physical infrastructure. This has been the rationale of growth centre scheme.

— Capital incentive in the form of investment subsidy scheme have not been successful in reducing the skewed industrial growth. Infact it may be a better approach to consider harmonisation of incentives.

— While promoting spread of industrialisation, the policy essentially needs to find means of concentration of industries as the complementarity and competitive requirements make such cluster approach more successful. This ensures diversified industrial base and optimal utilisation of infrastructure and other resources. This is the reason why the growth of centres has been in a corridor or cluster of districts which are geographically inter-linked.

— In a geographically continuous and ethnic homogenous region, industrial development requires consideration of area specific approach. In these areas besides the problem of markets and non local resources there may be constraint of profit, project identification and ignorance about the resources. This has been the approach for development of backward areas in North East where a North East Development Bank has been set up to cater to the specific requirements of the region, identify areas of investment, infrastructure constraints, technological needs and adoption of a hand-holding approach for the enterpreneurs.

— In other backward districts where there is no geographical continuity, growth centres approach which provide the infrastructure and thereby reduces the cost of operation have better chances of being successful. However, regional dispersal is a national issue and rquires discussion at all levels for adoption of a comprehensive policy package.

In the first few months of the current fiscal year, industrial performance—both in production and sales—has not been impressive when compared to the previous year. The Economic Times Investment Bureau has estimated that the average growth in turnover of the sensex 30 companies (excluding IDBI, ICICI and SBI) will be between 9.10% as compared to 24% last year. The net profit growth is also expected to slow down to around 25% as against 46% last year. This along with the relatively poor performance of the infrastructure industries, the depressed stock markets, and slower growth of imports has cast a warning signal about industrial performance in 1996-97.

Taking care of weaker sections

The Ninth Plan document has to take care of the needs of the SCs/STs and the OBCs. They are the people who are not only poor but they are the politicized communities. Their votes have brought this coalition government at the Centre. The thirteen party government has rightly recognized their needs in the Common Minimum Programme. This document has reflected the aspirations of these people in their thrust areas. Let us look into the problems of each community one by one.

The peasant tradition: There are two occupational groups in the OBCs. The majority of them are the cultivating classes who depend on the family labour to sustain the farm production. It is the peasant tradition which is sustaining the farm production rather than the market economy which is generating enough profit. That is why they get involved in the farm production. If one takes into account the wages of each family labour who works in the farm, then the small farm economy is neither profitable nor sustainable. A major section of rural people are engaged in peasant production which is not working on market lines. The State has already withdrawn subsidies in terms of fertilizers and seeds. If they are going to be taxed as the urban rich, then the farm economy is going to collapse. Moreover, they are the victims of vicissitudes of the weather. A majority of our farmers depend on the weather.

It has been studied that because of the changes in ecology, They are the victims of the natural disasters like cyclone, flood and drought. The coastal region of India where a substantive population live, is prone to flood and cyclone. The State is unable to provide any system of insurance which can take care of their losses.

Yearning for quality: Moreover, the peasant families are conscious of health and education. To avail itself of both health and education facilities, each peasant family is spending money directly or indirectly, as the quality of education and health facilities provided by the public system is so poor. The government can charge educational cess from each peasant family. If the government can ensure them quality school education, they would gladly accept the proposal. The same thing can happen in the health sector if some form of health insurance can be created where both the peasant family and the government can can manage the contribution to sustain such a system. Only the landless families in the rural areas may not carry this financial burden. In the approach paper, allocation of resources in both primary education and primary health services has increased to some extent.

Upgradation of skills: The lower OBCs, who are working as artisans, have lost their market. No technological upgradation of their traditional technology has taken place. Furthermore, education provided by our school system is not creating any skills. Education without skills creates a lot of educated unemployed who do not fit either in the traditional economy or in the modern economy. The planning of education has to be done in such a manner that the duality of our economy is destroyed. Traditional economic activities have to undergo the process of modernisation which can sustain the modern economy. In this area of thinking, Gandhi's concept of basic education has to be applied in a changed form. The Ninth Plan approach paper has agreed to make special efforts in bringing about tehnological upgradation of the traditional sector of our economy.

The people of the SC community are without any productive assets. But they work as agricultural labour or do some economic activities which have an insignificant place in the modern economy. A section of the SCs who work as feshermen or cobblers are aleady threatened by the mechanized fishing and modern shoe factory. Can they be absorbed in the modern economic activities if proper skills are added to their traditional knowledge? Mechanisation of agriculture has affected their women, as they actively participate in agricultural operations. Feminization of poverty has affected nigatively both their level of nutrition and health. It has to be accepted that mechanization of agriculture cannot stop, but at the same time skill of this community has to be upgraded to be absorbed in a meaningful manner in agriculture. Theoretically, the State is providing them free education. Education to SCs is liked with the job opportunities in the State sector. As the State sector is shrinking, the job opportunities for these communities are reduced.The cost of educated unemployed in the SC community is an expensive affairs from the State point of view. Unless the State provides education which is directly liked with the skill formation from the modern economy point of view, it is indirectly creating a social volcano which can burst any time.

Globalization of Indian agriculture: Some Strategies in the Ninth Plan

Indian agriculture, which had hitherto been of a subsistence nature, is now poised for a take—off on the export front and is getting ready to face international competition. Our strategies for development of agriculture till recently were oriented towards ensuring food security to the population and food production itself was primarily meant for meeting the domestic demand. With the announcement of the new economic policy in 1991, the development perspective has changed and there is greater emphasis on producing for meeting the demand of the global market. The establishment of the World Trade Organization (WTO) in 1995 has further widened the sckope for exporting the agricultural produce.

India, by producing 186 million tonnes of food grains has achieved self—sufficiency on the food front. The credit goes to the hard toil of millions of farmers of this country who are wiling to experiment with innovations and accept new technologies of production and the dedicated agricultural scientists, extension workers and others who are directly or indirectly associated withthe implementation of the highyielding variety (HYV) programme and made the Green Revolution a success.

The agricultural sector in India has demonstrated an admirable performance over the past four decades, but still there is abundant scope to imporve for occupying the premier position in global market. This calls for a change in outlook and approach towards agriculture from the subsistence model to the commercial one. The Government of India is also considering granting status of industry to the agricultural sector. Boosting farm exports is also a priority area under the New Agricultural Policy (NAP). Considerable emphasis is there on food processing sector too. During the past few years all these factors have focused tha attention of corporate bodies, NRIs, multinational coompanies, etc on the agricultural sector, which is an encouraging and positive feature.

This paper is an attempt to suggest some strategies in the in the Ninth Five Year Plan (1997—2002) for the globalization of Indian agriculture.

Current status of agriculture

India has the unique advantage of diverse agro—climatic conditions which are conductive to growing a variety of tropical, subtropical and temperate crops including plantation and horticulture crops. India has a land area of 329 million hectares, of which the land available for crop production is 182 milion ha. Approximately 128 million ha (72%) are being covered under food crops. The ranking of the country in the world in terms of production and yield of major crops.

Horticulture Crops: The climatic features of the country are very congenial to the cultivation of a wide variety of horticultural crops on a commercial scale. India is the second largest producer of fruits and vegetables in the world. There is considerable scope for exports of both fruits and fresh vegetables in fresh and processed form. This sector has been assigned adequate priority in the national programme for agricultural development. The proposal is to increase the production of fruits to 60 million tonnes and vegetables to 120 million tonnes by AD 2000 to satisfy not only the domestic consumption but also export requirements. The world trade in floriculture is estimated at about $ 25 billion and increasing at 11 per cent per annum. Though India has been identified in the world market as a potential exporter for cut—flowers because of the present climatic and resource advantages, its share is very low (2%). The

Government of India has set an ambitious export target of Rs. 100 crore by the end of the VIII Plan for floriculture.

Mushroom Cultivation: In India, mushroom can be grown on commercial lines exclusively to meet the foreign market like Singapore, Malaysia, France, Germany, East Europe and West Asia. Availability of low cost technology, short gestation period of cropping, possibility of intensive indoor production, less labour deployment, etc make mushroom cultivation a profitable agro—business.

Sericulture: India is the only country in the world which produces four types of natural silk, viz mulberry silk, tusser silk, eri silk and muga silk because of favourable agro—climatic conditions. The important silk producing countries in the world are China, India, Japan, Russia and Korea out of which India ranks second. The Government of India has allocated a budget of Rs. 860 crore during the VIII Plan for sericulture.

Dairry and Poultry: India possesses the largest cattle population (cows, buffaloes, sheep, goat, pig) and ranks third in the world in milk production. the current production of meat and poultry products (excluding eggs) in India is estimated at over two million tonnes per annum. This sector too needs a boost not only to meet our own increasing demand but also to increase our exports.

Egg Production: India stands sixth in egg production with 27 billion eggs per annum and 25th in broiler production with 400 million broilers per annum. The world market of processed chicken is about US $ 5 billion which is very attractive for India. Among the countries importing opoultry from India are Oman, Saudi Arabia, the Maldives, Bahrain, and Hong Kong. A few corporate sectors have also entered into this industry with foreign collaboration. Our products are going to be cheaper in the global market once the subsidies which are very high in European countries are withdrawn/reduced and increased in our country in view of the recent GATT accord. *All these indicates tremendous potential and prospects for the globalization of Indian agriculture.*

Fertilizers

Four decades of planning and development has brought India to the frontline of fertilizer producing countries and is today the fourth largest producer of nitrogenous fertilizers in the world. There are, at present, 58 fertilizer units manufacturing a wide range of nitrogenous and complex fertilizers, including nine units producing ammonium sulphate as a by-product. Besides, there are about 80 units producing single super-phosphate. Production capacity of nitrogen has increased from a modest 85,00 tonnes in 1951-52 to 89.72 lakh tonnes as on 31 March 1995 and that of phosphatic fertilizers from 63,000 tonnes to 28.22 lakh tonnes of P^2O^5 during the same period. Against the nominal production of 16,000 tonnes of nitrogen and 11,000 tonnes of phosphate in 1951-52, the country proudced 79.45 lakh tonnes of nitrogen and 24.93 lakh tonnes of phosphate during 1994-95. Despite massive increase in the indigenous capacity production of fertilizers over the years, substantial imports, either in the form of finshed fertilizers or its raw materials and intermediates, are requied every year to meet the country's growing demand. The overall per hectare consumption of fertilizer nutrients in the country has been rising steadily and has now reached a level of about 68 kg from a mere 0.55 kg in 1950-51.

One large scale gas-based nitrogenous fertilizer plant, with an annual installed capacity of 3.34 lakh tonnes of nitrogen is presently under implementation at Shahjahanpur (UP) and likely to go on stream during 1995-96.

With a veiw to making fertilizers available to farmers at a price they could afford, the Retention Price Scheme was introduced in 1977. Its aim was to insulate farmers from the rising trend in fertilizer prices and to ensure that fertilizer consumption in the country did not suffer as its growing use was an essential component of the Green Revolution strategy of India's development. The scheme simultaneously aimed at ensuring reasonable return on investment to indigenous manufacturers and to attract further investment in this vital sector. The scheme proved its worth in terms of stimulating greater production and use of fertilizers and thereby contributing to greater agricultural production. Inspite of substantial increases in the prices of feedstocks, utilities wages etc. and consequent revision in the retention prices, the selling prices of fertilizers to farmers remained almost frozen for ten years between 1981 and 1991. Thus, while the objective of promoting increased use of fertilizer by farmers was served, this added to the quantum of subsidy borne by the Government year after year. The fertilizer subsidy bill borne by the Government went up from Rs. 375 crore in 1981-82 to Rs. 5,166 crore in 1994-95. Realising that the country could no longer afford to continue with a system which imposed a large and growing burden of fertilizer subsidy, the Government effected an increase of 30 per cent in the selling price of fertilizers in August 1991 after a gap of a decade. While this served to bring down the subsidy requirement from what it would have been in the absence of the price revision, it did not offer much relief in terms of the absolute amount of subsidy bill for the year because, inspite of 30 per cent price increase, fertilizers continued to be heavily subsidised and also because of the otherwise welcome growth in production and consumption of fertilizers.

A Joint Parliamentary Committee was set up to go into the verious aspects of fertilizer pricing and subsidy. Based on its recommendations, Government announced some major changes in the fertilizer pricing policy in August 1992. All price and distribution controls on phosphatic and potassic fertilizers were removed and the selling price of urea was reduced by 10 per cent with effect from 25 August 1992. However, the controlled price of urea was again increased by 20 per cent with effect from 10 June 1993.

To make production and marketing of phosphatic and complex fertilizers more competitive *vis-a-vis* imports in the wake of withdrawal of price and movement controls, various other corrective measures have been taken by the Government. These include: abolition of import durty on phosphoric acid-a basic raw material for phosphatic fertilizers, free availability of foreign exchange for import of raw materials and intermediates for manufacture of DAP and complex fertilizers at official exchange rates (till unification of exchange rates in March 1993) and lowering of railway freight for phosphatic and potassic fertilizers. In order to cushion the impact of increase in the prices of decontrolled fertilizers on farmers since *Rabi* 1992-93 season, a special subside of Rs. 1,000 per tonne on DAP and Muriate of Potash (MOP) and corresponding relief in the case of complex fertilizers was announced. From 1993-94, this special concession in the case of phosphatic fertilizers has been restricted to indigenous products only. These concessions have been extended during the current year 1995-96 also.

Power

Power generation during 1995-96 at 380.1 billion kwh recorded a growth of 8.3 per cent over 1994-95. Total generation of power during April-November, 1996 at 257.2 billion kwh, compared to 248.7 billion kwh during April-November, 1995 recorded a growth of 3.4 per cent.

While thermal and nuclear generation went up by 6.5 per cent and 4.1 per cent respectively, hydro generation declined by 7.7 per cent. Owing to the low Plant Load Factor (PLF) of thermal plants, heavy Transmission and Distribution (T&D) losses and other operational and technical inefficiencies, full benefits are not being derived even from existing capacities.

Thermal plants at present account for 74 per cent of total power generation and hydro electricity plants 24 per cent, with the balance 2 per cent being generated by nuclear plants. The installed capacity of power generation as on March 31, 1996 was 83,288 MW. During the first 4 years of the 8th plan (1992-97) capacity addition has been 14,799 MW as against the 8th Plan target of 30,858 MW. About 12 per cent of the total capacity addition during the first four years has been accounted for by hydro and the remaining by thermal units. Nearly half of the addition to capacity occurred in the Central Sector. 4.25 per cent was accounted for by the State Sector and the rest in the Private Sector. While the Central Sector has achieved 57.0 per cent of the 8th Plan, the State and Private Sectors achieved 42.3 per cent and 41.9 per per cent respectively. During the period (April-November) of the current year (1996-97) there has been a capacity addition of 53.460 MW of which 105.60 MW is in the private sector.

Several reasons have been identified for slippages in capacity creation in the Central and State sector. These include paucity of funds, delay in placement of order for main plant and equipment, delay in supply of equipment by suppliers, procedural delays in land acquisition, non-resolution of inter-state disputes, problems due to disturbed site conditions at some of the projects, unresolved issues in fuel linkages, suspension of work due to contract failures and resettlement and rehabilitation problems. Another important reason for slippages, particularly in State sector projects has been that the States saw the announcement of policy for private participation as an opportunity to cut back on their involvement in generation projects. As a result many projects that were scheduled for commissioning through the State sector resources have not been provided adequate funds for timely completion.

The PLF is an important indicator of operational efficiency of thermal power plants. The average PLF in the Central PSUs in 1995-96 and in April-November, 1996 was appreciably higher than that achieved by the State Electricity boards (SEBs). The low capacity utilisation of thermal power plants of the SEBs is largely due to deficiencies in management and operation, lack of proper maintenance and non-availabilty of coal of appropriate quality. There were wide inter-state variations in the average PLF of thermal plants and the average PLF in the case of Eastern and North Eastern regions continued to be much lower than the all India average during. 1996-97.

An action plan has been drawn up to improve the performace of the power sector in a phased manner. This involves short-term, medium-term and long-term measures and covers both the physical and financial aspects of generation, transmission and distribution of power. Short-term measures include overhaul and maintenance (O & M) of boileers and optimal operation of the regional grids. Significant improvements in the PLF of thermal power stations can be effected through medium-term measures like proper maintenance planning. In the long-term, the availability factor of the older thermal power plants can be improved by appropriate renovation and modernisation (R & M) programmes.

In the power sector, SEBs are responsible for distribution to all end users other than a small segment under the purview of privae distribution companies. As a result, in principle, all the electricity generated is to be sold to SEBs. But the financial condition of SEBs, though it differs from one state to the other, is fragile in most cases. The magnitude of losses incurred by SEBs over the period 1990-91 to 1994-95. The industry and agriculture sectors continued to be the two most important categories of consumers in terms of their relative shares, with SEB electricity charges set at much below the unit cost for the agricultural sector and above the unit cost for the industrial sector. In none of the SEBs does unit revenue realisation from the agricultural sector cover even a reasonable fraction of the unit average cost for the SEB, and this is leading to heavy financial losses. The commercial losses of SEBs which, in absolute terms, were a little over Rs. 4.000 crore in 1991-92, have shot up over a five year period to Rs. 10,941 crore in 1996-97 (RE). The hidden subsidy for the agriculture and domestic sectors has increased from Rs. 7,248 crore in 1991-92 to Rs. 19,227 crore in 1996-97 (RE) and is projected to further go upt to Rs. 21,580 crore in 1997-98. Introduction of proposed national minimum agricultural tariff of 50 paise/kwh, even if implemented, will leave uncovered a substantial proportion of the subsidy provided to the sector.

In addition the SEBs have continued to suffer from high T & D losses, which stood at 21.8 per cent in 1992-93, have come down marginally to 20.9 per cent in 1994-95. These figures are very high when compared with the international average of less than 10 per cent for the advanced countries of the world. A reduction in T & D losses by 1 per cent would result in saving of capacity of about 800 MW at present day consumption. These T & D losses are due to the sparsely distributed loads over large rural area, substancial amount of energy sold at low voltage level. under-investment in the power distribution systems, inadequated billing and high pilferage. Inherent losses in conductors and equipment can be brought down through system improvement schemes and the pilferage and theft of energy can be reduced through appropriate administrative measures.

Restoration of the financial health of SEBs and improvement in their operational performance continue to remain the most crucial issues in the power sector. In terms of Section 59 of the Electricity (Supply) Act, 1948, SEBs are required to earn a minimum rate of return (ROR) of 3 per cent on their net fixed àssest in service, after providing for depreciation and interest charges. This provision was to become operative from the accounting year of 1985. However the SEBs are yet to comply with this statutory stipulation. Whereas in 1992-93, the number of SEBs with a positive ROR were 11, there were only 6 such SEBs in 1994-95. Similarly, as against 5 SEBs with negative ROR in 1992-93, the number of such SEBs have increased to 9 in 1994-95. There were only 3 SEBs with a ROR Return of more than 3 per cent in 1994-95. The managerial and financial inefficiencies in the state sector utilities have in turn adversely affected future capacity addition and system improvement programme. On the one hand, the SEBs do not have enough resources to finance future programmes and, on the other, their ability to raise investible funds from alternate sources in limited due to their poor financial and commerical performance.

Diagnostic studies aimed at reform and restructuring of the State power sector with a view to improving its physical and financial performance have been initiated in several States namely Haryana, Uttar Pradesh, Rajasthan, Gujarat and Andhra Pradesh. Similar studies are being considered in Kerala and Karnataka. the State of Orissa has provided the framework for reform envisaged through the enactment of a reform legislation, namely "The Orissa Reform Act, 1995" made effective from 1.495. A few other states are also considering similar steps.

The net budgetary support to the Central PSUs under the Ministry of Power as a proportion of the approved plan outlay has been declining steadily over the years. It stood at about Rs. 719.5 crore in 1996-97 and this amounted to only 10.6 per cent of total plan outlay. Owing to the decline in budgetary support, the central PSUs have to mobilise resources through internal and extra budgetary resources (IEBR). During 1995-96, the PSUs wer able to mobilise resources amounting to Rs. 3,593.8 crore as against the approved allocation of Rs. 4,326.9 crore under IEBR. Against the total plan outlay of Rs. 6,923.5 crore for the year 1995-96, the actual utilisation (Provisional) is of the order of Rs. 5,760.3 crore. During 1996-97, the IEBR component constitutes Rs. 4,565.5 crore (67 per cent) of the total approved plan outlay of Rs. 6,790.3 crore.

In view of the paucity of resources with Central/State PSUs as well as the SEBs and the need to bridge the gap between the rapidly growing demand for the supply of electricity, there is a policy to encourage greater investment by private enterprises in the power sector. This policy, which has the objective of mobilising additional resources for capacity addition in power generation and distribution had been formulated in 1991, and is currently under implementation. The policy to invite private participation in the power sector also covers areas of transmission and distribution besides generation. The response to the policy has been expressed in putting up more than 124 power projects (requiring clearance of the Central Electricity Authority) for a total capacity of 67281 MW and involving and investment of about Rs. 2,46,472 crore. In addition, there are several projects (MOU/LOI projects costing up to Rs.

100 crore and Projects awarded through competitive bidding and costing up to Rs. 1000 crore) which are being set up by the private sector with the approval of the concerned State Government itself

In order to make the policy more attractive, the tariff notification has been amended twice to offer an assorment of incentives to investors. The Government has revised the hydro tariff guidelines to boost private investment in hydro-electric projects. To bring about private investment in the renovation, modernisation and upgradation of old power plants, the Government has finalised the policy and the guidelines have been issued. The Govenment has also taken steps to encourage captive/co-generation plants by industries. In order to encourage short gestation period projects, the Government has decided to permit setting up of power projects based on heavy fuel oils such as napha, heavy petroleum stock (HPS), low sulphur heavy stock (LSHS), heavy furnace oil (HFO), furnace oil (FO) and natural gas, wherever available, as primary fuel.

Under the current structure, the Independent Power Producers (IPPs) generally sell powers to SEBs which distribute power. Since most SEBs are financially distressed, the security package for an IPP is crucial to the success of a power project. As an initial measure to attract private capital into the power sector, the Government of India had agreed to extend counter-guarantees to State-guarantees for the SEB's payment obligations to generating companies in respect eight fast track private power projects. This was a confidence building measure necessary for the initial batch of projects. Though these guarantees increase the comfort-levels of lenders in the initial phases, extensive use of these measures can lead to large contingent liabilities that would over-expose the concerned governments. Other options for securing the revenue stream of IPPs include

Escrow Accounts, Guarantees from Multilateral Development Banks and Direct sale to high tension customers. The status of these eight fast track IPPs for which counter-guarantees have been or will be extended. Most of these projects are expecting financial and technical closure soon.

To facilitate the setting up of large sized thermal/ hydel power plants in the country, and to derive economies of scale, projects having a capacity of 1000 MW or above and supplying power to more than one stae are being considered as Mega projects. The SEBs and the State Government have been advised to introduce a more competitive element in the process of selection of selection of developers and award of projects. A notification was issued in October, 1995 enhancing concurrence of the Central Electricity Authority from Rs. 100 crore to Rs. 400 crore in the case of generating companies. The limit has been further enchanced to Rs. 1000 crore in September, 1996.

Capative power generation units in industry are used to supplement the power drawn from the grid and as a stand-by in case of power cuts. As of now, the country has an installed captive generation capacity of more than 10,000 MW. The policies relating to captive generation have also been liberalised. A 50 per cent thershold level has been prescribed for the industry's own consumption from the capative unit, and capacity in excess of this level can be sold to the grid.

In view of the widening gap between demand and supply and the huge capital cost involved in the installation of new power plants, a movement has been launched to make consumers aware of the need to save energy. Moreover, the Government is vigorously promoting energy accounting and monitoring systems. Energy audits have been carried out in a number of industrial units to identigy energy saving opportunities and eliminate wastage and to ensure that industries adopt the recommendations ofthese energy audits. Steps have been taken to improve the efficiency of domestic electrical appliances and agricultural pump sets and to promote the usage of fuel efficient engines and motors in both agricultural and transport sectors. Efforts are also being made to encourage co-generation of electricity in such industries as sugar, paper, cement, pertrochemicals and fertilisers.

The Government is working on a three-pronged strategy to overcome the existing structural constraints, technical inefficiencies and financial constraints. These include short and long-term measures to meet the power supply situation, encourage greater doses of private capital in power generation and facilitate reforms and restructuring in the state utilities. The Chief Ministers of different States met on 16th October, 1996 and 3rd December, 1996 to discuss and deliberate upon issues pertaining to the power sector. In the course of these deliberations a national consensus evolved for improving the performance of the power sector in a time bound manner and a Common Minimum National Action Plan for Power was adopted.

Non-conventional energy

The non-conventional sources of energy are capable of solving the twin problems of energy supply in a decentralised manner and helping in sustaining cleaner environment.

A new strategy and action plan for the remaining period of the Eighth Plan has been formulated. Against the original Plan target of 500-600 mw, the new action plan envisages a four-fold increase aiming at a target of 2,000 mv of renewable energy, through mobilization of institutional financing (including bilateral and multilateral funding) and purely private sector investments stimulated through entrepreneur development and a package of incentives. Policy changes have been made in both solar photovoltaics and solar thermal fields to encourage market development and minimize direct subsidies. This opening up of the market especially for solar photovoltaics, has resulted in greater competition, modernization and cost reduction and in overcoming programme infirmities and encouraging genuine entrepreneurs. Rapid growth of solar photovoltaic and solar hot water industry has started as a result of introduction of incentives and soft loans against the budget-drive subsidy programme. Policies have been pursued to encourage direct foreign investment and collaborations including tapping of NRIs have shown interest and are in the process of setting up of projects such as wind farms, solar plants in the states of Andhra Pradesh, Gujarat, Karnataka, Madhya Pradesh and Kerala.

Inter-agency and inter-ministerial contacts have been pursued to bring about greater involvement of user agencies. Initiatives have been taken to promote renewable energy applications in Defence, Railways, Tele-communications and similar establishments. Initiatives have also been taken to develop joint programmes with the Rural Electrification Corporation for promotion of decentralised renewable systems in villages still remaining unelectrified.

India is today recognised as one of the pioneer country in the field of renewable sources of energy. A three-fold strategy has been pursued by the Ministry of Non-conventional Energy Sources (MNES) for the promotion of new and renewable sources of energy (NRSE). This includes: (a) providing budgetary resources of Government for demonstration projects; (b) extending institutional finance from Renewable Indian Energy Development Agency (IREDA) and other financial institutions, for commercially viable projects, with private sector participation and external assistance from multilateral agencies like World Bank, GEF, ADB etc.; and (c) promoting private investment through fiscal incentives, tax holidays, depreciation allowance, facilities for wheeling and banking power for the grid and remunerative price for the power provided for the grid. The MNES intends to promote a new community of 'energy entrepreneurs' whereas the Government will act as the 'mission leader' giving a special focus and direction to the NRSE sector.

Power generation

The total potential for wind energy in the country is estimated to be 20,000 mw. The Central Government intends to create a wind energy capacity of 500 mw in the Eighth Five year Plan. With the achievement of this target India would become a major wind power producer in the world. Asia's largest wind farm cluster of 150 mw is located at Muppandal in Tamil Nadu.

A comprehensive wind mapoing programme to identify prospective sites for wind farming has been undertaken, 179 wind mapping and 83 wind monitoring stations are operational in the country. Eighty sites have so far been identified in the states of Tamil Nadu, Andhra Pradesh, Gujarat, Karnataka, Kerala, Madhya Pradesh, Maharashtra and Lakshadweep. The total capacity of wind energy to be generated is expected to be 3,000 mw in these areas. The installed capacity in the wind farm sector is 370 mw and a number of projects are under installation in tamil Nadu, Gujarat, Andhra Pradesh, Kerala, Karnataka and Madhya Pradesh. Several major developers, particularly from United States such as Cannon, Ford, Seawest, Carter Wind Turbines, Optimum Power, etc., are actively working on large proposals. So far 500 million units of energy has been generated and fed to the grids.

Small hydro power development programme

MNES is dealing with the implementation of small hydro power projects upto three mw. The new strategy and action plan aims at achieving a goal of 600 mw of energy power generation during the Eight Plan period through small hydro power projects. This is three times the target originally envisaged for the Eighth Five Year Plan . Around 2,000 potential sites with an estimated capacity of 5,000 mw have been identified in various states including potential states of Uttar Pradesh, Arunachal Pradesh, Orissa, Andhra Pradesh, Kerala, Madhya Pradesh, Himachal Pradesh, Punjab and the target of 600 mw in the Eighth Plan is expected to cover almost 1,000 sites in different states. To encourage exploitation of this potential, Ministry has announced a composite scheme for survey, investigation and DPR preparation under which cent per cent cost of survey and investigations and 50 per cent of the cost of DPR preparation is provided as grant. 44 projects aggregating 29 mw for survey and investigation, 36 projects aggregating 52 mw for DPR preparation and in addition 87 projects aggregating to 94.5 mw have been sanctioned under the Ministry's capital subsidy scheme for actual implementation of SHP projects.

Projects of 114 mw capacity have so far been installed and projects worth 220 mw capacity are under implementation. It is anticipated that the potential of small hydro power projects upto 15 mw per site in the country may exceed 10,000 mw. The state governments of Kerala, Karnataka and Tamil Nadu have already signed MOUs with private developers and agreed to lease out a number of sites for private investments in small hydro power projects.

Portable mini-hydel sets

In view of the remoteness and lack of infrastructure and grid in various areas, particularly in the hilly areas, an innovative scheme for providing 50 portable micro-hydel sets upto 15 kw capacity each for local communities in these areas was also launched. A UNDP/GEF project on optimizing development of small hydel resources in the Himalayan and sub-Himalayan regions become operational with a UNDP contribution of US dollar 7.5 million and counterpart funding of Rs. 22 crore. Thirteen hilly states will participate in the project under which a Master Plan will be evolved and twenty demonstration projects will be installed.

Biomass based co-Generation

Bagasse based co-generation new programme, launched in January 1994, envisages creation of 300 mw power generation capacity during the Eighth Plan. The programme is targeted at around 420 existing and around 90 new sugar mills, where a potential of 3,500 mw of power generation is estimated. The thrust of the programme is towards upgradation of existing co-generation facilities of sugar mills, which basically cater to captive steam and power requirements, to ensure generation of surplus power. A salient feature of the programme is the demonstration project scheme, under which 10-12 selected state-of-the-art projects in major sugar producing states will be provided with 30 per cent subsidy by the Ministry. USAID/GEF have approved a project for alternative biomass co-generation during off-season with funding support of US dollar 12.5 million for technical assistance and to leverage financing for such projects in selected sugar mills. Programmes are also being developed for direct biomass combustion and grid-connected gasification projects using woody biomass and agricultural residues.

Solar photovoltaic systems

The solar photovoltaic systems are currently being used in the country on a commercial basis for powering a variety of lower power applications in rural, remote and un-electrified areas for lighting and water pumping, power for railway signalling, rural telephones, microwave repeater stations and TV transmissions. Under the new strategy and action plan,one lakh number of solar lanterns initiated for both socially oriented and market oriented schemes. So far, 30,000 solar lanterns have been distributed under the programme. Over 60,000 solar photovoltaic systems with total capacity of four mw have been installed in the country. The socially oriented programme specially meant for designated areas and provide subsidy of 50 per cent of the cost. Solar photovoltaic systems with total capacity of 25 mw are proposed to be installed during the Eighth Plan period.

In August 1993 the Ministry has launched a demonstration project for the deployment of 1,000 solar photovoltaic (SPV) water pumps for agriculture and related uses at a cost of about Rs. 28 crore. So far, 397 pumps have been installed and orders for 625 have been booked. Seven manufacturers have finalilsed business plans and some of them have secured loans from IREDA.

The first two 100 kw partial grid interactive solar photovoltaic power projects at Kalyanpur in Aligarh district and Saraisadi in Mau district of Uttar Pradesh have been commissioned. A concept of strengthening of substations with small additions of 20 to 25 kw PV capacity to enhance grid stability is also under examination. In pursuance of the special emphasis being accorded by Government of India for generation of grid quality power from non-conventional energy sources, the Ministry has received several proposals of about 10 mw capacity from prospective promoters in the private sector for establishing grid interactive solar photovoltaic power plants which are being negotiated on build, own and operate (BOO) basis. Three preliminary proposals from American companies have already been received.

Solar thermal programme

Technologies for solar water heating systems and solar cookers have been developed and are being commercialized. Solar thermal systems for various other applications like, solar air heating, crop drying, timber seasoning and water desalination have also been developed and the new action plan envisages their commercialization. Solar thermal systems are today supplementing thermal energy requirements at various temperatures from 60-380 degree celsius for different domestic and industrial applications including process heating and power generation. One lakh LPD solar water heating system at 8 degrees celsius installed at the Hindustan Spinning and Weaving Mill, Bombay. About three lakh sq.mt collector area has been installed in the country for various domestic and industrial applications. There are about 3.5 lakh solar cookers used in the country. Solar water heating systems have vast potential to save electricity in domestic and commercial sectors and furnace oil in industrial sector which otherwise are being used for hot water supply. A provision in municipal law is beingmade for mandatory installation of solar water heating systems in functional buildings. All state governments have been requested to issue directives to local bodies under their control to extend this decision to buildings in private sector by making suitable provision in building bye-laws.

A proposal for setting up a 35 mw size solar thermal power project at Maithania village, Jodhpur, Rajasthan based on line focussing collectors has been under the consideration of the Ministry. Detailed feasibility and project reports have been prepared which are under discussion with World Bank, GEF and Government of Germany for soft loan financing.

Rural energy programme

So far 21.85 lakh numbers of family type biogas plants

and 196 lakh improved *chulhas* havebeen installed. Under the new strategy and action plan, it is envisaged to install 10 lakh numbers of bio-gas plants during the Eighth Plan period as against 7.5 lakh numbers envisaged earlier. The strategy for the universalisation of rural cooking energy programmes envisages covering 20-25 per cent of the potential beneficiaries by the end of Eighth Plan.

Integrated Rural Energy Programme (IREP) has been transferred to the Ministry of Non-Conventional Energy Sources from Planning Commission with effect from 1 April 1994. The IREP provides a comprehensive framework for macro level planning of energy requirements of rural areas. The programme is being implemented taking block as a unit, and has been extended in 552 blocks so far. To enhance the effectiveness of the programme at the field levels, inputs from ongoing rural energy programmes are being harmonized and increased involvement and concentration of renewable energy programmes is being planned.

Biomass programme

Biomass occupies a predominant place as an energy source in rural India. Fuel-wood requirement has gone upto around 166 million tonnes per year, the availability has declined to about 28 million tonnes, resulting in a deficit of 138 million tonnes per annum. It has been estimated that India is having about 93.69 million hectare of waste lands out of which about 20 million hectare is productive non-forest land which would be able to produce 400 million tonnes fuel-wood per year equivalent to 60,000 mw of power. Ministry of Non-Comventional Energy Sources have initiated biomass programme with a view to increase bio-productivity fast-growing short rotation fuel-wood species, suitable for plantation under the given set of agro-climatic conditions through scientific input and to evolve methodologies/ package of practices for increasing the productivity to around 40 tonnes per hectare per year compared to the average forest tree production rate of 0.5 tonnes per hectare per year. Biomass yield ranging from 12 tonnes to 36.8 tonnes per hectare per year have been achieved by the established Biomass Research Centres.

Animal energy programme

Of the total energy generated in the country, the contribution of animal energy is close to 50 per cent. This is mailny for farming operations and transportation. The MNES has launched a national programme in this field in March 1994. The programme is implemented in close coordination with the Ministry of Agriculture and involve comunity awareness campaigns about the role of animal energy, support for improvement in equipment, devices and transport vehicles which are animal driven. Under the programme, 15 models of improved bullock carts have been developed.

Energy from Urban and Industrial Wastes

Large quantities of wastes (solids and liquids) are generated in India in urban, municipal and industrial sectors and mostly find their way into the environment with little or no treatment which results in their natural biodegradation with consequent release of methane into the atmosphere. These resources can offer viable option for energy generation with attendant benefits of reducing emission green house gases and minimising environmental pollution. Considering the far reaching environmental benefits by proper utilisation of various wastes hitherto causing pollution problem, UNDP have agreed to provide technical grant out of GEF fund for development of high rate biomethantion process for energy recovery from all such wastes. In the first phase of the activity concerning utilisation of wastes, a national programme under the GEF assisted project for development of high rate biomethantion processes has been initiated in the Ministry. A National Energy Board has been set up as an apex body to formulate policy and over all management.

Industry

Attainment of industrialisation over the last 48 years has been striking feature of Indian economic development process which was launched as a conscious and deliberate policy in the early fifties. In pursuance of this policy, large investment has been made in building up capacity over a wide spectrum of industries. Industrial production has made rapid strides in terms of variety, quality and quantity. There has been a substantial diversification of industrial base during this period with the consequent ability to produce a very broad range of industrial goods. Self-reliance has been achieved in basic and capital good. Indigenous capabilities have now been established to the point of virtual self-sufficiency so that further expansion in various sectors such as mining, irrigation, power chemicals, transport and communication can be based primarily on indigenous equipment. Process of industrialisation has also fostered entrepreneurship and development of a wide variety of technical, managerial and operative skills. Today, the country is in a position to provide consultancy services as well as managers, technicians and skilled workers for setting up industrial projects abroad.

The Industrial Policy Resolution of 1948 marked the beginning of the evolution of Indian Industrial Policy. The resolution not only defined the broad contours of the policy, it delineated the role of the State in the industrial development both as an entrepreneur and as an authority.

Successive policy resolutions also reiterated this basic tilt in favour of the public sector. The Industrial

Policy Resolution of 1956 gave the public sector a strategic role in the economy. It categorised industries which would be the exclusive responsibility of state or would progressively come under state control and others. Earmarking the pre-eminent position to the public sector, it envisaged private sector co-existing with the State and thus attempted to give the policy framework flexibility.

The Industrial Policy initiatives undertaken by Government since July 1991 have been designed to build on the past industrial achievements and to accelerate the process of making Indian industry internatinally competitive. It recognises the strength and maturity of the industry and attempts to provide the competitive stimulus for higher growth. The thrust of these initiatives has been to increase domestic and external competition through extensive application of market mechanism and facilitating forging of dynamic relationships with foreign investors and suppliers of technology. The process of reform has been continuous.

As on 31 March 1993 there were 245 central public sector undertakings, comprising of eight in the construction sector, 72 in services and remaining 165 in the manufacturing. The number of CPSUs as indicated above exclude nine companies, six insurance companies and three financial institutions with Central Government investment but without direct responsibility of management.

The total capital employed in the 245 CPSUs increased from Rs. 1,179.91 billion in 1991-92 to Rs. 1,399.33 billion in 1992-93. The overall rate of return on capital employed in the PSUs also increased from 2.0 per cent in 1991-92 to 2.43 per cent in 1992-93.

The number of small scale units as at the end of 31 March 1994 were 2.38 million comprising of 1.77 million registered units and 0.61 un-registered. The overall production in the small scale sector during 1993-94 has been estimated to have reached Rs. 2,416.5 billion. The total value of exports of these units has been Rs. 177.85 billion in 1992-93.

Industrial development

As a result of sound policies pursued over the years, tremendous development has taken place in India industry, which stands today on a sound footing. However, there are certain infrastructural weaknesses which need to be tackled to ensure further growth, says the author.

Indian industry has undergone a sea change since Independence. From a situation, where even a pin had to be inported, India has reached a stage when it is going to manufacture 50-seater and 100-seater passenger aircraft. What is more, the Indian consumer today has a wide variety of goods to choose from. The Indian market place is today loaded with a range of goods. Whether it is newer models of cars, scooters or mlobikes, washing machines, sooking range or mixies there ia large variety to choose from. Gone are the days when choices were limited and one had to wait almost a year to get delivery of a new car or a scooter. One can today walk into a show room and drive out. With a choice available to the consumer the quality of goods have also shown distinct improvement.

Indian industry at the time of Independence was at a rudimentary stage. It was confined to cotton and jute textiles, which accounted for 56.5 per cent of value-added in manufacturing sugar (6.6 per cent), engineering (8.4 per cent), steel (7.6 per cent), chemicals (4.1 per cent) and cement (2.1 per cent). Modern industry formed only six to eight per cent of national income in Independence India in 1950, with small scale enterprises and mining contributing 12 to 14 per cent. A feature of India's industrial sector soon after Independence was the virtual absence of capital or producers goods industry. Indian industries had to rely almost wholly on imported machinery and machine tools. In 1950, India met 89.8 per cent of its need for machine tools through imports, producing internally only Rs. 30 lakh worth of machine tools and portable tools.

Foundation laid

The foundations of modern India's industrial economy was laid by Jawaharlal Nehru, who led the country to freedom and thereafter as Prime Minister for nearly 17 years, built the country's economy form a scratch. This was done through the public sector, whose foundations were laid by Nehru, as the private sector did not have the resources to undertake huge infrastructure projects, like Bhakra hydro-electric power project, or steel plants like Bhilai, whom the great visionary described as the temples of modern India. Nehru realised that without the basic infrastructure industries, the foundations of a modern industrial economy could not be laid. If this war true in 1950, it is equally true today as infrastructural bottlenecks are constraining growth.

Two policy resolutions

Industrial growth after Independence was facilitated by the Industrial Policy Resolution of 1948, followed by the Industrial Policy Resolution of 1956, which had as its objective, the acceleration of the rate of economic growth and the speeding up of industrialisation as a means of achieving a socialist pattern of Society. In 1956 capital was scarce and the base of entrepreneurship was not strong enough. Hence the 1956 Industrial Policy Resolution, gave primacy to the role of the state to assume predominant and direct responsibility for industrial development. Special importance was given in the two resolutions of 1948 and 1956 to the development of steel, heavy engineering, machine tools and heavy chemicals industry.

The industrial policy resolution of 1948 has a small number of industries to be reserved for production by the public sector. These included the production and control of atomic energy and ownership and managment of railways. However, coal, iron and steel, aircraft manufacturing, shipbuilding, manufacture of telegraph and wireless equipment (except radios) and minerals were reserved for production by Central or State government undertakings.

The 1956 industrial Policy Resolution added some more industries to the list. The original thinking was that as far as the public sector was concerned, it should enter fields where private sector would find it difficult to invest. By 1956, this had changed to an absolute preference for state ownership of industries and the public sector was supposed to capture the commanding heights of the economy.

Education and ninth plan

Education is the lifeline of development, be it spiritual or economic, scientific or technological, national or global. In the 21st century, countries will be measured by the education and health status of their population and not by GDPs and GNPs. The foremost component of education is its definition, aims, goals and objectives translated into an effective and practical policy. Included in this policy are a national curriculum, teaching strategies and evaluation procedures for measuring stated outcomes. *Hence, an education policy and curriculum is to educational institutions what a blueprint is to an architect.*

The education of an individual can be divided into five stages, namely preschool, primary, secondary, tertiary and adult education. *The stage of preschool education is to the nation and educational institutions what a foundation is to a building.* Both require a lot of specialization, knowledge and planning. Both are areas where we cannot afford to make a single mistake, else the entire structure will come tumbling down, or, we will have a scenario as highlighted they are both invisible. *Further, just as a building can only be constructed with locally available materials, so too, a successful education policy and curriculum must reflect the culture, the needs, the norms, the language, and the values of its people.*

Last but not least just as the construction of a building does not start from its roof, so too, there cannot be a downward extension of the education policy and curriculum. However, an examination of our education system over the length and breadth of the country, reflects just that! CBSE, ISC and IB (International Baccalaureate diploma) have become the focus and objective of our education system with an overdose of formal learning, texbooks, an overemphasis, on English language, an inappropriate age for admissions, and proliferation of private schools and teaching shops.

There are many problems with the Ministry's perception, namely.

1. The most basic issue is that the new policy on education (NPE 1992) notwithstanding, the focus of our education system is CBSE, which neither prepares the children for life nor for the existing international competitive ethos—a point that MHRD has chosen to ignore. The problems as highlighted are an outcome of the deliberate ignorance of education by the MHRD in the past:
2. As per National Council of Applied Economic Research (NCAER) report, excluding drop-outs, 55 million primary school children have never stepped into a school. Not only does it burgeon child labour

statistics, these children and their parents know that the existing system does not prepare their children for life. So rejection of the system through child labour, and, poverty make for an excellent scapegoat. *Instead of applying itself to the curriculum issues as highlighted by the Yashpal Committee report and advise the Planning Commission to make 'Education Policy' as the springboard to success, the MHRD has chosen to indulge in populist programmes like NSPE and DPEP.*

3. There has been a sharp rise in our interest payments and interest rates as highlighted. But the MHRD has chosen to borrow further from commercial international banks to fund a dead end UEE programme.

4. The statutory transfer and enforcement of elementary education from the Directive Principles of the Constitution to Fundamental Human Right, will in all probability backfire. *Instead of decentralizing power and placing it in the hands of the people, it has the capacity to further empower and strengthen the bureaucrats.*

5. Further, for the past 50 years, the government has demonstrated a stubborn lack of will to implement the Directive Principles of the Constitution. What is so sacrosanct about Fundamental Rights? Do we have a democratic education policy in place? Is the infrastructure in place? Do we have the required and trained human power, ready to take the plunge? Have the PRIs really placed the power into the hands of the 'real' people or is it still concentrated in the secretariats of the Union and State governments? Have we really reached the monitoring and supervision stage to dare statutory enforcement of primary education? Have we really dumped the frivolous and cantankerous educational issues into the Indian Ocean?

6. *There is a contradiction in allowing the corporate sector and private sector into primary education as well as making it free and compulsory through statutory enforcement.*

7. Last but not least is the issue of funding and finance. A glance at the primary education trend during the eight five year plans, and the continuous tussle at the State-level of financing primary education vs other sectors, it is a foregone conclusion that primary education will emerge a loser.

Recommendations

With the colossal expenditure just on incentives to attract students through midday meals, free textbooks and uniforms, and scores of other expensive programmes, a question on everybody's lips is: After all this expenditure and programmes, do the students learn anything? If so, what do they learn? Is the acquired information useful to them? Despite such heavy funding through borrowed and taxpayers' money and the numerous populist programmes, why are the dropout rates so high? What is the correcd message–privatization of primary education or free and compulsory primary education? How does the government explain 10 per cent of rural population attending private schools vs 2 per cent in 1986? Why are we spending so heavily on a dead-end adult education programme? How has the programme benefited them if during the VIII Plan unemployment and underemployment has increased while self-employment and salaried employment has declined.

If we want to outbeat the competitive ethos and emerge a winner without being a drain on the exchequer, the following suggestions need to be placed on the front burner:

1. Define education, literacy and development such that

the entire nation understands it, accepts it and fully embraces it.

2. The focus of the education policy must shift from the 3 Rs to the 3 Hs, i.e. the head, heart and hand—an education policy towards self-reliance and self-employment. The way we have defined education, literacy and development, we are only trying to catch our shadows, knowing fully well that shadows cannot be caught.
3. Justify the logic for transferring education and health to the sector—charity syndrome. Such segregation and compartmentalization only fuels deficits and inflation.
4. Ours is the typical case of the candle burning upside down! It is indeed very sad that during the Ninth Plan, primary education is to be guided and pushed forward for achieving the 7 per cent growth rate against the NPE (1992) grain of separating jobs from education.
5. The issue is not one of resource crunch but one of will power, imagination and magnanimity to shun the powers and material gains accrued through chairs. The issue is one of redefining our education policies, be it industry, agriculture, employment, etc. The issue is one of redefining our education policy so that rural-urban dichotomies, gender dichotomies, rich-poor dichotomies are reduced. The issue is one of having the will to implement the new policy. The issue is one of demonstrating flexibility and tolerance to other points of issue is one of shedding fear and hypocrisy.

Ninth plan & employment programmes

In working out the size of the wage employment programmes, we have to ensure that at least one member of every family below the poverty line gets employment for a minimum of 100 days in a year to cover the seasonal unemployment. The 38th round of NSSO has estimated about 44 million families below the poverty line in rural areas (in 1983—84) and providing employment to one member each of such families for 100 days would requre employment generation of 4,400 million mandays. If we take the poverty estimates of the 43rd round of NSSO and average size of family as 4.5, there are about 30 million families who are below the poverty line. To provide 100 days of employment to one member of each family, 3,000 million mandays will be required. At present, abut 24 million persons have got themselves registered under EAS and this figure would go up as EAS will be implemented throughout the country (till October 1996, EAS was limited to 3,206 blocks only). The poor people seeking employment could roughly go up to 35 million or so, when EAS would be extended to the entire country in 1997—98. During the normal years, we, therefore, have to generate about 3,000—3,500 million mandays in a year to meet the assurance of 100 employment to all those rural poor who need and seek employment. At present, the weighted average minimum wage is about Rs. 30 per manday and taking into account the wage material ratio of 60:40, thecost of generation of one manday would be Rs. 50. For generation of 3,000—3,500 million mandays,l we would reqquire Rs. 15,000—16,500 crore every year. Given the resources, it may, however, not be possible for the Indian economy to support such a massive programme. But then, the implementation of the Maharashtra EGS show that all the poor may not turn up for the kind of work provided under wage employment programmes. The actual requirement of funds would be somewhat less than the projections above. *The provision of Rs. 60,000 crore in the Ninth Plan for rural employment, the major portion of which would go to the wage employment programmes, should, therefore, be sufficient to take care of the lowest rung of poverty.*

The wage employment programmes in India started from the experimentation/pilot phases, in the 1960s and the 70s and then consolidated in the 80s and are now moving towards a scenario which guarantees employment, although it is beyond the economic capacity of the Centre for the present. We are in the assurance kind of scenario, where the implementation of EAS would certainly mitigate the hardships of the poorest of the poor in the rural areas by providing employment and food security in terms of increased purchasing power and distribution of food grains. The point that the present wage employment programmes in India are based on the vast experiences of the implementation, would strengthen our optimism in the Ninth Plan in which we would be moving towards a full employment situation. It is also heartening to note that during the Ninth Plan, EAS along with JRY would become perhaps the largest wage employment programme of its kind anywhere in the world.

Budget to impart growth impulses

The 1997—98 Union Budget has broken new grounds in terms of carrying forward the liberalisation process and tax reforms by attempting to impart growth impulses to the economy. The Budget initiatives are important for more reasons than one presumably because the macro economic parameters of the economy were onthe downswing throughout most of the last year of the Eighth Plan (1997—98) with inflation rearing its head, trends in industrial production and foreign trade remaining none too ecouraging and capital markets coasting on thin trading for even blue chip companies. The 1997—98 Budget, as such, was expected to address these serious maladies so as to ensure that the economic activity gathered momentum and also to herals hope for realising the seven per cent growth target set for the Ninth Plan for which 1997—98 Budget is the inaugural year.

The Finance Minister Mr. P. Chidambaram did not dash hopes on all these things as the Budget he presented was a deft exercise in attempting to satisfy every constituency—be it salaried class, trade and industry, investors, both domestic and foreign and instiitutionals. In a master stroke, the Finance Minister attempted to rope in only one segment under the tax net and that is the services sector which is now contributing 40 per cent to the GDP. The logic is that "services" are products as much as "manufactured goods" and it was historic underestimation of this segment that had led to the neglect of any attempt to bring this into the tax net. But the credit for bringing services under the tax net must redound to the glory of the reform architect Dr. Manmohan Singh who initiated a modest but momentous beginning by introducing services tax on telephones and stock brokerage. Later, it was extended t advertising, courier and radio paging. From nowhere, the services tax fetched Rs. 970 crore for the exchequer in the fiscal year 1996—97.

It is but natural that the 1997—98 Union Budget should extend the services tax to some more aeas. The Finance Minister did not hesitate to do so and in his second budget after assuming office in July 1996, Mr. P. Chidambaram has confined his tax mobilisation effort to mop up Rs. 1205 crore only by bringing a few more services under the tax net and revising postal rates. The Budget for 1997—98 extends the service tax to cover a host of well—known services embracing transportation of goods by road, consulting engineers, custom house, steamer and clearing and forwarding agents, air travel agents, tour operators and car rental agencies, out—door caterers, pandal contractors and *mandap* keepers and man—power recruitment agencies. While the proposals on service tax are estimated to yield a revenue of Rs. 1200 crore in a full year, in the next fiscal year, a credit of Rs. 900 crore alone is being taken into account. The remaineder Rs. 305 crore for next year is being realised by revision of tariffs for some postal services, the proceeds of which would be for the development of postal services and in partially bridging the deficit on the numerous services being provided by the Postal Department.

A particularly noteworthy feature of the 1997—98 Budget is that it has given away massive customs tax relief amounting to Rs. 2625 crore and the reason for that as provided by the Finance Minister was that "our goal must be to achieve rapid and broad-based growth." While Mr. P. Chidambaram reduced the peak rate of customs duty from 50 to 40 per cent in a bid to align the country's tariff structure with international standards, he also reduced customs duty on capital goods from 20 to 15 per cent. Some of the intermediate inputs which witnessed cuts include steel industry inputs, cold rolled coils of iron andsteel, duty on ships brought for breaking, organic and inorganic chemicals, dyes, pigments, paints and varnishes, glues, enzymes and modified starches.

In tune with the tenet of emerging cooperative federalism, which is the hall—mark of the 13—party coalition government at the Centre, the Budget has accepted the alternative devolution formula seeking to bring in all taxes collected bythe Centre into a single divisible pool and apportion 29 per cent to the States as recommended by the Tenth Finance Commission.

The Budget of 1997—98 is a veritable bag of sops for Indian corporates and tax—payers as duty was cut across—the—board. In personal income tax, the existing rates of 15, 30 and 40 per cent is proposed to be replaced by 10, 20 and 30 per cent. The rate would be 10 per cent in the slab of Rs. 40,000 to Rs. 60,000, 20 per cent in the slab of Rs. 60,000 to Rs. 15,000 and 30 per cent for all income above Rs. 150,000. The limit on standard deductions has been raised to Rs. 20,000 which would apply uniformly to all salaried tax—payers. In widening the tax net, the Budget proposed an amendment of Section 139 of the I.T. Act by which residents of large metropolises who satisfy economic criteria such as ownership of a four—wheel vehicle, telephone, flats and undertaking foreign travel in the previous year should voluntarily file their tax returns. Failure to do so would entail a simple notice from the I.T. Department. Yet another related scheme announced in the Budget pertains to the Voluntary Disclosure Scheme (VDS). Following the mandate of the National Development Council (NDC), the Minister announced the VDS to tap black money for productive purposes by which any disclosed income would be taxed at the revised highest rate of 30 per cent, the states would receive 77.5 of the proceeds on this score while the balance would be spent on bolstering the Basic Minimum Services. The scheme would start on a date to be notified by the Finance Minister and end on December 31, 1997. Some category of people would not be liable to secure immunity under this scheme and they include those held for offences under the Drugs and Psychotropic Substances, Arms Act, ordinarily punishable under the IPC and the Anti—Corruption Act.

Outlook

1. The financial sector has a vital role in promoting efficiency and growth. It intermediates the flow of funds from those who want to save a part of their income to those who want to invest in productive assets. The efficiency of intermediation depends on

the width, depth and diversity of the financial system. Till about two decades ago, a large part of household savings was either invested directly in physical assets, or put in bank deposits and Government small saving schemes. It is only since the late eighties that the equity market has started to play a role in this intermediation process. Other markets and short-term money markets, remain relatively segmented and underdeveloped. In recent decades, the Government and its subsidiary institutions and agencies, have had an overwhelming and all encompassing role. This has played a part in slowing the evolution and development of thse markets. The extensive system of controls, rules, regulations and procedures, directly or indirectly affects the development of these markets. We need to clear this web in the interest of both savers and those who invest in productive assets. Tax deductions and exemptions cannot be a substitute for reforms of policy and procedures. they can, however, create further distortions.

2. The two most serious problems in the financial system are the lack of flexibility in intermediary behaviour and the segmentation of various markets and sets of financial intermediaries. Well developed markets are interconnected; demand-supply imabalances in one market overflow into related markets thereby dampening shocks and disturbances. This inter-connection also ensures that interest rates and returns in any market, reflect the broad demand-supply conditions in the overall market for savings. A rise in the demand for funds for investment, above the existing flow of funds from savings, leads to a rise in the interest rate or rate of return in all markets. The time lag may differ from market to market depending on economic factors.

Conversely, a decline in demand for funds for investment below saving, leads to a fall in interest rates across the board. This does not happen in segmented markets. Adjustment in interest rates is also delayed by the slow speed of response of intermediaries and their lack of flexibility. Because of the historical role of the government and its subsidiary organisations in controlling and directing all financial activity, the autonomy and flexibility if intermediaries was greatly circumscribed. Consequently, adjustment to demand-supply imbalance in each segment was also very slow. Over the last five years a series of reforms. The widening and acceleration of reforms will increase the flexibility and responsiveness of the intermediaries and promote integration.

Outlook

1. The anuual (point-to-point) inflation rate in the first half of the currint financial year (April-September) ranged between a low of 4.2 per cent to a high of 6.6 per cent. The price rise of this magnitude could be regarded as modest given the hefty increase of 18 per cent in the administered prices of petrolium products in early July, 1996. Even in the next two months October-November 1996, the annual price rise was still below 7 per cent. However, there was a clear indication of inflationary pressures resurfacing due to the persistant rise in the prices of many of the agricultural commodities—mainly foodgrains—right from the middle of current financial year. By the end of December 1996, the annual inflation rate had crossed 7 per cent. The normal seasonal decline in the post-harvest period generally seen during November-December did not happen this year and hence the uptrend in prices was unabated in the third quarter of 1996-97. The containment of

inflationary pressures in 1996-97. The containment of inflationary pressures in 1997-98 will require prudent fiscal and monetary policies and appropriate supply side policy measures to control price increases in primary articles.

Balance of payments

The development so far in 1996—97 in the balance of payments, the Survey says, point to an easing of pressure on the current account and to buoyancy in capital inflows. The deficit on trade account in 1996—97 is expected to be lower than in the previous year, largely due to a sharp deceleration in the growth of non—petroleum imports. The improvement in trade deficit would be partly offset by anticipated decline in invisible receipts, reflecting an increase in payment for factor services and some decline in private transfers.

The current account deficit is expected to decline from 1.7 per cent of GDP in 1995—96 to less than 1.4 per cent of GDP in 1996—97. Net capital inflows in 1996—97 are likely to be nearly three—fold over the previous year, largely because of buoyant inflows under non—resident deposits and foreign investment flows, including Euro—equities, and a sizable build—up of foreign exchange reserves. The foreign currency assets of the RBI rose by over US $ 2.8 billion from about US $ 17 billion at the end of March 1996, providing cover of about 5.5 months of imports.

The Survey says, exports during April—December period of 1996—97 grew only by 6.4 per cent as against 19.7 per cent during the previous three years. Among the significant reasons for the decline are slow down in world trade growth in 1996 (by about three percentage points). The latest trend in the growth rate of exports suggests that the initial impact of trade liberalisation is petering out and the trade flows are reverting to their normal trend determined by world demand and domestic activity. Despite the export slow down, self reliance as measured b;y the coverage of imports by exports, has risen by 88.2 per cent in April—December 1996 from 86.7 during 1995—96.

On the capital account, foreign investment continued to dominate capital fows. Total foreign investment (direct plus portfolio) during April—December 1996 surged to over US $ 4 billion, which is more than 50 per cent higher than in the corresponding period of 1995—96. This revival followed a modest decline in such investment flows from US $ 4.9 billion in 1994—95 to US $ 4.3 billion in 1995—96, mainly due to a sharp fall in the issue of Euro–equities. Foreign direct investment flows were US $ 2.1 billion in 1995—96. During April—December 1996. FDI flows were US $ 1.5 billion in the corresponding period of the previous year. Portfolio investment, comprising investment by FIIs and Euro—equities, doubled to over US $ 1.1 billion in the corresponding months of 1995—96.

India's external debt declined from US $ 99.0 billion at end—March 1995 to 92.2 billion at the end of March 1996. The downsizing of external debt resulted in a decline in debt—to—GDP ratio. The share of concessional debt in total debt remains stable at about 45.5 per cent. The share of short—term debt was 5.5 per cent at end—March 1996 and is low by international standards.

The survey does not provide current estimates of either poverty or employment generation, saying that the methodology of estimation is currently under the review of the Planning Commission. However, it says the government has accorded high priority to poverty alleviation programmes through an increase in the Central Plan allocations for social sectors and poverty alleviaton theweaker sections, specially scheduled castes and scheduled tribes and women have been given importance in special programmes of poverty alleviation and employment as well as in several other programmes. The Public Distribution System has also been streamlined recently in order to target the poorer sections of the population.

As outlined in the Update of the Economic Survey, fiscal deficit, reliable economic infrastructure services and broad–based employment—generating growth remain the key challenges for ecomomic policy. About fiscal deficit, as the Survey itself puts it "the normally difficult task of expenditure management will be accentuated in the coming years by the challenge of accommodating the recommendations of the Fifth Central Pay Commission." Further, as it says "the responsibility for fiscal consolidation and prudence does not rest with the Central Government alone."

About the infrastructure sector, as the Survey rightly puts it, the crux of the problem is of heavy investment. Both for infrastructure and other investment requirements of the economy, the country would need an inflow of foreign direct investment of US $ 10 billion per year as against US $ 2 to 3 billion currently. The Survey rightly exhorts al concerned to "learn from the pragmatic nationalism of China which received around US $ 40 billion of investment in 1996. We must also learn from the flexibility and speed of Indonesia, which modified its policies rapidly in response to perceived competition from China and India, to double foreign investment inflows between 1994 and 1996."

About poverty alleviaton, as the Survey puts it for the vast majority of the people it would have to be through job opportunities stemming through labour intensive Growth. For those at the margins of a market driven economy "the effective provision of minimum social services and special programmes for employment and poverty alleviation, fulfil an essential need." The basic goal, as the Survey puts it "should be to enhance sustainable benefits to the poorest segments of the society, while reducing administrative duplication and wastage and minimising well—known leakages."

Cultural relations

The primary objective of the Indian Council for Cultural Relations (ICCR) is to establish and strengthen cultural relations and mutual understanding between India and other countries. One of the major activities of the Council is administering scholarship schemes for international students. There are at present 1,792 international students from around 70 countries pusruing a variety of courses on scholarships. Two new scholarship were instituted in the memory of the late Appa Saheb Pant, the first Commissioner of India in Kenya, and the Okita Memorial Scholarship at the request of the family of the former Japanese Foreign Minister, the late Dr. S. Okita.

The ICCR celebrated the birth anniversary of its founder, Maulana Abul Kalam Azad on 11 November as 'International Students Day'. Special get-togethers and cultural programmes were arranged on this occasion for international students and Indian students.

Festival of India in China held in May 1994 has been one of the major highlights of ICCR in 1994. Some o fth other major events include 'India Today 1994' in Australia, which was inaugurated by the Vice-President of India; the India Trade Fair at St Petersburg; 'India in Dubai'; the 125th Death Anniversary Celebrations of Miraz Ghalib in Mauritius; and the 'India Night' at Alter Opera, Frankfurt. During April-december 1994, the ICCR sponsored visits of 17 cultural troupes abroad. The ICCR also organised performances by a number of incoming delegations and several Indian cultural programmes in honour of visiting delegations and several Indian cultural programmes in honour of visiting delegations/VVIP functions.

On the occasion of 125th Birth Anniversary of Mahatma Gandhi, the ICCR organised a major exhibition titled 'Ashoka-Gandhi-Nehru-The Healing Touch' at the Tokyo Fuji Art Museum in October 1994. Other exhibitions organised by ICCR during 1994 are the exhibition of Indian Children's Paintings (Republic of Korea) and the Children's Paintings (Cairo). The ICCR also presented busts of Gandhiji to the USA (for installation at International Peace Garden, Salt Lake City, San Francisco) and Cuba (for installation at Central Park, Havana) and that of Gurudev Rabindranath Tagore to Japan (for installation at Soka University Campus).

The Council sponsored and assisted 45 Indian scholars, intellectuals, academics and artists to participate in seminars, symposia, study tours, etc., abroad in 21 countries and received 78 visitors from 11 countries. The ICCR organised the International Symposium of India Studies (ISIS) during November-December 1994 at Kovalam, Kerala in which 31 scholars from vrious parts of the world participated.

In keeping with India's foreign policy that has a cultural dimension for promoting greater people-to-people contact, the Council has set up cultural centres in Geogetown, Jakarta, Moscow, Port Louis, Paramaribo, Cairo, Berlin, London, Tashkent and Almaty. These centres, except in Berlin and London, impart lessions in Indian music, dance, *yoga* and languages and organise lectures,l symposia, exhibitions, essay competitions, performances of dance and music, staging of plays, screening kof films and publication of news bulletins. ICCR presently has 18 professors teaching Indian languages, Indology and allied subjects in Belgium,

Bulgaria, China. Finland, France, Hungary, Indonesia, Republic of Korea, Mauritius, Poland, Thailand, Turkey, Trinidad and Tobago.

In August 1994, Ted Tanen from American Secretariat of the Indo-US Sub-Commission on Education and Culture visited India and had meetings with the Indian Co-Chairman of the Sub-Commission, Shri Salman Khurshid and several other leading persons, in various cultural and academic fields. The Press Information Bureau in collaboration with the ICCR sponsored the visit of four women delegates from the media to participate in the 'Women & Media' programme in the USA in October 1994. The ICCR hosted the visit of four Indian film directors from USA to India to participate in the film festival'From India to America; New Directions in Indian American Films and Video' in New Delhi and Bombay in December 1994 organised by the Smita Patil Foundation in collaboration with the Indo-US Commission and Whitney Museum of American Art, USA.

The 28th Maulana Abul Kalam Azad Memorial Lecture was delivered on 9 September 1994 by Secretary General of the United Nations on 'Current World Challenges as Reflected in the United Nations Today' and the 29th Lecture was delivered on 12 January 1995 by Tan Sri Ghazali Shafie, former Malaysian Minister for Foreign Affaisrs, Home and Education. Renowned Canadian environmentalist Mr. Naurice FS Kong was nominated for the Jawaharlal Nehru Award for International Understanding, 1992.

The Council brings out six quarterly journals in different languages: English (*India Horizons and Africa*), Hindi (*Gangananchal*), French (*Recontre Avec L'Inde*), Spanish (*Papeles de la India*) and Arabic (*Thaqafatul Hind*). A special issue of Indian Horizons on India-China

Relations was brought out on the occasion of Festival of India in China and is considered to be one of the finest and most comprehensive books available on the age-old contacts between the two countries. The ICCR co-published *India and Egyypt: Influences and Interactons* and *'The Divine Peacock: Understanding Contemporary India'.*

The ICCR also participated in the 11th New Helhi World Book Fair, the Exhibition of Indian Books in China, the Australian Book Fair in Sydney, the 46th Frankfurt Book Fair, the Exhibition of Indian Books in Male, the Special Book Exhibition in New Delhi and the Book Exhibition of ICCR publications at New Delhi. The ICCR gifted 1,050 books to institutions, distinguished persons, academicians and opinion makers in 35 countries and 200 musical instruments, audio/video tapes and art objects to institutions in 18 countries.

Promotion of cultyre

Centre for cultural resources and training

Centre for Cultural Resources and Training (CCRT) was set up in May 1979 as an autonomous organisation by the Government of India. The CCRT took over the scheme 'Propagation of Culture' among college and school students which was being implemented by Delhi University, since 1970. The Centre is under the administrative control of Department of Culture, Ministry of Human Resource Development.

The broad objectives of the CCRT have been to revitalise the education system by creating an understanding and awareness among students about the plurality of regional cultures of India and integrating this knowledge with the education. The main thrust is on linking education with culture and making students aware of the importance of culture in all development programmes. The training being imparted stresses on the role of culture in science and technology, housing, agriculture, sports, etc. An important component of training is creating an awareness amongst students and teachers of their role in solving environmental pollution problems and conservation and preservation of the natural and cultural heritage. To fulfil these objectives, the Centre organises a variety of training programmes for teachers, educators, administrators and students throughout the country. It has also been organising academic programmes on Indian art and culture for foreign teachers and students. Workshops are conducted in various art activities lilke drama, music, narrative art forms, etc., to provide practical training and knowledge in the arts and crafts. In these workshops, teachers are encouraged to develop programmes inwhich the art form can be profitably utilised to educational curriculum.

The CCRT organises various educational activities for school students, teachers and children belonging to governmental and non-government organisations under its extension and community feedback programmes, which includes, educational tours to monuments, museums, art galleries, craft centres, zoological parks and gardens, camps on conservation of natural and cultural heritage, camps on learning crafts using low cost localilty available resources, lectures and demonstrations by artists and experts on various art forms, demonstrations by artists and crafts persons in schools.

The CCRT collects materials on the arts and crafts of the country in the form of audio recordings, slides, photographs, films and written texts in order to disseminate the information on culture and provide participants and other research institutions with material on the arts of India. The Centre also aims to disseminate information and foster an understanding of Indian culturre amongst teachers, administrators, educators and students. Publications for institutions and members of the community are prepared on topics related to aspects of Indian culture and ecology and the natural environment.

The CCRT implements the Cultural Talent Search Scholarship Scheme, which was taken over from the Department of Culture in 1982. The scheme provides scholarships to outstanding children in the age-group of 10 to 14 years studying, either in recognised schools or belonging to families practising traditional, performing or other arts to develop their talent in various cultural fields particularly in rare art forms. The scholarship continues till the age of 20 years or first year of university degree. The Centre has also instituted CCRT Teacher's Award which is given every year to selected teachers in recognition of the outstanding work done by them in the field of education and culture.

Zonal cultural centres

Zonal cultural centres have been conceptualised with the aim of projecting cultural kinships transcending territorial bounds. The idea is to arouse and deepen awarreness of the local cultures and how these merge into zonal identities and eventually into the rich diversity of India's composite culture. Besides, these are also intended to document, preserve and to sustain the vanishing art forms and oral traditons. The involvement of artists and creative people has been in built in the set-up through a system of autonomous governance.

The seven zonal cultural centres established under the new scheme are: (i) North-Zone Cultural Centre, Patiala; (ii) East Zone Cultural Centre, Santiniketan; (iii) South Zone Cultural Centre, Thanjavur; (iv) west Zone Cultural Centre, Udaipur; (v) North-Central Zone Cultural Centre, Allahabad; (vi) North East Zone Cultural Centre, Dimapur and (vii) South-Central Zone Cultural Centre, Nagpur. The participation of states in more than one zonal cultural centre according to their cultural linkage is a special feature of the composition of the zonal centres.

Ramakrishna mission institute of culture

The Ramakrishna Mission Institute of Culture, Calcutta is engaged in the promotion of thought, knowledge and education. Apart from being engaged in cultural activities at national and international level, the Institute also maitains several schools of instructions.

Indira Gandhi national centre for the arts

Indira Gandhi National Centre for the Arts (IGNCA) was established to commemorate the memory of the late Prime Minister, Mrs Indira Gandhi. This Centre launched on 19 November 1985 as a fully funded autonomous trust, is visualized as a centre encompassing the study and experience of all the arts-each for its own integrity, yet within a dimension of mutual interdependence, inter-relatedness with nature, social structure and cosmology. Through diverse programmes of research, publication, training, creative activities and performance, the IGNCA seeks to place the arts within the context of the natural and human environment. the fundamental approach of the Centre in all its work is multi-disciplinary and inter-disciplinary.

The Indira Gandhi National Centre for the Arts, comprises five main divisions viz. (i) Kala Nidhi; (ii) kala Kosa; (iii) janapada Sampada; (iv) Kala Darshana and (v) Sutradhara. During 1994-95, the reference library of Kala NIdhi Division added 2,204 selected works of eminent authors to its collection, 478 rolls of microfilms of rare Indian manuscripts from abroad and 1,532 microfiches from SMPK, Berlin University of Vienna were also added to its collections. The Kala Kosa Division under its programme of *Kalathttvakosa,* a lexicon of fundamental concepts of Indian arts, is engaged in the preparation of its volume engaged in the preparation of its volume III and IV. The institution organised a 17 day workshop on 'Manuscriptology and Palaeography' in collaboration with Shri Lal Bahadur Shastri Rashtriya Sanskrit Vidyapeetha as part of training programme for younger generation of researchers from within IGNCA and outside. During the year, the Janapada Sampada Division under its *Loka Parmapara* programmes, recieved interim reports on various projects including Santhal Perception of Sound", "Seed and Earth in Oral Tradition of Vraja", etc. Under its publication programme, a number of manuscripts were assigned to the co-publishers. The first and second issues of IGNCA Newsletter, *Vihangama*, have been brought out during the year and the third issue is under publication. The Kala Darshana Division organised a number of exhibitions abroad in collaboration with Mr. Jacques Pimpaneau of Musee Kwok On, France, photographic exhibition of photographs by David Ulrich titled Hawalii Landscape of Transformation; and Raja Deen Dayal Exhibition at Bombay and Bhopal. The IGNCA also co-sponsored a session on "Cave art of India and China" at Dunhuang (China), and deputed three delegates to participate in the International Seminar held there as a part of the Dunhaung Academy Golden Jubilee celebrations.

Centenaries and anniversaries

One of the important activities undertaken by the Government of India has been the commemoration of the centenaries ofdistinguished Indians who have left an indelible impression on the history and life of our country. National committees are set up for centenaries which are considered to be of such importance. Year long programmes are drawn up by the committees for implementation during the centenary year. These programmes normally include organisation of national seminars, installation of statutes, other functions, stamp release, publications and exhibitions. The Department of Culture also provides financial assistance to registered voluntary organisations for celebrating the centenaries of outstanding personalities which are not taken up for celebration by the Government of India. Another mode of organising centenaries is where one or more state governments are requested to set up the centenary committee and the Government of India on its part organises a few programmes like release of commemorative postage stamps, seminars/lectures, publication, etc.

Gandhi smriti and darshan samiti

Gandhi Smriti and Darshan Samiti (GSDS) was set up by the Department of Culture in 1948 primarily to maintain and look after the national memorial where gandhiji was assisinated and now called 'Gandhi Smriti', and a permanent photo exhibition at Rajghat called' Gandhi Darshan', which was created at the time of Gandhiji's birth centenary in the year 1969. The institution has brought out a number of books on Gandhi, communal harmony and national integration. It also publishes a quarterly newsletter to create awareness about the GSDS and also organises annual Gandhij Memorial Lecture by an eminent scholar both in India and abroad.

The year 1994-95 happens to be the 125th birth anniversary year of Gandhiji and, therefore a series of programmes commenced with an inaugural function at Vigyan Bhawan on 2 October 1994 chaired by the President. The Samiti has since organised a programme of painting by the children, a photo exhibition put up at Paris on the eve of the 1st UNESCO Gandhi Memorial Lecture delivered by the Prime Minister; a massive programme of creating awareness for the youth in all the districts of Kerala; another programme involving several thousand youths and others for creating awareness about the literature on Gandhi. Programmes have also been organised for women, especially for those elected for Panchayats. Orientation programmes comprising discussions, film shows, visit to an exhibition and cultural programmes in several rural settings were the other highlights. The GSDS also participated and collaborated in the regional Conference organised by UNESCO on tolerance in April 1995 at New Delhi.

Maulana Abul Kalam Azad institute of asian studies

Maulana Abul Kalam Azad Institute of Asian Studies, under the administrative control of the Department of Culture is the centre for research and training of the life and works of Maulana Abul Kalam Azad and with the study on social, cultural, political and economic movement in Asia from the middle of the 19th century. The Institute also maintains library of books, newspapers, still photographs and materials on the secular traditions of modern India and events of the 19th century which is suitable for the public to collect papers and library sources for study and research from India and abroad. It also maintains personal museum at the former residence of Maulana Abul Kalam Azad. The Museum highlights the life and works of Maulana Abdul Kalam Azad as a distinguished national leader and thinker.

Festival of India

All festivals have a common purpose of creating a greater awareness amongst the people of the receiving country of India's rich cultural heritage and contemporary development in vrious spheres of modern India. This helps to generate an appropriate climate of goodwill and understanding for mutual exchanges in different spheres including technology, commerce and tourism on a more permanent footing. The main thrust of the Festival of India has been to project its multifaceted cultural life, while also highlighting scientific and technical progress and advancement through a series of exhibitions, programmes of performing arts as well as through seminars, readings, workshops, youth meetings, sports festivals etc.

The Festival of India in China was inaugurated on 9 May 1994 at Ply Plaza at Beijing by the Human Resource Development Minister and his Chinese counterpart. The inaugural ceremony consisted mainly of performing art event with the underlying theme 'Harmony'. Eight Indian films were screened at different venues in China during the Festival of India. The National Institute of Fashion technology mounted fashion shows during the festival.

The Performing Arts programme for the Festival of India in China was the single largest component among the festival events. About 75 performers visited China during the period of festival. Indian handicrafts combine varied styles and colours, fine workmanship, profound traditions and have a distinctive national flavour, *Karigari* provided a glimpse of these patterns of handicraft traditions that have survived in India for many thousand years. It was inaugurated on 10 May 1994. In this exhibition, an effort was made to give the viewers an impression of Indian science as a whole, in all its rich diversity through Indian experience in science and technology in its long history of 4500 years.

Around 1500 titles, mostly recent and some old titles of perennial value, brought out by almost 150 publishers were displayed at the exhibitions in China. The books selected for the exhibitions in China covered a wide range of subjects such as arts, history, biography, literature, philosophy, religion, social sciences, technology and books of general reference.

Education

Education was one of the goals of the India's freedom movement and Mahatma Gandhi, even while leading the epic struggle against colonial power, evolved an alternative, community based system of education. Rooted in the struggle for Independence, several articles in the Constitution of India bring into focus the general principles governing educational development in the country. At the time of Independence in 1947 India inherited an educational system which was not only quantitatively small but was also characterized by striking regional and structural imbalances. Only 14 per cent of the population was literate and only one child out of three had been enroled in primary school. The low levels of enrolment and literacy were compounded by acute regional and gender disparities. Recognizing that education is vitally linked with the totality of the development process, the reform and restructuring of the educational system was accepted as an important area of state intervention.

Accordingly, the need for a literate population and universal education for all children in the 6-14 age group was provided with a precisely defined and delineated framework in the Indian Constitution as well as in successive Five Year Plans. The Constitution makes an elaborate legislative, administrative and financial distribution of powers between the state governments and the union government. Decisions regarding the organisation and structure of education are largely the concern of the states. Within the overall policy framework, each state determines independently the educational structures to be adopted. However, the Union GOvernment has clear responsibility regarding the quality and character of education.

The Central Advisory Board of Education (CABE), set up during the pre-Independence period in 1935, continues to play a lead role in the evolution and monitoring of educational policies and programmes, the most notable of which are the National Policy (NPE), 1986, Programme of Action (POA), 1986, and a revised NPE and POA (1992).

Educational management and planning

In addition to policy formulation, the Department of Education shares with the states the responsibility for educational planning. Till the Sixth Plan, education was taken to be a social service rather than an imput in the development process. But now education is considered pivotal in social and economic development through development of human resources.This is reflected in the National Policy on Education, 1986 and in the budgetary allocation of resources. The Eighth Plan outlay for education (Centre and states) at Rs. 19,599.7 crore is higher than the Seventh Plan expenditure of Rs. 7,633.1 crore by 2.6 times. In keeping with this set up, the Central plan outlay for education has been substantially increased from Rs. 1,541 crore in 1994-95 to Rs. 1,825 crore in 1995-96. There has also been an *inter se* shift in the allocation of resources within the education sector from higher education to elementary education. The outlay on elementary education is up by 24.5 per cent to Rs. 651.04 crore in 1995-96. Further the outlay consists of Rs. 409.11 crore for secondary and physical education, Rs. 245.55 crore for university and higher education, Rs. 234 crore for adult education and Rs. 253.41 crore for technical education. Plan expenditure on different sectors of education (percentage) is given in table 1.

The National Policy on Education (NPE) 1986, a landmark in the educational development of the country was reviewed by a committee under the Chairmanship of Acharya Ramamurthi in 1990. Its recommendations were considered by the Central Advisory Board of Education

(CABE) Committee on Policy under the Chairmanship of Shri N.Janaradhan Reddy, then Chief Minister, Andhra Pradesh which submitted its report on 22 January 1992. The Report was considered by the CABE which recommended certain modifications. Consequently, a Revised Policy Formulations containing the modifications recommended by the CABE were tabled in the Parliament on 7 May 1992. Subsequently, a revised Programme of Action (POA) was prepared to opertionalise the policy and the revised POA, 1992 was tabled in the Parliament on 19 August 1992.

Five thrust areas viz,. adult literacy, primary education, decentralisation of management of education, vocational education and technical education, have been identified to achieve Universalisation of Elementary Education to make education relevant to the needs of the community and also to meet new challenges of liberalisation and globalisation of the economy.

Tribal development: need for a Fresh Perspective

The total Scheduled Tribe population in India, as per 1991 census, is about eight per cent of the entire population in the country. Of this, aboupt 55 per cent Scheduled Tribe population are concentrated in central region; roughly 28.14 per cent in western religion, 12.02 per cent in north eastern region; 4.22 per cent in southern region; and the remaining in other regions. Since Independence, the Government of India continued to emphasize the programmes and schemes for raising the socio-economic levels of the tribal people. *One of the main tasks of planning was to identify and remove the large disparities that existed in the country across regions and social groups.* A number of Departments and Ministries in the Union and State governments had been entrusted with the task of implementing the constitutional provisions to ensure speedy development of the Scheduled Tribes. The financial allocation for their development had also been increased. *Yet, why is there no perceptible improvement in their condition? Is there something wrong with the policy and planning as also the implementation?*

Approach to policy and planning

As for the general policy approach to tribal development, it is pertinent to go back to the statements made by Dr. Rajendra Prasad and Jawaharlal Nehru, and the proposals of the Planning Commission for the Second Five Year Plan. They constitute, as a matter of fact, the policy statements towards tribal development.

Dr. Rajendra Prasad, the first President of India, indicated that "there should be no idea of forcing anything on the tribals either by way of religion, language, or, even mode of living and customs. Facilities for education and for general improvement in their economic life should be provided for them, and it should be left to them to choose whether they would like to be assimilated with, and absorbed by the surrounding society, or would like to maintain their own separate tribal existence."

"They are our own people and our work does not end with the opening of so many schools, and so many dispensaries and hospitals. Of course, we want schools, hospitals, and roads and all that, but to stop there is rather a dead way of looking at things, what we ought to do is to develop a sense of oneness with these people, a sense of unity and understanding. We must approach the tribal people with affection and friendliness and come to them as a liberating force. If they feel you have come to impose yourselves upon them, or, that we go to them in order to try and change their methods of living, to take away their land to encourage our businessmen to exploit them, then the fault is ours, for is ours, for it only means that our approach to the tribal people is wholly wrong."

Strategy of tribal development: TSP approach

The strategy for development of the Scheduled Tribes is based on the TSP (tribal sub-plan) approach which came into operation since 1974-75 (V Plan) in 16 States (now 18 States) and two Union territories. The main objective of the tribal sub-plan is to (i) raise the socio-economic condition of the tribal population and strengthen infrastructure in the tribal areas, and (ii) to protect and promote tribal interests through legal and administrative support.

The programmes are now being implemented through (i) 194 Integrated Tribal Development Projects (ITDPs) comprising generally blocks/*tehsils* with 50 per cent or more Scheduled Tribe population; (ii) 277 pockets of tribal concentration (Modified Area Development Approach Projects) having a total population of 10,000 or more, and Scheduled Tribe population of 50 per cent or more; and (iii) 90 primitive tribe projects or micro-projects.

The tribal sub-plan has a two-fold thrust, viz (i) socio-economic development of the tribal areas, and (ii) socio-economic development of the tribal families.

It was expected that during the Seventh Plan period, there would be cent per cent coverage of Scheduled Tribe population under the tribal sub-plan. Benefits were also proposed to be extended to the scattered Scheduled Tribe population which was not covered by any specific project through family-oriented programmes. It may be mentioned that the tribal population coverage during the Sixth Plan period was only 75 per cent. During the Seventh Plan, the following were the objectives under tribal sub-plan approach: (i) taking up family beneficiary programme through raising productivity-level of the beneficiary families in the field of agriculture, horticulture, animal husbandry, small industry, etc. (ii) elimination of exploration of the tribals in the sphere of alienation of land, money-lending, debt bondage, forest, etc. (iii) human resource development through education and training programmes, (vi) infrastructure development, (v) development of vulnerable tribal areas and groups like, forest villagers, displaced tribes and tribal women; and (vi) upgradation of environment of tribal areas.

For the year 1985-86, the target of tribal families to be economically assisted was fixed at 8.35 lakh, and the achievement reported was 8.3 lakh families. For 1986-87, the target fixed was 8.35 lakh tribal families and for 1987-88, a tentative target of assisting 8.50 lakh tribal families had been kept.

Special Central Assistance: Under tribal development, Special Central Assistance (SCA) is an additive to the State Plan efforts for Scheduled Tribes. The Eighth Plan had a target to cover 46.50 lakh families. Against this, 28.69 lakh families were covered during the first three years of the Plan (8.88 lakh in 1992-93; 10.42 lakh in 1993-94; and 9.39 lakh in 1994-95). This constituted 61.7 per cent of the target. To improve the literacy rate among tribal women, a new scheme was introduced since 1992-93, and is being implemented through non-governmental organizations in 48 districts with tribal concentration where female population is less than two per cent.

Financing tribal sub-plan: There are four sources for financing tribal sub-plan programmes: (i) Special Central Assistance (SCA) administered by Ministry of Welfare, (ii) State Plan funds, (iii) centrally-sponsored schemes, and (vi) institutional finance.

Since the V Plan period, with the launching of the tribal sub-plan approach, special programmes for extremely backward tribe groups had been taken up. These were micro-projects or projects for primitive tribal groups. These primitive tribal groups had three criteria for their identification: (i) almost stagnant population, or extremely low growth rate facing the danger of extinction, (ii) having are pre-agricultural level of technology, and (iii) extremely low level of literacy.

Another important factor was the ecosystem in which they lived. There were also other factors which entered into the situation of each of these tribal groups calling for a sensitive and in-depth study of each, precedent to enforcement of any action plan.

The Planning Commission also mentioned that particular care need to be taken of the small primitive tribal groups, some of which were on the verge of extinction.

The Dhebar Commission (1961) alluded to them as the 'lowest layer}, and listed 50 tribes in various States which were in an extremely underdeveloped state. During the V Plan period, the Ministry of Home Affairs identified 52 tribal communities as primitive, their estimated population being 10 lakhs. During the VI Plan period, an additional 20 tribal groups were identified raising their total number to 72 with an estimated population of 14 lakhs. Now the clusters of tribal concentration have gone up to 90.

There had been emphasis since the V Plan period on preparation of a project report for each of these groups relative to its situation. Nevertheless, there had been considerable neglect in this regard. Apart form the continued misery of conditions in which they lived, the risk of extinction of some of these tribes was also great.

Principle of panchsheel

According to jawaharlal Nehru, avenues of tribal development should be pursued within the broad framework of the following five fundamental principles:

1. People should develop along the lines of their own genius and we should avoid imposing anything on them. We should try to encourage in every way their own traditional arts and cultures.
2. Tribal rights in land and forest should be respected.
3. We should try to train and build up a team of their own people to do the work of development and administration. Some technical personnel from outside will be needed in the beginning. But we should avoid introducing too many outsiders into tribal territory.
4. We should not over-administer those areas or overwhelm them with a multiplicity of schemes. We should rather work through, and not in rivalry to their own cultural and social institutions.
5. We should judge results, not by statistics, or the amount of money spent, but by the quality of human character that is involved.

Role of tribals

The proposals of the Planning Commission for the Second Five Year Plan also emphasized that the tribals themselves must play their part in schemes of their own development:

"Welfare programmes for the tribal people have to be based on respect and understanding of their culture and traditions, and an appreciation of the social psychological and economic problems with which they are faced. In their implementation, the confidence of the people, and in particular, the understanding and goodwill of the elders of the tribal communities are of the highest importance. It is necessary that the welfare extension workers should be found as far as possible from amongst the educated youths in tribal communities. In the adoption of new techniques, tribal leadership has a major role. Tribal people have to be assisted largely through their own institutions. Details of development programmes should be formulated in consultation with members of Advisory councils, leaders of tribal opinion, and institutions engaged in the study of tribal problems. The tribal people feel that these programmes area response to their own urge for better standards of living and the development of their own culture. If the programmes are implemented with popular support, they will give the tribal people a sense of partnership and integration with the nation as a whole."

These statement of the national leaders and the Planning Commission briefly set out the schemes of tribal development.

The overall policy approach towards the tribals had been (i) isolationist, (ii) assimilative, and (iii) integrationist. The first approach is: 'let them choose their own way, let them remain isolated, touch them not.'

The second approach is 'to absorb them and assimilate them.' The third approach is 'to integrate them into the national mainstream, let them develop a sense of oneness with other people, a sense of unity and understanding.'

Health care scenario

The post-Independence era has witnessed the development of a vast health care infrastructure in the country to control major public health problems. However, ever growing population, changing lifestyles and emergence of new disease have increased the health care burden resulting in a widening gap between what is possible and what is affordable, says the author.

India is one of the pioneers in the health service planning with a focus on primary health care. The Bhore

Committee report which laid the foundation of the health care system in Independent India preceded the Alma Ata declaration by three decades. At the time of Independence, the country's health care infrastructure was mainly urban and clinic based. These hospitals and clinics provided curative care to patients who came to them. Outreach of services in the rural areas was very limited; there were very few preventive and rehabilitative services available.

From the First Five year Plan efforts were made to build up primary, secondary and tertiary care centres and to link them through appropriate referral system. National Programmes for combating major public health problems were evolved and implemented. These efforts have resulted in a discernible impact on mortiality with Crude Death rate (CDR) deslinning from 27 in 1951 to 9 in 1995 Sample Registraton system (SRS 1995 provisional). However the morbidity due to communicable and nutrition related diseases has not shown a parallel decline. In addition, there is now an increasing morbidity due to non—communicable diseases and newly emerging infections such as those with HIV.

Rural health

Over the last Eight Plan periods the Rural Primary Health Care infrastructure has been built up throughout the country. Adequate number of subcentres and PHCs have been created so that at the national level the norms for these have been met by the end of the Seventh Plan. Efforts are underway to build adequate number of Community Health Centres (CHCs) so that there is effective emergency services available in rural areas. However the staffing of these infrastructure is often inadequate and lack of key personnel have come in the way of effective delivery of health and family welfare service and implementation of the major national programmes. Yet another problem has been in building up of effective referral services between these three tiers of health services.

There is a need to assess the requirement of personnel based not only on population, but also on the basis of workload, distance to be covered, and problem in utilization of health services by the population. Flexible approach to recruitment of staff if necessary on contract basis has to be taken up to ensure that programmes do not suffer due to lack of key personnel.

Urban health

In 1991 it was estimated that nearly 30 per cent of India's population lived in urban areas. Urban migration over the last two decades had resulted in rapid growth of urban slum population. Though initially the health care services were mainly urban based, the existing services have become inadequate to serve the needs of the growing population. Realising this unmet felt need for health care, several organisations including Municipalities, State Governments, non-governmental organisations and externally aided projects undertook efforts to create necessary infrastructure and provide the manpower there. Unlike the rural health services, there has not been any clear cut and well organised efforts to provide primary secondary and tertiary care services in geographically defined areas in urban health care. Efforts have been initiated to build up appropriate linkages between centres providing primary health care services and those providing secondary and tertiary care in the same areas, so that there is optimal utilisation of the available health care facilities.

Population and family welfare

1. The family Welfare Programme has helped in containing the growth rate of population. Total Fertility Rate has declined from 4.5 in 1981 to 3.5 in

1993 as per the estimates of Sample Registration System (SRS). The Crude Birth Rate has decreased from 33.9 per provisional estimates of the SRS. The Crude Death Rate has also declined from 12.5 to 9 per thousand population over the same period. The Infant MOrtality Rate dropped from 110 per thousand live births in 1981 to 74 in 1995. The annual average exponential population growth rate has come down marginally from 2.22 per cent during 1971-81 to 2.14 per cent during 1981-91. The population, however, continues to grow as the decline in birth rate has not been as rapid as the decline in the death rate.

2. There are, however, inter-State differences in the achievements of the Family Welfare Programme. At one end of the spectrum are the States like Kerala, Tamil Nadu and Goa which have already achieved replacement level of fertility. At the other end, are the large States like Uttar Pradesh, Madhya Pradesh, Rajasthan and Bihar where fertility levels and bjirth rates continue to be higher than the national average. Therefore, decline in the rate of growth of population for the country as a whole depends upon how the large northern States perform in the family welfare programmes in the future. Unless effective steps are taken to bring about significant improvements in the programme, the performance in containing the growth of population at the All India level may not change significantly.

3. Recognising the close relationship between high birth rates and high rnfant mortality, high priority has been accorded to the Maternal and Child Health (MCH) programme since 1985. In order to achieves the main objective of MCH, (i.e. to improve the health status of women and children and to reduce maternal, infant and child morbidity and mortality

rates), the Universal Immunisation Programme (UIP) was launched in 1985. From the year 1992-93 the UIP has been strengthened and expanded into the Child Survival and Safe Motherhood (CSSM) programme. Under this programme, apart from strengthening the existing MCH, initiative has been taken to expand the pilot projects on Acute Respiratory Infection Control and Traditional Birth Attendants training. For this, a provision of Rs.350 crore has been made in the 1996-97 budget as against Rs.220 crore in 1995-96 (BE).

4. From 1.4.1996, the Family Welfare Programme is being implemented on the basis of the "Target Free Approach" (TFA). This approach envisages replacement of the system of setting contraceptive targets from the top by a system of decentralised participatory planning at the Primary Health Centre level.

5. Pursuant to the World Health Organisation (WHO) goal to eradicate poliomyelitis (polio, a major crippling childhood disease) by the year 2000 A.D., the Pulse Polio Immunization (PPI) was launched in 1995-96. About 87 million children aged 0-3 years were administered as supplemented dose of oral polio vaccine on 9.12.1995 and 93 million on 20.1.1996, irrespective of their routine immunisation status. Since PPI received an overwhelming response from the public, the exercise was repeated on 7.12.1996 and 18,1.1997 covering about 120 million children in the age group of 0-5 years.

6. A Special School Health Check-up Scheme for Primary School Children was carried out in 27 States/UTs in July 1996, and in the remaining 5 States between August and October 1996. The objectives of this Scheme were to detect common

health related problems among primary school children; to conduct screening of children for appropriate referral and check up; to generate health awareness in the community; and to ensure arrangements for follow up and treatment at higher level medical facilities. Reports from 441 districts show 75.9 per cent coverage of schools and 84.9 per cent coverage of enrolled children.

7. In order to foster community involvement in the Family Welfare Programme, two new schemes have been started on a pilot basis. Under one of these, one revenue village in every district, among villages with a population of 500 or more, will be given an award of Rs. 2 lakh for achieving a reduction in the Crude Birth rate, Infant Mortality Rate and Child Mortality Rate. The second schemes aims to integrate family welfare and health care into the ongoing National Wastershed Development Project for Rainfed Areas (NWDPRA) of the Ministry of Agriculture. Under this scheme, the watershed level community based management structures, known as the 'Mitra Krishak Mandal' (MKM) will conduct surveys and prepare watershed level family welfare and health care plans. An amount of Rs. 5000 will be given to each village in the watershed areas, for specified activities like emergency obstetric care and purchase of essential medicines.

8. The Prenatal Diagnostic Techniques (Regulation and Preventation of Misuse) Act, 1994, has been brought into force from 1st January, 1996. This Act makes it illegal to use prenatal diagnostic techniques like amniocentesis for determining the sex of the foetus, a practice that often leads to abortion of female foetuses. Statutory machinery for implementation of the Act has been established.

Housing

Housing is a State subject but the Union Government is responsible for the formulation of policy with regard to programmes and approaches for effective implementation of the social housing schemes, particularly those pertaining to weaker sections of the society. The National Housing Policy is enunciated in the Five Year Plan and the state goverments implement the schemes in accordance with the plan priorities and local requirements.

National housing policy

In tune with the policy of the Government, a National Housing Policy (NHP), taking into account the developments on national and international scene on Shelter Sector after 1988 and also in the light of comments received from state governments and different sections of the community has been evolved. Special emphasis has been given in the policy paper on the specific needs of rural housing. The policy document outlining the strategy under the Eighth Plan has since been endorsed by Parliament in 1994. The long term goal of the NHP is to eradicate houselessness, to improve the housing conditions of the inadequately housed and to provide a minimum level of basic services and amenities to all. It recognises that the magnitude of housing task calls for involvement of various agencies including government at different levels, cooperatives, the community and the private sector. The policy envisages a major shift in Government's role to act more as a facilitator than as provider. The needs of vulnerable sections of society will continue to be atended to by the Government. It envisages to facilitate housing activity of the lower and middle income groups and to encourage within the framework of housing policy and local planning, the voluntary agencies in efforts to upgrade shelter, extend basic services, augment incomes and promote environmental conservation. The policy has been incorporated in the Housing Chapter on the Eighth Plan.

During the Eighth Plan, emphasis will be on social housing schemes including Minimum Needs Programme projects in rural areas, strengthened role of HUDCO, shelter for the homeless, technology transfer, housing information system and housing for Central Government employees. All the state governments have been requested to formulate detailed action plans for implementation of the policy.

Action for improved cities

In most cities and towns of India there are NGOs whose focus is the improvement of the urban environment and the condition of the urbanites.

The Bombay Environmental Action Group's efforts have been focused on Bombay and Maharashtra, but the fallout is expected to be experienced in many urban centres. The group has used environmental advocacy and public interest litigation to bring about a rethinking on siting of failities, unplanned growth and pollution.

The Ahmedabad Study Action Group's activities include programmes for slum children, income supplementing programmes for women, low-cost housing, biogas plants and policy research on poverty-related issues.

The Self Employed Women's Association, Ahmedabad, represents a merger of labour, cooperative and women's movements and has promoted cooperatives of rag-pickers, roadside vendors and hawkers, and has been campaigning for the rights of unroganized workers in the non-formal sector.

The Society for the Promotion of Area Resource

Centres (SPARC), Bombay works in training and mobilization of the urban poor.

The KKNSS, Bangalore is a federation of slum dwellers, one of the few peoples' organizations of thi kind.

Slum improvement

The Government has taken several initiatives to cope with the burgeoning problem of urban housing. Slum upgrading became a part of official housing policy in 1972. The rationale of slum upgrading is that *in situ* improvement of existing communities is socially preferable to relocation or redevelopment. Under the scheme of Environmental Improvement of Urban Slums, water supply including drinking water taps, open sewer drains, storm water drains, street lighting, etc., are provided to notified slums.

In 1986 the Scheme of Urban Basic Services was launched as a centrally sponsored scheme with teh objective of promoting woman and child survival and development, low-cost water supply and sanitation, and other community welfare activities through community participation.

The Government seeks to completely eliminate the practice of manual scavenging by conversation of dry latrines and construction of low cost sanitation units.

Pollution abatement

The Government has recently announced a comprehensive Pollution Abatement Policy which seeks to combine regulation with fiscal incentives, encourage clean technologies, make voluntary action attractive and promote people's participation.

Recycling

A whole economy runs on recycling in Indian cities. In

Ahmedabad alone, a hundred factories are exclusively involved in converting plastic picked from the roadside into recycled products. Apart from the used paper which is sold to old paper dealers, 60 tonnes is picked up an recycled. Foundry wastes are ground, undergo magnetic extraction and are made into manhole covers. Rags are sold on a large scale for cleaning machines in factories. The total amount of recycling in Ahmedabad by the informal sector alone is estimated to be 200 tonnes per day, providing employment to 100,000 people, at Rs. 20 to Rs. 30 a day, which is higher than the minimum wage.

Rural and urban integration

Rural and urban integration has been a neglected aspect of decentralized planning. The district planning has been nothing more than assembling the various sectoral programmes implemented by various State departments at district level. For the first time, the 74th Constitutional Amendment (243 ZD) has made provision for integration of the rural plan with the urban plan but only at the district level. It is one of the lacunae of the 73rd and 74th Amendments that they have not made provision for integration of rural areas with urban areas below the district level. No State government including that of Kerala, has made such provision. Therefore, it is suggested that economic development and social justice plans prepared by Nagar Panchayats and Municipal Councils for establishing spatial linkages and effective participatory planning.

District planning committee

A District Planning Committee (DPC) will be constituted as per Section 53 of the Kerala Municipality Act, 1994. The welcome feature of this Section is that the chairperson of the DP and the District Collector have been made Chairperson and Secretary of this Committee respectively. This provision of the Kerala Act should also be emulated by other States.

State council for panchayats

Section 266 of the Gujarat Panchayat Act provides for a State Council for Panchayats to co-ordinate and advise the Panchayats. The Panchayat Minister shall be its Chairperson. Among others, Presidents of Zilla Panchayats shall be its members. Kerala may incorporate a modified provision in its Panchayat Act making the Chief Minister as its Chairperson.

The above critique of the Kerala Panchayat Raj Act shows that although the Act contains certain positive features which could be emulated by other States, it does not provide an enabling environment for participatory planning because vital issues affecting local government are still in the domain of either the government or its suggestions for its improvement have been offered. If these suggestions are incorporated in the Act they will ensure autonomy of action by the people through the Panchayats. Such provisions in the Act are very important to provide a sound base for capability building of the Panchayats. In this way, Kerala's enlightened and politically conscious people could practise participatory planning in a more effective way. The example of the Goa Panchayat Act is worth mentioning her.. Because of its Section 68, the Querium Panchayat was able to drive out an American multinational corporation "Du Pont" which wanted to construct a factory in its jurisdiction to produce nylon.

The history of Panchayati Raj in the State reveals that the institutions have not become vibrant for participatory planning and the prime mover in enlisting people's participation in development has been the voluntary sector. The Ernakulam model of literacy, the Kalliasseri model of participatory planning and the

Alappuzha model of economic empowerment of women have been success stories, acclaimed across the would and could be emulated elsewhere.

Participation of the poor in local development has been ensured by way of reserving seats for them in the Panchayats. But a critical examination of various provisions shows that the Kerala Panchayat Raj Act fails to give autonomy to the people in their actions through Panchayats, because the vital issues affecting local government have been in the domain of the State government. Thus, for making Panchayats strong institutions in order to enlist people's participation, Kerala may be benefited from other States like Gujarat, Rajasthan, Assam, Punjab, Manipurm West Bengal and Karnataka. If functional, administrative and financial autonomy is ensured for the Panchayats by amending certain provisions of the Act as suggested in this paper, it may provide a sound base for a sustainable democracy and participatory planning at the local level.

Rural development and employment

Rural development implies both the economic betterment of the people as well as greater social transformation. Increased participation of people in the rural development process, decentralization of planning, better enforcement of land reforms and greater access to credit and inputs go a long way in providing the rural people with better prospects for economic development. Improvements in health, education, drinking water, energy supply, sanitation and housing coupled with attitudinal changes also facilitate their social development. Rural development is, in fact, the pivot of administration at the Central, State and district levels in India. Various steps for the betterment of villages have been taken from time to time. Rural development has remained one of the constant and increasingly conscious goals of our Five Year Plans from their inception. As such, in the Ninth Five Year Plan also, high priority has been given to rural development and employment.

Rural poverty is inextricably linked with low rural productivity and unemployment including underemployment. Hence, it becomes necessary to improve productivity and increase employment in rural areas. Moreover, more employment needs to be generated at higher output. It is true that over the last two decades there has been a considerable decline in the incidence of rural poverty. However, a large number of persons continue to live below the poverty line. Hence, there is a need for continued direct State intervention for poverty alleviation. While the programmes for self-employment and supplementary wage employment would continue in the Ninth Five Year Plan, these would be redesigned in order to make them more effective as instruments of poverty alleviation. Apart from this, they would be integrated with the various doctoral programmes as well as the area development programmes within the umbrella of the Panchayati Raj institutions.

The decline in rural poverty is attributable both to the growth factor and to the special employment programmes launched by the government in order to generate more incomes in the rural areas Hence, in its more limited interpretation, rural development has been confined to a direct attack on poverty through special employment programmes, area development progra-mmes and land reforms. Some of these programmes are discussed below.

IRDP

The Integrated Rural Development Programme (IRDP) is a self-employment programme aimed at enabling poor families to cross the poverty line, via access to income-generating assets and training. During the Eighth Plan, a system of concurrent evaluation of the IRDP was introduced. Various rounds of the concurrent evaluation revealed that while it had been successful in providing incremental income to the poor, in most cases this was not enough to enable them to cross the poverty line. Thus to make self-employment programmes more effective in the Ninth Five Year Plan, there will be a shift in strategy under IRDP. Several modifications have been made in order to improve the efficacy of the programme via higher levels of investment, better infrastructural support and strengthening of linkages, as also by a shift towards a group/cluster approach.

TRYSEM

Training of Rural Youth for Self-Employment (TRYSEM) aims to enable the rural youth to take up self-employment ventures in different spheres across sectors by giving them assistance under IRDP. During the Ninth Plan, TRYSEM will be revamped in its design, curriculum and method of training in order to improve the employment opportunities of the poor. It will focus on activities in which the rural youth are already engaged and where there exists a potential for skill up gradation or else on activities which would enhance production under the group-cluster approach.

DWCRA

The success of several women's groups under Development of Women and Children in Rural Areas (DWCRA), which is based on a group approach, suggests that group dynamics work if people are organized into homogenous self-help groups for taking up income generating activities. A mechanism for replicating the successful DWCRA groups would be evolved. Besides, a greater integration of DWCRA with IRDP and TRYSEM will be attempted to provide women's groups with greater access to financial resources and training.

In the Ninth Plan, a new initiative for social mobilization will be taken up, for creation self-managed institutions of the poor. A mechanism for training of social animators to assist the poor to from their own organizations and articulate their felt needs and aspirations would be taken up.

JRY and EAS

The Jawahar Rozgar Yojana (JRY) was the only wage employment programme at the beginning of the Eighth Plan. The primary objective of the programme is generation of supplementary employment and creation of rural infrastructure required for more sustained employment. However, funds under this scheme went into every single village, though the amounts varied as States were allocated resources on the basis of the incidence of poverty. Apart from JRY, there is another wage employment programme known as the Employment Assurance Scheme (EAS). Both these schemes provide employment for a short duration in the form of casual manual work, during the lean agricultural season. So far, the EAS is being implemented in 3,206 blocks but will be universalized by 1997-98. In the Ninth Plan, this scheme would also be implemented through the PRIs.

IAY and MWS

In order to provide a greater thrust to shelter and irrigation facilities for the weaker sections, the Indira Awaas Yojana (IAY) for rural housing and the Million Wells Scheme (mws) for provision of open wells/family water harvesting structure were made separate independent schemes since January 1996. In the Ninth Plan, IAY will receive a greater thrust as it is one of the identified basic services for complete coverage in a time-bound manner. The scope of MWS will now be expanded to include borewells/tubewells and lifting devices.

DPAP and DDP

The area development programes confined to drought-prone and desert areas were reviewed and redesigned in an attempt to restore the ecological balance through soil and moisture conservation. Preparation of watershed plans for a unit of 500 hectares with involvement of all members residing in the watershed was made mandatory. Training of functionaries in area planning and watershed management will be expanded.

Land reforms

Access to land remains a key element of the anti-poverty strategy in rural areas because rural poverty is largely among the landless and marginal farmers. In the Ninth Plan, emphasis has also been given to land reforms. The programme of action for land reforms would include the following: (i) detection as well as redistribution of ceiling surplus land; (ii) updating of land records on a regular basis; (iii) tenancy reforms providing for recording the rights of tenants and share-croppers; (iv) consolidation of holdings; (v) preventing alienation of tribal lands; (vi) providing access on a group basis to the poor on wastelands and common property resources; (vii) leasing-in and leasing-out of land will be permitted within the ceiling limits; (viii) preference to women in the distribution of ceiling surplus land and legal provisions for protecting their rights on land.

The extent of poverty and employment scenario

The major problems that confront India are poverty and unemployment. And both are interrelated. There is a lot of controversy regarding the estimates of poverty in the country. Estimates of Tendulkar and Jain show that rural poverty has increased from 37.5 per cent in 1990-91 to 39.7 per cent in 1993-94. On the other hand, urban poverty has declined from 35 per cent in 1990-91 to 30.9 per cent in 1993. The upshot of the argument is that even in 1993-94, around 40 per cent of the rural population (around 250 million) and 31 per cent of the urban population (around 65 million) were below the poverty line, or food insecure in terms of not having enough calories.

The continuance of poverty at such a colossal level has created great distortions in the economy. There are several reasons why poverty has persisted in rural areas. One obvious factor which has hurt the poor is the sharp increase in the prices of food grains. During the last five or six years, procurement prices of food grains have increased considerably recultural labourers. Secondly, the rural poor appear to have been left out of the gains of increased productivity in the agricultural sector. Thirdly, the rate of growth in employment in rural areas (both males and females), during the period 1987-88 to 1993-94 was significantly lower as comparesd to the urban areas as shown in .

According to the 50th Round of the NSSO, while 'Open' unemployment at a little over 6.0 per cent, remained more or less unchanged. And casualization increased with a corresponding decline in self-employment, both in rural and urban areas. Casual wage employment increased from 31.2 per cent in 1987-88 to 33.5 per cent in 1993-94, while self-employment declined from 53.6 per cent to 51.9 per cent. Regular salaried employment also declined from 15.2 per cent to 14.7 per cent.

The census figures have given an alarming new for Indian planners again. The data paint a dismal picture both with regard to increase in population and unemployment. By 2040, India is set to become the world's most populous country with a population of 126 crores. And as far as unemployment situation is concerned, one-third of the populztion—300 million were estimated to be without work in 1994.

This implies that unless some effective steps are taken to control population, the rate of employment will increase in future.

The approach paper, however, recognizes that a sustained and long-lasting solution to gthe problem of poverty depends on the creation of adequate employment opportunities through a broad based programme of development and economic growth. Therefore, in the Ninth Plan, a great deal of emphasis has been given to agriculture and rural development. And agriculture has been delinked from rural development in order to emphasize the development of irrigation, watershed development, animal husbandry schemes, social forestry and so on.

Grouping women for economic empowerment

Indian Development planning has always aimed at removing inequities in the process of development to ensure that the fruits of development are an equal privilege of all. In recent years it has become increasingly evident that women are lagging behind a great deal both in availing of the benefits of development and as participants in the process of development due to several socio—economic—cultural—political impediments. This has become a cause for concern since women number several millions and constitute nearly half of our populaltion.

In the early years of planning the concern for gender took a welfarist perspective which manifested itself in the form of grants, waivers, subsidies and freeships for girls and women in a few relevant programmes. But these concessions did not elicit the required level of participation. In the later half of the

1970's the focus shifted from merely welfare to development and greater emphasis on integration of women into the mainsteam of social and economic development. In due course many social and economic programmes like NOn Formal Education for Grils, Integrated Rural Development Programme... were evolved exclusively for women or with a percentage set aside solely for them. The benefits derived from these programme had to be sustained and this was posing a challenge. Studies have shown that 'practical gender gains' in improved livelihood, education, nutrition and sanitation are not sustained and easily reversed if the 'strategic need' to give 'women a voice' in the decisions that so directly affect their lives, is not adequately taken care of. The strategy in the 1990's has shifted to empowerment of women and 'giving them a voice'.

It is in this context of empowerment and given the vulnerability and powerl;essness of the individual women in the existing socio—economic set up that 'Grokup' strategies acquire great relevance. The formation of small informal functional groups of women would give them 'visibility' and create micro level power pockets. Further, grouping would initiate a learning process through sharing of ideas, skills and interactive capacity and in course of time women would learn to articulate their needs resulting in more appropriate participatory and grassroots level plans for them. Some social barriers would also be broken in the process'. Many groups in recent years have started cutting across barriers of religion and caste and working together harmoniously for economic betterment.

Poverty hits women the hardest, as they balance means and ends at the household level and many a time skip a meal to let the rest of the household avail of the little that is available. These women are subject to economic and social discrimination, and credit is not easily available to them. Millions of our women live in poverty and their social empowerment would have littlerelevance without first empowering them on the economic front. The World Bank studies have shown that enhancement of women's earnings would hav a more profound effect on the welfare of the family as a whole since 'increases in wmen's income result more directly into better health and nutrition for children. Thus grouping women for economic empowerment is of great importance.

The programme for Development of Women and Children in Rural Areas (DWCRA), launched in 1982—83, inaugurated an era for systematically organising women in groups for enhancing their earnings on a self–sustaining basic and increasing their access to and utilisation of services like health, child care and adult education, among others. The programme called for formation of groups of 10—15 women who would collectively engage in an activity. A revolving fund of Rs. 15000 (presently enhanced to Rs. 25000) was made available to each group for credit and administrative needs. Supplementing of staff by inclusion of an additional gram sevika and appointment of a lady officer to the post of Assistant Project Officer to oversee implementation to the programme were called for. Subsequently with a view to fortifying the programme further and increasing awareness a Community Based Convergent Services (CBCS) component and Information, Education and Communication (IEC) component were included. Upto early 1996, over 1.3 lakh groups covering 2.2 million women were formed. Almost all the districts in the country (except a handful of exclusively urban ones) are presently covered under this programme.

Formation of Thrift and Credit groups of women for self help and economic self reliance has also been encouraged by the government. A Rashtriya Mahila

Kosh (RMK) was set in 1993 for extending credit with low transaction costs to poor and needy women and women's groups through Non Governmental Organisations. At present (as in July, 1996), the scheme is being implemented in the fifteen states of Andhra Pradesh, Bihar, Haryana, Himachal Pradesh, Gujarat, Karnataka, Kerala, Maharashtra, Madhya Pradesh, Manipur, Orissa, Rajasthan, Tamil Nadu, Uttar Pradesh, and West Bengal through an network of one hundred and four Non—Governmental Organisations.

The Indira Mahila Yojana (IMY) launched in 1995 aims at coordinating and integrating sectoral programmes relevant to women like health, education, water, sanitation, housing and others at local, block and district levels and increasing their awareness and income through group activities and participation with the aim of empowering women. Indira Mahila Kendras would be established at village level and Indira Mahila Block Kendras at Block level for this purpose. The programme would be a Centrally sponsored scheme. Non—Governmental Organisations would also be involved in this process. The Programme has been sanctioned for a period of seven years commencing from 1995—96. During the inception year it was to cover two hundred blocks on a pilot basis and a thousand blocks each year in the subsequent years. The Central Governemnt would provide a one time grant of Rs. 5000 to each Indira Mahila Kendra. Further funds provided at block level would be used for payments of honoraira to individuals who involve themselves in awareness camps, mobilisation of groups, training group members and functionaries and helping survival of groups through creation of outlets for marketing.

Delivery system: need for streamlining

An area of priority in the Ninth Plan is to improve

project implementation and delivery mechanisms and to ensure that the intended benefits actually reach the people. Further, several social sector programmes are formulated without addressing the isssue of sustainability of benefits and most programmes run with ever-increasing government budgets and thus pre-empt resources which could find better alternative uses. *The Ninth Plan must introduce necessary correctives to reverse many of the unsustainable trends in the implementation of poverty alleviation programmes. Just allotting higher outlay for rural development will mean nothing unless a major streamlining takes palce in the implementation and delivery systems.*

The existion schemes whose delivery costs are disproportionately high or which fail to make the desired impact should be considered for reorientation and discontinuation. It is necessary to shelve such schemes whose delivery cost exceeds, say 15 to 20 oer cent of the total cost of operating the programme. *Monitoring and evaluation of programmes have to be made equally effective and purposeful.* Therefore, the Centre, States and the grass roots level organizations/institutions would need to be involved to ensure the effectiveness of the system. It is encouraging that the Planning Commission would bring out compendium of evaluation studies and give wider publicity of the findings of research studies conducted and sponsored by it. This would be helpful for a meaningful public debate on issues involved.

An overall increase in the level of real wages of the unorgainzed workers will also help empowering them to be able to secure maximum advantage from the other developmental programmes of the government. The very concepts of democratic decentralozation and empowerment of the people imply a steady reducation in the paternalistic role of the State and increased emphasis on empowerment of the people themselves. It is hoped that during the Ninth Plan there will be much more attention on bringing about awareness among the unorganized workers as also on providing effective redressal mechanisms to enforce their rights. The approach document of the Plan rightly observes that one of the most important weaknesses of the Indian social sector programmes has been is inabiligy to inform the target benefiviaries about the schemes that are available and to which they have a rightful clain. The Ninth Plan will, hopefully, stress the creation and deployment of an effective information dissemination system,and the necessary redressal mechanism for making the demands effective.

Finally, of course, there is no unique way to describe an ideal gorwth process. It can be hoped that the Ninth Plan will lay down foundations for a more progressive process of planning than has been the case so far. Growth involves a dynamic interaction of linked changes. The economic endocrine gland has to be clear as to how much other matters mingt have advanced. As such, it can also be argued that little attention is required to any particular rate of economic growth so long as it is positive.

Wouldn't it then make little sense to worry whether a baby will end up five or six feet tall when the real anxiety should be whether the baby can be safely brought through the problems of infancy, childhood and adolescence? The slower rate of growth, once under way, can pick-up speed and, of course, can slow down too. But the higher gorwth rate has the prospect of slowing down only. It is desirable to have a steady growth as it has more possibility of ending up with the fastest rate of growth of the economy just as the movement on a highway gives to the motorest the highest speed. The crux of planning is to find the turnpike and reach it. Also gorwth is no longer the guarantor of trickle down effects. To what extent these plan promises are taken care of in the Ninth Plan, can be anybody's guess.

Issues of capacity building

The world Conservation Strategy has recommended greater public participation in planning and decision-making concerning the use of living resources and proposed environmental education programmes and campaigns to build support for conservation. The Panchayati Raj is institutionalization of public participation in planning and decisison-making in rural India. The following issues can be listed for capacity building in Panchayati Raj for environment protection and improvement.

Institutional issue

Through Panchayati raj institutions are not directly linked with the Indian federal system, they are closely related with State governments. Most State government departments, particularly departments of agriculture, education, public health, forests and finance have close functional relationship with PRIs. The activities of State governments may be broadly analysed as general administration, technical assistance in the fields ofpersonnel, financial assistance, correction of errors, excesses and negligences. State governments provide administrative guidance and advice to PRIs n problems and issues. The 73rd Constitutional Amendment Act 1992 has strengthened the organizational aspects of PRIs. The success or failure of the object of environment protection through PRIs would largely depend on administrative ability, leadership and motivation of personnel. It becomes even more significant because of the fact that administrative capability is an important means of converting programme inputs into outputs with economy and efficiency. The administrative and transforming quality of the leadership would significantly determine the administrative capability of the Panchayati Raj. The administrative capability involves the ability to mobilize, allocate and combine the actions that are needed to achieve the objectives of environment protection.

Legal issue

India is one of the few countries of the Third World which has enshrined in its Constitution a commitment to environment protection and improvement. The environment law ia a new division of law. Even though it appears to be of recent origin and yet it not a sudden creation. Many provisions dealing with the environment are scattered in pieces and found in different enactments. The Environment (Protection) Act 1986 was enacted with the objectives of protection, regulation of the discharge of environment pollutants; handling of hazardous substances; speedy response in the event of accidents threatening environment safety and health. The World Conservation Strategy has suggested reviewing and strengthening of legislation concerning living resources to ensure that it provides sufficiently for conservation, paying particular attention to enforcement as also to remove loop holes. The lack of proper co-ordination and co-operation among the administrative institutions is an important loophole. A greater degree of co-ordination and co-operation between Central, State and local governments is needed for the implementation of environmental programmes. The other important weakness of the legislative enactments is its lack of recognition of the crucial role that the PRIs can play. The involvement of PRIs as the eyes and ears of the government in terms of grass roots monitoring of environmental quality, needs to be duly recognized. In due course, as experience is gained, particularly with regard to the respective roles of PRIs, enactment of new legislation for environment protection could be considered.

Technical issue

Though PRIs are not sound in their organization for technical tasks and do not have technical and professional experts, decentralization below the State level ensures technical expertise of a high order required for environment protection and improvement in rural India. The Ashok Mehta Committee on Panchayati Raj has asserted that technical assistance and organization of a high order is necessary to sustain the momentum. The State governments have the requisite competence in this regard and the decentralization process at the district level is now under way. When the process of administrative decentralization is already taking place, analysis of the changes, and the ensuring emphasis on development point to the need for democratic management or rural development below the State level so that the entire programme can be effectively implemented, co-ordinated and supervised. The inescapable conclusion is that the first point of decentralization should be at the district level. District heads of sufficient competence are already stationed here. Their capabilities ae also being upgraded. The district is also traditionally a unit of administration to which all are acclimatized. Further, it is the key planning unit for evolving the overall strategy, resource allocation including credit and the delineation of the different types of projects. The establishement of a strong Panchayat tier at the district level appears to respond both to the organizational needs within district and the demands of emerging links with the State.

Financial issue

Despite the emphasis on the active role to be played by PRIs, they were not, much effective in the past. A number of efforts were undertaken to bring forward the Constitution Amendment Bill 1992, to provide constitutional status to Panchayati Raj bodies and to strengthen them by making suitable provisions for this durability, continuity, adequate representation to all the sections of society and financial allocations. The Act has empowered the State legislatures to authorize the Panchayats to levy, collect, and appropriate suitable local taxes and also provide for making grants-in-aid to the Panchayats from the Consolidated Fund of the State. In addition, a Finance Commission has to be constituted once in every five years to review the financial position of the Panchayats and make suitable recommendations to the State on the distribution of the funds between the State and the local bodies. The Central Finance Commission shall also suggest measures necessary to augment the Consolidated Fund os a State to suppliment the resources of the PRIs in the State. Thus, a large amount of assured funds will flow to the PRIs involvement in environment protection and improvement.

In rural India, all the life support systems are now under serious stress and strain. Both human and animal population pressures have reached a level where the flora, fauna, soil and water and also atmospheric conditions are getting more and more depleted and pollutted. Consequently, in a predominantly agricultural country, the renewable base of land resources has been eroded and environmental degradation has taken place in the name of development. The Panchayati Raj institutions have existed for long in India, but these institutions have not been effective in environment protection and improvement. Against this backdrop, the 73rd Constitution Amendment Act assumes greater importance. Now it will no more be possible for any State government to fiddle with these institutions, as has been the case in the past. The continuation of these institutions will automatically result into strengthening of both horizontal and vertical linkage with the administration at different levels. This, in turn, will provide these institutions an opportunity to play their legitimater role in environment protection and improvement. Besides this, PRIs can play an educative role in environmental matters for younger generation as well as adults, with due consideration to the underpriviledged. This is essential in order to broaden the basis for an enlightened opinion and responsible conduct by individuals, enterprises and communities in protecting and improving the environment in its full human dimension.

Global action for sustainable food security

The commitment of the international community to ensure food and nutrition security to every child, woman and man on our planet has been reiterated at several international conferences held during this decade. Some of them are:

1990	World Summit for Children, New York.
1992	International Conference on Nutrition (ICN, 1992), Rome.
1992	UN Conference on Environment & Development (UNCED, 1992), Rio de Janeiro.
1993	World Conference on Human Rights (WCHR, 1993), Vienna.
1994	International Conference on Population & Development, Cairo.
1995	UN Conference on Social Development, Copenhangen.
1996	World Food Summit, Rome.

Despite such high level political reaffirmation of the need to achieve speedily the goal of "Food for All", over 800 million human beings now suffer from hunger and malnutrition. Hidden hunger, arising from the deficiency of the essential micronutrients is widespread. Endemic hunger is now more due to the lack of adequate income at the household level than due to the lack of food in the market. Both poverty as well as non-food factors such as environmental hygiene, sanitation and lack of safe drinking water are becoming major contributors of food insecurity at the level of communities and individuals. A majority of the food insecure live in Asia.

There is also increasing concern about the earth's capacity to produce adequate food for the growing population. The increase in human population, now mostly confined to the developing countries, coupled with enhanced purchasing power leading to greater capability to buy food and increasing urbanisation will lead to a higher growth rate in demand for food as well as more diversified food products in the coming millennium. Thus, on the one hand, there will be need for intensification and diversification of agriculture, particularly in the developing countries, on the other, the ecological foundations essential for sustainable advances in crop and animal productivity are getting eroded. This situation has led to the ringing of alarm bells by experts concerning the earth's capacity to produce adequate food to meet growing needs. Lester Brown has concluded; "Constraints imposed by the earth's natural systems, the environmental degradation of land and water resources and the diminshing backlog of yield-raising agricultural technologies are slowing the growth in world food production, raising questions about the earth's population carrying capacity. The earth's capacity to produce enough food to satisfy expanding demand is now emerging as the overriding environmental issue as the world approaches the 21st Century".

The year 1998 will mark the bicentenary of Malthus's essay on population. The onward march of science and technology, supported by appropriate public policies, has so far helped humankind to keep Malthusian forebodings on the population-food supply equation at bay. It is, however, becoming increasingly clear that without concerted national and global action to arrest environmental degradation, promote economic and gender equity and check population growth, the Malthusian spectre may still come true in the next century. The Food and Agriculture Organisation of the United Nations (FAO) therefore, organised a World Food Summit in Rome from November 13 to 17, 1996.

At this Summit, a Rome Declaration on World Food Security and a World Food Summit Plan of Action were adopted.

The Declaration makes a commitment to reduce the number of undernourished people to half their present level no later than 2015. It also states:

"We will pusue participatory and sustainable food, agriculture, fisheries, forestry and rural development policies and practices in high and low potential areas which are essential to adequate and reliable food supplies".

"We will strive to ensure that food, agricultural trade and overall trade policies are conducive to fostering food security for all through a fair and market-oriented world trade system".

The Plan of Action includes the following seven commitments:

1. Create an enabling political, social and economic

environment designed to create the best conditions for the eradication of poverty, and for durable peace.

2. Implement policies aimed at eradicating poverty and inequality and improving physical and economic access to sufficient, nutritionally adequate and safe food and its effective utilization.
3. Pursue participatory and sustainable food, agriculture, fisheries, forestry and rural development policies and practices in high and low potential areas.
4. Ensure that food, agricultural trade and overall trade policies are conducive to fostering food security for all.
5. Prevent and be prepared for national disasters and man-made emergencies.
6. Promote optimal allocation and use of public and private investments to foster human resources, sustianable food agriculture, fisheries and forestry systems, and rural development, in high and low potential areas.
7. Implement, monitor and follow-up the Rome Plan of Action at all levels in cooperation with the international community.

The above plan of action integrates the principles of (a) conservation of the ecological foundations essential for sustainable advances in agricultural productivity and production, (b) sustainable production through ecotechnologies and (c) equity in acces to food through an appropriate blend of national and international action in the area of entitlements and employment. The Science Academies Summit held in Madras in July, 96, recommneded that all nations may provide an overall public policy support to action at these three levels through the enactment of a National Food and Livelihood Security Act designed to achieve the following objectives:

(i) That every individual has the physical, economic, social and enviormental access to balanced diet that includes the necessary macro-and micronutrients, safe drinking water, sanitation, environmental hygiene, primary health care and education so as to lead a healthy and productive life.

(ii) That food originates from efficient and environmentally benign production technologies that conserve and enhance the natural resource base of crops, animal husbandry, forestry, inland and marine fisheries.

Capacity-building for sustainable development

Integrating environemntal considerations into development planning is not an easy task. Unless concern is backed by an ability to take ameliorative action, little can be achieved. India has been very conscious of this and has, over the past few decades, taken important steps to increase its capacity to handle environmental issues.

The initiatives have come equally from the Government, NGO's and individuals. Many collaborative and joint programmes exist today between the Government and the NGO's.

Environment and development problems are complex and there cannot be generalized and simplified solutions. Answers have to be found which are ecologically, economically and socio-culturally consistent in the particular milieu. Given the size and diversity of a country like India, this task becomes extremely difficult.

Expertise is requied in framing appropriate policies and legislation, in planning, in creating mechanisms for implementation, in education and public awareness. India also needs to be able to bring its perspective to global forums and participate in evolving international treaties, protocols and conventions. Most importantly, with the increasing emphasis on decentralized decision—making and the stress on micro-planning, this capacity-building is taking on a greater urgency. Capability is required to enable decisions to be made in a decentralized manner—decisions which are not imported solutions, but are appropriate to the particular situation.

Government efforts

Addressing the plenary session of the UN Conference on Human Environment in Stockholm in 1972, Prime Minister Indira Gandhi and said, "Even though our industrial development is in its infancy and at its most difficult stage, we are taking various steps to deal with the incipient environmental imbalances, more so because of our concern for the human species, whic is also imperilled." It was at her initiative that a National Council Environmental Planning and Coordination (NECPC) was set up in 1972 to identify and investigate the problems of preserving or improving the human environment in the country. and to propose solution to environmental problems.

Another Empowered Committee, the Tiwari Committee, was set up in 1980 to review and recommend legislative measures and administrative machinery for ensuring environmental protection. On the recommendation of this Committee, the Department of Environment was set up in 1980 as the focal agency in the administrative structure of the Central Government for planning, promotion and coordination of environmental programmes. This department became part of the new Ministry of Environment and Forest in 1985.

The Ministry is the apex body under the Government of India for planning, promotion and coordination of environmental and forestry programmes. Its activities include conservation and survey of flora and fauna, prevention and control of pollution, afforestation and regeneration of degraded areas, impact assessment, forest conservation and research, and education and information. The National Wastelands Development Board and the Ganga Project Directorate are major components of the Ministry.

Most of the states have also set up their own Departments of Environment, Pollution Control Boards and other associated bodies. Various other ministries and departments, including those of Urban Development, Oceanography, Non-Conventional Energy Sources etc., at the state and central levels, are also concerned with different aspects of the environment. Greater coordination among these various agencies—government and non—government would strengthen environmental efforts. State Governments are in the process of involving themselves seriously in environmental planning.

Non-government efforts

The Directory of Environmental NGOs, brought out by the World Wide Fund for Nature - India (WWF-I) in 1989, lists about 850 NGOs working in this field, but there are porbably at least four times this number. Their involvement is clearly seen. As the Secretary General of WWF-I says, "India's impressively large body of NGOs is becoming active on the environmental front because fo the increasingly clear nexus between meaningful, equitable, sustainable economic growth and the conservation of the environment. For instance, the National Environmental Awareness Campaign promoted by the Ministry has successfully encouraged many NGOs whose primary concerns are rural development, appropriate technology, civil rights, women's development, tribal welfare etc. The interaction between NGOs and State Governments is largely confined to functional matters (clearance, information, advice etc.) whereas for financial and technical support various central departments and agencies have to be relied upon. However now there is a concerted effort by the Government to use their expertise for their own programmes."

The NGOs range from clubs which encourage and assist in adventure travel, exploration, and dissemination of knowledge about an ecosystem to agencies which deal with various issues like creating gainful employment, wastelands development, afforestation, rehabilitation of tribals, and with preparation of educational materials and aids. They may be as small as groups of two or three persons, or as large as organizations with an eight-thousand-strong membership.

One of the most important signs of environmental awareness in India is the rise of people's movements which are challenging existing socio-political structures and development models, and are showing alternative paths. These have led not only to action at the grassroot level, but are also helping to shape developmental policies.

ENCYCLOPAEDIA OF INDIAN GOVERNMENT: PROGRAMMES AND POLICIES

ENCYCLOPAEDIA
OF
INDIAN GOVERNMENT:
PROGRAMMES AND POLICIES

Vol. 18

Coal Industry

Edited by

Satish Tiwari

ANMOL PUBLICATIONS PVT. LTD.

NEW DELHI - 110 002 (INDIA)

ANMOL PUBLICATIONS PVT. LTD.
4374/4B, Ansari Road, Daryaganj
New Delhi - 110 002

Encyclopaedia of Indian Government: Programmes and Policies

First Edition, 2000
ISBN 81-261-0515-1 (Set)

PRINTED IN INDIA

Published by J.L. Kumar for Anmol Publications Pvt. Ltd., New Delhi - 110 002 and Printed at Mehra Offset Press, Delhi.

Contents

Preface

Encyclopaedia of Indian Government: Programmes and Policies contains authoritative information on about fifty departmental policies and their future developmental programmes.

Organised to be completed in 40 volumes, this gigantic work covers Agriculture; Atomic Energy; Chemicals and Fertilizers; Coal; Commerce; Communication; Culture; Defence; Education; Environment and Forests; External Affairs; Finance; Food & Consumer Affairs; Food Processing Industries; Health and Family Welfare; Home Affairs and Internal Security; Human Resources; Industry; Information and Broadcasting; Labour; Law, Justice and Company Affairs; Non-conventional Energy Sources; Ocean Development; Parliamentary Affairs; Personnel, Public Grievances and Pensions; Petroleum and Natural Gas; Planning and Programme Implementation; Planning and Statistics; Posts and Telegraphs; Power; Rural Development; Science and Technology; Social Justice and Empowerment; Space; States Affairs; Steel; Steel and Mines; Sugar and Edible Oils; Surface Transport; Textiles; Tourism; Urban Development; Water Resources; Women and Child development etc.

Based on the information derived from authoritative sources, this work contains authentic facts and figures. I am deeply beholden to all the scholars whose writings are cited or substantially made use of in the present work. I am also thankful to Anmol Publications Pvt. Ltd. for undertaking publication of this encyclopaedia. I am solely responsible for shortcomings in presentation of matter.

Encyclopaedic in nature, this will prove a dependable reference work for scholars and academics besides those appearing for different competitive examinations.

—**Satish Tiwari**

1

Introduction

The Ministry of Coal has the overall responsibility of determining policies and strategies in respect of exploration and development of coal and lignite reserves, sanctioning of important projects of high value and for deciding all related issues. Under the administrative control of the Ministry, these key functions are exercised through the public sector undertakings, namely, Coal India Ltd. and its subsidiaries and Neyveli Lignite corporation Limited.

Other than Coal India Ltd. and Neyveli Lignite Corporation Ltd., the Ministry of coal also acts in close association with Singareni Collieries Company Ltd. which is a joint sector undertaking of Government of Andhra Pradesh and Government of India sharing the equity capital of SCCL in the ratio of 51:49. As on 1.1.1999 the coal resources of India (down to a depth of 1200 m) have been estimated by the Geological Survey of India at 208751.50 million tonnes. Currently, lignite deposits in the country have been estimated at 29360 million tonnes, most of which, occur in Tamil Nadu. Other states where lignite deposits have been located are Rajasthan, Gujarat, Kerala, Jammu &:Kashmir and U.T. of Pondicherry.

Coal planning

During the year 1998-99, one project in the Coal Sector

was sanctioned by the Government, till 31.12.98. The details are given below:-

Name of project	Company	Capacity (mty)	Capital Cost (Rs. Crs.)
Jharkhand OC	CCL	1.00	110.89

Coal production

Coal production achieved during the year 1998-99 has been 206.31 million tonnes as compared to the production of 206.36 m.t. achieved during same period of the previous year i.e. 1997-98. Company-wise details are given below:

(In million tonnes)

Company	Target (Apr-Dec. 98)	Actual production (Apr-Dec. 98)
CIL	188.43	183.40
SCCL	21.80	18.32
Others	4.93	4.59
Total	215.16	206.31

About 88% of the total coal production in the country comes from the collieries of Coal India Ltd. CIL is also the biggest supplier of coal in the country.

Consumer satisfaction

To improve consumer satisfaction, a comprehensive Action Plan was introduced in Oct '92 to install Coal Handling Plants (CHPs) in the Subsidiaries of CIL to improve the bulk handing of coal. It was further decided to ensure that, as far as possible, all coal sale and despatches to consumers at the loading points are processed through Coal Handling Plants, Weighbridges etc. to ensure correct quality and quantity. The following table indicates companywise number of existing major CHPs as on 31/12/98 and existing operating capacities of Major CHPs as on 1/4/98, vis-a-vis 31/12/98.

Company	No. of major CHPs on (31/12/98)	Existing operating of major and mini CHPs (in MTY) on 1/4/98	Total coal handled capacity (in MTY) in1997-98 including washeries as on 31.12.98
ECL	47	23.80	23.80
CCL	21	32-35	33.25
CCL	23	37.08	36.80
NCL	8	34.70	37.20
WCL	59	35.07	35.17
SECL	54	46.57	45.57
MCL	13	3730	38.70
Total/CIL	225	247.27	250.49

The Central Government is empowered under section 4 of the Colliery control Order, 1945, as continued in force by the Essential Commodities Act, 1955 to fix the gradewise and colliery-wise price of coal. The prices of the administered grades of coal were last revised w.e.f. 17.6.94.

The price notification had been amended in December 1995, January 1996 and April 1996 to enhance the differential between run of mine, steam and slack coal, to increase the transportation charges and also to provide for additional prices for coal produced from Ramagundem OCP of SCCL and Rajmahal OCP of Eastern Coalfields Limited.

Following the recommendations of Bureau of Industrial Costs and Prices (BICP), a decision was taken by the Government to deregulate the prices of all grades of coking coal and A, B, C grades of non-coking coal and this decision was implemented with effect from 22.3.96. Subsequently in consideration of a recommendation of the Committee on Integrated Coal Policy, the Government decided the deregulate the prices of soft coke, hard coke and D grade of non-coking coal and this decision was implemented with effect from 12.3.97.

The Government also decided to allow CIL and SCCL to fix prices of E, F and G grades of non-coking coal once in every six months by updating the cost indices as per the escalation formula contained in the 1987 report of the BICP and necessary instructions to this effect were issued to CIL and SCCL on 13.3.97.

Following these instructions, CIL fixed their coal prices on 1.4.97, 1.10.97 and 21.8.98 and SCCL did so on 15.3.97 and 29.8.98. The latest average base price of CIL coal as fixed on 21.8.98 is Rs. 585.19 per tonne whereas the latest average base price of SCCL Coal as fixed as on 29.8.98 is Rs. 753.31 per tonne. After 1st January 2000, the prices of E, F and G grades of non-coking coal may be fixed by CIL and SCCL in relation with the market prices.

2

Organisation

The Ministry of Coal is responsible for development and exploitation of coal and lignite reserves in India. The subjects allocated to the Ministry under the Government of India (Allocation of Business) Rules, 1961, as amended from time to time, are as follows:

i) Exploitation and development of coking coal, non-coking coal and lignite deposits in India.

ii) All matters relating to production, supply, distribution and pricing of Coal.

iii) Development and operation of coal washeries other than those for which Ministry of Steel (Ispat Mantralaya) is responsible.

iv) Low Temperature carbonisation of coal and production of synthetic oil from Coal.

v) Administration of the Coal Mines (Conservation and Development) Act, 1974 (28 of 1974).

vi) Administration of the Coal Mines Provident Fund and Miscellaneous Provisions Act, 1948 (46 of 1948).

vii) Administration of all residual matters relating to the Coal Mines Labour Welfare Organisation since abolished with effect from 1.10.1986.

viii) Administration of the rules under the Mines Act, 1952 (32 of 1952) for levy and collection of excise duty on coke and coal produced and despatched from mines.

ix) Administration of Coal Bearing Areas (Acquisition and Development) Act, 1957 (20 of 1957).

x) Administration of Public Sector Enterprises dealing with coal and lignite.

xi) Administration of Mines and Minerals (Regulation and Development) Act, 1957 (67 of 1957) and other Union laws in so far as the said Act and other laws relating to Coal and Lignite and use of sand for stowing purposes.

xii) All business incidental to the administration of above activities including matters concerning the State Governments.

At the Secretariat level, the Ministry is headed by a Secretary who is assisted by one Additional Secretary, three Joint Secretaries (including the Financial Adviser), one Project Adviser, seven Directors/Deputy Secretaries, seven Under Secretaries, eleven Section Officers, one Desk Officer, one Asstt. Director (Official Language) and one Deputy Controller of Accounts and their supporting staff.

Coal companies

The Ministry has under its administrative control the Coal India Limited, a Public Sector Undertaking, with its 8 subsidiary companies. The Coal India Limited with its headquarters at Calcutta is the Holding company in respect of its subsidiaries. It is also the apex body in coal industry and is responsible for laying down the policy guidelines and coordination work of subsidiaries. It also does the investment, planning, manpower, management, purchase of heavy machineries, financial budgeting etc.

on behalf of all its subsidiaries. The Ministry of Coal has also under its administrative control the Neyveli Lignite Corporation (NLC) with Registered Office at Chennai and Corporate Office at Neyveli in Tamil Nadu. The Company is engaged in the exploitation of lignite deposits.

Organisations under administrative control of ministry of coal

The following subordinate offices and autonomous organisations are functioning under the administrative control of this Ministry:

i) Coal Controller's Organisation, with headquarters at Calcutta-a subordinate office.

ii) Coal Mines Provident Fund Organisation, with headquarters at Dhanbad —an autonomous organisation.

iii) Commissioner of Payments Office, with headquarters at Calcutta— a subordinate office.

Coal controller's organisation

The Coal Controller's Organisation is a subordinate office of the Ministry of Coal, having its headquarters at Calcutta and field offices at Dhanbad, Asansol, Ranchi, Sambalpur, Bilaspur, Nagpur and Delhi. The Coal Controller has various statutory functions derived under the under noted Acts and Rules:-

1. Colliery Control Order, 1945

2. Coal Mines (Conservation & Development) Act, 1974 and coal Mines (conservation & Development) Rules, 1975

3. The Collection of Statistics Act, 1953 (32 of 1953) and the Collection of Statistics (Central) Rules, 1959.

4. Coal Bearing Areas (Acquisition and Development) Act, 1957 (20 of 1957).

Apart from the above the Coal Controller has been assigned some functions under the Mines and Minerals (Regulation and Development) Act, 1957. Apart from the above statutory functions, the Coal Controller has also to discharge the following responsibilities:

(a) to look after the residual work of the World Bank Loan relating to pre-nationalisation period.

(b) to look after the residual work of the erstwhile Coal Board.

(c) to attend to legal matters/court cases arising out of the various statutes which the Coal Controller has been made responsible to administer.

Coal Controller's Organisation performed the following main functions during 1998-99 (upto Dec. 98)

Grant of permission for opening

Under clause 14 of the Colliery Control Order, 1945, the. Coal Controller granted 33 permissions for opening and reopening of seams and mines, during 1998-99 (upto Dec. 98)

Conservation and utilisation of coal

Under the guidance of Coal Conservation and Development Advisory Committee, the office of the Coal Controller carries out assessment of the actual expenditure incurred by the coal mines on the stand stowing jobs and also makes necessary recommendations to the CCDA for grant of assistance for stowing and protective work as provided under the Coal Mines (Conservation and Development) Act, 1974. Subsidy is given for road development and for scientific development work in the coal companies.

The Coal Conservation and Development Advisory Committee funds projects to study and recommend means for restoration of ecological balance in the coal mining areas. It has also been decided by the Coal Conservation and Development Advisory Committee to commission a study for minimising the bulk movement of high ash content coal by the washing of non-coking coal and transportation of washed coal to the remote parts of the country by rail-cum-sea route.

The Budget Estimates for 1998-99 is :-

	Head	Amount (Rs. In Crs.)
(a)	Stowing and Protective Works and Research and Development	60.00
(b)	Development/Construction of Roads and Rail infrastructure.	60.00
	Total	120.00

During 1998-99 (upto Dec. 98), four meetings of the Coal Conservation and Development Advisory Sub-Committee were held on 28.7.98, 29.7.98, 30.7.98 and 31.7.98 for scrutinizing the proposals/applications for various works for the year 1998-99 and also for claims of assistance for the period from October '97 to March '98.

Generally the CCDA fund is released in two spells during every financial year. The following amounts have been recommended by the Committee in their 44th Meeting held on 14.10.98 as indicated under the different heads below:—

I	Conservation	
	Protective works, water Management	Rs. 3,13,91,369
	and Bund at Medapalli	Rs.21,91,40,920
II	Road/Rail	Rs.32,48,70,000
	Total	Rs. 57,54,02,289

Road development works

The Company-wise break-up of construction/development of roads in coalfields areas for the year 1998-99 is as under:-

Sl. No.	Coal Co.	Amount Recommended (Rs. In lakhs)
1	ECL	128.42
2	BCCL	193.00
3	CCL	1175.00
4	WCL	100.00
5	NCL	160.00
6	NEC	760.00
7	SECL	542.28
8	MCL	---
9	TISCO	30.00
10	SCCL	160.00
	Total	3248.70

Cases under coal bearing areas (Acq. & dev.) act. 1957.

The receipt of Notification U/S 4(l) & 7(l) and issue of No Objection report U/S 8 of Coal Bearing Areas (A & D); Act, 1957 are indicated below:-

	Receipt of Notification	Issue of Report U/S-8
U/S-4(l)	NIL	4
U/S-7(l)	13	—

Collection of excise duty

During 1998-99 an amount of Rs. 78,66,01,393.00 was collected against Rs. 107,12,76,458.00 being the Revised Estimate.

Quality surveillance activities quality control division

The Coal Controller is authorised under the Colliery Control Order, 1945 to monitor the quality of coal despatched from collieries and settle the complaints of consumers against grading and substandard supply of Coal. Due to rising complaints on quality and related problems, Quality Control Cell was formed under the aegis of Coal Controller to undertake joint sampling and resolve disputes between suppliers and consumers of coal.

This division with its headquarters at Calcutta and 7 field offices to cover the 6 subsidiary coal producing companies and one at Delhi was set up. The break-up of this setup is as follows:—

1. Asansol — Collieries under ECL
2. Dhanbad — Collieries under BCCL
3. Ranchi — Collieries under CCL.
4. Sambalpur — Collieries under MCL.
5. Bilaspur — Collieries under SECL.
6. Nagpur — Collieries under WCL.
7. New Delhi — Inspection of coal for Northern India consumers, especially, power houses.

Each of the field offices is headed by one CGM/GM level executive working in the capacity of OSD. Each of these field offices is supported by the compliment of junior level executives and technical staff.

The total strength of this setup is 407 consisting of 56 executives and 351 non-executives, technical and nontechnical staff. The field office at Singrauli (NCL) stopped functioning since December, 1997. The performance of Quality Control Cell during the year 1998-99 is given below:

	Percentage coverage of sampling		
Company	Power	Others	Totals
ECL	53.08	9.71	43.77
BCCL	93.75	6.87	43.35
CCL	74.34	10.72	58.67
SECL	43.18	14.86	38.94
MCL	48.73	5.48	37.68
WCL	69.59	8.53	58.33
Overall	57.75	8.81	45.41

Sampling activity

Company	No. of Samples Drawn/analysed	No. of sample conforming Decl. Grade	% Conformance to be Decl. Grade
ECL	5816	5004	86.04
BCCL	4943	2868	58.02
CCL	4252	3026	71.17
SECL	6591	4503	68.32
MCL	3309	2664	80.51
WCL	6925	4768	68.85
Total	31836	22833	71.72

Inspections

Company	No. of memos issued	No. of collieries needing Spl. care	No. of collieries needing grade revision
ECL	332	3	1
BCCL	106	10	3
CCL	418	2	1
SECL	148	2	2
MCL	3362	Nil	Nil
WCL	60	1	1
Total	4426	18	8

Statutory Complaints

Company	No. Received	No. Disposed of	Nos. under investigation
ECL	NIL	NIL	NIL
BCCL	3	2	1
CCL	3	3	NIL
SECL	5	NIL	5
MCL	NIL	NIL	NIL
WCL	1	I	NIL

Coal mines provident fund organisation

The Coal Mines Provident Fund Organisation is an autonomous body established under the Coal Mines Provident Fund and Miscellaneous Provisions Act, 1948 and is responsible for administering the Coal Mines

Provident Fund Scheme, 1948, Coal Mines Deposit Linked Insurance Scheme, 1976, and Coal Mines Pension Scheme, 1998.

These three schemes are administered by a Tripartite Board of Trustees, consisting of Govt's representatives, employers' representative and employees representatives. CMPF Organisation has 23 Regional Offices and its headquarters is at Dhanbad (Bihar). The sanctioned establishment of the organisation now consists of 71 officers and 1532 staff.

Coal mines provident fund scheme

During the year 1998-99 (upto Dec.'98), the total number of units covered stood at 965 excluding coke plants operating in Private Sector. During 1998-99 (upto December '98), 4492 persons were enrolled as new members of the Fund, while the exit was 20,337. The number of live subscribers of the Fund stood at 7,79,354 at the end of December '98.

During 1998-99 (upto December '98) Provident Fund contributions including voluntary contributions amounting to Rs. 608.22 crores were received in the Coal Mines Provident Fund raising the total contributions received to Rs. 8242.40 crores. The net accretion by way of contribution and interest there on less refund and advances upto December'98 amounted to Rs. 12988.54 crores, which, however does not include interest on investment.

The entire accumulation in the fund are invested in accordance with the guidelines laid down by the Ministry of Finance. The total face value of the Fund's investment upto December '98 stood at Rs. 13,434.21 crores. During 1998-99 interest has been allowed on members' accumulation at the rate of 12%.

Refund from Provident Fund during 1998-99(upto Dec'98) together with the advances paid are indicated below:-

	No. of claims settled	Amount paid (Rs. In crores)
Refund of provident fund	20,337	449.92
Marriage advance	17,884	60.84
Education advance	217	0.35
House building advance	5,409	34.59

The cost of administration of CMPF Scheme is met out of the Administrative Charge 3% paid by the Coal companies.

Coal mines deposit linked insurance scheme

In the event of death of an employee in harness who was a member of Coal Mines Provident fund, his/her nominee is entitled to receive in addition to the Provident Fund, an amount equal to the average balance, in the account of the deceased during the preceding 3 years, subject to a maximum of Rs. 10,000/-

In accordance with the Scheme, the employers are required to contribute at the rate of 0.5% of the aggregate wages of covered workers. The Central Government is also required to pay half of the amount contributed by the employers under the scheme. During 1998-99 (upto December '98), employer's contributed a sum of Rs. 0.83 crores on this account.

During 1998-99 (upto December'98) an amount of Rs. 20,000 was paid as Deposit Linked Insurance Benefit in the cases of 2 deceased employees. For meeting the cost of administration of this scheme, employers contribute @ 0.1 % of aggregate wages and the Central Government contributes 50% thereof.

Coal mines pension scheme, 1998

One of the most important landmarks in the history of Coal Mines Provident Fund Organisation was the introduction of Coal Mines Pension Scheme, 1998 notified by the Central Government on 5th March, 1998.

In exercise of the powers conferred by Section 3E of the Coal Mines Provident Fund and Miscellaneous Provisions Act, 1948 (46 of 1948) and in supersession of the Coal Mines Family Pension Scheme, 1971, the Central Government has framed the Coal Mines Pension Scheme, 1998. The Coal Mines Pension Scheme has come into force with effect from the 31th day of March, 1998 and on that day its members were 7,82,578 coal workers, working in different coal Mines within the Country. The highlights of the Scheme are:-

Corpus of the fund and its sustainability:—

The Pension Fund consists of the following:

(a) net assets of the Coal Mines Family Pension Scheme, 1971 as on the appointed day;

(b) an amount equivalent to two and one-third percent of the salary of the employee, being the aggregate of equal shares of the employee and the employer from their respective contributions to the Fund, to be transferred from the appointed day from the Fund of employee;

(c) an amount equivalent to two percent of the salary of the employee from the first day of April, 1989 or the date of joining, whichever is later, upto the 31th day of March, 1996 and two percent of the notional salary of the employee from the 1st day of April, 1996 or the date of joining, whichever is later, to be transferred from his salary;

(d) an amount equivalent to one increment to be calculated on the basis of the salary of the employee as on the first day of July, 1995 or the date of joining, whichever is later, to be transferred from the first day of July, 1995 or the date of joining, whichever is later, from the salary of the employee;

(e) an amount equivalent to one and two-third percent of the salary of the employee to be contributed by the Central Government from the appointed day; Provided that in the case of an employee whose salary exceeds rupees and thousand six hundred per month, the contribution payable by the Central Government shall be equal to the maximum of the amount payable on the salary of rupees one thousand six hundred per month only;

(f) amounts to be deposited by new optees in terms of the provisions of the Scheme.

In 1998-99 (upto Dec '98) Rs. 142.20 crores was diverted to Pension from Provident Fund. Net accretion in the Pension Fund as on 31.12.98 (without Government Shares and interest) is Rs. 1623.40 crores. The Commissioner shall be responsible for valuation of the Pension Fund every third year by an Actuary to be appointed by the Board of Trustees.

Coverage

(a) All employees who are members of the ceased Coal Mines Family Pension Scheme, 1971 and are on rolls on 31st March, 1998.

(b) All such employees who are appointed on or after 31st March, 1998.

(c) All such optee members who opted for membership of the Pension Fund in Form PS- I and PS-2 as the case may be.

Benefits

(a) Monthly Pension.

(b) Disablement Pension.

(c) Monthly widow or widower pension.

(d) Children Pension.

(e) Orphan Pension

(f) Exgratia Payment.

During 1998-99, 1217 claims have been settled and Rs. 11.79 crores disbursed.

Commissioner of payment

The office of Commissioner of Payments was setup in pursuance of the Coking Coal Mines (Nationalisation) Act, 1972 and the Coal Mines (Nationalisation) Act, 1973 for the purpose of disbursement of amounts payable to owners of coal mines or group of coal mines nationalised in 1972-71.

Initially, there were two offices of Commissioner of Payments, one for determining compensation etc. for nationalised coking coal mines and coke over plants with headquarters at Dhanbad and another for nationalised non-coking coal mines with headquarters at Calcutta. After the work of Dhanbad Office had been disposed of substantially, that office was wound up and its residual works were transferred to the office of the Commissioner of Payments, Calcutta.

3

Coal Companies

The Coking Coal Mines Ordinance was promulgated by the Government of India on 16.10.1971 under which except the captive mines of TISCO and IISCO, the management of all coking coal mines was taken over by the Government. A new company called Bharat Coking Coal Limited was formed as a subsidiary company of Steel Authority of India Limited to mange the taken over mines. These mines were subsequently nationalised w.e.f. 1.5.1972.

Later on the management of 711 coal mines was also taken over by the Government with effect from 31.1.1973 and they were nationalised w.e.f. 1.5.1973 and a new Government Company namely Coal Mines Authority Limited (CMAL) with headquarters at Calcutta, was set up by the Government in May, 1973 to manage noncoking coal mines. The CMAL was organised as a unitary structure on divisional pattern with four Divisions, the Central Division, the Eastern Division, the Western Division and the CMPDIL.

The mines of erstwhile National Coal Development Corporation were brought under the Central Division of the CMAL. In September, 1975 CIL was formed as a Holding Company with five subsidiaries namely Bharat Coking Coal Limited (BCCL), Central Coalfields Limited(CCL),Eastern Coalfields Limited (ECL),

Western Coalfields Limited (WCL) and Central Mine Planning and Design Institute Limited (CMPDIL). In view of the projected increase in production and investment contemplated for CCL and WCL group of coal mines and in view of their extensive geographical spread resulting in day to day administrative, technical and communication problems etc. two more coal companies, namely, Northern Coalfields Limited and South Eastern Coalfields Limited were formed w.e.f. 28.11.1985.

Considering the prospects of Orissa Coalfields, being the growth centre for the VIII and IX Plan periods, a new coal company was formed bifurcating South Eastern Coalfields Limited (SECL). The new company Mahanadi Coalfields Limited was incorporated on 3rd April, 1992 with its headquarters at Sambalpur (Orissa) as fully owned subsidiary of Coal India to manage the Talcher and IB-Valley Coalfields in Orissa.

CIL have now 8 subsidiaries viz. Bharat Coking Coal Limited (BCCL), Central Coalfields Limited (CCL), Eastern Coalfields Limited (ECL), Western Coalfields Limited (WCL), South Eastern Coalfields Limited (SECL), Northern Coalfields Limited (NCL), Mahanadi Coalfields Limited (MCL) and Central Mine Planning and Design Institute Limited (CMPDIL).

The CMPDIL is an engineering, design and exploration company set up for preparing perspective plan(s), rendering consultancy services and undertaking exploration and drilling work to establish coal reserves in the country and collection of detailed data for preparation of projects for actual mining. The other seven subsidiaries of CIL are coal producing companies.

CIL and its subsidiaries are incorporated under the Companies Act, 1956 and are wholly owned by the Central Government. The coal mines in Assam and its neighbouring areas are controlled directly by CIL under the unit North Eastern Coalfields. In addition to CIL and its subsidiaries there is another Coal Company in Public Sector namely SCCL, which is a joint venture of Government of Andhra Pradesh and Government of India sharing SCCL's equity capital in the ratio of 51:49.

Coal India Limited

CIL the holding Company with headquarters at Calcutta, is headed by a Chairman-cum-Managing Director in schedule 'A' scale of pay who is assisted by three Functional Directors, namely Director (Technical), Director (Personnel and Industrial Relations) and Director (Finance) who are all in Schedule 'B' scale of pay. Each Subsidiary Company has its own Board of Directors headed by a Chairman-cum-Managing Director in schedule 'B' scale of pay. In addition, there-are four functional Directors (in schedule 'C' scale of pay) in each of the six production companies of BCCL, ECL, CCL, NCL, SECL and WCL viz. Director (Personnel), Director (Finance), Director (Planning and Projects) and Director (Technical).

In MCL there are at present three posts of functional Director namely Director (Technical), Director (Personnel) and Director (Finance). CMPDIL also has four functional Directors on its Board of Directors who are designated as Director (Technical), director (Coal Production and Utilisation), Director (Planning and Design) and Director (Research, Development and Technology).

In addition, there are several part-time or nominee directors on the Board of CIL and its subsidiaries who are appointed in accordance with the Articles of Association of the Company and Government guidelines prescribed in this behalf from time to time. The authorised share capital of CIL as on 31.3.98 was Rs. 8,904.18 crores divided into:

i) 90,41,800 Non-cumulative 10% redeemable preference shares of Rs. 1000/- each — Rs. 904.18 crores

ii) 8,00,00,000 Equity Shares of — Rs. 1000/0 EACH

Rs. 8000.00 crores

Total — Rs. 8904.18 crores

The paid-up capital of CIL as on 31.3.98 was Rs. 7220.54 crores comprising of Rs. 904.18 crores of Non-cumulative 10% redeemable preference share capital and Rs. 6316.36 crores of Equity Capital issued to the Government of India, including Rs. 256.93 crores worth of Equity Shares issued to the Government of India towards the value of land acquired. The authorised share capital of the subsidiary companies of CIL as on 31.3.98 is given below:—

Subsidiary company	Authorised Share Capital Rs in crores
Bharat Coking Coal Limited	2500.00
Western Coalfields Limited	800.00
Central Coalfields Limited	1100.00
Eastern Coalfields Limited	2500.00
Northern Coalfields Limited	1400.00
South Eastern Coalfields Limited	1300.00
Mahanadi Coalfields Limited	500.00
Central Mine Planning and Design Institute Limited	50.00

CIL is mainly responsible for laying down corporate objectives, approving and monitoring performance of subsidiary companies in the fields of long-term planning, conservation, research and development, production, sales, finances, recruitment commissioning and execution of new as well as on going projects, man management, production, consumer satisfaction etc. In addition, subsidiary companies perform related functions, such as maintaining liaison with concerned State Governments, acquisition of land, execution of welfare programmes, maintenance of safety standards, improvement of industrial relation etc. In addition to the above functions, CIL has directly under its control the development and exploitation of the coal mines in the North-Eastern states, and the coal marketing network spread throughout the country.

Working results of coal India Ltd. for the year 1996-97

CIL and its Subsidiaries have earned a pre-tax profit of Rs. 1803.99 Crores in the year 1997-98 against Rs. 1137.42 Crores for the year 1996-97. Company-wise position is shown below:

Company	1997-98 Profit (+)/Loss(-)	1996-97 Profit +)/Loss(-) (Rs. in crores)	
ECL	(–) 541.89	(–)	341.15
BCCL	(–) 140.91	(–)	322.81
CCL	(–) 85.67	(+)	15.52
NCL	(+) 759.34	(+)	728.65
WCL	(+) 628.29	(+)	525.21
SECL	(+) 693.20	(+)	580.72
MCL	(+) 654.11	(+)	326.65
CMPDIL	(+) 3.30	(+)	2.91
CIL	(+) 540.82	(+)	442.06

The profit figure of the subsidiary companies for the year 1997-98 as shown in the table above are before dividend payments. In case of CIL the profit of Rs. 540.82 Crores includes income of Rs. 706.60 Crores from dividend received from subsidiaries. The profit figure of the subsidiary companies for the year 1996-97 as shown in the table above are before dividend payment. In case of CIL the profit of Rs. 442.06 Crores includes income of Rs. 789.30 Crores from dividend received from subsidiaries. The Company-wise dividend provided by the subsidiaries and included in the Accounts of CIL for the year 97-98 are as follows:

Company	Rs. in Crores
NCL	196.68
WCL	153.65
SECL	185.30
MCL	170.97
Total	706.60

In the last hearing of BIFR held on 22.12.97, the financial position and the trend of physical performance were submitted by BCCL. Taking note of the fact that net worth of the Company had become positive and there was significant all-round improvement in the performance achieved by the company, the Bench agreed to take BCCL out of BIFR.

The Bench, however, observed that, as the accumulated loss of the Company was still more than 50% if its enhanced paid up share capital and the company continued to make losses, BCCL would continue to be under watch by BIFR under section 23 of SICA. In pursuance thereof, the company is required to send a progress report to BIFR. In compliance with Section 23 (1) of the Sick Industrial Companies Act, 1985 ECL had sent form CC, duly filled in, alongwith necessary enclosures to the Secretary, BIFR on 23rd November, 1995.

Subsequently, as a result of networth becoming negative a reference was made to BIFR as per the requirement of Section 15 (1) of SICA on 26th November, 1997. ECL continued to be a Sick Industrial Company during the financial year 1997-98, till the restructuring of capital by conversion of debt of Rs. 1179.45 Crores into equity was made effective on 31.3.98. On consideration of the facts of the case and submissions made during the hearing on I June, 1998, the Bench noted that the Networth of ECL has rendered positive and the Company was no longer a Sick Industrial Company as per the provisions of the Act.

Central Mine Planing Design Institute Limited (CMPDIL)

Central Mine Planning and Design Institute Limited, a subsidiary of Coal India Limited is engaged in the work of exploration, project planning, detailed designing of system and subsystems, coordination and integration of applied research and development, absorption of new techniques of coal mining, beneficiation and utilisation of coal, perspective planning and demand assessment and caters to the total planning and designing needs of new coal projects and reorganisation of existing mines for optimal production of coal.

The company headquarters is located at Ranchi. It has its Regional Institutes located at Asansol, Dhanbad, Ranchi, Nagpur, Bilaspur, Singrauli and Bhubaneshwar to render doorstep service to the coal producing companies located in these areas. In addition, one more Regional Institute was opened on 24th January, 1992 at Tura (Meghalaya) to render services to Meghalaya, Arunachal Pradesh, Nagaland and Assam.

Consultancy service outside CIL

In addition to satisfying the planning requirement of CIL and its subsidiary companies, CMPDIL is also offering expert consultancy services to CIL as well as outside organisations. During the year 1997-98, expert consultancy services were provided to CIL and its subsidiary companies in the field of Environmental Management and Monitoring, Remote Sensing, Energy Audit, Physico-mechanical Test on Rock and Coal Samples, Subsidence Studies, Strata Control, Non Destructive Testing (NDT), Controlled Blasting, Vibration Studies and Explosives Utilisation, Mining Electronics etc.

Consultancy services outside CIL

During the year 1997-98, 13 outside jobs were completed for 13 organisations. Some of the important clients/ organisations to whom services were provided are,

Associated Cement Companies Ltd. U.P. Bhumi Sudhar Nigam Ltd. The Indian Iron and Steel Co. Ltd. Tamil Nadu Electricity Board, Metallurgical and Engineering Consultants (India) Ltd. etc.

Presently, 23 outside consultancy jobs are in hand for 21 organisations like Madhya Pradesh electricity Board, Punjab State Electricity Board, the Singareni Collieries Co. Ltd., Directorate General of Hydrocarbons (under Ministry of Petroleum & Natural Gas), Steel Authority of India Ltd., Meghalaya Industrial Development Corporation Ltd., Tata Iron and Steel Co. Ltd. etc. In addition to above, assistance was also provided to private entrepreneurs for preparing project report and rendering technical know-how for special smokeless fuel plants. The major achievements in international consultancy efforts during the year 1997-98 are as follows:

i) In terms of agreement signed with M/s. National Development Corporation Tanzania, the financial feasibility report for the mines, the power plants, and the EIA report were submitted in July, 1997. The client approved the report in October, 1997.

ii) As a part the implementation of a research programme for an environment friendly Coal Utilisation System in India, in cooperation with an organisation namely Centre for Coal Utilisation, Japan and CMPDIL entered into an agreement on 6th February, 1998. Site Survey and visits to related authorities/plants were completed by CCUJ and CMPDI in February, 1998. The final report was submitted by CMPDI in April, 1998 to the complete satisfaction of the client.

iii) CMPDI alongwith Montan Consulting, Germany was awarded a project on "Implementation of Clean Coal Technology through coal beneficiation" funded by

Asian Development Bank (ADB). Based on the discussions held at ADB, Manila in May, 1997 on the Draft final report, necessary modifications were carried out in the CMPDI portion of the report and' submitted in August, 1997 to Montan for compilation and submission to ADB.

iv) In its bid to internationalise its activities, CMPDI has signed Memorandum of Understanding with M/s. DMT, Germany during the year for undertaking joint consultancy work abroad.

Bharat Coking Limited (BCCL)

The Company has its headquarters at Dhanbad in Bihar. It had under its charge nationalised Coking Coal Mines and two mines namely Moonidih and Sudamdih transferred to it from the erstwhile National Coal Development Corporation Ltd. All these mines were reorganised into units/areas for administrative and operational convenience.

BCCL is the major producer of prime coking coal. Medium coking coal is also produced in its mines in Mohuda and Barakar areas. In addition to production of hard coke and soft coke, BCCL operates a number of sand gathering plants, a network of aerial ropeways for transport of sand, and nine Coal Washeries, namely Dugda - I, Dugda - II, Bhojudih, Patherdih, Lodna, sudamdih, Bakora, Moonidih and Rohula.

BCCL was referred to the Board for Industrial and Financial Reconstruction (BIFR) on 23.11.95 under section 15 of the Sick Industrial Companies (Special provisions) Act, 1985, as it had become sick within the meaning of the said Act. The networth of the company had become negative. A revival package for revival of the company was submitted to the BIFR for their consideration and decided to review the performance of the company in May, 1997.

The performance of BCCL was again reviewed by the BIFR in August, 1997. Finding the networth of BCCL positive following an internal exercise of capital restructuring among CIL subsidiaries, BCCL was taken out of the proceedings of BIFR. This decision was taken in the hearing before the BIFR on 22.12.97.

Southern East Coal Limited (SECL)

South Eastern Coalfields Ltd. with headquarters at Bilaspur (MP) was incorporated under the Companies Act, 1956 on 28.11.1985 but for accounting purposes, it started functioning independently from 1.4.86. The Company covers Korba (East), Korba (west), Baikunthpur, Chirimiri, Hasdeo, Sohagpur, Jamnuna-Kotma and Johilla areas in Madhya Pradesh. Despite separation of coalfields in Orissa from its jurisdiction, SECL continues to be one of the leading coal producers among the subsidiaries of CIL.

Western Coalfield Limited (WCL)

This company has its headquarters at Nagpur (Maharashtra). It covers at present all the coalfields in Maharashtra and the three coalfields namely Kanhan, Pench and Patharkheda in Madhya Pradesh. WCL meets to a large extent, the requirement of industries and power stations in western region of the country.

Eastern Coalfields Limited (ECL)

The company has its headquarters at Sanctoria in West Bengal. It covers the Ranigan coalfield in West Bengal and Mugma and Rajmahal coalfields in Bihar. This company produces coal to meet requirements of loco and other industries which require relatively higher grades of coal. ECL was referred to the BIFR on 23.11.95 under section 23 of the Sick Industrial Companies (Special Provisions) Act, 1985 as more than 50% of its net worth was eroded.

However, it was not registered as a sick company by the BIFR. At the end of the financial year 1996-97, the networth of the company again became negative and it was referred to the BIFR, as a sick industrial company. The BIFR heard the ECL case on 1.6.98 for determination of its sickness. However in hearing, BIFR did not register ECL as a sick company considering the fact that its net worth became positive following the capital restructuring exercise of CIL.

Central Coalfield Limited (CCL)

This company has its headquarters at Ranchi in Bihar and covers Bokaro, Ramgarh, Giridih, North and South Karanpura coalfields of Bihar. Apart from several nationalised mines, it owns most of the mines of former National Coal Development Corporation Ltd. The company produces medium coking coal (raw and washed), noncoking coal, soft coke and hard coke.

Northern Coalfield Limited (NCL)

Northern Coalfields Limited with headquarters at Singrauli (M.P.) covers the entire Singrauli Coalfields situated in the two states of Uttar Pradesh and Madhya Pradesh. The company was incorporated under the Companies Act, 1956 on 28.11.1985; but for accounting purposes, it started functioning independently from 1.4.1986 only.

Mahanadi Coalfields Limited (MCL)

Mahanadi Coalfields Limited with its headquarters at Sambalpur, was incorporated under the Companies Act, 1956 as another subsidiary compan y of CIL on 3.4.1992. Its areas of jurisdiction comprise Talcher and IB valley coalfields in Orissa.

North Eastern Coalfields (NEC)

North Eastern Coalfields, with its headquarters at Margherita is a unit directly controlled by CIL and is responsible for development and production of coal in the North Eastern States. The present mining activities are confined to Assam and Meghalaya. The area has large proven reserves of low ash, high calorific value coal but its high sulphur content prevents its coal to be used directly as metallurgical coal.

Singareni Collieries Company Limited (SCCL)

SCCL is a joint undertaking of Government of Andhra Pradesh and the Government of India. The equity capital is shared in the ration of 51 : 49 between Government of Andhra Pradesh and the Central Government respectively, The Headquarters of the company is at Kothagudem in Andhra Pradesh. In 1994, SCCL was under reference to the BIFR as a sick industrial company within the meaning of section 3(1) (0) of the Sick Industrial Companies (Special Provisions) Act, 1985. A turnaround package for rehabilitation of SCCL approved by the Government of India in consultation with Government of Andhra Pradesh and the company, was submitted to the BIFR.

Following this, the BIFR vide its order dated 10.1.95 decided that it was no longer necessary to pursue the case of the company under the provisions of the Sick Industrial Companies Act, 198 ember 1996 the company was referred to BIFR as a potentially sick company under the above cited provision of the Act.

Though the accumulated losses of SCCL have now marginally been reduced, about 85% of the company's equity has been eroded. A capital restructuring package for improving the financial and operative performance of the company is under consideration of the Government.

Details of coal mines in coal companies

The Company-wise details of working mines in CIL, SCCL and other companies in the country alongwith the number of mines closed since nationalisation are given below:

Company	Number of working mines	Number of mines closed since nationalisation
ECL	120	57
BCCL	89	16
CCL	68	13
NCL	09	01
WCL	90	38
SECL	95	17
MCL	22	--
NEC	07	-
CIL (Total)	500	142
SCCL	70	11
TISCO	8	--
IISCO	3	--
DVC	1	--
Bihar State Mineral Development Corporation Ltd.	1	--
J & K Minerals Ltd.	4	--
Bengal Emta Coal Mines Ltd.	1	--
Total	588	153

Captive coal mining

Considering the need to augment thermal power generation and to create additional thermal power capacity during the VIII Plan period, the Government decided to allow private participation in the power sector. The Coal Mines (Nationalisation) Act, 1973 was amended with effect from 9th June, 1993 to allow coal for captive consumption for generation of power, washing of coal obtained from a mine and other end uses to be notified by Government from time to time in addition to the existing provision for captive coal mining for production of iron and steel. The amendment was carried out in Sec. 3(3)(a)(iii) of the 1973, Act by a Gazette

Notification dated 9.6.93. Under this amendment, another Gazette Notification has been issued on 15.3.96 to allow production of cement as an end use for captive mining of coal.

The June, 1993 amendment to the act as well as the Gazette notification of 15.3.96 apply to both the public sector and private sector companies desiring to mine coal for captive consumption. The restriction of captive mining does not apply to the state-owned coal mineral development Undertakings like CIL, SCCL. Neyveli Lignite Corporation and Mineral Development Corporation of the State Government. One hundred and Five Captive Mining Blocks (105) in the command area of CIL with an estimated reserve of 27563 million tonnes have been identified for Captive Mining.

4

Coal Exploration

Exploration of coal reserves

Exploration of coal reserves in the country is carried out in two stages. In the first stage, Geological Survey of India (GSI) undertakes Regional Exploration for locating potential coal bearing areas on a continuous basis. In order to supplement the efforts of Regional Exploration, services of GSI and Mineral Exploration Corporation (MECL) have also been engaged for carrying out Promotional Regional Exploration.

In the second stage, Detailed Exploration is carried out. Central Mine Planning and Design Institute Ltd. (CMPDI) directly as well as through Mineral Exploration Corporation., State Govts. and private agencies carry out detailed exploration, for the purpose of mine planning and exploitation of coal reserves for meeting the demand of different sectors of the economy.

The detailed exploration in the command area of SCCL is carried out departmentally. Priorities of various projects/blocks, taken up for Detailed Exploration, are decided taking into account factors like emerging demand and its location, availability of infrastructure for coal evacuation and techno-economics of the mine development including coal quality. Coal Companies of Coal India Ltd. (CIL) and CMPDI have identified blocks proposed to be retained by CIL to sustain a production level during 2006-07 (final year of X plan) for another 30 years i.e. upto 2036-37. These blocks retained by CIL are termed as CIL blocks. All other blocks which have not been retained by CIL are termed as Non-CIL blocks. A study was carried out to assess the total requirement of detailed drilling in non-CIL blocks. A document titled Perspective Plan for Exploration for IX Plan in Non-CIL Blocks Under the Command Areas of Coal India Ltd. was prepared in December, 1997 The detailed drilling in Non-CIL blocks by CMPDI and MECL is in progress as per the approved programme of 98-99.

An exercise has also been carried out to assess the total requirement of drilling in CIL blocks. A perspective plan titled "Perspective Plan of Detailed Exploration in CIL Blocks for IX Plan" has been prepared by CMPDI in June 98.

Coal resources of India

As on 1.1.1999, the coal resources of India (upto the depth of 1200m) have been estimated by the Geological Survey of India at 2,08,751.50 in tonnes. The state-wise distribution of coal reserves is given in the table.

(In Million Tonnes)

States	Proved	Indicated	Inferred	Total
Andhra Pradesh	7,094.82	3,313.78	2,928.67	13,337.27
Arunachal Pradesh	31.23	11.04	47.96	90.23
Assam	259.37	26.83	34.01	320.21
Bihar	34,401	28,420.83	5,934.77	68,756.60
Madhya Pradesh	12,502.72	21,795.24	8,474.47	42,772.43
Maharashtra	3,927.53	1,357.37	1,684.17	6,969.07
Meghalaya	117.83	40.89	300.71	459.43
Nagaland	3.43	1.35	15.16	19.94
Orissa	9,623.1	21,990.91	17,447.19	49,061.20
Uttar Pradesh	574.8	487	0	1,061.8
West Bengal	10,570.36	10,981.29	4,352.06	25,903.71
Total Coal	79,106.19	88,426.53	41,219.17	208,751.89

Categorisation of reserves

Reserves have been categorised as under:

(In Million Tonnes)

Type of Coal	Proved	Indicated	Inferred	Total
Gondwana Coals	78,694.33	88,349.21	40,821.33	207,864.87
Tertiary Coals	411.86	77.32	397.84	887.02
Total	79,106.19	88,426.53	41,219.17	208,751.89
Coking				
Prime Coking	4,614.35	698.71		5,313.06
Medium Coking	11,250.53	10,692.09	1,214.91	23,157.53
Blendable/ Semi-Coking	482.16	904.04	221.68	1,607.88
Sub-Total (Coking)	16,347.04	12,294.84	1,436.59	30,078.47
Non-Coking	62,759.15	76,131.69	39,782.58	178,673.42
Total	79,106.19	88,426.53	41,219.17	208,751.89

Exploration activities

CMPDI continued its detailed exploration programme during '98-99 for providing exploratory and production support drilling in view of the increasing, demand projection for coal. The main emphasis has been on proving high grade, power grade and metallurgical grade coal resources for Xth and subsequent plan periods. For the purpose of Detailed Exploration, CMPDI has deployed, besides its own drilling resources, the resources of MECL, State Govts. of M.P. and Orissa and of private agencies. The monthly average number of drills deployed by all agencies during the period April to December, 1998 was 83 to 85. The detailed exploration activities were conducted in 115 blocks spread over 23 coalfields in the states of Assam, West Bengal, Bihar, M.P., Maharashtra and Orissa.

Drilling

During the period April to December 1998, a total of 1,96,739m of drilling has been carried out for detailed coal exploration. Agency-wise drilling performance during the period under review has been given below:

Agency-wise drilling achievements during April to December 1998

Agency	Annual target	Achieved April-Dec. 1998	Av. no. of drills operated	Productivity (m/dr/mth)	%Achieved against annual target
CMPDI	192,000	135,638	46 - 48	327	70.64
MECL	62,500	53,780.95	26	227	86.05
State Govts.					
M. P.	5,000	4,870.48	8	65	97.41
Orissa	5,000	1,960.80	1	163	39.22
Pvt. Parties	1,500	488.5	2	33	32.57
Total	2,66,000	196,738.73	83. 85	261	73.96

During the period under report, CMPDI drills have recorded a productivity of 327 per month for all metre per drill per month. The overall productivity per drill agencies has been 261 m as against 223m achieved during last year. Coal Company command area wise and agency wise details of drilling for detailed coal exploration for April to December 1998 are given in the table below:

Agency/coal Company 1998-99	Annual Target (m)	Achievements in April-Dec '98 (m)	% Achievement against Annual Target
CMPDI			
RI-I/ECL	26,500	18,788.70	70.90
RI-III/CCL	35,000	24,684.55	70.53
RI-IV/WCL	35,500	24,717.00	69.63
RI-V/SECL	49,000	36,462.80	74.41
RI-VI/NCL	11,500	7,226.00	62.83
RI-VII/MCL	34,500	23,758.95	68.87
Total	192,000	135,638.00	70.64
MECL			
RI-I/ECL	12,000	8,209.20	68,41
RI-III/CCL	6,500	8,858.00	136.28
RI-IV/WCL	21,000	12,259.20	58.38
RI-V/SECL	23,000	24,454.55	106.32
Total	62,500	53,780.95	36.05

Agency/coal company	Annual target (m) 1998-99	Achievements in April-Dec. '98 (m)	%Achievement against annual target
State Govt.			
DGM, MP/SECL			
RI-V/SECL	5,000	4, 870.48	97. 41
DGM Orissa/MCL			
RI-VII/MCL	5, 000	1,960.80	39.22
Total	10,000	6,831.28	68.31
Pvt. Parties			
NECF	1,500	488.50	32.57
Grand total	266,000	196,738.73	73.96

Drilling in Non-CIL Blocks : Out of the total 2,66,000 m of drilling proposed for 1998-99, 37,500 m will be drilled in Non-CIL blocks (19000 m by CMPDI and 18,500 m by MECL). The agencywise and Coal Company command area wise drilling carried out during April to December 1998 is given below: Table: agency and company command areawise drilling in non-CIL blocks during April to December, 1998

Agency	RI/Company command area	Annual target 1998-99 (m) Dec. 1998 (m)	Achievement April to	Achieve ment against annual target
CMPDI	RI-III/CCL	9,000	10,066	111.84
	RI-VII/MCL	10,000	5,784	57.84
CMPDI Total		19,000	15,850	83.42
MECL	RI-I/ECL	12,000	8,209	68.41
	RI-III/CCL	6,500	5,002	76.95
MECL Total		18,500	13,211	71.41
Grand total		37,500	29,061	77.50

Apart from detailed exploratory drilling, CMPDI has carried out 12,416 m of noncoring blast hole drilling for production support work in CCL area.

The SCCL continued its detailed exploration in 7 blocks during the year 1998-99. Production support drilling work, and generation of additional subsurface data for the Longwall projects have also been taken up. The MECL has carried out their promotional drilling activity in 5 sectors. Progress is low due to acute shortage of essential items. In addition, delay in clearance of permission to drill in the forest areas and remoteness of the area of operations with inadequate transport facilities and sensitive law and order situation are the main constraints, Heavy monsoon during the period also hampered the progress.

New exploration camp

During the period April to December 1998, CMPDI has increased the installed capacity from 45 to 48 operating drills. A new exploration camp named Utkal has been established in Talcher coalfield with one operational drill and the capacity of the camps at Bisrampur and Amadand (Sohagpur Coalfield) has been enhanced by adding one drill each from April/June 1998.

Geophysical surveys

Geophysical logging: During the period under report following tasks have been completed in different Coalfields in the command area of ECL, CCL, WCL, SECL and MCL:

Total no. of boreholes logged	91
Total depth logged	21296 meter
Total no. of loggers deployed	6

Surface Geophysical Surveys have been carried out in different Coalfields of ECL, BCCL, CCL, WCL, SECL and MCL as detailed below:

i) Resistivity profiling : 3 5.13 line km

ii) Vertical Electrical Sounding (Resistivity) : 24 nos.

iii) Seismic Refraction Survey :6.85 line km.

iv) HRSS Survey :8 line km

v) Magnetic Survey :12.2 line Km

A total of 15 geophysical reports were submitted upto December '98.

S&T project: The In-seam seismic survey equipment was received in March '97 and inspection of the equipment was carried out. The equipment was tested by CMRI for intrinsic safety to work in underground mines. The test report of CMRI was sent to DGMS for clearance. Some clarifications were bought by DGMS which was submitted and an Interim approval for field trial was obtained in March '98.

Meanwhile data processing work station was installed for processing of In-seam and other data. Field trial/ installation of the equipment was conducted in association with supplier's representatives (M/s CME, China) in two panels of seam no. XVIII in Moonidih underground mine and 'test report of the same was submitted in September '98. On the basis of this report an application for granting final approval for the use of this equipment in any Indian underground coal mine has been submitted to DGMS. The application is under process.

Hydrogeological investigations

CMPDI continued to provide production support work apart from water supply projects, environmental data generation schemes, modelling and control of water system projects and other hydrogeological investigations.

Drilling and construction of one deep tube well for drinking water supply to drilling camp, Singrauli was successfully completed.

Chemical laboratory

During the year 1998-99 (upto December, 1998), a total of 1876,27 meter of coal cores from CCL command areas covering Gondalpara & Karimati blocks of North Karanpura CF, Padrangi Rabodh, Pundi South & Tapin South of West Bokaro CF, Jhirki West, Asnapani, South Swang Extension, Govindpur blocks of East Bokaro CIF have been processed for quality evaluation in CMPDI laboratory. Samples from Quality Control Departments of CCL, ECL & NCL were processed for chemical analysis of various parameters. A total no. of 3950 samples were analysed by Chemical Laboratory.

Under the outside consultancy job, 230 samples from M/s Coal Controller's organisation, Ranchi were analysed.

Petrography laboratory

The Coal Petrography Laboratory carried out 359 determinations (Maceral analysis and reflectance measurement) of coal of North Kathara, Pipradih and Asnapani blocks of East Bokaro Coalfield, Pundi South, Parej East & Topa blocks of West Bokaro Coalfield; Rohne-Rautpara, Chano-Ribka blocks of North Karanpura Coalfield; Saunda & Urimari blocks of South Karanpura Coalfield; Shyampur, Madhukunda & Raniganj blocks of Raniganj Coalfield; Hingula block of Ib valley Coalfield.

The laboratory also handled following two R&D projects. One funded by S&T fund and the other one by CIL's R&D fund.

S&T Project: A project for Development of Methodology for Characterisation of Indian coals by Computer Aided Petrographic Image Analysis has been taken up. Supply order has been placed for procurement of the equipment. Conventional petrography studies of 5.00 samples have been completed.

CIL's R&D Project: R&D project for Resource Survey, Characterisation and Blending status of low-volatile coking coal for their use in steel industry duly approved by CIL's R&D Board has been initiated. The procurement, of equipment is under progress. Meanwhile ten samples from Dhori area of East Bokaro coalfield and 8 samples from lower seams of Jharia Coalfield have been collected for laboratory scale washability test and other studies. Washability test on 5 samples of East Bokaro coalfield have been completed and petrographic studies on 100 samples from Kalyani VI/VII/VII seams and Amlo VI/VIII seam of East Bokaro Coalfield have been completed.

Remote sensing

Remote sensing is an established technology for mapping regional geological structure as well as creation of environmental data & its monitoring by way of preparation of various thematic maps. Following jobs have been taken up by Remote Sensing Cell during the period 1998-99 (till December '98):

(i) Land use Mapping of Ib Valley Coalfield based on Satellite data for three cut-off periods, i.e. 1986,1992 and 1998 has been completed for Mahanadi Coalfields Ltd., in connection with preparation of Regional Environmental Management Plan for the Ib Valley coalfield.

(ii) Up-to-date Landuse Mapping of Singrauli Coalfield and Siltation Study of GBP Sagar based on Satellite data of January 1998, has been completed for Northern Coalfields Ltd., for monitoring the changes in landuse pattern due to mining and other industrial activities,

(iii) Land use mapping of Mand-Raigarh Coalfield based on satellite data for the year 1988 and 1998 is under progress for creation of environmental data base.

(iv) Large scale (1: 10,000) thematic mapping based on remote sensing data of Korba coalfield is under progress for South Eastern Coalfield.

(v) Sodic Land Mapping of Allahabad district, Uttar Pradesh, based on satellite data is under progress for Remote Sensing Application Centre (RSAC), UP Govt. in connection with their on-going Sodic Land Reclamation Project.

(vi) Letter of Intent from Mahanadi Coalfield Ltd. has been received for preparation of Thematic maps of Talcher Coalfield for creation of environmental data would be taken up on finalisation of the limit of the target area by MCL.

Documentation

A total of 20 Geological Reports have been prepared and submitted during the period April to December 1998.

Reserver estimation

Geological Reports prepared so far have established a reserve base of 2.84 billion tonnes, of which 1.99 billion tonnes is under "Proved" category and 0.85 billion tonnes is under "Indicated" category. Of the total reserve of 2.84 billion tonnes, 2.70 billion tonnes of reserves are for non-coking coal sand 0. 14 billion tonnes are for coking coals.

Coal bed methane studies

CMPDI has entered into a new field of resource assessment of Methane associated with coal seams / coalbed, popularly known as Coalbed Methane (CBM).

A demonstration project titled " Coalbed Methane Recovery & Commercial Utilisation" has been planned in association with United Nations Development Programme (UNDP) and is being taken up with assistance from Global Environment Facility (GEF) and

UNDP. Two mines, Moonidih and Sudamdih in Jharia coalfield of Bharat Coking Coal Limited (BCCL) located in the State of Bihar have been identified by UNDP experts. Ministry of Coal and UNDP have signed the project document.

The Standing Scientific Research Committee (SSRC) of Ministry of Coal has approved this project and recommended part funding from S & T fund. The said project was approved by EFC and clearance from MOEF has been obtained. GEF/UNDP and Government of India (GOI) are the collaborators of the project. The Central Mine Planning & Design Institute (CMPDI) will be the implementing agency on behalf of GOI. Approval of CCEA is awaited for undertaking this demonstration project.

During the year, Directorate General of Hydrocarbons (DGH), Ministry of Petroleum and Natural Gas has approached CMPDI for identification and delineation of suitable blocks for CBM prospecting and exploitation. CMPDI has taken up studies in Raniganj, Jharia, North Karanpura, East Bokaro, West Bokaro and Sohagpur coalfields and submitted study reports.

Forest cover maps over the major coalfields of CIL

The CCDA/Ministry of Coal sanctioned Rs. 44 lakh for a project titled "Creation of Digital Data Base Map Showing Forest Cover in Major Coalfields of CIL" on 29.3.97. The detailed objective of project includes creation of integrated maps of each coalfield showing mines, status of exploration, areas of proved, indicated and inferred category of reserves, forest cover based on the vegetation maps prepared by Forest Survey of India and topographical features based on Toposheets published by Survey of India.

5

Planning and Foreign Collaboration

History of coal mining in India dates back to 1744, when coal was first mined in the Raniganj coalfield in West Bengal. Annual production was stagnant at 70 million tonnes during late sixties and early seventies and was inadequate to meet growing demand of coal for generation of power and for other industrial and metallurgical purposes. The oil crisis of early seventies spurred the Government into taking a hard look at the coal sector. Recognising the importance of coal, a primary source of energy in the national economy and the massive investment needed to meet the huge demand, coal industry in India was nationalised in phases in 1972 and 1973.

The primary goal for nationalised coal industry was to ensure a scientific approach to exploration and exploitation of coal deposits with due attention to safety, conservation and environmental aspects while accelerating the production level through substantial investment so as to reduce India's dependence on oil.

Eighth five year plan period (1992-97)

Coal demand

At the time of formulation of 8th Five Year Plan, Planning Commission had assessed country's raw coal demand in 1996-97, the terminal year of the 8th Plan at

311 million tonnes. To meet this demand, Planning Commission had indicated an indigenous coal production of 308 million tonnes for the year 1996-97. The growth rate in demand of coal was estimated to be 6.3% per annum during this plan period. Against original projection of 8th Plan, year-wise demand assessed by Planning Commission for each of the

Annual Plans is given below:

(million tonnes)

Year	Demand	
1992-93	256.70	(5.80)
1993-94	268.80	(6.00)
1994-95	268.50	(5.00)
1995-96	288.00	(6.70)
1996-97	325.00	(7.70)

The growth rate in coal consumption in the first 3 years of 8th plan has only been 4.4% .

Due to sluggish growth in coal consumption coal production targets were kept lower with a view to liquidate the pit head stocks. The demand again started picking up in the 2nd half of the 8th plan particularly during the years 1995-96 and 1996-97.

The demand for the year 1996-97 indicated by the various coal consuming sectors had suddenly shown a sharp increase.

The power sector alone asked for 210 mt. (plus 5.00 mt. of middling) of coal in the year 1996-97 as against 185.30 mt. (plus 4.70 mt. of middling) indicated for the year in the beginning of the 8th plan and 194.00 mt. (plus 5.00 mt. of middlings) asked for at the time of Mid Term Appraisal carried out in Sept., 94.

On the other hand, as a result of various constraints, including those of finances, land acquisition, forestry clearance, geo-mining condition and transportation, the coal companies indicated a domestic production of only 288.65 mt.

While a stock liquidation of 2 mt. was accepted, another 5 mt. was offered from stock in Korba coalfields provided the Railways were able to provide the necessary transportation facilities.

As a result of this, the Planning Commission had indicated that there would be a gap of 25.35 mt. in demand and supply of coal in the country during 1996-97.

Production

To meet the demand as discussed above, target and actual coal production during the Eight Five Year Plan period are given below:—

(in million tonnes)

Company	1992-93		1993-94		1994-95	
	Target	Actual	Target	Actual	Target	Actual
ECL	26.50	24.05	25.50	22.60	26.50	24.85
BCCL	28.00	28.06	28.10	29.04	28.50	28.75
CCL	32.00	32.38	33.50	33.52	34.40	31.21
NCL	30.70	30.70	31.40	31.41	32.50	32.50
WCL	25.00	25.75	26.00	26.50	27.00	27.24
SECL	44.88	46.04	46.60	47.54	48.00	50.00
MCL	21.92	23.14	23.30	24.29	25.00	27.33
NEC	1.00	1.10	1.10	1.20	1.1:0	1.19
Total CIL	210.00	211.22	216.00	216.10	223.00	223.07
SCCL	23.40	22.51	24.00	25.21	25.60	25.65
TISCO/ IISCO/ DVC	4.80	4.38	5.00	4.73	5.00	4.98
Grand Total	238.20	238.11	245.00	246.04	253.60	253.70

(In milliontonnes)

	1995-96		1996-97	
Company	Target	Actual	Target	Actual
ECL	29.50	27.80	31.50	29.649
BCCL	30.75	27.81	29.50	27.136
CCL	35.00	30.76	35.20	32.213
NCL	35.00	35.20	37.00	37.010
WCL	28.25	29.01	29.50	31.225
SECL	50.75	53.17	52.50	55.304
MCL	30.75	32.70	36.00	37.365
NEC	1.00	0.80	0.80	0.752
Total (CIL)	241.00	237.28	252.00	250.654
SCCL	28.00	26.77	30.20	28.730
TISCO/ IISCO/ DVC	5.50	6.00	6.45	6.280
Grand Total	274.50	270.05	288.65	285.664

Man productivity

The productivity measured as output per man shift (OMS) in tonnes, achieved during 8th Five Year Plan is given below:—

(figures in tonnes)

Year	CIL			SCCL		
	UG	OC	Overall	UG	OC	Overall
92-93	0.55	3.80	1.46	0.70	4.46	1.04
93-94	0.55	4.00	1.52	0.71	4.38	1.05
94-95	0.56	4.36	1.63	0.69	4.63	1 08
95-96	0.54	4.73	1.75	0.74	3.66	1.17
96-97	0.59	4.88	1.82	0.74	4.25	1.20

It is apparent from the above table that man productivity has increased over the years both in Coal India Limited and Singareni Colliery Company Ltd.

Plan expenditure

At the time of finalisation of 8th Five Year Plan, Ministry of Coal had requested for a total plan outlay of Rs. 19,374.07 crores. However, the plan size was approved at Rs. 12,357 crores. The net budgetary support was indicated as Rs. 1795 crores (14.53%) and another Rs. 986 crore was proposed to be met from external assistance routed through the budget. The details are as under:—

(Rs. in crores)

	Outlay for 8th Five Year Plan period	
	Proposed (at 1991-92 prices)	Approved
Coal India Ltd.	11669.00	8520.00
Singareni Colliery Company Ltd.	2967.38	1850.00
Neyveli Lignite Corporation (Mines)	1700.69	800.00
S & T,		87.00
Regional Expl.	100.00	25.00
EMP Measures		75.00
Total (Coal S Lignite)	16437.07	11357.00
NLC Power	2937.00	1000.00
Grand Total	19374.07	12357.00

The Plan outlays as approved by Planning Commission for successive Annual Plans during the 8th Five Year Plan and actual expenditure are given below:

(Rs in Crores)

Year	CIL	SCCL	S&T, Reg. Exp. and others
1992-93			
BE	1850.00	409.00	23.00
RE	1760.00	409.00	23.00
Actual	1808.47	406.45	18.24

(Contd.)

1993-94			
BE	1901.00	642.20	17.00
RE	1720.00	560.00	17.00
Actual	1687.92	544.98	15.91
1994-95			
BE	2062.90	483.40	23.50
RE	1850.00	550.00	22.99
Actual	1604.56	516.58	4.84
1995-96			
BE	2260.00	516.00	43.82
RE	1203.78	335.75	25.10
Actual	1503.63	259.35	14.79
1996-97			
BE	2143.00	538.97	52.80
RE	1310.83	325.00	28.00
Actual	1530.45	250.06	28.07

The net budgetary support as percentage of actual plan expenditure in coal and lignite sector including S & T projects, during the 8th Five Year Plan had been as given below:—

Year	Not Budgetary Support (In %)
1992-93	13.54
1993-94	8.50
1994-95	12.55
1995-96	12.59
1996-97	7.33

The pace of plan expenditure suffered mainly due to the fund constraints arising out of non realisation of market borrowings as envisaged and non revision of coal prices of the regulated grades of coal. Besides, large amounts of outstanding undisputed coal sale dues from State Electricity Boards to Coal India Limited and Neyveli Lignite Corporation had also adversely affected the Plan expenditure. This had resulted in reducing the production potential. The financial resources constraints have also affected advance action to be taken for the projects which are to yield production during the 9th Five Year Plan.

Ninth five year plan period (1997-2002)

Coal demand

At the time of formulation of 9th Five Year Plan Working Group on Coal & Lignite, constituted by Planning Commission had assessed country's raw coal demand in 2001-02, the terminal year of the 9th Plan at 405.00 million tonnes. To meet this demand, Planning Commission had indicated an indigenous coal production of 359.60 million tonnes for the same period. The growth rate in demand of coal was estimated to be 3.8% per annum during this plan period. Against original projection of 9th Plan, year-wise demand assessed by Planning Commission for each of the year is given below:—

(million tonnes)

Year	Demand	Middlings
1997-98	323.40	(6.80)
1998-99	325.38	(7.50)
1999-00	331.08	(5.90)
2000-01	392.80	(7.60)
2001-02	412.20	(7.70)

Production

The target for the first year of 9th Five Year Plan (1997-98) was fixed at 298.00 million tonnes. The total production during the year has been recorded as 295.93 million tonnes (provisional) i.e 99.30% of the targeted figures, The target for coal production during the year 1998-99 has been fixed at 306.50 million tonnes. The projected target for 1998-99 is kept 2.85% higher over the of 1997-98. The estimated raw coal demand of 325.38 mt is proposed to be met from an indigenous production of 306.50 mt, 2.65 mt of stocks liquidation from CIL and import of coking coal of 10. 14 mt for steel sector, totalling to 319.29 mt. This still leaves a gap of 6.09 mt between demand and supply. The all India coal demand assessed by Ministry of Coal for the year 1999-2000 is 331.03 million tonnes (plus 5.90 million tonnes of middlings). Against this demand, availability of Coal in 1999-2000 is indicated as under:

(in million tonnes)

Coal India Limited	270.90
Singareni Collieries Company Ltd.	31.00
TISCO/IISCO/DVC	6.80
Import	13.79
Draw down of Stock	0.20
Gap	8.34
Total	331.03 (5.90)

Thus the gap between demand and supply will be 8.34 million tonnes.

(in million tonne)

Company	1997-98		1998-99			1999-2000
	Target	Achievement (Provisional)	Target	Anti/ R.E.	Actual upto Nov.98	Target
ECL	32.50	27.43	32.00	29.50	17.60	30.50
BCCL	30.70	30.92	32.30	29.60	17.63	30.30
CCL	34.00	33.20	35.00	33.50	18.36	35.50
NCL	37.00	37.12	37.00	37.00	21.02	38.00
WCL	30.50	32.51	32.00	32.50	19.90	33.00
SECL	55.50	56.63	58.70	57.80	37.23	60.00
MCL	39.50	42.17	41.00	42.50	28.96	43.00
NEC	00.80	00.68	00.85	00.60	0.27	0.60
Total (CIL).	260.50	260.69	268.85	263.00	160.12	270.90
SCCL	31.00	28.94	31.00	30.23	15.55	31.00
TISCO/ IISCO/DVC	6.50	6.31	6.65	6.65		6.80
Grand Total	298.00	295.93	306.50	299.88		308.70

Man productivity

The productivity measured as output per man shift (OMS) (actual) in tonnes. The actual figures for the first 2 years of the 9th FYP i.e. 1997-98 and the targeted figure for the year 1998-99 are given below:

(figures in tonnes)

Year	CIL			SCCL		
	UG	OC	Overall	UG	OC	Overall
97-98 (Provisional)	0.57	5.07	1.93	0.76	3.50	1.31
98-99 (Targeted)	0.60	5.73	2.01	0.82	4.07	1.36
98-99 (Anticipated)	0.60	5.73	2.01	0.82	3 58	1.36
99-2000	0.60	5.29	1.95	0.79	3 58	1.36

Ninth five year plan outlay

The 9th Five Year Plan outlays are yet to be finally approved.

Plan expenditure

BE, RE and Actual (Provisional) upto the month of December, 1998 are given below:—

(Rs. in crores)

Year	CIL	SCCL	S and T, R.E., EMSC. and other schemes
1998-99			
BE	2517.00	331.57	92.13
RE	1700.00	280.00	57.10
Actual (Prov)	1084.25	130.90	3.00

Lignite sector

Eight five year plan period (1992-97)

The Planning Commission had fixed a lignite production target of 74.30 million tonnes for 1992-97, and 16 MT in the Annual Plan 1996-97. To meet this lignite production target and also power generation, coke and urea production, the Planning Commission had approved the following Eighth Plan outlay for Neyveli Lignite Corporation Limited:

Eighth plan outlay

(Rs. in crores at 1991-92 prices)

Mining Sector	800.00
Power Sector	1000.00
Total NLC	1800.00

The actual lignite production, power generation urea and coke production figures viz-a-viz targets since 1992-93 are given below:—

Year	Lignite (million tonnes)	Power Gen. (million units)	Urea (tonnes)	Coke (tonnes)
1992-93	13.30	8358.00	129,200	262,000
Actual	13.31	8324.12	108,591	172,606
1993-94				
Target	14.50	9923.00	129,000	262,000
Actual	14.15	9396.42	111,018	226,998
1994-95				
Target	15.00	10457.00	122,400	240,000
Actual	14.41	10893.00	105,543	240,878
1995-96				
Target	15.50	10640.06	122,400	240,000
Actual	17.21	12267.67	104,560	249,140
1996-97				
Target	16.00	10685.00	124,000	240,000
Actual	17.35	12704.56	119,049	215,172

The plan outlays as approved by the Planning Commission, Revised Estimates and the actual expenditure figures during period 1992-93 to 1996-97 in respect of Neyveli Lignite Corporation Limited are as under:

(Rs. in crores)

Year	BE	RE	ACT
1992-93			
Mining	123.00	117.18	43.37
Power	278.00	262.21	147.64
Total	401.00	379.39	191.01
1993-94			
Mining	162.00	124.00	43.24
Power	233.00	191.00	94.25
Total	395.00	315.00	137.49
1994-95			
Mining	211.40	121.01	112.82
Power	117.28	100.75	67.58
Total	238.68	221.76	180.40
1995-96			
Mining	387.24	288.41	136.03
Power	179.14	120.78	45.35
Total	566.38	409.19	181.38
1996-97			
Mining	311.55	325.65	135.96
Power	247.58	201.58	67.81
Total	559.13	527.23	203.77

Annual plans 1997-98 and 1998-99

The actual provisional figures for the year 1997-98 and target of lignite production, power generation, urea and coke production for the year 1998-99 and 1999-2000 are given below:

Year	Lignite (million tonnes)	Power Gen. (million units)	Urea (tonnes)	Coke (tonnes)
1997-98				
Target	16.50	11365.00	124,000	240,000
Actual (Provisional)	18.10	13402.27	102,690	233,963

(Contd..)

1998-99				
Target	17.50	11715.00	105,000	240,000
Actual	11.86	8798.17	30,491	128,005
(Provisional upto Nov., 98)				
1999-2000				
Target	17.50	12431.00	96,000	240,000

Expenditure

Budget, Revised Estimates, Actual (Provisional) 1997-98, BE and RE for the year 1998-99 and BE for the year 1999-2000 for NLC are as under:

(Rs. in crores)

Year	BE	RE	Actual (Prov.)
1997-98	584.77	327.50	168.28
1998-99	1112.05	750.00	315.10
1999-00	872.62	N.A.	N.A.

Foreign collaboration

To meet country's growing demand for coal, foreign collaboration with the advanced coal producing countries are considered for:

a) bringing in new technologies both in underground and opencast sectors for efficient management in the coal industry and skill development and training etc.

b) seeking bilateral funds for import of equipments which are not manufactured in the country.

c) bringing foreign financial assistance to meet the investment requirement.

Keeping these objectives in view, Joint Working Group on coal had been set up with France, Germany, Russia, Canada, Australia and China. Ministry of coal is also the nodal Ministry for the Joint Commission with Poland. The priority areas, inter-alia, include acquisition of modem underground mining technology, introduction of high productive opencast mining technology, working underground in difficult geological conditions, fire control and mine safety. Training of Indian personnel as well as assimilation of the technology are an important consideration. With the liberalisation of the economy, greater thrust is being given to get the foreign investments/assistance on the basis of cost competitiveness. Indian coal PSUs are now also offering their expertise to other developing countries viz China and Tanzania.

Cooperation with Canada

The expansion phase of Rajmahal opencast project of Eastern Coalified Limited from 5 Mty to 10.5 Mty has been completed by the Canadian Commercial Corporation on a turn-key basis with financing of the Canadian goods and services by Export Development Corporation of Canada. Presently there is no active cooperation with Canada in the coal sector.

Cooperation with France

France has developed expertise in thick seam underground mining with the introduction of advanced technologies like Blasting Galleries and Longwall Sub-level Caving. It has assisted India in introduction of blasting gallery method at East Katras (Bharat Coking Coal Limited) and Chora (Eastern Coalified Limited). France has also assisted in the introduction of sub-level caving technology at East Katras mine of Bharat Coking Coal Limited.

France had also cooperated in the introduction of high face longwall mining technology in Kottadih Project of ECL.

GDK-10 (Block B) and GDK-8 incline projects in SCCL were taken up for introducing blasting gallery technology in collaboration with France. These two project have already been completed. SCCL has signed another contract for introducing Blasting Gallery method at VK-7 project, which is under implementation.

Training Centre at Burradhemo (Eastern Coalified. Limited) had formally been inaugurated in April, 1994 and phased training programme with the French assistance were successfully completed. This Training Centre will be used to impart training to the personnel of coal mining companies.

In order to strengthen the cooperation between two countries and broaden the scope of cooperation especially in coal industry, a Joint Working Group on coal was constituted, which used to meet annually to address the various problems covering bilateral cooperation. In view of the declining cooperation with France in the field of coal, it has been decided to merge this Working Group with the proposed Working Group on Energy.

Cooperation with U.K.

In January, 1997 an Indo-British Coal Forum (IBCF) was established to foster greater cooperation between the two countries in coal sector. The Forum provides a platform for mutual consultations and cooperation between the coal industries of both the countries under the auspices of the Govt. of the India and U.K.

The activities which are envisaged under the MOU include sharing of latest know-how technology, organisation of meetings for exchange of information, identification of suitable projects as well as methods of funding, introduction of compatible technology for more efficient management in Indian Coal Industry and skill development etc. Four meetings have been held till now-in persuance of these objectives.

Cooperation with Poland

Ministry of Coal is acting as the nodal Ministry for Indo-Polish Joint Commission on Economic, Trade,

Scientific and Technical Cooperation. The last meeting (14th) of the Joint Commission was held in January, 1996. The Commission has 4 sub-committee on (1) Coal Mining and power (2) Trade (3) Industry and (4) Science and Technology which also deliberated simultaneously. The Projects which were taken earlier in coal sector with Poland have since been completed but the Polish Coal Industry has offered their expertise in underground mining, washery construction, Thermal Power Generation, mine safety and rescue. In furthering Indo-Polish Cooperation in coal sector, it was also agreed by the representatives of both sides to form Working Group for coal sector. The first meeting of the Indo-Polish Working Group on Coal was held in Warsaw, Poland on 14th of October, 1998. The Working Group was established under the aegis of Indo-Polish Joint Commission for Economic, Trade. Technical & Scientific cooperation. The Indian delegation was led by Secretary (Coal).

Co-operation with Russia

The erstwhile USSR was assisting CIL in the implementation of the Nigahi opencast project (Northern coalfields Ltd.), Khadia opencast project (Northern Coalfields Ltd.), Jhanjra underground project (Eastern Coalfields Ltd.) etc. The cost of the imported equipment for these projects was funded from the credit, IMP while the payment for deputation of experts for rendering technical assistance was made in Indian Rupees under the Bilateral Trade plan. Indo-Russian Working Group on coal has so far met five times. The projects which are currently going on with Russian co-operation are Master planning of Talcher, Ib valley and Korba coalfields, Slope stability study of internal dumps in mines of NCL.

Co-operation with Germany

Major thrust of assistance with Germany is in the Lignite sector. In coal sector, Germany had earlier assisted CIL in studying underground voids in Eastern Coalfields and on a project for subsidence and strata control in multi-seam working in underground mines, Further assistance on the project for subsidence and strata control in multi-seam working in underground mines is envisaged. CMPDI has signed Memoranda of Understanding with M/s Rheinbraun Engineering and Wasser GmbH, M/s Montan Consulting GmbH and M/s DMT for undertaking consultancy work jointly. CMPDI had undertaken an ADB funded Technical Assistance project on Implementation of clean coal technology through coal beneficiation in collaboration with M/s Montan Consulting GmbH.

Co-operation with China

During the visit of the Govt. of India delegation under the leadership of Coal Minister a Joint Working Group had been constituted for bilateral cooperation between the Indian and Chinese coal industries. So far four meetings of the Joint Working Group have been held. Chinese side had signed three agreements for longwall projects in SECL in Sept. '95. These contracts are under various stages of execution. During the last meeting of the Working Group, the Indian side had shown their renewed interest for the development of opencast mines in China with Indian technology and expertise. Chinese response to CMPDI's offer for development of XIANFENG opencast mine in China is awaited.

Co-operation with Australia

Australia had assisted Central Coalfield Ltd. in implementation of Piparwar opencast project on turn-key basis. The import costs for this project were financed by concessional loan from the Export Finance and Insurance Corporation of Australia.

6

Personnel Industrial Relations and Safety Manpower

Human resource management in Coal India is one of the strategic functions as the industry is labour intensive. The achievement of business objectives demand optimal demand optimal utilisation of available manpower. The cost of employing this manpower is high, as such continuous efforts are made for development and deployment of surplus women employees has also been started to derive, benefits from their utilisation. To maintain profitability, mechanisation and introduction of new technology is being continually attempted for which supply of for which supply of skilled manpower is ensured wherever necessary. All round efforts are made by the companies to improve labour productivity with references to current status of manpower in Coal India.

The Coal India management attaches considerable importance to Human Resource Development at all levels, Concerted action has been taken by the management to exercise strict control on fresh induction of workers, training and development of existing employees with a view to ensure skill upgradation and also to achieve rationalisation by retirement of workers through natural separation and under voluntary retirement scheme.

The company has been able to achieve substantial reduction in the employees strength and increase in the productivity.

Coal India Ltd. and its subsidiary companies prepare the Annual Manpower Budget for all the units starting from colliery, projects and areas up to the company headquarters level, The budget takes into consideration the designationwise and skillwise requirement of manpower and their deployment in different units and establishments.

The company has now undertaken a comprehensive exercise to identify the surplus manpower in companies like ECL, BCCL & CCL and has also fixed the targets for bringing about rationalisation in manpower strength.

Efforts are also on to identify the workers who are trainable and who could be gainfully employed by intra - company and inter - subsidiary transfers. The company is faced with a major problem of mismatch of workers due to the provision for employment of next of kin in case of death and permanent physical disablement. The management has started a dialogue with the unions to bring about suitable modification in the provision.

Coal India Ltd. has a well-laid down system of Manpower Audit in all the companies. Standing Committee for Manpower Audit have been formed at company headquarters to monitor and control issues relating to manpower and their deployment. The company has also introduced fortress checking so as to ensure that there is effective check in the actual deployment of workers and the salary being paid to the employees. The Voluntary Retirement Scheme introduced by CIL is getting encouraging responses from the employees.The total number of workers retired under the scheme is given to the next page.

During 1997-98, a sum of Rs. 80 crores was sanctioned from the National Renewal Fund for implementation of Voluntary Retirement Scheme in ECL & BCCL. For the current financial year i.e. 1998-99, a provision of Rs. 160

crores has been made in the budget for implementation of VRS in these two companies, Out of this Rs. 30 crores have already been sanctioned and 7600 employees are expected to be covered under VRS. A provision of Rs. 160 crores has also been proposed in the 1999-2000 budget for VRS.

Year	No. of workers retired (under VRS)
1988-89	1,182
1989-90	1,661
1990-91	900
1991-92	1,587
1992-93	6,232
1993-94	5,455
1994-95	9,967
1995-96	1,538
1996-97	1,905
1997-98	4,912
1998-99	5,052
Total	40,391

The total manpower of CIL and its subsidiaries as on 31.3.98 was 6,11,689 as compared to 6,24,463 as on 31.3.97 and stands at 5,95,201 as on 31.12.98.

Corporate HRD plan

A Corporate HRD Plan for the period 1996-2000 AD has been developed by Coal India Ltd. on the basis of review of performance of HRD during last five years and strategic HRD Plan developed for next five years. The annual plan was worked out to integrate the efforts of HRD in all the training centers, located in different subsidiaries. The strategy was to utilise available in-house training infrastructure as well as meeting the needs with the help of existing training capabilities.

Training Strategies

The HRD strategies focused on the following areas:

— To facilitate availability of skilled manpower through planned development of existing employees.

— To conduct basic and refresher training for operators and maintenance personnel with reference to HEMM equipment.

— To prepare employees for acquiring statutory qualification through intensive coaching as well as grooming eligible employees for departmental examination aimed at career growth.

— To conduct general development programmes for workmen and supervisors for integrating them with the state-of-art Technology as well as enterprise.

— To train Management Trainees, through a standard scheme.

— To develop senior executives from M- 1 to M-3 level through centralised in-house programmes organised at IICM, Ranchi.

— To develop senior executives through nomination to courses organised by reputed institutes and professional bodies in India and facilitate inter-organisational exposure to assimilate development in the areas of technology and management science.

— To develop employees through training opportunities abroad available from foreign Governments manufacturers and international seminars and courses and to help & enhance managerial and technical competence of employees working in strategic positions.

The number of employees trained during 1998-99 (April' 98 to Dec. '98) in Coal India Ltd., is given below: -

Category	Employees trained			
	Abroad	Outsidethe company	In house	Total
Executives	22	1,406	5,585	6,991
Supervisors	4	142	5,824	5,970
Workers	8	347	15,263	15,618
Total	34	1,395	25,672	28,579

These employees were trained in training centers, as well as in areas also. 9.11. As on 30.11.1998, the Singareni Collieries Company Limited, a joint-venture of the Union Government and the State Government of Andhra Pradesh, had on its roll 1,10,044 men, as per the following breakup:

Category		Men on roll (as on 30.11.98)
I. Daily rated Non-Excavation:		
1. Category - I	...	19091
2. Category - 11	...	6832
3. Category - III	...	2738
4. Category - IV	...	11567
5. Category - V	...	14006
6. Category - VI	...	4386

Excavation:

1. Special Grade	...	94
2. Grade "A"	...	495
3. Grade "B"	...	898
4. Grade "C"	...	837
5. Grade "D"	...	688
6. Grade "E"	...	205
II. Monthly paid		
1. Executives	...	2442
2. Non-Executives	...	6191
III. Piece rated		
1. Regular Fillers	...	26396
2. Badli Fillers (including Badli Workers)	6191	
Total.	...	1,10,044

Management development and training abroad

Type of Training	1998-99 allocation	Utilisation up to Nov., 98
Short-term training course in the field of Coal with Emphasis on Colliery level Managers at Australia.	3	3
Total	3	3

The three Executives as shown above were sent to Australia.

The number of Executives and non-executives of SCCL who have been sent abroad and elsewhere in India for training in management development programme (up to 31st December, 1998) is given below:

Category	Abroad	(SCCL) India	Total
Executives	3	67	70
Non-Executives	-	10	10
Total	3	77	80

In-house training

SCCL has an integrated plan drawn up for the year 1998 -99 for utilisation of In-house training facilities for the development of Executives, Supervisors and Workmen. SCCL has identified certain areas for Human Resource Development as listed below: -

(a) Intensive training for upgradation of skill to meet the demand of skilled and highly skilled personnel.

(b) Training of Operators and maintenance personnel for various HEMM equipment.

(c) Coaching of Supervisors for statutory examinations conducted by Director General of Mines Safety.

(d) Implementation of JET's training scheme.

A special drive to groom executives through planned management development efforts which may facilitate succession in the long run. The table below indicates the number of employees trained during the year 1998 - 99 (Up to Dec., 98):

Category		Employees Trained (Up to Dec., 98)
Executives	...	279
Non-Executives	...	229

Wage revision

The pay structure of the executives of Coal India Limited is due for revision w.e.f. 1.1.1997. The Government of India had appointed a Pay Revision Committee during October, 1996 to examine the present structure of pay, allowances, perquisites and benefits for Central Government PSUs Board Level functionaries, below Board level executives and non-unionised supervisory staff. A decision on the report of Committee is awaited.

Wages in coal sector

The wage structure and other conditions of service (including fringe benefits, welfare measures etc.) of the unionised employees (i.e. other than executives) in the coal industry are settled by negotiations in the Joint Bipartite Committee for the Coal Industry (JBCCI) consisting of representatives of management and the 5 (five) Central Trade Unions. The unionised employees of the entire Coal Sector are from the roal India Limited and its subsidiaries, the Singareni Collieries Company Limited and the captive coal mines of TISCO and IISCO. Five National Coal Wage Agreements have so far been signed as per details below: -

National coal wage agreement	Date of which signed	Period covered by the agreement
N.C.W.A. - I	11.12.1974	1.1.75 to 31.12.78
N.C.W.A. - II	11.08.1979	1. 1.79 to 31.12.82
N.C.W.A. - III	11.11.1983	1.1.83 to 30.12.86
N.C.W.A.-IV	27.07.1989	1.1.87 to 30.06.91
N.C.W.A. - V	19.01.1996	1.7.91 to 30.06.96

National coal wage agreement-VI has become due from 1.7.96. The Joint Bipartite Committee for the Coal Industry has been constituted on 3.4.1997. Pending finalisation of the agreement, the employees are being paid Interim Relief @ 12% of Basic Pay & FDA as admissible as on 30.6.96 in terms of a Memorandum of Understanding arrived at on the 19th May, 1997 between the representatives of the Management and the five Central Trade Unions. Further deliberations are in progress for finalisation of the 6th round of wage negotiations.

Industrial relations

The industrial relations in CIL and its subsidiary companies have remained cordial contributing to growth in production, productivity and reduction in mandays lost due to strikes.

Strikes and bandhs

The following steps have been taken to maintain Law & Order in the coalfields:

a) Deployment of CISF in affected areas.

b) Communications network strengthened.

d) The job of transportation of coal is being awarded to ex-servicemen and co-operative agencies.

d) Company employees holding sensitive posts are transferred at periodic intervals.

e) Steps have been taken to protect employees from the clutches of moneylenders operating in the coalfield areas. Co-operative Credit Societies are functioning in collieries which are granting loans at convenient rates of interest to employees with an aim to prevent them from the clutches of money lenders. System of payment of wages through bank has also been introduced in some of the Subsidiaries.

f) Efforts are made to get major civil works like

construction of quarters, roads, bridges etc. done through Public Sector Companies.

Signarent collieries company limited (SCCL)

The Industrial relations are not satisfactory, due to the influence of banned Peoples War Group .and multiplicity of Unions.

In SCCL, as on date there are 77 Odd Registered Trade Unions, mostly Craft Associations operating in SCCL which are varying with one another to establish their respective strength/existence.

The details of, mandays lost and production lost (tonnes) during the last three years are furnished hereunder:

Year	No. of Strikes	Mandays Lost (Provl.)	Production Lost (T) (Provl.)
1995-96	191	36,79,892	33,02,740
1996-97	310	10,04,021	9,64,759
1997-98	355	9,08,015	7,76,742

The details of Strikes, Mandays lost and production lost (in tonnes) during the period April '98 to December, 98 and corresponding period of April, 97 to Dec., '97 are furnished hereunder for perusal.

SI. No.	Year	No. of Strikes	Mandays lost	Production lost (In tonnes)
I.	1998-99 (April-Dec., 98)	104	18,06,923	15,68,130
2.	1997-98 (-April-Dec.,97)	281	8,44,673	6,98,201

A mechanism has been evolved to have a periodical meetings with the Recognised Union and the Representative Status Unions at various levels to amicably settle all issues/problems of the workmen. It is noted that with the application of above mechanism, there has been a downward trend in the number of strikes.

Workers participation in management

The management continued its efforts to strengthen employees participation in the management through mutual discussions with operating central trade unions at CIL Hqrs. and subsidiary companies in different joint bipartite fora.

These efforts have brought about an overall improvement in the service conditions of our employees and the work culture in the organisation. These have contributed a great deal in improving the industrial relations scenario in the organisation.

Status of land acquired under CBA act

The Coal Bearing Areas (Acquisition & Development) Act, 1957 (CBA Act) is a Central Act for the acquisition by the State of unworked land containing or likely to contain coal deposits or of rights in or over such land and matters connected therewith.

Safety

One of the primary objectives of nationalisation of coal mines in India was to bring about an improvement in the safety scenario which has been embodied in the Mission of Coal India Ltd. with this in view the Safety Policy of Coal India has been formulated and implemented. Coal India Ltd. has also created an Internal Safety Organisation in each subsidiary as well as the holding company level. As a result of a sustained thrust on improvement in the safety scenario by implementation of various safety measures it has been possible to bring down the number of fatalities, serious injuries and the rates of fatality and serious injury per million tonne of coal produced progressively as shown in the table below:-

	1975	1995	1996	1997	1998 (Jan-Dec.)
Fatalities	233.00	115.00	110.00	112.00	99.00
Fatality rate per million tonne of coal production	2.62	0.50	0.44	0.43	0.38
Serious injury	1515.00	612.00	505.00	519.00	407.00
Serious Injury rate per million tonne of coal produced	19.49	2.65	2.02	1.99	0.95

Safety measures

In order to bring about a continuous improvement in the safety scenario the following measures were adopted:

1. Thrust on DISASTER PREVENTION through

 (i) Repeated Safety Audit of mines and continuing implementation of the recommendations of the same and monitoring thereof. At present the Third Safety Audit of mines is being done.

 (ii) Priority inspection of highly gassy (Degree III) mines and fiery mines by ISO officials and follow up corrective action for removal of deficiencies.

 (iii) Environmental Monitoring of degree III gassy and fiery mines to take corrective action before a dangerous situation can build up by constant vigil and monitoring the parameters which are indicative of accumulation of inflammable gas or the progress of heating leading to a possible outbreak of fire.

 (iv) Measures against possible dangers of

inundation of underground mines are being taken like strengthening of embankments, barriers, diversion of jores etc.

2. Monthly review of safety performance of the companies in CMDs meets with analysis of each and every accident and formulation/revision of strategies for their prevention.

3. Increased thrust on use of scientific methods of roof support through Rock Mass Rating based Support Plans for mines and roof Bolting Systems of Support especially in the freshly exposed roof area.

   Exercise for standardisation of manufacture of Quick Setting Cement Capsules in collaboration with Central Mining Research Institute underway.

4. Examination of Annual Operation Plans of mines by the Internal Safety Organisation (ISO) of the companies.

5. Safety clearance of production districts before commencement of operations.

6. A major thrust on inspections of the mines by officials of the ISO of CIL as well as subsidiary companies in addition to inspections by trade union representative members the CIL Safety BOARD, THE Standing Committee on Safety in Coal Mines, the Workmen's Inspectors and the mine level Safety Committees.

7. Monthly monitoring of the Safety Status of all mines of CIL on a computerised database report (SSR-I AND SSR -II) and thrust on rectification of deficiencies observed.

8. Training and Retraining of the workers, supervisors and officials of the mine through VTC, HRD etc.

Reviewing of safety status of coal mines

The safety status of coal mines is being continuously monitored at different levels. At the mine level the Safety Committees, where workmen are represented, review the safety status of every mine. Workmen's Inspectors make inspections of the mines and the reports of the inspections are rigorously acted upon. Bipartite Committees of management and workmen's representatives review the safety status of each and every Area. At the subsidiary company headquarters level Tripartite Committees which include representatives of the Directorate General of Mines Safety (DGMS) also review the safety performance of the company, and suggest measures for further improving the safety standards.

The Coal India Safety Board, comprising representatives of the coal companies, the workmen, DGMS, the Ministry of Coal review and deliberate on safety measures to be taken for improving the safety performance of CIL bi-annually.

The safety situation of the coal mines is also reviewed bi-annually by the Standing Committee on safety in Coal Mines chaired by the Hon'ble Minister of State for Coal.

Workers participation in safety management

Participation of workmen in the management of safety has been a priority area for CIL and institutions like Workmen's Inspectors, Safety Committees, Area level Bipartite Committees, company level Tripartite Committees and the CIL Safety Board have been set up and ensure that workmen are involved in all measures for safety at the workplace.

Mines rescue services

During 1998-99 the modernisation programme of the mines Rescue Services of Coal India Limited was continued. Six main rescue Stations (RS), twelve Rescue Rooms with Refresher Training Facilities (RRRTs) and eleven Rescue Rooms have been established and are functioning in various subsidiaries.

Old outdated main rescue equipment are being replaced by modern equipment in a phased manner. Modem training galleries have been provided at all main Rescue Stations and RRRTs. These are being equipped with modern gadgets.

Out of thirteen additional Rescue Rooms being constructed to ensure that Rescue Teams reach within half an hour of receiving information construction of seven Rescue Rooms have been completed as planned in 1997-98. These are being equipped.

Several incentives have been introduced for attracting suitable persons to serve in the Rescue Services. Shortage of field volunteers have been made up by and large.

New technology equipment like infra-red imager, paging system, etc. have been introduced. Trial is under way for development of cordless radiocommunication system for use by Rescue Teams in rescue/recovery work below ground.

One large diameter drill machine for evacuation of miners trapped below-ground has been procured from abroad and supporting equipment have been procured from indigenous sources. The machine has been put on trial commissioning at Amritnagar site of ECL.

A large number of high capacity submersible pumps and horizontal pumps have been procured and kept in readiness for large scale dewatering of mines should the need arise.

Action has been taken to repair and commission two mobile winders procured by CIL for use in emergency.

Accident statistics

Functioning of public grievance cell

Although there is no formal P.G. Cell in this Ministry, the PRIW Section attends to the work relating to public grievance. *The grievances of the following nature are dealt with:*

(i) Individual grievances of retired employees of Coal Companies regarding non payment of gratuity, PF, Family Pension, DA etc.

(ii) Grievance of working employees of Coal Companies regarding age dispute, retirement on medical ground, employment on compassionate grounds etc.

(iii) Grievance representation received from the workers' Unions, and organizations companies, which go into contract with CIL or its subsidiaries in connection with work. Mainly, the grievances relate to nonpayment of outstanding bills.

Standard grievance redressal machinery is in existence in the Ministry of Coal. Every Wednesday of the week is generally being observed as a meetingless day. Shri G.B. Mukherjee, Joint Secretary, in the Ministry of Coal has been designated as the Director of Public Grievance. He hears grievances on every Wednesday from 11.00 AM to 1.00 PM.

A Board depicting the name, designation, telephone number, meeting time etc., of the Director Grievance has been displayed at the reception counter at Shastri Bhavan. Organisations under the administrative control of the Ministry have also been advised to display similar Boards at their reception counters.

During 1998-99 (up to December, 1998) about 120 public grievance cases were received in the Ministry. Out of these, 104 cases have been disposed of and only 16 cases are in hand.

The Coal India Limited an organisation working under the administrative control of Ministry of coal has a vast net work consisting of nine subsidiaries. All companies have standard public grievance redressal machinery. The Public Grievance Cell in the Coal India Ltd. is headed by the Chief General Manager (Personnel) who is assisted by two more officers, one each from the Marketing Division and the Administration Deptt. of Coal India Limited. As per the information received through quarterly returns on public grievance cases, the subsidiary companies had received about 373 public grievance petitions during 1998-99 (up to December, 1998). Out of these 305 cases have been disposed of and only 68 cases are pending.

A grievance redressal machinery is also functioning in Neyveli Lignite Corporation Limited. During 1998-99 (up to Dec. 1998), 676 public grievance petitions were received. Out of this 673 have been disposed of and only 3 petitions are pending.

7

Employees Welfare and Social Security Scheme

Welare

Welfare of Coal miners has the same importance as production, productivity and safety. The Coal companies are paying greater attention to the welfare of their workers. Every effort is being made to improve the living conditions of the coal miners. The ,thrust is on improving the basic necessities such as housing, water supply and medical care. Emphasis has also been laid on improving the general environmental and ecological conditions in the coalfield areas. In order to create a sense of belonging and involvement at work, top priority is given by the management to provide housing, medical and educational facilities etc. The results of the welfare measures taken in different areas are as under:

Housing

At the time of nationalisation, in Coal India Ltd. and its subsidiaries there were only 1, 18,366 houses including substandard houses. The availability of these houses has increased to 3,98,656. The housing satisfaction has now reached 67.28%. The coal companies are making all out efforts to further improve these facilities.

In SCCL as on 31.12.98, 45,706 Nos (including CISF) quarters have been provided for employees of SCCL and 507 quarters are under construction.

Water supply

In Coal India Ltd. & its subsidiaries as against 2.27 lakhs population having access to potable water at the time of Nationalisation in 1973, presently 23.37 lakhs population has been covered under water supply scheme. This was as a result of the concerted efforts made by the Coal companies.

In SCCL, the population covered under water supply is 8,24,800 and all the residential quarters have been provided with water supply.

Medical facilities

The Coal India Ltd. and its subsidiaries are extending medical facilities to its employees and their families through various medical establishments starting from the Dispensary level to the Central and Apex Hospitals in different parts of the coalfields.

There are 86 hospitals with 5,929 beds, 438 dispensaries, 697 ambulances, 1,743 doctors including specialists in CIL and its subsidiaries to provide medical services to the employees.

Besides, 26 Ayurvedic dispensaries are also being run in the subsidiaries of Coal India Ltd. to provide indigenous system of treatment to workers.

SCCL is running 7 hospitals with a combined strength of 1140 beds, 43 allopathic and 2 Ayurvedic dispensaries situated at different localities The Health Education programmes and Immunisation drives are also organised in the areas. To promote family planning SCCL has also conducted 2152 operations in its hospitals and dispensaries during April 1998 to Dec., 98. The company is also running a Nursing School recognised by the Andhra Govt.

Educational facilities

The primary responsibility of providing educational

facilities lies with the State Governments. However, CIL on its part has been providing financial assistance to certain schools like DAV Public Schools, Kendriya Vidyalaya, Delhi Public School and other educational institutions run by the State Government. In addition, as part of its Community Development Programme, CIL and its Subsidiary Companies are also providing financial assistance by way of grant-in-aid to certain privately managed schools functioning in and around coalfield areas.

At present, 1,248 educational institutions are functioning within the operational areas of CIL's subsidiary companies against 287 at the time of nationalisation.

SCCL is running 16 high schools and I upper primary school to cater to the educational needs of worker's children. Special classes for mentally retarded children are being run in the school at Godavari Khunj. A Women's Junior College is also run by the company.

Statutory/non-statutory welfare activities

Statutory welfare measures

In accordance with the provision of the Mines Act 1952 and Rules and Regulations framed thereunder, subsidiaries of Coal India Ltd. are maintaining various statutory welfare facilities for the coal miners. On the surface of mines, canteens, creches, pit head bath and rest shelters are being maintained for the convenience of the employees.

There are 466 canteens, 90 creches, 122 pit-head baths and 675 shelters running in the Coal India and its Subsidiaries.

Under the statutory provisions the following schemes are in operation in the Coal India Ltd. & SCCL: -

(i) Coal Mines Provident Fund.

(ii) Coal Mines Pension Scheme.

(iii) Gratuity.

Non-statutory welfare measures

Co-operative stores

In order to supply essential commodities and consumer goods at a cheaper rate in the collieries, 11 central co-operatives and 153 primary co-operative stores are functioning in the coalfield areas of CIL. For protecting the employees from falling under the trap of moneylenders, 155 co-operative credit societies have also been established in the coal companies.

There are 3 Super Bazar Complexes, 18 Sales Depots and 44 Sales Counters working in SCCL areas. The following facilities are also provided by SCCL to its workers.

1. Free supply of 200 Kg. coal per month to the workers not having LPG connection For those owning the LPG connections, the cost of LPG Cylinders is reimbursed in a financial year. 53,366 LPG connection holders avail of this facility now.
2. 3 Community Halls at Yellandu, Manuguru and Ramagundem areas.
3. 12 Parks and 114 Canteens are provided in the various areas.

Banking facilities

The Management of coal companies are providing infrastructural facilities to the various nationalised banks for opening their branches and extension counters in the coalfields for the benefit of their workers. Workers are educated to draw their salaries through 244 nos. of banks/extension counters and they are also encouraged to develop saving habits, which will ultimately reduce the menace of moneylenders in the coalfields.

Ecology and tree plantation

The Coal India is well aware of the need for improvement in ecological conditions in order to provide a better environment to workmen and to local inhabitants in the mining areas. They have been making concerted efforts to keep the environment free from pollution. The subsidiaries of CIL have been undertaking the work of regular development of green belts. The plantation is done on waste and reclamation land.

During the year 1998-99, the coal companies had a target of 61.73 lakhs tree plantation. Against this target, they have raised plantation of 59.43 lakh (prov.) tree so far. In SCCL, the company has raised about 76.09 lakh seedlings in the last 31 years. It is proposed to plant 7,84,375 seedlings in 325 Ha. of land during 1999-2000.

8

Neyveli Lignite Corporation Limited

Lignite reserves in the country have been estimated at around 29360 million tonnes. Out of the above 3300 MT spread over 480 sq. km. is in the Neyveli Lignite fields in Cuddalore District and about 2000 m.t. has been identified as mineable under the presently adopted mining paramerters.

Geological reserves of about 1167 MT of lignite have been identified in Jayamkondacholapuram of Trichy District of Tamilnadu. In Mannargudi and East of Veeranam, geological reserves of around 19,500. MT and 1420 MT of lignite have been estimated respectively.

Lignite reserves at Neyveli are exploited by NLC which was incorporated as a private limited company in 1956 wholly owned by Govt. of India. With effect from 7th March 1986, the Corporation was converted into public limited company.

Existing projects

NLC is an integrated complex consisting of two Lignite Mines, two Thermal Power Stations, a Fertilizer Plant based on Furnace Oil/LSHS and a Briquetting & Carbonisation Plant. The capacity of the various units is as under:

Mine-I	...	6.5	m.t.y.
Mine-II	...	10.5	m.t.y.
TPS-I (linked to Mine-I)	...	600	MW
TPS-II (linked to Mine-II)	...	1470	MW
Fertilizer Plant (Urea)	...	152,000	T/annum
(achievable capacity)	...	129,200	T/annum
Briquetting & Carbonisation Plant (Leco)	...	327,000	T/annum
(achievable capacity of Coke)	...	262,000	T/annum

Mine-I)

The first lignite mine which is in operation since 1961 with a capacity of 6.5 MT per annum using continuous mining technology viz. Bucket Wheel Excavators, Mobile Transfer Conveyors and system Of conveyors which are used for extraction ınd transportation of lignite and Overburden. Spreaders are used for dumping of overburden. The technology and the equipment have been imported from Germany and German credit was availed for import of Specialised Mining Equipments.

Thermal power station-I

The Thermal Power Station-I (capacity 600 MW) has 6 units of 50 MW each and three units of 100 MW each. The nine units of this power station were commissioned between May' 62 and Sept. 1970. The equipments of this power station were imported from the then USSR under Indo-Soviet assistance Programme. The erection was entirely carried out by Indian Engineers/workers under the supervision of experts from USSR. Entire power generated from this Thermal Power Station after meeting NLC's requirement is fed into the Tamil Nadu Electricity Board grid which is the sole beneficiary.

Mine-II :

Second Mine was implemented in two stages, In the first

stage the production capacity was 4.7 M.T. per annum and in second stage it was increased to 10.5 M.T. -and the expansion was completed in Dec.' 91 with the commissioning of last overburden system. Specialised Mining Equipments, viz. BWEs, Spreaders, Mobile Transfer Conveyors were imported from Germany with sizable indigenous content. The conveyors for Second Mine were supplied by M/s. Elecon Engineering, India.

Thermal power station-II:

The second power station was implemented in two stages. Under Stage-I 210 MW of 3 units were commissioned between March' 86 to March' 88. Boilers were supplied by M/s.Trans-Electro, Hungary and Turbo Generators by M/s.Franco Tosi of Italy.

Under Stage-II, 4 units of 210 MW each were commissioned between March 1991 and June 1993. Equipments were supplied by M/s. BHEL, India. Power generated from the Second Thermal Power Station after meeting the NLC's internal requirements is being shared by the Southern States viz. Tamilnadu, Andhra Pradesh, Karnataka, Kerala and Union Territory of Pondicherry in accordance with the formula on sharing of the power stations set up in the Central Sector.

Fertilizer plant

Fertilizer Plant with an installed capacity of 1.52 lakh tonnes of Urea per annum was commissioned in 1966. The equipments of the Fertilizer Plant were supplied by M/s. PINTSCH PAMAG, M/s. Linde of West German-, and M/s. Ansaldo of Italy. Achievable capacity of this plants had been subsequently assessed in 1983-84 as 129,200 Tonnes per annum. Initially the plant used raw lignite as feed stock. However, due to certain operational and technological constraints, the plant was switched over to LSHS/Furnace Oil as feed stock since July 1979.

Briquettting and carbonisation plant

Briquetting and Carbonisation Plant was commissioned in 1966 with an installed capacity of 3.27 LT of Carbonised briquettes (Leco) per annum. The equipments were supplied by consortium of M/s. West German firms. The achievable capacity has been subsequently assessed as 2,62,000 T of Coke per annum. Coke is used in Electro chemical, Electro metallurgical industries as a reluctant and in tea sector as a versatile fuel for drying and also as substitute for coal, in cement and paper industries. In the process of low temperature carbonisation adopted in the plant base chemicals vital to the chemical industries viz. Carbolic acid, Orthocresol, Metaparacresol, Xylenol, Multivalent phenol and neutral oil are also produced.

Projects under construction

First mine expansion project:

The expansion of First Mine Project from 6.5 MT to 10.5MT per annum was sanctioned by Govt. of India in March' 92 with a capital cost of Rs.1336.93 crores. In the meanwhile, Ministry of Coal, Govt. of India had instructed to stop further commitment on 26.8.93 due to uncertainties in the sanctioning of TPS-I Expansion and finalising the funding Agency. Subsequently, Ministry of Coal vide their letter dt. 6th Oct.' 94 informed that the embargo imposed on the expansion of Mine-I Expansion projects should be treated as withdrawn.

Accordingly, NIT was issued in Nov.' 94 for Specialised Mining Equipments. After evaluation conditional LOI was issued for 2 Nos. of Bucket Wheel Excavators and 1 No. Spreader in December' 95. The linked project of TPS-I Expansion (2 X 210 MW) was sanctioned by Government of India in February' 96. Loan agreement (Foreign fund) with M/s KfW was finalised in March' 97. The conditions of LOI was withdrawn in March' 97 and the effective date of contract was reckoned as March' 97. Supply of components for BWEs and Spreader commenced in April' 98 and June' 98 respectively and erection works commenced in August '98 and October' 98.

2000 mm conveyors system has been commissioned in Dec.' 98. For 2400 mm conveyor system, supply of material commenced since May' 98.

The new surface bench system commissioning is scheduled in April' 2000 and attaining full production stage by November' 2002.

Life extension programme of TPS-I

Life Extension, Programme of units in Thermal Power Station-I sanctioned by Govt. of India with a capital cost of Rs. 315.23 crores in March' 92. Till 31.03.98 three 50 MW unit (unit 1, 2, 4) and three 100 MW unit (Unit 7, 8 & 9) were released for LEP works and re commissioned. During the year 1998-99, unit-3 was recommissioned on 23.06.98 after completion LEP works.

Unit-5 (50 MW) was released for LEP works during 01/98 and re commissioned on 29.10.98. Unit-6 (50 MW) was released for LEP works during 07/98 expected to be completed in 03/99, thus completing the LEP programme.

Thermal power station-I expansion (2x210 MW) :

Government of India sanctioned for installation of 2 units of 2-10 MW for expansion of first Thermal Power Station on 12th February' 96 at a cost of Rs. 1590.58 Crores. M/s. MECON was appointed as Project consultant for Thermal Power Station - I Expansion on 4.1.95.

Tender for the Main Plant Package on ICB basis was floated on 22.2.96. Tender opened on 5.8.96. Since none of the bidders met the Qualifying Requirements either wholly or partly, re-tendering was issued on 8.4.97 after relaxing/ revising the Qualifying Requirement. On request of bidders and insistence of KFW tender opening date was postponed by 10 weeks and was opened on 08.08.97. Price covers including financial package was opened on 09.02.98 and after evaluation and with the approval of Board, LOA was issued on 10.12.98 to M/s Ansaldo, Italy for Main Plant Package (A 01), Civil works have been commenced on 27th September '98. Contract in four split up was approved and advance paid for FE portion in November' 98. Supply of material commenced on 18.12.98.

— For Lignite handling system (A 02), LOA issued in July '98 and civil vegetation clearing work is under progress.

— LOI for 400 KV and 220 KV Switch yard (A 08) was issued in 10/98. Soil investigation work has been started.

— Construction power supply (D 05) work completed in December' 98.

— Bid evaluation is under progress for other packages.

Status of civil works at site

Construction Facilities and Plant Boundary (C01), site work is in progress. 97% of work has been completed against the schedule of 100 %.

In respect to General Civil Works (C02A), 72.25% work has been completed against the schedule of 94 %.

The commissioning schedule of units are Unit-I - 11/2001 & Unit-II - 05/2002.

Mine-I A:

Government of India on 26th February' 98 sanctioned the Mine-IA Project - 3 Million Tonnes of lignite per annum subject to obtaining Environmental Clearance from Ministry of Environment & Forests (MOE&F) at an estimated cost of Rs. 1032.81 Crores at Neyveli. Advance action for procurement of major equipments was initiated and tender issued on 28th February' 98. Technical Covers for the packages viz. Bucket Wheel Excavator (3 Nos), Spreader (4 Nos.), MTC (5 Nos.) and Conveyor System & Transport Crawler were opened between 14th to 16th May' 98. Technical discussions are under progress. Conditional EMP clearance was obtained on 16.05.98 from Tamil Nadu Pollution Control Board (TNPCB), and it was sent to Ministry of Environment and Forest, GOI on 21.05.98. An Expert committee for Environmental appraisal of mining projects consisting of 14 experts has been formed by Ministry of Environment and Forest. Site clearance was issued on 22.09.98 from the Ministry of Environment & Forests (MOE&F) with some conditions.

Reply for the conditions has been prepared and sent to Ministry of Environment & Forests on 06.10.98. The expert committee meeting was held on 23.11.98. A subcommittee has been formed and the committee visited Neyveli on 21st & 22nd of December' 98. Additional information for EMP clearance has been submitted on 26th December' 98.

Price covers were opened for Spreader Conveyers and Transport Crawlers on 14.12.98 and for BWEs and MTC on 28th December' 98. Evaluation is under progress. Environment clearance is expected from MOE&F.

Revamping of fertilizer and B&C plant

Fertiliser plant

A report was prepared by M/s. Project and Development India Ltd., Sindri for installation of single ammonia reactor and accessories in place of existing 3 reactors at an estimated cost of Rs. 50.00 crores for safe operation of the ammonia plant and to improve the capacity utilisation of ammonia and urea plant. LOI was issued to M/s PDIL in May' 97 and manufacture is in progress.

Civil works have commenced in December' 98 and is in progress. Supplies with regard to steel and electrical equipments were commenced. The revamping of Ammonia plant is expected to be completed by 7/99.

B&C plant:

The technology adopted in the B&C Plant (commissioned in 1966) is old and outmoded. The plant was designed to match the environmental pollution control existing at that time. Since then the legislation regarding environmental pollution has been made more stringent and the plant has to be modernised taking this aspect into consideration as also the safety factor and to counter the ageing which is causing frequent breakdowns.

As an interim measure for enhancing the safety for the operation of the Carbonisation Plant, the revamping of instrumentation system of the Carbonisation Plant and a system for the supply of inert gas for blanketing Carboniser units has been taken up. Instrument revamping work has been completed in all carboniser unit.

Performance of existing projects

Overburden removal, lignite production, gross power generation and its export, production of urea and coke during the year 1998-99 April' 98 to December' 98 are indicated below:

Product	Unit	April' 98 to December' 98	
		Target	Actual
Overburden	LM3	650.50	690.74
Lignite	LT	129.50	13172
Power Gross	MU	8270.00	9669.88
Power Export	MU	6745.00	7990.54
Urea	LT	0.86	0.35
Coke	LT	1.78	1.42

Productivity

The productivity performance in 1997-98 and 1998-99 for different units is indicated below:

Output per manshift (OMS)

Unit		1997-98	1998-99 (Apr. '98 to Dec, '98)	
		Actual	Target	Actual
Mine-I (013+ Lig.)	Tonne	100.27	85.63	94.23
Mine-II (OB+ Lig.)	Tonne	108.16	95.34	100.65
T.P.S-I KwHr.	9028	6716	9988	
T.P.S-II KwHr.	19487	10876	17953	
Fertiliser Tonne	0.3058	0.2458	0.1230	
B & C Plant Tonne	1.02	0.68	0.64	

The PLF achieved by TPS-I and TPS-II during 1997-98 and 1998-99 April' 98 to December' 98 are as under :

Unit	1997-98	1998-99 (Apr. '98 to Dec. '98)	
	Actual	Target	Actual
T.P.S-I based on LEP	83.73	74.30	80.07
based on 600 MW	65.59	59.85	69.15
T.P.S-II	77.31	60.31	71.45

Financial performance

NLC has been making profits since 1976-77. During 1997-98 the Corporation earned a pretax profit of Rs 448.90 crores. The Corporation has earned pretax profit of Rs. 301.69 Crores (Prov.) during 1998-99 (Up to December '98). The cumulative profit amounted to Rs. 1794.45 Crores as on 3 1.3.98.

The sales turnover in 97-98 was Rs. 1475.80 Crores against Rs. 1351.92 crores during 1996-97- highest ever since inception. The sales turnover during 98-99 (up to December' 98) was Rs. 1094.69 Crores (Provl.) as against Rs. 1067.23 Crores during the corresponding period of last year.

Productwise sales during 1998-99 (Up to December' 98) is as under:

Product	Value (Rs. in crores)
Lignite (sales to outsiders)	50.37
Power (including transmission charges)	965.17
Urea (including retention price)	39.42
Coke	39.73
B&C By products & others	0-00
Total	1094.69

NLC has accumulated outstanding dues in respect of electricity supplied to the various Southern Region Electricity Board to the extent of Rs. 962.22 Crores as on 31.12.98. Efforts are continuing to realise the dues as well as to prevent a further build up of arrears.

Lignite exploration

Lignite reserves in India have been currently estimated at around 29360 million tonnes. The state wise distribution of lignite reserves is as follows:-

State	Area	Geological reserves (M.T.)	
Tamilnadu	Neyveli	3300	000
&	Bahur	575	
Pondy	Jayarnkondachola puram	1167	
	Mannargudi	19500	26118
	East of Veeranam	1420	

Kudikadu	133	
Perambalur	23	
Rajasthan		1496
Gujarat		1505
Jammu & Kashmir		128
Kerala		108
Total		29355

Contractual exploration & drilling activities

A quantum of 2100 m was earmarked for carrying out drilling during the period 1998-99. This meterage is essentially aimed for filling up of gaps in information in the proposed Mine-I A area which is located just east of the present Mine-I.

Promotional drilling activities

The 31st Sub-Committee/Coal and Lignite has recommended a total meterage of 55,000 m for the year 1998-99 MECL for lignite exploration for the country. The break up details for the meterage allotted to different states are given below.

S.No.	Area	Meterage	Gravity survey in Sq. Kms.
1.	Tamil Nadu	30000	--
2.	Rajasthan	20000	300
3.	Gujarat	5000	--
	Total	55000	300

Tamil Nadu

Out of total quantum of 30,000 metres of drilling programmed for Tamil Nadu, 20,000 metres would be drilled in Mannargudi basin, 5000 metres in Neyveli basin and the remaining 5000 metres would be drilled in East of Veeranam. As against the target of 30000 metres, MECL had completed 21639 metres in 74 bore holes during April' 98 to December' 98 including 1 bore hole in the region for scanning in Thanjavur district.

Mannargudi block:

A total quantum of 12237 metres of drilling was completed involving 38 boreholes by MECL during April' 98- December' 98. The lignite thickness ranges from 8.8 to 64 metres at depths ranging from 178 metres to 318 metres. The lignite occurs mostly in 3 to 4 seams.

East of Veeranam

Drilling was taken up in May' 98 on 800 m grid restricting up to 1: 15 ratio. During the period April' 98 to December' 98, MECL has completed 7747 m involving 30 boreholes. The lignite thickness ranges from 7 to 23 metres at depths ranging from 181 to 255 metres.

Neyveli Basin

In order to trace the continuity between Jayamkondam block and East of Veeranam, few bore holes were proposed. During the period April' 98 to December' 98, MECL has completed 1400 m involving 5 boreholes. The first bore hole was down to 325 m and the bore hole was proved to be barren. In the second bore hole the lignite thickness was of 4.8 meters at depths ranging from 165 to 182 metres in 2 seams.

Rajasthan

During the period April' 98 to December' 98 MECL has completed 9818.70 m involving 34 bore holes in Sindhari block of Barmer district. The results are very encouraging and the cumulative thickness of lignite is around 15 to 20 m. In Chokla block drilling was taken up for checking gravity anomalies and up to December '98 a quantum of 1115.20 m have been drilled involving 4 boreholes.

Gujarat

Drilling was taken up in Gujarat till October' 98. Drilling was not taken up in Ustia region of Kutch district during November' 98. During the period April' 98 to December' 98 a quantum of 1598.60 m have been drilled involving 10 boreholes and were proved to be barren.

Gravity survey (Rajasthan) :

As against a target of 300 Sq. Km. MECL had completed 175.24 Sq.Km. covering areas in Kolasar and Nagarsar in Bikaner. District and Chokla block in Barmer district.

Research and development

The Research and Development activities- were continued during the year. The details of various R&D activities being carried out are given below:

I) Ministry of coal S & T projects:

1) Biological method of employing VAM fungi in Neyveli Mine spoil/ashpond soils in tree plantation:

It is a joint project implemented by NLC and Madras University. Field experiments are in progress at ash pond TS-I, CARD, Corporate Office and Mine-II. In the above said sites 20 different types of fruits and forest tree species were planted with VAM and Bio fertiliser inoculation to know the effect of VAM on tree species. The growth performance is being monitored. Application of VAM fungi has improved the growth and biomass of various tree species when compared to untreated one.

2) Flyash utilisation in agriculture :

This is a S&T project jointly implemented by NLC and CFRI. It is proposed to study the effect of fly ash application in two types of soil (Red soil and Mines soil) and crop response in short/long term basis. Paddy was cultivated as a third crop at Mine-I with various levels of fly ash. Application of fly ash at the rate of 20 T/ha has registered more grain and straw yield of rice. In CARD site maize was raised as a third crop with grade levels of fly ash. Application of fly ash at 200 T/ha registered maximum grain yield in maize. In Mine-I site, 4th crop green manure and at CARD site 4th crop groundnut is in progress.

3) Pond ash reclamation and possibilities of utilisation of industrial waste for developing green cover:

This is a joint project recently approved by Ministry of Coal and implement CARD, NLC and Annamalai University with an outlay of Rs. 112.70 lakhs. In this project it is proposed to develop green cover in the abandoned ash pond area advanced biological reclamation techniques. Preliminary survey and surface oil sample collection is in progress. Action has been initiated for g infrastructural facilities like construction of shed, accommodation for project construction of observatory borewell, etc.

II) Foreign collaboration in the field of science & technology projects

I) Lignite energy research institute (LERI)

N.L.C is implementing a project to upgrade CARD into a National level LIGNITE ENERGY RESEARCH INSTITUTE (LERI) with assistance from UNIDO. The project will provide a centre for excellence in lignite related technology. Further it helps to bridge the gap in technical capabilities available at CARD in the field of lignite usage and its associated environmental problems. The project covers various sections as follows:

a) Analytical section

b) Information Technology section

c) Energy and Environmental section

d) Lignite treatment section

e) New project section

Sophisticated Instruments like TGA/DTA which can be used for advanced combustion research was procured. Order has been placed for HTC Furnace- and Autoclave and equipments were received. Studies on high temperature carbonisation/ liquifaction of slurry are under progress.

The National Experts, Shri P.M. Belliappa on Environment Management and Dr. Kuppuswamy on Data Management System visited NLC and shared their expertise in R&D activities in LERI.

UNIDO has floated tender for the combustion studies on lignite (slagging and fouling) and gasification of lignite at Neyveli. The equipments for combustion studies here arrived at site. Civil works are in progress and electrification tender is under finalisation.

The purchase and commissioning of entire computer network were completed during October' 98.

2) Environment management:

Large scale mining and power generation in a limited area may have several impacts on the environment. In order to assess the prevailing environmental status and undertake mitigative measures air, water and soil are regularly monitored by NLC.

Ambient air quality monitoring is being conducted throughout the year at six locations in and around Neyveli on every alternate day (3 x 8 hour basis) as per CPCB guidelines. The pollutants monitored are suspended particulate mater (SPM), Sulphur dioxide (SO_2) and Oxides of Nitrogen (Nox). Respirable dust and noise levels are monitored twice a year as per the guidelines of Director General of Mines Safety. The effluent samples from various industrial units are also regularly analysed by CARD as well as TNPCB lab.

Corporate Environment cell is regularly conducting co-ordination meeting with unit environment cell members from different units to sort out various environmental standards,

3) Training and development:

CARD has been extending faculty services to NLC training division, Annamalai University and National Power Training Institute. CARD also extends guidance for undertaking project works to students from various institutions/colleges and universities.

Manpower

The total manpower of NLC as on 31.12.98 is indicated below:

Category	Technical	Non-technical	Total
Executives	2884	443	3327
Supervisor	1402	612	2014
Staff	3036	2685	5721
Workmen	7469	2870	10339
Total	14791	6610	21401

Industrial relations

The Industrial Relations atmosphere in NLC signifies employee friendly attitude of the Management which shows greater care in dealing with Human Resources.

The recognised Unions and Associations in turn are looking beyond their own problems to realise their responsibility to be more responsive to the needs of increasing productivity. Thus the overall Industrial Relations scenario continues to be cordial.

— An understanding was reached on 26th July '98 between the Joint Council of Associations and NLC for the payment of Interim Relief for Executives pending finalisation of Wage revision.

— An understanding was reached in Sept. '98 between the Joint Council of Unions/Associations and NLC for the issues relating revision of LTC/LTA, QPPR/Incentive.

Welfare

Housing:

The sprawling residential township with a maze of roads, excellent drainage systems, waste disposal arrangements, water facility and other recreational facilities provide the perfect ambience for the employees and their dependents to feel comfortable, secured and create the atmosphere of being well cared for by the Management.

As high as 21,510 houses nestled in the green canopy of trees make NLC Township a place ecologically balanced and environment friendly to live in to achieve of quality of work life. It is abound with facilities for quality education up to college level, medical care, recreation, religious needs and shopping.

Medical services :

NLC Hospital is contemplating the best posture it can take in providing a wide range of Health Care Services to it's employees, dependent population and other rural communities (over 3,00,000). It engages in four broad areas of activity:

(i) Operation of the General Hospital (369 bedded acute-care Hospital).

(ii) Operation of 5 peripheral dispensaries to ensure better accessibility in the area of outpatient care to residents.

(iii) Operation of community Health programme to help the surrounding rural populations meet their basic medical needs. Eye Camps, Polio, Screening Camps and General Community Health Screening form part of this programme. During the year 1997-98, as many as 8 camps were conducted which include a major Opthal Screening Camp for implanting IOL to selected rural patients with cataract problems.

(iv) Operation of occupational Health services to ensure optimal Health, safety and well being of employees and first aid care at plant level.

Family welfare

NLC Hospital has been signed out as the best Medical Institution in the State for reforming sterilisation with zero failures. During the year 1998-99 up to Dec. '98 as high as 687 sterilisation were performed. Little more than one half of them (324) were rural beneficiaries.

Education

The NLC township is teeming with over 35 schools and a college for meeting the educational needs of children of employees and children from nearby villages. Drawing support from private participation, NLC offers quality education with most of the children making appreciable grades at High School and +2 levels. 18 NLC managed schools have also come into the limelight in the recent years for achieving excellence in the school and college curriculum. NLC has also instituted number of scholarship scheme to harness the full potentials of children.

Sports

The bottom-line equations of NLC include programmes and facilities for the development of sports among employees as well as students. This goal is best served by the development of sports stadium that house facilities for conducting state and national level tournaments. Schools make best use of these facilities to give equal importance to sports activities that help the students achieve overall development. The Sports Control Board is behind planning sports ' activities and developing facilities to meet the growing needs for sports and leisure time games.

Concern for social welfare

NLC's concern for social welfare is highlighted by it's commitment to serve the cause in general and more particularly of physically, mentally and socially handicapped population of Neyveli and beyond through Organisations such as Neyveli Health Promotion and Social Welfare Society and SNEHA Opportunity School. While the former upholds the specific needs of physically handicapped and destitute women through rehabilitation programmes the latter offer timely succour to mentally retarded children in making them useful and productive members of the society. NLC has not only provided infrastructure facilities for the operation of these programmes but more importantly extend financial support for their sustained growth.

Human resource development

Training is the powerful tool which NLC utilises effectively to harness its vast human resource potential, manage their career development and plan for enriching their skills/professions in line with the technological advancement. The training complex with modem facilities organise various training programmes to make the employees update their knowledge. The demands for continuing education at shop-floor level are also fully met.

To nourish managerial excellence, executives, professionals and skilled workmen are sent for training outside in premier training institutions in India and abroad. Training facilities offered by equipment manufacturers are also being utilised before installing new equipments/

machineries. Details of training during 1998-99 up to December '98 are

Details	April '98 to December '98
In-house programme	7461
Deputation training within India	900
Training abroad	21
Total	8382

Energy conservation

Separate cell is functioning with adequate staff to continuously monitor conservation of energy in the production units as also service units and township.

Indigenisation

Indigenisation is a continuous process and separate cell continuously monitoring the items to be indigenised in various units of NLC During 199798, 54 items were indigenised with a value of over Rs. 101.73 lakhs.

Hon'ble Members of the Sub-Committee on Coal of the Standing Committee on Energy visited Neyveli on 16th & 17th September '98 and held discussion with CMD and Directors on "Lignite Reserves and their exploration programmes and lignite sales, despatches & realisation of dues."

Hon'ble Members of the Committee on Papers laid on the Table - Rajya Sabha visited Chennai between 23.09.98 and 25.09.98. Held discussion with CMD and Directors on 25.09.98.

Indian Institution of Industrial Engineering, national headquarters, informed vide their letter dated 3d October '98 that Coal India Productivity Award 1997-98 for the organisations has been conferred to NLC in recognition of contribution to productivity improvement through application of I.E. Techniques.

Shri Dilip Ray, Hon'ble Minister of State for Coal and Shri Swam Singh Boparai, K.C., IAS, Secretary to GOI, Ministry of Coal visited Neyveli on 26th October '98 and went around the production units and reviewed the NLC's. production performance and status of on-going projects.

The 42nd Annual General Meeting of the Company was held at Chennai on 23 d November '98.

NLC Mine-I had bagged the All India first prize for the longest accident free period for the years 1995 and 1996 awarded by Union Ministry of Labour.

NLC Mine-II had bagged the All India second prize for the longest accident free period for the year 1996 awarded by Union Ministry of Labour.

9

Progressive Use of Hindi

In the year 1998, the Ministry of Coal continued to make sustained efforts to promote Hindi in all its subordinate offices and in all the companies under its administrative control. As a matter of fact, the previous records of the Ministry highlight the achievements and performance of the Ministry in the promotion of Rajbhasha.

The Ministry of Coal was awarded " Indira Gandhi Rajbhasha Shield" four times i.e. in 1990 (Ist prize) 1991, 1995 and 1996. Instructions received from the Deptt. of Official Language are regularly circulated to the subordinate offices and companies to impress that the statutory provisions of the "Official Language Policy" must be implemented both in letter and spirit. Special appeals/ circulars are also being issued from time to time to persuade officers and staff to resort to increased use of Hindi. To facilitate noting and drafting in Hindi, number of standard drafts in Hindi were circulated for use in various sections of the Ministry.

The Official Language Rules, 1976 make it obligatory that all the, letters received in Hindi or those bearing signature in Hindi even though written in English, must be answered only in Hindi Language. In order to ensure this, arrangements were further strengthened to segregate such letters at the stage of receipt itself and stamp them with the fascimile "to be replied in Hindi" to avoid their getting mixed up with other letters and also to ensure that they were properly attended to and replied in Hindi only.

In the Ministry, an overwhelming percentage of officers and staff have already acquired working knowledge of Hindi. To enhance their capability and confidence to work in Hindi, employees are nominated and got enrolled in the Hindi Teaching Scheme of the Ministry of Home Affairs.

A library with several books of Hindi is also provided in the Ministry. Some of the Coal Companies and subordinate offices also have libraries in their Headquarters and subordinate offices. Most of the books in these libraries are in Hindi or in Regional Languages. In order to motivate the employees to read more Hindi books, Rajbhasha Pustakalaya is being run by the Bharat Coking Coal Ltd. At Koyla Bhawan, Dhanbad.

In the Coal India Ltd. a holding company of the Ministry of Coal, Rajbhasha Karyanwayan Samiti was constituted for effective implementation of Rajbhasha Policy. Coal India Ltd. also continues to publish Hindi edition of all its publications during the year under review. The use of Hindi has been propagated through various publications like Khanan Bharti, Jyotsna, Saurav, Pallav, Vasundhara, Sampada and Pratibimb on a regular basis.. Special issue of "Kalyani" was brought out in Hindi by the Coal Mines Provident Fund.

In the Ministry of Coal "Hindi Pakhwara" was celebrated on 9.11.98 to 21,11.98 in which several officers/ staff participated overwhelmingly. During "Hindi Pakhwara", the Minister of State of Coal had appealed to the officers/staff of the Ministry to do their maximum official work in Hindi. The appeal of the Union Home Minister issued by the Official Language Department was also circulated in the Ministry of Coal and its all subordinate offices/Coal Companies. An "Award

Distribution Function" was held under the Chairmanship of the Secretary (Coal). He distributed the awards to the winners in various competition organised during the Hindi Pakhwara. On this occasion two renowned poets, Dr. Ganga Prasad Vimal and Dr. Jagdish Chaturvedi were also invited to grace the occasion. A "Hindi Workshop" was organised in the Ministry from 9.9.1998 to 11.9.1998 so that officers/ staffs of the Ministry could do noting and drafting in Hindi more precisely and effectively. Efforts had also been made to increase progressive use of Hindi and achieve the targets mentioned in the Annual Programme of the Deptt. of Official Language and upkeep a suitable environment to maintain it.

10

Progress of Computerisation

Year 1998-99 witnessed rapid advancements in Information Technology front in the Ministry of Coal. In close cooperation with NIC, an IT infrastructure is created in the Ministry with latest technology tools in tune with the fast changing field of information technology.

Windows NT based high speed ethernet LAN has been established in the Ministry. All sections and officers have been equipped with Windows 95 based Pentium workstations enabling them to work on latest GUI packages like WORD, EXCEL, Internet Explorer, Outlook Express etc. This LAN is part of larger state of art network the Shastri Bhawan Intranet. Users can connect into the gain secure access to all Internet features wide web, telnet and ftp.

Coal workgroup has been created which facilitates different sections in the Ministry to securely share information providing speedy day to day operations. Many valuable resources are also being shared over this network proving it to be quite cost effective.

Besides this, the Ministry has a Pentium server under Unixware 2.01 operating system which provides multi user environment for over fifty terminals.

Ministry of Coal with NIC has planned, designed developed and implemented databases and information systems on various key parameters to strengthen the monitoring, streamlined and safe storage and fast retrieval of data in desired formats. These include :

— Trends Monitoring System on Production Despatches & Stocks
— Product-wise monitoring on production & despatches
— Daily result monitoring
— Rail Movement monitoring
— Demand & Offtake
— Consumer wise Despatches
— Project monitoring
— Equipment monitoring
— Coal Linkages to Power Houses
— Annual Budget Monitoring
— System for phasing of budget
— Expenditure Control System
— Parliament Questions System
— Pendency monitoring system
— Document Tracking system
— Information System on VIP References
— ACC Decisions Monitoring System
— Incumbency Database
— Public Grievances Monitoring System
— Facilitation Counter Information System
— Target Oriented On-Line Tasks/Events Monitoring
— Payroll
— GPF accounts system

Ministry has reviewed the requirements of periodic and regular data/information from its PSUs for monitoring and planning at different levels in the ministry and has designed, with the help of NIC, various MIS formats. Ministry has circulated these standardised MIS formats among Coal PSUs from where data/information is regularly required.

Ministry has initiated efforts to bring all its Coal Companies, its subsidiaries and other agencies under administrative control, on computer network to transfer/ capture files and on-line interaction using high speed computer communication network.

Ministry of Coal has achieved increased user awareness on usage of computers. Tendency to work on the computer has been developed in all the users in the Ministry. Extensive use of computers has virtually sidelined the time consuming manual working in the Ministry.

Ministry of Coal has arranged with NIC to train their staff on the new Windows LAN environment and applications implemented for their use. On the job training has been planned and imparted to the users to avoid inconvenience for the users in finding time from their busy day schedule for training. Various familiarisation programs and training classes are being arranged with NIC to enable officials to be updated with the latest developments.

Ministry of Coal is planning to systemise various systems - already implemented with the help of NIC to get maximum throughput. New applications in latest state of art software packages are also being designed with the help of NIC which will enable users to work in GUI environment.

Ministry of Coal has initiated the process of looking into Y2K related problems both within the Ministry and in subordinate offices. It is closely monitoring Y2K compliance in applications, hardware and software packages being used by the Ministry so that all problems are sorted out well in time.

11

Mineral Law and Policy

Mineral law and policy

The Ministry of Steel and Mines, Department of Mines, continued the ongoing process of consolidating the steps taken in the wake of enunciation of the National Mineral Policy, 1993.

These policy changes have attracted many multinational companies for investment in mineral exploration and mining. Forty three proposals for prospecting over large areas in pursuance of the October, 1996 guidelines covering an area of about 60,000 sq. kms. in the States of Rajasthan, Gujarat, Maharashtra, Uttar Pradesh and Bihar have so far been cleared. Out of these, 20 Prospecting Licences involving an area of about 30,000 sq. kms. in the States of Rajasthan, Gujarat, Maharashtra and Bihar have been granted during the first nine months of 1998-99. Prospecting Licences have been granted in favour of Indian subsidiaries of well-known international mining companies like BHP Mineral of Australia, Meridien Peak Resources of Canada, Metdist of UK, Phelps Dodge Corporation of USA and Rio Tinto of UK. Aerial prospecting has already been completed over an area of more than 18,000 sq. kms. in Rajasthan and the licencees are very upbeat about the anomalies found so far. Further, a Secretary-level Inter-Ministerial Committee has been set up to facilitate removal of bottlenecks pertaining to grant of security clearance for undertaking aerial exploration, import of aircraft and its inspection etc. and the Department of Mines has been designated as the nodal agency. It is expected that the tempo will pick up during the next financial year.

The Foreign Investment Promotion Board (FIPB) has so far cleared 51 proposals involving Foreign Direct Investment (FDI) of about Rs. 3158 crores in the mining sector. Out of these, 12 proposals with FDI amounting to Rs. 474 crores were cleared in the first nine months of 1998-99.

To further operationalise the policy initiatives, the Government is considering greater delegation of powers to the State Governments and major procedural simplification by amending the Mines & Minerals (Regulation and Development) Act, 1957.

A National Committee under the Chairmanship of Secretary (Mines), co-chaired by Secretary, Ministry of Environment and Forests was constituted on 15.4.1998 to monitor and review environmental aspects of mining activities.

Mineral development

The total value of mineral production (excluding atomic minerals) during 1998-99 is estimated to be Rs.40,677 crores.

Public sector undertakings

In conformity with Government policy to balance the autonomy of PSUs commensurate with accountability and to set mutually acceptable targets, Memoranda of Understanding (MOU) were signed for 1998-99 with NALCO, BALCO, HZL, HCL and MECL. Greater autonomy is expected to result in quicker decision making, enhancing efficiency and increasing productivity of the

MOU signing PSUs.

National aluminium company ltd. (NALCO) made a net profit of Rs.625.43 crores (PBT) during 1997-98. The project of expansion of capacity of NALCO's Aluminium Smelter from 2,30,000 TPA to 3,45,000 TPA and that of the Captive Power Plant from 720 MW to 840 MW at a cost of Rs.2062 crores (June, 1997 price level) has been approved by the Government. The project is to be completed within 51 months from the date of Government's approval i.e. 3.2.1998. Currently, the project is under implementation by NALCO. The project of expansion of bauxite mines from 2.4 MTPY to 4.8 -MTPY and that of Alumina Refinery from 0.8 MTPY to 1.575 MTPY at a cost of Rs.1664.60 crores is also progressing as per schedule.

Bharat aluminium company ltd. (BALCO) achieved the highest ever turnover of Rs. 848.51 crores for the year 1997-98 and earned a net profit of Rs. 134.79 crores (PBT) in 1997-98. The project of setting up of new Cold Rolling Mill at a cost of Rs. 157.50 crores is under implementation by the Company.

Hindustan zinc ltd. (HZL) had a record sales turnover of Rs.1233.74 crores and earned a profit of Rs.201.77 crores (PBT) during 1997-98 which is, the highest since the inception of the Company. Two of its major units - Rampura-Agucha Lead Zinc Mine and Debari Zinc Smelter have been accredited with ISO 9002 Quality Management Certification.

Granite development council

The Granite Development Council was reconstituted vide Resolution dated 24.4.1998 for the development of granite industry and export of granite from the country. An Expert Committee was also constituted vide Resolution dated 27.4.1998, which will work under the overall guidance and supervision of the Granite Development

Council for examination of rates of royalty and dead rent fixed by different States and to suggest some broad uniformity in these rates for the overall development of the granite industry.

The geological survey of India

Surveys: A total, of 430 sq.km. was covered by systematic mapping in the North Eastern Region. Out of the country's total mappable area of 3.146 million sq.km., about 3.083 million sq. km. i.e. 98% (approx.) has so far been covered by systematic geological mapping.

Mineral investigations: In connection with mineral investigations, 2893.76 sq.km. of large scale mapping, 48.53 sq.km. detailed mapping and 53319.45 m. of drilling were done.

Additional reserves/resources established in the course of mineral exploration during the year are as follows:

- 1373 million tonnes of coal in Talcher, Godavari valley, Tattapani-Ramkola, Mand-Raigarh, Hasdo-Arand, Rajmahal and Raniganj coal fields.
- 1.64 trillion cu.ft. of Coal Bed Methane (CBM) in Birbhum and eastern part of North Karanpura coal field.
- 0.63 million tonnes of gold ore with an average grade of 3.54 g/t Au in Chikkanahalli South Block, Karnataka.
- 0.70 million tonnes of gold ore with 7.20 g/t Au in Dona East Block, Andhra Pradesh.
- 0.125 million tonnes of gold ore with 2.6 g/t of gold in Marupar-Kitari area, Maharashtra.
- 0.85 million tonnes of ore with 2.25% Pb+Zn (lead+zinc) in South Sindesar Ridge of Dariba-Bethumni belt, Rajasthan.

- 1.14 million tonnes of ore with 3.82% Pb+Zn in Latio-Ka-Khera East Block of Dariba-Bethumni belt, Rajasthan.
- 0.484 million tonnes of molybdenum ore with an average grade of 0.11 % Mo in Marudipatti Central block, Tamil Nadu.
- Re-categorised reserve of 884 million tonnes of SMS Grade and Cement Grade Limestone in Litang river valley block, Meghalaya.
- Potential zones of basemetal mineralisation have been delineated in Banskhapa-Pipariya block, Betul district, M.P.
- Significant gold values have also been reported from Puttumala West block and Kottathara block (7.6 ppm. average grade gold) in Kerala, Sonadehi prospect (upto 11.76 ppm gold) Bastar district, M.P.
- Several kimberlite pipes have been identified in Andhra Pradesh and Karnataka. These include three kimberlite bodies in Kalyandurg area of Anantapur district, Andhra Pradesh, one in Muligiripalle, and one in Yagapur in Karnataka. It may be mentioned here that this is the first report of kimberlite emplacement within the Closepet Granite. One of the three kimberlite bodies at Kalyandurg has yielded one microdiamond. Processing of a total of 972 tonnes of material from Anumpalle, Dibbasanipalle and Golapalle Kimberlite bodies has produced 24 diamonds weighing 3.58 ct. 2 diamonds weighing 2.15 ct. and 15 diamonds weighing 2.28 ct.
- A high platinum rich breccia zone (5.95 pprn to 7.15 ppm Pt.) has been identified in the southern extension of the already known PGM-mineralised zone of Boula-Nausahi area, Orissa.

- High incidence of Cesium and Lithium have been reported from Beku Pegmatite body in Chhotanagpur Gneissic Complex in West Bengal.
- A 10 m. wide band of high grade limestone extending over 20 km. from Gempalle to Lingala, in Cuddalore district, Andhra Pradesh, has been reported.

Expedition to antarctica : An area of about 1000 sq.km. was geologically mapped on 1:50,000 scale in the eastern part of Muhling-Hoffmanfjella. GSI is participating in the ongoing XVIIIth Expedition to Antarctica.

International co-operation

The first meeting of the Indo-South African Working Group on Geology and Mineral Resources, set up in pursuance of the Agreement on Co-operation in the fields of Geology and Mineral Resources signed between the two countries was held in South Africa from the 13th to the 19th August, 1998. At the end of the Working Group meeting, a Protocol was signed in Cape Town on the 18th August, 1998.

The 12th meeting of the Indo-French Working Group on Mineral Exploration and Development was held in Paris on the 7th and 8th October, 1998. The meeting prioritised five new projects amounting to FF 48.95 million (Rs.35.77 crores) and recommended for inclusion under the Indo-French Financial Protocol. The cooperation with BRGM, France, has so far resulted in flow of FF 137.88 million (Rs.100 crores approx.) assistance to upgrade equipment and skills in the GSI, IBM, MECL and some State Geological Departments.

The 5th meeting of the Indo-Russian Working Group on Ferrous and Non-Ferrous Metallurgy was held in Moscow on the 24th and 25th November, 1998. The Russians have offered technology transfers, including upgradation of old Soviet Hot Rolling Mill and Aluminum Smelter of BALCO in Madhya Pradesh.

The first 'Pride of India' Exhibition was held in Vietnam from the 14th to the 17th January, 1998. HZL and NALCO had set up stalls in the exhibition which were widely appreciated. Following the success of the first exhibition, the 2nd 'Pride of India' Exhibition was held in Hanoi from the 23rd to 26th October, 1998. The prospects of the Pac Lang Joint Venture gold project between HZL, La-Source, France and Vietnam Minerals Corporation was discussed with the Vietnamese authority.

Science & technology

The entire demand of nickel in India, which is presently around 25,000 MT, is met through imports. In order to produce this important metal in the country, technology has been developed through a collaborative project between HZL and CSIR. A Technology Proving Plant (TPP) at an estimated cost of Rs.10 crores is being set up at Regional Research Laboratory, Bhubaneswar The cost of TPP is being equally shared by HZL and CSIR. The foundation stone was laid by the Minister of Steel & Mines on 7.9.1998. If the TPP is successful, commercial production of nickel through chromite overburden, which is available in plenty, will be undertaken.

National mineral awards

The National Mineral Awards for 1997 were presented by the Minister for Steel & Mines at a function held on 24.12.1998 in New Delhi. Twelve Awards carrying a cash prize of Rs.50,000/- each were made to outstanding scientists/technologists in recognition of their meritorious contribution in their respective fields. The 'Award of Excellence' carrying a cash prize of Rs.1,00,000/- was conferred on Prof. K.S. Valdiya of the Jawaharlal Nehru Centre for Advanced Scientific Research, Bangalore, for his sustained and significant contributions in the field of geosciences.

Other events

The Department of Mines including its Public Sector Undertakings (PSUs) and Subordinate offices participated in the 5th International Mining and Machinery Exhibition (IMME'98) organized by the Confederation of Indian Industry (CII) at Pragati Maidan, New Delhi from the 26th to the 29th October, 1998.

A 'Mega Event' was organized by the Department of Mines to celebrate the 50th year of India's Independence at Nagpur from the 6th to 8th August, 1998. The Indian Bureau of Mines, a subordinate office of this Department, also celebrated its Golden Jubilee.

12

Department of Mines

Main functions

The Department of Mines is responsible for survey and exploration of all minerals, other than natural gas, petroleum and atomic minerals; for mining and metallurgy of non-ferrous metals like aluminium, copper, zinc, lead, gold, nickel etc. and for administration of the Mines and Minerals (Regulation and Development) Act, 1957 in respect of all mines and minerals other than coal, natural gas, petroleum and atomic minerals. A list of subjects allocated to the Department of Mines, subordinate offices, public sector undertakings and research institutions under the administrative control of the Department of Mines is given at Table I & 11.

Organisational structure

Headed by the Secretary, the Department of Mines comprises an Additional Secretary, an Additional Secretary and Financial Adviser, who is common for the Department of Steel and Department of Mines, two Joint Secretaries, one Adviser (S&T), five Directors, three Deputy Secretaries, one Senior Principal Private Secretary, five Under Secretaries, one Deputy Director (Official Language), one Principal Private Secretary, fifteen Section Officers, seven Private Secretaries, one Junior Scientific Officer and one Assistant Director (Official Language). Besides this, the Department has a technical wing comprising one Industrial Adviser, one Additional Industrial Adviser, two Development Officers and two Additional Development Officers. The total number of sanctioned posts for the Secretariat of the Department of Mines is 51 Gazetted and 198 Non-Gazetted posts. In addition, there is a Chief Controller of Accounts assisted by a Pay and Accounts Officer and 35 Non-Gazetted staff in the Pay & Accounts Office.

List of subjects allocated to the department of mines

(i) Legislation for regulation of mines and development of minerals within the territory of India, including mines and minerals underlying the ocean within the territorial waters or the continental shelf, or the Exclusive Economic Zone and other Maritime Zones of India as may be specified from time to time by or under any law made by the Parliament.

(ii) Regulation of mines and development of minerals other than coal, lignite and sand for stowing and any mineral declared as prescribed substances for the purposes of the Atomic Energy Act, 1962 (33 of 1962) under the control of the Union as declared by law, including questions concerning regulation and development of minerals in various states and the matter connected therewith or incidental thereto.

All other metals and minerals not specifically allotted to any other Ministry/Department such as aluminium, zinc, copper, gold, diamond, lead and nickel.

Planning, development and control of and assistance to all industries dealt with by the Department.

Subordinate offices

There are three Subordinate Offices under the Department of Mines, namely :-

(1) Geological Survey of India (HQ, Calcutta)

(2) Indian Bureau of Mines (HQ, Nagpur)

(3) Controller of Mining Leases (HQ, Nagpur)

Public sector undertakings

There are six PSUs and one Joint Venture Company under the Department of Mines, namely :-

(1) National Aluminium Company Ltd. (NALCO), Bhubaneswar;

(2) Bharat Aluminium Company Ltd. (BALCO), New Delhi;

(3) Hindustan Zinc Ltd. (HZL), Udaipur;

(4) Hindustan Copper Ltd. (HCL), Calcutta;

(5) Mineral Exploration Corporation Ltd. (MECL), Nagpur;

(6) Bharat Gold Mines Ltd. (BGML), Kolar Gold Fields (Karnataka);

(7) Sikkim Mining Corporation (a company jointly owned by the Government of Sikkim and the Central Government).

Research institutions

There are three Research Institutions under the Department of Mines, namely:-

(1) Jawaharlal Nehru Aluminium Research Development and Design Centre, Nagpur.

(2) National Institute of Rock Mechanics, Kolar.

(3) National Institute of Miners' Health, Kolar.

Organisations under department of mines

Survey and exploration

Geological survey of India:

Regional exploration, geological mapping, surveys on land, sea and airborne surveys and priority assignments to GSI.

Mineral exploration corporation ltd:

MECL is responsible for detailed exploration of various minerals/ores by drilling and exploratory mining and proving reserves for their eventual exploitation.

Regulation and conservation

Indian bureau of mines:

Engaged in promoting, conservation and development of mineral resources of the country.

Controller of mining leases:

The Officer deals with the work relating to modification of all such mining leases which have been granted before 1972 i.e. the date when the provisions/amendments to the MM (R&D) Act, 1957 for the purpose were made.

(The State Governments have also framed Minor Mineral Concession Rules for regulation and development of minor minerals).

Minig and processing

Bharat aluminium company ltd.:

Incorporated on 27th November, 1965 with an integrated Alumina/ Aluminium Complex at Korba in Madhya Pradesh.

Bharat gold mines ltd.:

Incorporated on 22nd March, 1972 to own and manage the mines at Kolar Gold Fields (Karnataka) w.e.f. 1.4.1972.

Hindustan zinc Ltd.

Incorporated on 10th January, 1966 after the Govt. of India took over erstwhile Metal Corporation of India to own, manage and develop the mineral and smelting capacities for the strategic zinc and lead metals in the country.

Hindustan copper Ltd.:

Incorporated in November, 1967, it is presently the sole indigenous producer of primary copper in the country.

National aluminium, company Ltd.:

Incorporated on 7th January, 1981 to implement the BauxiteAlumina-Aluminium Project in Orissa.

Sikkim mining corporation (in which central Government has 49% equity participation):

It produces polymetallic ore which is treated in the concentrator plant producing copper, lead and zinc concentrates.

13

Survey and Exploration

Survey and exploration

The Geological Survey of India (GSI), a premier Earth science organisation in the country, has been rendering services to the nation and the scientific community at large in meeting the geoscience information requirements in diverse fields, natural resource build–up and the country's multifarious developmental missions. In the post–Independence era, there has been an added emphasis on locating and harnessing the natural resources for meeting the growing demands of various developmental sectors such as mineral/metal, power (thermal, hydro and nuclear), agricultural, irrigation, transport and communication, etc. Management of risks caused by natural hazards such as floods, landslides, earthquakes, defining and delineating areas prone to environmental degradation and providing geological inputs to optimise sustained development in the rural and urban sectors are gradually becoming important functions of the Survey.

The upgradation of geoscientific expertise through training and induction of modern technology and sophisticated tools coupled with R&D efforts also received attention. Creation of computerised database for management of geoscientific information and dissemination to the user agencies, both Government and private sectors, has become an important activity of the organisation. These activities of the Survey have benefited almost all the major segments of the Indian economy

The functions of the Geological Survey of India encompass a wide spectrum of earthscience activities such as geological, geophysical and geochemical mapping, specialised thematic studies, ground and airborne geophysical surveys, marine surveys, geoenvironmental studies, geotechnical and seismotectonic surveys and various laboratory studies.

The thrust areas of GSI's activities have evolved with the changing national priorities throughout the last eight Five Year Plans and are presently oriented in the light of the objectives and goals set for, the 9th plan. GSI has moulded its role suitably in tune with the economic reforms and liberalisation measures introduced during the period.

The Airborne Mineral Survey and Exploration (AMSE) Wing of GSI is engaged in airborne geophysical survey for the preparation of geophysical maps. The geophysical data sets are followed up by ground evaluation aimed at prospecting and exploration of minerals (including oil/hydrocarbon resources).

The Marine Wing of GSI continued off–Shore geoscientific surveys with the help of deep sea going research vessel, R.V. Samudra Manthan and two coastal research vessels, R.V. Samudra Kaustubh and R.V. Samudra Shaudhikarna, the latter two being deployed within the territorial waters along the East and West coasts respectively. The near shore areas within the bathymetric depth of 0–10m, where coastal research vessels cannot manouvre, were surveyed by hiring small mechanised boats and utilising portable equipment.

Mineral exploration

Mineral search and appraisal by the Geological Survey of India was tailored to meet the thrust areas envisaged for the 9th Plan with particular stress on prognostication for gold, diamond, basemetal and platinum groups of minerals.

Dimension Stone Granite (DGS) has of late assumed great importance due to its ever increasing demand in the export market. Accordingly, GSI has formulated the Phase – 11 programme (1997–98 to 2000–2001) with a more comprehensive objective to cater to the demands of this expanding industry,

During 1998–99, a total of 167 programmes on mineral investigation were taken up. Region–wise breakup of these programmes is given in the following table :

Minerals	*ER*	*NER*	*NR*	*SR*	*CR*	*WR*	*AM–SE*	*Total*
1	*2*	*3*	*4*	*5*	*6*	*7*	*8*	*9*
Coal/Lignite	14	–	–	[illegible]	13	4	–	36
Non–Ferrous minerals	2	1	2	–	3	11	2	21
Strategic & rare minerals	4	–	2	4	–	–	–	10
Gold	5	3	6	21	12	5	2	54
Diamond	2	–	–	5	3	–	–	10
Precious & Semiprecious minerals	–	–	–	–	–	1	–	1
Ferrous minerals	3	–	–	1	3	–	–	7
Limestone/ Dolomite	–	2	–	–	–	3	–	5

(Contd. . .)

Other Ind. minerals	2	–	1	3	1	1	–	8
Dimension stone	3	1	2	5	2	2	–	15

Geoscientific survey

Systematic geological mapping

The programmes on systematic mapping, however, did not get priority during the 7th and 8th Plans because of shifting priorities and shortage of required manpower to take up the additional work after fulfilling the prioritised programmes. Moreover, the areas left for systematic geological mapping are mostly unapproachable areas of the North–Eastern region, in the States of Arunachal Pradesh, Manipur, Nagaland, Mizoram and Meghalaya; of the northern Himalayas in the States of Jammu & Kashmir and Uttar Pradesh; Jarwa inhabited islands of Andaman & Nicobar; Abhujmar Plateau of Madhya Pradesh and parts of Andhra Pradesh. The output/coverage of this activity in many of these areas, has been aided by the support of airphotos, IRS imageries and digital image processing. The areas, so covered, however, will not be taken as mapping coverage on 1:50,000/63,360 scale but the information and findings of PRS inputs will be incorporated in compilation of quadrangle sheets.

The status of systematic geological mapping is given in the following table :

Specialised thematic studies

The multidisciplinary specialised thematic studies in selected areas were initiated a decade ago. The stress was laid on integrated inputs backed up by laboratory studies/analysis. This activity, in addition to resolving the problems on specific themes, is serving as the first logical step towards demarcation of potential mineralised zones outside the well defined areas.

(in thousand sq. km.)

Formation	*Total*	*Total Area area*	*Herd Rock Mapped*		*Quaternary area*	
area mapped			*Total*	*Total area*	*Total mapped*	*Total area*
Total area	3287.00	3083	2386.00	2206	901.00	877
Unappro–achable area	141.20	–	123.60	–	17.06	–
Mappable area	3145.80	3083	2262.40	2206	883.40	877
		(98% approx.)		(97.94%)		(99.27%)

Airborne surveys

The programme of airborne surveys of GSI has three components:

i) Multisensor Surveys with the Twin Otter aircraft of GSI.

ii) Aerogeophysical data processing.

iii) Ground evaluation of Airborne Geophysical Survey data.

Under the 15 year National programme with NRSA, GSI has covered 73% of the total target of 18,43,380 sq. km. by aeromagnetic survey till 1996–97.

Upgradation of the data acquisition and processing systems is going on as per schedule with training of scientists at Scintrex, Canada.

Marine survey

The Marine wing of the Geological Survey of India carried out cruises within the Exclusive Economic Zone (EEZ) by R.V. Samudra Manthan (RVSM). Within the territorial waters of the Bay of Bengal and the Arabian sea R.V. Samudra Kausthubh and R.V. Samudra Shaudhikama (RVSS) undertook surveys.

During the said period, RVSM surveyed in the regions west and east of Andaman Islands falling in the Bay of Bengal and the Andaman Sea, respectively. A total of 3015 Ikm (line kilometre) and 2765 Ikm of bathymetric and magnetic surveys respectively were carried out against a target of 1880 Ikm each of bathymetric and magnetic, respectively. Samudra Kausthubh covered 800 sq.km. against a target of 1000 sq. km. covering 350 Ikm of bathymetric and 150 Ikm of sub–bottom profiler against a target of 250 Ikm each in single cruise in the month of April, 1998.

Samudra Shaudhikama covered 1600 sq. km. against a target of 1200 sq. km. and covered 175 Ikm of bathymetric against a 220 Ikm target during the month of April '98 off Kundopur in the Arabian Sea.

Performance during 1998-99

Targets for the year 1998–99 (April 98 – March 99) and the achievements for the period April 98 – Dec. 98 and performance during the two previous years are indicated in the following table :

Mineral aearch & evaluation

Item		*96–97*	*97–98*	*98–99(+) Achieved upto Dec.'98*
Large Scale	T	3118.00	3945.90	2785.15
Mapping (sq.km.)	A	4048.00	4374.70	2928.46
Detailed	T	50.15	50.78	49.83
Mapping (sq.km.)	A	37.48	34.684	50.02
Drilling (metres)	T	1,47,698.00	1,28,210.00	89,810.00
	A	74,594.00	86,885.80	60,533.16

Survey and mapping

Airborne surveys

Item		*96–97*	*97–98*	*98–99(+)*
Multisensor Surveys by	T	25,000	20,000	[illegible],000
GSI Twin Otter aircraft		(12,500	(10,000)	(5,500)
(LKM/sq.km.)	A	18,746 (8,861)	3219	**Nil

Marine surveys (sq.km.)

Item		*96–97*	*97–98*	*98–99(+)*
Mapping in EEZ beyond territorial waters by R.V. Samundra Manthan	T	23,000	*78,000	As the Systematic Survey within EEZ has been completed only parametric studies are being taken

taken up

up

(Contd...)

	A	23,000	67,664	
Survey in territorial waters by two	T	2,000	*3,600	2200
coastal launches Ground	A	2,190	2,256	1900

Surveys (sq.km.)

Systematic	T	8,750	6,300	2507.60
Geological Mapping	A	7,542	3530	430.00
Specialised	T	7,148	7,430	7001.60
Thematic Mapping	A	6,649	4989	2775.00

Survey programmes

In connection with the multisensor airborne survey, an area of 9844 sq.km. encompassing 20,343 line km. of flying, was done over parts of Chattisgarh basin and in Betul district in two sectors, to locate kimberlite pipes and basemetal.

Mapping of an area of 57,324 sq.km. was carried out by R.V. Samudra Manthan in five cruises within the EEZ of India.

Systematic geological mapping of 430 sq.km. was carried out. Besides, specialised thematic studies on a large number of programmes were continued during the period under review.

Mineral search and evaluation

In connection with mineral investigation and evaluation, 2928.46 sq.km. of large scale mapping, 50–02 sq.km., of detailed mapping, and 60533.16 metres of drilling was achieved against the targets of 2785.15 sq.km., 49.83 sq.km. and 89,810 metres, respectively.

Coal and lignite

The national resource inventory as on 1.1.98, based on the data accrued through drilling by GSI and other agencies, indicated a total of 206.23 billion tonnes of coal. The all–India reserve of lignite stands at 29.36 billion tonnes as on 1.6.98.

GSI, during 1997–98 made a preliminary assessment of coal bed methane in Birbhum and North Karanpur coal fields based on in–situ reserves of coal and observed possible gas content. The total gas–in–place reserves amount to 1.64 trillion cu.ft. (Birbhum 0.87 billion cu.ft. and eastern part of North Karanpura 0.77 trillion cu.ft).

Gold

In the southern part of Dhanjori basin, search for gold in the QPC (Quartz Pebble Conglomerate) was intensified with induction of drilling. Detailed mapping and channel sampling were carried out in Sanudor block of Haludbari–Brauniya–Sanudar sector. The QPC is persistent over 450m strike length. Channel samples collected so far from Haludbari sector indicated an average grade of 0.75 g/t Au(gold).

Some of the prominent occurrences investigated have yielded a tentative additional reserve of 0.70 m.t. of 7.20 g/t Au in Dona East block, Jonnagiri belt, Kurnool district, Andhra Pradesh. A probable reserve of about 0.63 m.t. ore with an average grade of 3.54 g/t Au has been tentatively estimated in Chikkanahalli south block, Chitradurga belt, Chitradurga district, Karnataka. In Dugocha block in Manpura–Sanjela area, Dungarpur Dist., Rajasthan, geochemical sampling indicated gold values ranging from 0.12 ppm to 1.10 ppm in carbonate rocks. Significantly higher values of 2.09 ppm to 4.41 ppm Au have been recorded in the metavolcanic enclaves within the carbonates sequence. In Gurhar Pahar East Block, drilling carried out so far has intersected a number of mineralised zones analysing 0.5 to 1.0 g/t Au over width ranging from 1m to 16m. In Jammu & Kashmir, a programme of preliminary stream sediment sampling for placer gold and PGE was taken up in Taklung–Halne area, Leh district, Ladakh around the Kyun–Tso ultramafic body. In Sonadehi prospect Madhya Pradesh, the borehole SD–1 has intersected a 4.6m wide zone analysing 11.76 g/t gold at 1 g/t cut off. In Maharashtra several gold investigations were carried out in different prospects of Pular–Parsori Gold belt. viz. MaruparPular–Kosari block, Parsori East block. Parsori West block, and Pular (west) – Kosari–Kolari–Bhaonri and Ranmangli areas, Nagpur district. The Sonadehi prospect of M.P. and

Dona East block Jonagiri belt, Kurnool dist, AP seem to be promising.

Diamond

Regional search for kimberlite in basal Chhattisgarh Formation and the surrounding Saraipalli area, Raipur district, was taken up. Ground evaluation of aerogeophysical anomalies in parts of Raipur district and adjoining districts of Orissa are being continued during 1998–99 period for locating mineral targets including kimberlite. In Maharashtra, a multidisciplinary programme of search for kimberlite and lamproites was taken up in parts of Chandrapur, Nanded and Godchiroli districts. In Andhra Pradesh, two investigations were undertaken for search of new kimberlite bodies in the granite greenstone belts in Central segment of Wajrakarur Kimberlite Field (WKF), Anantapur district and Closepet Granite in the Kalyandurg area, Anantapur district, A.P. Three new kimberlite pipes (KL–1,2,3) have been, identified within Closepet granite in Kalyandurg area. A micro–diamond has been recovered from KL 2 body. Bulk samples from Anumpalle (P–10), Dibbasanipalle (P–11) and Golapalle (CC–4) kimberlite bodies from the Central segment of WKF were processed. So far, 24 diamonds weighing 3.58 ct were recovered by processing 659 tonnes of material from the Anumpalle body. A total of 225 tonnes of kimberlite material from Dibbasanipalle body was processed and two diamonds weighing 2.15 ct. were recovered. The Golapalle body produced 15 diamonds weighing 2.28 ct. from the processing of 88 tonnes of material. In Orissa, search for kimberlite/ Lamproite pipes in Indravati basin, Koraput and Nawarangpur district led to the identification of a number of prominent linements and a zone of high magnetic permeability near the northern margin of the basin.

Other minerals/metals

Mineral Commodities	*Reserve Estimated/ Significant finding*	*Areas*
1	**2**	**3**
Lead–Zinc–Copper	0.35 million tonnes of ore with 2.25%	South Sindeser Ridge, Dariba Pb+Zn.
Bethumni belt Rajasthan.		in
	1.14 million tonnes of ore with 3.82%	Latio–Ka–Khera East block of Pb+Zn. Dariba belt in
Bethumni Rajasthan.		
Manganese	0. 13 m. of Mn ore over a strike length of 220m and upto a	Parsoda block, Nagpur district Maharashtra depth of 30m.
Iron	Grab sampling of Iron ore indicated 56% to 68% Fe	IOG of Sumdargarh and Keonjhar
Platinum Group of Metals (PGM)	Chromite–ferrochromite breccia in gabboioc matrix, traced for 100m length with PGM content upto 7.88 ppm.	Bula Nuasalin arera, Keonjhar district, Orissa
Dimension Stone	1700 cubic meters of dimension stones (coloured grantie)	Cuttack, Dhenkanal Angul, Deogarh and Sambalpur district, Orissa.

Geoscientific survey

Marine Survey

	Target of 98–99	*Achivementss upto Dec. '98*
1	2	3
Coverage in EEZ (sq.km.)	As the systematic survey has been completed only studies will be taken up.	within EEZ parametric
Coverage in territorial waters (sq.km.)	2200	1900
Ground Survey		
Systematic Geological Mapping (sq.km.) on 1:50,000 scale	2507.60	430
Specialised Thematic Survey (sq.km.) on 1:25,000 scale	7001.60	2775.00

Specialised investigation

Geotechnical investigation

The association of the GSI in major civil engineering projects of the country continued during the year. Geotechnical services were rendered to 34 projects involving about 303 investigations mostly sponsored by different State Governments, majority of which are related to water resource development projects.

Geoenvironmental investigation

.2 The GSI carried out 54 items on environmental studies, majority of them pertaining to regional geoenvironmental appraisal. Some were oriented towards the environmental impact assessment of specific anthropogenic activities. Some others are related with coastal geodynamics and some were oriented towards seismotectonics.

The 9th Plan proposal of the GSI envisages programme of Development of Village Economy through Mineral Resources Appraisal (DOVEMAP). The study includes assessment of quaternary and recent deposits, comprising boulder, pebble, sand and clay which may be utilised for building and construction purposes. The programme has so far covered 199 villages in the States of Assam, Tripura and Meghalaya. Shallow level drilling also will be taken up, wherever needed, to assess the low value high yield mineral/material resource and ground water pollution.

Studies have also been undertaken for the arsenic pollution in groundwater of several districts of West Bengal. In this regard, collaborative project has been taken up with Indian Council of Agricultural Research and IIT, Kanpur. The geoenvironmental appraisal in parts of Calcutta Metropolitan District, a CMDA–GSI joint investigation, was continued.

Geothermal studies

Investigation to study the recovery/extraction possibility of Cs (cesium) in the field has commenced in July 1998.

In view of location of a large number of thermal springs in most seismically sensitive zones in the U.P. Himalayas, a programme for monitoring thermal manifestations in seismically sensitive zones like Gangnani in Bhagirathi Valley, Tapoban in Alakananda Valley, Deobata in Kali Valley has been proposed.

A MNES (Ministry of Non–conventional Energy Sources) sponsored project for assessment of power potential and direct heat utilisation possibilities from geothermal resources in Northern and Central India was taken up. Compilation of data is under progress.

Seismotectonic studies and natural hazards

GSI undertook investigations on seismotectonics with the aim to compile necessary database for assessment of seismic hazard potential of different parts of the country. With this view, the compilation of seismotectonic Atlas of India on 1: 1 m scale has been taken up and is in an advanced stage of finalisation.

The World Bank sponsored DST (Department of Science and Technology) project for setting up of the Khandwa telemetered network is progressing well. GSI has also been entrusted with the setting up of a broadband seismic observatory at Jaipur by DST.

At the request of Government of Maharashtra, GSI actively interacted with the Earthquake Rehabilitation Wing of Maharashtra for preparation of a seismic hazard map of Maharashtra in collaboration with Lamont Doherty Earth Observatory, U.S.A.

Laboratory and research

Laboratory studies including Research and Development activities in different disciplines of geoscience, constitute essential and integral components of most of the programmes/projects of GSI. To generate a database through laboratory studies and related research investigations, sophisticated analytical capabilities and infrastructural facilities in the disciplines of Petrology, Mineralogy, Geochemistry, Geochronology, Isotope Geology, Palaeontology, Photogeology, Remote Sensing and Geophysics have been developed. Linkage between the field investigations and optimum laboratory support needed for execution is built up in each of the schemes/ projects. In addition to the service programmes, the laboratory based divisions have taken up R&D programmes. Some of the findings in research investigations are as follows:

Petrological research has been oriented towards (1) granite–granulite relationship and crustal evolution of Chhotanagpur Gneissic Complex. (2) petrological studies of the Anorthosite massifs of Chilka, Orissa, for comparison of similar rocks in Antarctica and (3) evaluation of petro–tectonic implication of the granulitic suites, north of the Sausar Belt in the over all context of the tectono–thermal evolution of the Central Indian Mobile belt. A modest beginning in the field of experimental petrological studies has been made through a collaborative project with Allahabad University on lamproites of the Bokaro Coal Field.

In the field of Palaeontological studies the find of metazoans activity suggests thigmotactical locomotion, digging and tunnelling in the glauconite standstones of the Semri Group which indicates the appearance of metazoans to be at least 1100 m.y., contrary to the existing perception of 860 m.y.

Finding of post canines of tritheledontid cynodont in the Carnian Tiki Formation from where the earliest mammal was discovered is particularly significant because it underscores the validity of the tritheledontid – mammal transition rather than the trithylodontid – mammal hypothesis.

Study of cephalopods from the Jurassic of Kutch made it possible to demarcate the Bathonian–Callovian and Callovian–Oxfordian boundaries.

Geochronological and related isotope research was undertaken in southern Granulite terrain, peripheral areas of Bundelkhand Complex; Champanar Group of rocks of Eastern Gujarat and Mishmi Diorite Complex of Arunachal Pradesh.

Elagiri syenite and Alangeyarn syenite in Southern Granulite terrain yielded Ca 850 Ma age which coincides with the younger alkaline plutonism of the Eastern Ghat, Mobile Belt.

The age of the granite intruding the Parsoi Formation (Mahakoshal Group) in southern UP along the Narmada lineament suggests the upper limit of the age of Mahakoshal metasedimentary rocks to be older than 1.7 Ga.

In Gujarat, the granite intrusives into the Champanar Gneiss yielded an age of 950 Ma and the pre–Champanar Gneiss has shown the metamorphic age around 1200 Ma. This age indicates closer affinity to the rock suites of Central India, rather than those of the Aravallis. The Mishmi Dioritic Complex of Dibang Valley, Arunachal Pradesh, indicated the Mesozoic crystallisation age of 142+9 Ma with low initial Sr ratio. This Mesozoic age indicates a probable relation with the Karakoram Granite Complex.

Chernical laboratories of GSI have analysed 92,835 samples involving 8,81,357 determinations.

Information dissemination

Dissemination of geoscientific information through various publications, thematic maps etc. forms a very important domain of the GSI's activity.

During the period under review, thirty five publications were brought out and nine more are in different stages of printing.

Twenty five Quadrangle geological maps were printed bringing the total number of published Quadrangle sheets to 172 out of a total 284 sheets amenable to geological data collection and publication. Geological and Mineral Map of North East India on 1:2 million scale and one sea–bed map of Territorial Waters of India in parts of Bay of Bengal have also been released this year. The Geological Map of India on 1:2 million scale has been published.

Computerisation effort in GSI gained momentum since June, 1996 with the commencement of the major project of "setting up of the Geoscientific Data Centre in GSI" in collaboration with the BRGM, France. The project has provided necessary input in modernising the map production facility of GSI at Hyderabad and Digital Image Processing facility at Nagpur, besides setting up of state–of–the–art geoscientific data centres at Calcutta, Lucknow, Nagpur, Hyderabad and Jaipur. The Centre for study of Ore deposits and Metallogeny (CSOM) has also been set up under the project at Jaipur.

The National Data Centre will serve as the nodal information window for the geoscientific community and commercial entrepreneurs. Human resource development forms an integral part of this on–going project and 50 officers have been trained in specialised subjects for running different centres and broadening the expert base in the organisation.

As a part of the post–GSI–BRGM project and in conformity with the National IT policy, GSI has embarked upon an ambitious programme on Informatics aimed at launching multiple database programmes at different locations to achieve faster growth of digital database.

The collaborative programme between the GSI and several Indian institutes and organisations for creation of database of multi–themed georeferenced data for parts of Madhya Pradesh and Maharashtra is progressing well.

GSI has taken up a programme for creating a database on earthquakes recorded in India and adjoining countries covering 00–370 N latitudes and 680–980 E longitudes. Thematic earthquake hazard and probability maps on selected tectonically active areas have been generated.

Training

The Training . Institute of GSI with its centres located at different parts of the country imparts training to professionals from the GSI and State/Central Government Department, PSUs and some foreign countries. It conducts about 28 programmes per annum.

International participation

GSI continued co-operation with international organisations, as in previous years, through participation in bilateral and collaborative programmes, various geoscientific projects under CGMW (Commission of Geology and Map of World), UNDP (United Nations Development Programme), SAARC (South Asian Association for Regional Cooperation) etc. and acted as the nodal agency for IGCP (International Geological Correlation Programme) in India.

GSI – BRGM, France collaboration programme involved upgradation and development of professional skills in GSL Now it is taking a turn towards supply of equipment like drill rigs. The possibility of Indo–Vietnam, Indo–China and Indo–Canada collaboration in selected fields is being explored. A collaborative proposal with Mauritius for mapping of their EEZ is under consideration.

Several fields like assistance in improvement of analytical facilities in GSI, supply of ground geophysical instrument, etc. have been identified for collaborative venture between India and Australia. Collaboration with South Africa is on the anvil. The GSI participated in the Indo South African Working Group meeting held in South Africa during August, 1998.

Under the existing Indo–Bhutan cooperation programme, GSI continued to render services in the fields of geological survey, mineral exploration, geotechnical investigation for hydroelectric and communication projects.

In order to fulfil the aim of effective manpower development, GSI organised 19 (nineteen) training courses on core disciplines and management.

During 1998–99, twenty two scientists went abroad for specialised training/attending seminars and eight officers participated in international seminars/ symposia held in India.

Expedition to antarctica

The GSI participated in the XVII Antarctica Expedition with a two member team. An area of about 1000 sq. km. was geologically mapped on 1:50,000 scale in eastern part of Muhlig–Honffmanfjcela between long. 6^0 30'–7^0 E and Lat. 71^0 40' – 72^0 S. It is also participating in the ongoing XVIII Antarctica Expedition.

Mineral exploration corporation limited

The Mineral Exploration Corporation Limited (MECL) was set up on 21.10.1972 to undertake detailed systematic mineral exploration and allied works in order to establish reserves of various minerals/ores in the shortest possible time so that the large time gap entailed between the discovery of a prospect and its eventual exploitation could be curtailed. The Corporation has been carrying out these functions by steadily enlarging its volume and scope of activities during the last 26 years and has so far established about 86,671 million tonnes of reserves of various minerals, besides estimating 471 billion cubic meters of coalbed methane resources in 7 coalfields in India.

MECL is the premier exploration agency in the country now. It carries out exploration activities under two major heads (a) Promotional, on behalf of Government of India, in which the projects are funded by Central Government on the basis of detailed exploration schemes formulated by the Company, in the perspective of demand vs. availability as well as national priorities and (b) Contractual, on behalf of other agencies including Public Sector, Private Sector and State Government, as per contract executed by MECL with them. The company is also diversifying into commercial mining of selected minerals and coal sampling to increase its revenue.

With its Headquarters at Nagpur, MECL has been carrying on operations all over the country. The activities of the company are carried out through separate divisions formed for attending to specific functions. The operational divisions comprise, Geology, Drilling and Mining. Support services are provided by Finance Division, Materials Management Division, Personnel & Administration Division ' Commercial Division and Planning & Monitoring Division. It also has a full fledged Information Technology Centre at Nagpur.

Physical performance

The production of drilling & mining, and the submission of geological reports during the year 1998-99 vis-a-vis previous three years are given below:

Production	*1956-96 Actuals*	*1996-97 Actuate*	*1997-98 Actuals*	*Target for 1998-99 (Budget estimate)*	*1998-99 Actuals upto Dec. '98*	*1998-99 estimated (Revised estimate)*
1	*2*	*3*	*4*	*5*	*6*	*7*
Drilling (Mtrs)	1,60,626	1,80,261	1,75,551	2,00,000	1,55,502	2,00,000

(Contd...)

Mining (Mtrs)	2,079	3,758	5,215	5,500	3028	5,000
Final Geological Reports (Nos.)	50	65	71	40	45	–

Financial performance (operating results)

(Rs. in crores)

Details	*Actuate for the Previous 3 years.*			*Annual Budget Estimates*	*Actuals 1998-99 Upto*	*Annual esti-mates*
	95-96	*96-97*	*97-98*	*1998-99*	*Dec'98*	*1998-99 (Revised Estimate)*
Income	35.40	41.15	51.58	63.50	42.09	63.50
Operating Cost	41.41	38.34	49.39	58.34	38.37	56.45
Interest and transaction loss	3.38	4.03	0.94	6.96	0.64	1.00
Depreciation and amortisation	2.93	2.94	3.71	5.00	2.96	5.00
Net profit before income tax and dividend	-12.32	-4.16	-2.86	-6.80	0.12	1.05

Sales performance

Details	*Actuate for the Previous 3 years.*			*Annual Budget Estimates*	*Actuals Upto Upto*	*Annual esti-mates*
	95-96	*96-97*	*97-98*	*1998-99*	*Dec'98*	*1998-99 (Revised Estimate)*
Sales	35.40	41.15	51.13	63.50	42.09	63.50

Ongoing projects

The priority in exploration continues to be for energy minerals i.e. coal and lignite. In addition, exploration for lead, zinc, copper, molybdenum, uranium, gold, iron ore and diamond was also continued.

Under the promotional programme, exploration is in progress for the following :

Promotional exploration on behalf of the department of mines

a) Copper at Kalapahar and Singhana in Rajasthan
b) Bauxite at Amtipani-Dipakujam block in the state of Bihar.
c) Copper at Dhadkidih in the state of Bihar.
d) Molybdenum at Vellampatti in the state of Tamil Nadu.

Priority regional exploration for coal and lignite on behalf of the ministry of coal

a) Coal in the command areas of Singareni Collieries Company Ltd. and Coal India Ltd. in CCL, SECL & WCL areas)
b) Lignite in the states of Tamil Nadu. Rajasthan & Gujarat.

A brief review of major Exploration programmes undertaken during 1998-99 (Upto December '98) is given below :-

Coal : Major exploration activities of MECL continued to be for coal, in which exploration was continued on contractual basis on behalf of Coal India Ltd, and also on behalf of Ministry of Coal under priority regional exploration programme. Total 102,543 m. of drilling and 693 m of mining/mine construction work was completed in various blocks of Bihar, West Bengal, Madhya Pradesh, Maharashtra and Andhra Pradesh for Coal India Ltd. and

Singareni Collieries Company. Under Priority Regional Exploration programme on behalf of Ministry of Coal, against an allocation of 75,500 m for the year 1998-99, 48,761 m of drilling representing 65% has been completed.

Copper : Detailed exploration for copper Surahari block in Jhunjhunu dist., Rajasthan was concluded and geological report was submitted, establishing therein 4.960 million tonnes of copper ore reserves with average grade of 0.92% Cu. Drilling work is in progress at Kalapahar and Singhana blocks (Rajasthan) where 4843m of drilling has been carried out till Dec.'98.

Uranium : Mine construction work for Uranium was continued at Jaduguda (Bihar) as a contractual work for UCIL and 552 m. of mining was achieved during 98-99. Mine construction work at Narwapahar commenced, where 462 m of mining was carried out upto 'Dec.'98.

Lead-Zinc : Mine Construction work at Balaria, Mochia, on behalf of HZL (Rajasthan) was continued and 617m of mining has been completed upto Dec.'98.

Bauxite : Exploration for bauxite at Amtipani-Dipakujam, district Gumla. on behalf of Department of Mines, was continued . A total of 2,893 m of drilling and 115 m of pitting work has been achieved during the current year upto Dec.'98. The contractual work at Baphlimali on behalf of UAIL commenced during November '98 and 566 m of drilling has been achieved.

Iron Ore : Exploration work at Kudremukh Iron ore on behalf of KIOCL was concluded where 1,634 m. of drilling was carried out. Besides, developmental mining on behalf of OMC at Gandamardhan has also been completed during the year and 363 m of progress has been achieved.

Lignite : Exploration for lignite was continued on behalf

of Ministry of Coal under priority regional exploration programme and a total 55,000 m of drilling was allocated in the states of Tamil Nadu, Rajasthan, Gujarat and Maharashtra for priority regional exploration, against which 36,139 m of drilling has been completed in 1998-99 upto Dec.'98. Besides 250 m of drilling for lignite was completed on behalf of RSMDC. Thus, the total drilling achievement in lignite including contractual and priority regional exploration during 1998-99 is 36,389 m.

Gold : Exploration for gold was concluded in Chinmulgund Project with 1707 m. of drilling. Geological report was submitted establishing 1.36 million tonnes of gold ore reserves with 4.51 g/tonnes.

Significant findings based on MECL's endeavour

a) Total 2430 million tonnes of coal reserves were established (264 million tonnes of cooking coal and 2166 million tonnes of non-cooking coal).

b) 380 million tonnes of lignite reserves established in Sindhari and Gadiyala blocks in District Barmer and Bikaner, Rajasthan.

c) Total 5 million tonnes of Copper Ore reserves were established at Surhari copper deposit, Dist. Jhunjhunu, Rajasthan under promotional programme funded by Department of Mines.

d) 1.36 million tonnes of gold ore reserves with 4.51 g/ tonnes of gold were established at Chinmulgund block district Haveri, Karnataka.

e) MECL has established fully equipped Remote Sensing centers at Ranchi and Patna on turnkey basis for Government of Bihar. The revenue generated on account of this activity stands at around Rs. 46 lakhs.

Expansion & diversification

In order to expand the activities of the company,

vigorous marketing efforts were made through competitive biddings and discussions/negotiations, besides entering into MOUs and collaborative programmes with different clients, within India and abroad. The results of these efforts, in brief, are as under:

- Three work orders, valued at Rs.479 lakhs were received from various clients during 1998-99, through competitive bidding. In addition, work orders for undertaking coal sampling for five washeries in CCL command areas have been received.
- Memorandum of Understanding signed with :
  i) CSIR/CFRI for coal sampling and analysis work.
- CCL & SAIL, for coking coal sampling and analysis work for washeries at Kathara, Kargali and Rajrappa area.
- Discussions were held with
  i) GIPCL-for taking up balance drilling work for lignite exploration and for developmental drilling in Vastan area.
  ii) WCL-regarding coal sampling and analysis work at Nandan Washery.
  iii) Central Material & Soil Research, Ministry of Water Resources for Geotechnical activities and related work. A brochure on Geotechnical endeavour was prepared and presented.
  iv) HZL authorities regarding Geophysical work and also for detailed exploration of lead-zinc in Kayar block district Ajmer, Rajasthan. Exploration of Kayar block is

proposed to be taken up in collaboration with M/s.Boart Longyear, Canada.

v) RSMDC officials at Udaipur for Lignite exploration at Nagore, Rajasthan.

vi) ANETCO, Oman regarding consultancy work in Oman.

vii) BARC officials to undertake Remote Sensing studies in western Rajasthan and environmental studies in Bundelkhand region Stage-II, Phase-III. The revised cost estimate for environmental studies is being submitted and the work is likely to be awarded soon.

viii) BALCO representatives, for bauxite exploration at Bodai-Daldali, Dist. Rajnandgaon, M.P.

ix) Negotiations/discussions with SICON/VED for taping of CBM in Vidarbha, Maharashtra State is in progress.

x) Discussions were held with WCL authorities regarding coal sampling and analysis work.

- Agreement for Geological & Geophysical work at Deri block, Rajasthan, submitted to M/s.METMIN for ratification.
- Review of exploration for copper in Singhana block (Phase-II) was prepared and sent to Department of Mines, Government of India
- Nominated members participated in the different meetings held to organise the Mega Event of Department of Mines for celebration of the Golden Jubilee of Indian Independence.
- Agreement was signed with UCIL for excavation

or ore pass system for vertical shaft and other development work at Narwapahar Project.

➢ The draft MoU sent to IICT, Hyderabad for quality of Singareni Collieries despatched.

➢ **MECL participated :**

i) MECL participated in the Seminar and Exhibition held at Nagpur from 06.08.98 to 08.08.98 on the occasion of the "Mega Event" organised by Department of Mines.

ii) In Jharkhand Udyog Mela at Ranchi, from 9th to 13th, October, '98 organised by Chhotanagpur Small Scale Industry. Activities of MECL were exhibited through posters and multi media presentation.

iii) In Metals & Metallurgy 1998 exhibition at New Delhi, from 7th to 10th October, '98, where activities and products of MECL were shown through posters, exhibits and multi media presentation.

iv) In Exhibition "IMM-98 International" from 26th to 29th October, '98 at New Delhi. Highlights of MECL works and services offered were presented through trans slides to the multinational companies and investors.

v) In an exhibition organised by Association of Exploration Geophysics (AEG) at Nagpur, from 28th to 30th October, '98. Highlights of MECL work specially of Geophysics were displayed through posters and multi media presentation.

vi) In an international exhibition "Pride of India" at Hanoi, Vietnam, from 23rd to 26th October, '98. Highlights of MECL activities were presented to multinational companies and investors.

Programme for diversification

As a part of its diversification programme, MECL intends to enter into commercial mining of limestone, dolomite, silimanite and fluorite in the state of Maharashtra, in collaboration with Maharashtra State Mining Corporation (MSMC). So far the indications are positive and the proposal may be through in 1999-2000.

MECL has been identified as third party Agency for Coal Sampling and Analysis. MECL has already taken up Coal Sampling and Analysis work at Jarangdih for CCL-SAIL, at Korba and Baikunthpur for SECL-NTPC and at Dhanbad for BCCL-SAIL. From the identified quantum of work the expected revenue during 1998-99 would be around 50 lacs.

Energy conservation

Mineral Exploration Corporation Limited carries out exploratory drilling and mining for various minerals through different projects located at remote places of the country. The equipments used for exploration work are mainly driven by diesel engines. The electrical energy consumption for physical work at sites is practically at the minimum (e.g. lighting in mine face). The following steps are being continued in order to curtail the expenditure on POL and promote POL conservation.

a) Machineries/Vehicles consuming excessive POL are timely withdrawn from operations for overhauls/repairs.

b) MECL has set up Regional Maintenance Centre at Nagpur, Ranchi and Hyderabad for monitoring the conditions of machineries/vehicles deployed at projects. Regular/periodical maintenance of machineries/vehicles is being carried out to reduce consumption of fuel, breakdowns and improve performance.

Energy conservation is attempted in 2 ways:

Direct - by avoiding/minimising wastage :

All the drilling personnel have been advised to avoid/ minimise wastage of fuel, lubricants and other consumables.

Indirect - by carrying out periodical maintenance of all machinery and vehicles:

Regional Maintenance Centres have been set up at Nagpur, Ranchi and Hyderabad for monitoring the condition of the drills, machinery and vehicles deployed at various projects of the MECL for taking up their periodical and preventive maintenance for reducing breakdowns and improving their performance. This will help to reduce the consumption of fuel, lubricants, etc.

Computerisation

MECL has updated Computer Hardware and Software and a new Information Technology Centre to cater to the requirements of Fields and Corporate Office.

The technology upgradation in terms of procurement, installation and commissioning of latest Computer hardware and software was done. New Computers (Pentium) were installed at RMC's, Sr. Manager (Geology) Offices and user Divisions for computerised data entry and processing to improve upon efficiency and quality of work.

The computerised data processing related to geological modelling applications, geostatistical application, MIS, Salary, costing, Billing and other miscellaneous jobs continued during 1,998-1999.

Action taken on abatement of pollution and environment protection

The exploration activities of MECL do not cause any

pollution. However, MECL is carrying out Environmental studies for helping the exploitation agencies to plan measures for possible avoidance of pollution and environmental degradation at the time of mining. Baseline data is being collected for Environmental Impact Assessment (EIA) in various exploration projects and a report on the same is included in geological reports of the project. MECL has also taken up "Site Characterisation" studies for selection of suitable and safe places for disposal of hazardous wastes.

During the year 1998-99 MECL has submitted 3 reports on environmental studies.

1) Project Granite Bundelkhand Phase-II MP : Site characterisation studies for identification of suitable site for disposal of hazardous wastes.
2) Base line status of environment at Chinmulgund gold project, Dist. Haveri, Karnataka.
3) Project Granite Jaisalmer, Rajasthan. Site characterisation studies for identification of suitable site for disposal of hazardous wastes.
4) Base line environmental study is in progress in Mannargudi Lignite Project Tamil Nadu, Amtipani Dipakujam Bauxite Project, Bihar and Dhadkidih Copper Project, Bihar.
5) Remote sensing studies for Kutch and Saurashtra region is in progress.
6) Report on land use/land cover studies for Surahari-Kalapahar block was submitted.
7) Remote sensing report on Mohan block, Bander Coalfield, Dist. Chandrapur, Maharashtra was submitted.

Salient aspects of the work being done by advisory boards/ councils

During 1998-99, MECL participated in the 2nd "Standing Committee on Promotional Projects" (SCPP) formed by the DOM, held on 30.7.98 in which three proposals were approved for execution under promotional activity sponsored by the Government.

MECL participated in the 33rd Central Geological Programming Board meeting held during Sept. '98 at Calcutta. MECL programmes were reviewed in subcommittee meetings on coal/lignite, non-ferrous metals, noble metals, ferrous minerals, etc. held during the year.

MECL participated in the meetings of the State Geological Programming Board of Maharashtra, Kerala, West Bengal, Andhra Pradesh, Tamil Nadu and Gujarat and had close interaction.

Perspective oin non-ferrous metals

During 1998-99 (upto December '98) the company has carried exploration for copper ore and took part in target reach for lead-zinc ores. The details are given below:

Copper ore

i. The exploration for copper ore in Surhari block, Khetri copper belt, District, Jhunjhunu, Rajasthan was concluded in June '98 with completion of 4373 m. of exploratory drilling. 1.0 sq. km. of geological mapping and other associated jobs. The Geological report was submitted in October 1998. A total of 4.96 m.t. of copper ore reserves with 0.92% of Cu were established Kalaphar block, Khetri belt, Rajasthan is in progress. Against an annual work programme of 5600 m in these blocks, 1044 m has been achieved in

Singhana block and 2873 m in Kalaphar block. It is planned for intimation of work in Singhana block after completion of exploration in Kalapahar block.

Among the new projects

ii. The exploration for copper ore commenced in Dhadkidih Area, Singhbhum copper belt, Bihar in the month of July 1998 and work is in progress. The objective of the exploration is to confirm the strike and depth continuity of the lodes, static correlation and structure of lodes, estimates of reserves/grade and estimate beneficiation characteristics. So far, total of 5354 m of drilling has been completed upto December '98.

In the non ferrous sector, the annual work programme of MECL for the year 1998-99 includes 10,650 m of drilling for copper ore against which 10197m has been achieved upto December 1998.

Research & development activities

Following Science & Technology scheme is in progress :

1) Evaluation of metal content in basemetal and allied ores by geophysical logging.

– The administrative approval from the Department of Mines in respect of revised cost estimate for the project has been obtained vide letter no. 1(17)/86 - Met.-IV (Vol-II) dated 10.9.97. This is for supporting the expenditure to be incurred by MECL to undertake the commissioning of the imported equipment procured under this scheme.

– Full commissioning of the equipment by M/s Scintrex, Canada. The firm offer from the company has been obtained. The equipment shall be dispatched for upgradation at M/s Scintrex by the end of February '99

- Against the grant of Rs. 53.06 lakhs received during 1998-99, the sum of 23.06 lakhs would be utilised for this scheme.

New schemes

- Further, three new S&T proposals were put up in the SSAG meeting held on 19.12.97, New Delhi.
- The Committee has approved the scheme entitled "Development of electromagnetic tomography and buried electrode method for geotechnical studies and mineral exploration". Administrative approval for the scheme from DOM has been received vide letter No. 14(25)/96 Met-IV dated : 12.02.98. Out of the Rs. 53.06 lakhs received for S&T project during 1998-99 Rs. 30 lakhs shall be utilised for purchase of equipments for which specifications of equipment have already been collected. The global tender has been floated in January '99. The tender would be opened by March '99.
- In respect of other two schemes viz. (i) Development of geoenvironmental evaluation system (GENES) and development of model data bank/model for geo-friendly mines for selected minerals/ mining districts and (ii) Conceptual geological ore body modelling of Gadag Gold Field, Karnataka, the committee directed to re-submit the schemes after discussions with different organisations and necessary modifications.
- A meeting was held at Nagpur, as per the directives of SSAG, for review and modification

of the scheme of "GENES" and development of model data bank/model for geo-friendly mines for selected minerals/mining districts. Experts on environment from GSI and IBM participated. The modified scheme is being put up to DOM.

Industrial relations

As per the approval of the Department for pay revision, the pay and allowance of Executives under IDA pattern effective from 1.1.92 have been implemented with effect from 1.7.98 which has boosted the morale of front line executive and reduced the gap between CDA and IDA executives.

Contingent workmen of Bhopalpalli KTK-5A Project were on illegal strike w.e.f. 16.7.98. However, due to intervention of RLC(C)/ALC(C), Hyderabad, the contingent workmen called off the strike and have resumed their duties with effect from 21.8.98 and normal work has started at Bhopalpalli KTK-5A Project. The period of strike from 16.7.98 to 20.8.98 has been treated as "No work No pay" basis.

Pay Revision of all IDA executives (including Board Level) is due from 1-1 -1997 and Wage Revision of Unionised Regular employees is due from 1-4-1997. The Board in its 138th meeting held on 9th September, 1998 has approved payment of adjustable Interim Relief @ 10% of the basic pay subject to a minimum of Rs. 280/- per month to all I.D.A. employees on the roll of the Company, which is being paid.

At Chinoor Project Office, about 30 to 35 Ex. Contingent Workmen retrenched from MECL earlier, held demonstrations from 06.10.98 to 11.10.98 and also gheraoed the Project Office. Their main demand was regularisation of their services as per the CGIT, Jabalpur Award. MECL officials at the project explained the current status of the award and informed that the matter was subjudice as such and requested that they refrain from agitations, but they could not be persuaded. They continued their agitation from 13th to 16th October '98. Meanwhile, our officers met Mandal Revenue Officer, Chinoor on 13.10.98 and apprised him of the position. Mandal Revenue Officer, held discussion with these Ex. Contingent Workmen and requested them to call off their agitation immediately and not to precipitate since the matter was already subjudice. However, his request was turned down by these persons. On 14.10.98, ALC (C) and Labour Enforcement Officer, Mancherial also visited our project and held discussions with MECL officers at Chinoor. The matter was explained to him and he was requested to intervene in the matter so that the agitation was withdrawn. Accordingly, both ALC(C) & Labour Enforcement Officer, Mancherial requested them to withdraw their agitation immediately. On the request of the team of officials from CHQ and RMC Hyderabad, ALC(C), Mancherial visited the Chinoor Project Office on 16.10.98 and held prolonged discussions with the representatives of the agitating persons and they were impressed to withdraw the agitation/gherao immediately. They were agreed that MECL, can commence its operation from 19.10.98. It is worthwhile to mention that the regular employees of the Chinoor Project did not support or participate in this agitation and also had shown exemplary courage in dealing with the situation.

Perspective plan for women's welfare

We stand for raising and improving the socioeconomic status of women. For this purpose, we provide them training to acquire new skills for their career development. We also propose to organise programmes to educate women against social evils like dowry, regionalism, communalism, etc. depending upon availability of funds.

Welfare of tribals and minorities

Welfare of SC/ST's : MECL has given due importance to meet the socio-economic needs of the tribals and minority communities living in and around each camp/project site. However, in view of continued financial constraints being faced by the Company, no welfare activities were undertaken during the period under review. However, if any proposal for minor welfare activities is received for the upliftment of the weaker sections of the society, the same will be considered on the merits of each case keeping in view the fund availability.

Special recruitment drive for SCs & STs Keeping in view the difficult financial position of the Company and the surplus manpower, it has been decided to keep all recruitments including under "Special Recruitment Drive" in abeyance.

Personnel position as on 31.12.98 including SC/STs

The overall representation of SC/ST in MECL is 21.98% as on 31.12.98 and representation of SC/ST is as under:

Group	*Approved Strength*	*Total no. of Employees*	*SC*	*ST*	*% of SC*	*% of ST*
1	2	3	4	5	6	7
A		433	63	21	14.55	4.85
B	600	72	10	3	13.89	4.17
C		1703	243	115	14.27	6.75
D		1090	156	114	14.31	10.46
Total	2500	3298	472	253	14.31	7.67

Overall Percentage of SC/ST -21.98%

Employment of SC/ST/EX-SM/PH/LDP/minorities as on 331.12.1998

Group	*Total*	*SC*	*ST*	*Ex-*	*Physi-*	*LDP*	*Minori-*
		No. of			*Service*	*cally*	
ities			*Emplo-*			*men*	*Handi-*
			yees				*capped*
Executives	505	73	24	03	01	–	43
Non-Executives	2793	399	229	25	11	–	257
Total	3298	472	253	28	12	–	300

Export/import performance

The Company is neither exporting nor importing any goods.

Mou rating of PSU's achieved

The MOU rating of the company for last four years is given in the table below :

Year	*Composite Score*	*Rating*
1994-95	4.55	Poor
1995-96	2.20	Very good
1996-97	2.15	Very good
1997-98	2.27	Very good

Progressive use of hindi in official work

In accordance with the policy of Government of India for extensive use of Hindi for official purpose, all out efforts were made for progressively increasing the use of Hindi in official work,

HINDI DIWAS/PAKHWADA was organised at CHQ and other establishments of MECL from 01-09-98 to 14-09-98. At CHQ, Nagpur various competitions were conducted to encourage the use of Hindi among employees. Many executives and non-executives participated in these programmes. Concluding function of Hindi Pakhwada and Hindi Diwas was held on 14-09-98 which was presided over by the CMD, MECL. He also distributed prizes to the winners of various programmes. CMD, MECL appealed to the employees to encourage the use of Hindi in official work and complimented the employees who had participated in various programmes during Hindi Pakhwada. The function was attended by a large number of employees.

Abbreviations

1. AEG – Association of Exploration Geophysicists
2. ALC (C) – Assistant Labour Commissioner (Central)
3. BARC – Bhabha Atomic Research Centre
4. BCCL – Bharat Coking Coal Ltd.
5. CBM – Coal Bed Methane
6. CCL – Central Coalfields Ltd.
7. CFRI – Central Fuel Research Institute
8. CSIR – Council of Scientific & Industrial Research
9. DOM – Department of Mines
10. GIPCL – Gujarat Industrial Power Corporation Ltd.
11. HZL – Hindustan Zinc Ltd.
12. IICT – Indian Institute of Chemical Technology
13. KIOCL – Kudremukh Iron Ore Company Ltd,
14. MOIL – Manganese Ore India Ltd.
15. NTPC – National Thermal Power Corporation
16. OMC – Orissa Mining Corporation

17. POL – Petrol & Other Lubricants
18. RLC (C) – Regional Labour Commissioner (Central)
19. RMC – Regional Maintenance Centre
20. RSMDC – Rajasthan State Mineral Development Corporation
21. SAIL – Steel Authority of India Ltd.
22. SECL – South Eastern Coalfields Ltd.
23. SICOM – State Industrial Corporation of Maharashtra
24. UAIL – Utkal Alumina Industries Ltd.
25. UCIL – Uranium Corporation of India Ltd.
26. VED – Vidarbha Economic Development
27. WCL – Western Coalfields Ltd.

14

Regulation and Conservation Indian Bureau of Mines

The Indian Bureau of Mines (IBM) is a subordinate organisation under the Department of Mines, Ministry of Steel and Mines. It is engaged in the promotion, conservation and scientific development of all the mineral resources of the country, other than coal, petroleum and natural gas, atomic minerals and minor minerals.

Towards this end it performs regulatory functions, namely enforcement of the Mines and Minerals (Regulation and Development) Act 1957, Mineral Concession Rules 1960 and Mineral Conservation and Development Rules 1988 and the relevant provisions of the Environmental Protection Act 1986. It also undertakes scientific, tech no-economic, research oriented studies in various aspects of mining, such as geological studies, ore beneficiation and environmental issues.

It provides Technical Consultancy services to the mining industry for the geological appraisal of mineral resources, and the preparation of feasibility reports of mining projects, including beneficiation plants. It prepares Mineral Maps and a countrywide inventory of mineral resources of leasehold and freehold areas. IBM also functions as the Data Bank of Mines and Minerals and publishes statistical periodicals. It also brings out technical publications/monographs on individual mineral commodities and bulletins of topical interest. It advises the Central and State Governments on all aspects of mineral industry, trade and legislation.

IBM imparts training to technical and non-technical officials of IBM and also persons from the mineral industry and other agencies in India and abroad.

Organisational set-up

The IBM is organised into four functional divisions, namely, (i) Mines Control and Conservation of Minerals (MCCM) Division, (ii) Ore Dressing and Technical Consultancy Division, (iii) Mineral Economics, Statistics, Research and Publication Division, and (iv) Planning and Co-ordination Division having two sub-divisions :

(a) Administration, Establishment matters (including training), accounts with all other administrative and financial matters; and

(b) Planning and Co-ordination.

IBM has its headquarters at Nagpur and twelve regional offices at Ajmer, Bangalore, Bhubaneswar, Calcutta, Chennai, Dehradun, Hyderabad, Jabalpur, Marvao (Goa), Nagpur, Ranchi and Udaipur and two sub-regional offices at Guwahati and Nellore.

The IBM has well equipped ore dressing laboratories and pilot plants at Nagpur. Ajmer and Bangalore.

Performance review

The performance of IBM in respect of its main activities during the period under review is indicated in Annexure-1. During the year 1998-99 (upto Nov., 1998), 1758 violations of Mineral Conservation and Development Rules (MCDR) 1988 were pointed out in respect of 721 mines and 498 violations were fully rectified. Forty one prosecutions were launched in various courts. Six cases were decided in favour of IBM and 28 cases were compounded.

Cumulative number of mining plans received by the IBM at various Regional Offices since its introduction upto the end of November, 1998 were 8583. Out of these, 6645 mining plans were approved, 937 rejected, 723 withdrawn by the parties and 148 were pending with the parties for modification with reference to the comments conveyed to them after scrutiny. 121 mining plans were under scrutiny with the IBM at various Regional/Zonal offices and 9 mining plans were pending with the Directorate of Mines

Safety for their comments. However, the status of disposal of mining plans during 1998-99 (upto Nov. 98) is given in Annexure-I separately.

Measures for abatement of pollution and environmental protection

The IBM continued its activity of educating the mine-owners about pollution control and environmental protection in mines by organising Mines Environment and Mineral Conservation (MEMC) Weeks. The celebration of MEMC Weeks in the regions of IBM has promoted environmental awareness in the mining industry. During 1998-99 (upto November, 1998) two such programmes were organised under the aegis of the Bangalore Regional Office.

The IBM approves the mining plans which constitute a basic pre-requisite for the grant/renewal of mining leases and for the existing mines. Environment Impact Assessment and Environment Management Plan are the integral parts of the mining plan through which adequate environmental protection during mining operations is ensured.

Preparationo of Mineral Maps

During the year 1998-99 (upto Nov., 1998) preparation/updation of mineral maps of copper, lead and zinc in AP, Bihar, Gujarat, Karnataka, Orissa, Rajasthan and Sikkim covering about 14,000 hectare area alongwith corresponding forest overlays was in progress.

Mineral Beneficiation

Mineral beneficiation studies including mineralogical testing and chemical analysis is intimately related to both conservation and development of mineral resources. During the year 1998-99 (upto Nov., 1998), 51 ore dressing investigations, 45,537 chemical analyses and 1,713 mineralogical examinations were completed. Besides, 7 in-plant studies were carried out during the period.

The task of compelling a compendium of R&D facilities for processing of ores/minerals over the years since India's independence, was entrusted to IBM by the Ministry. Accordingly, a compendium entitled "R&D Facilities for processing of Ores/Minerals in India" was prepared in IBM and was released by the Hon'ble Minister for Steel & Mines, Shri Naveen Patnaik.

Inventory of mineral resources and market survey report

Computerisation of National Mineral Inventory (NMI) updated as on 1.4.97 was completed for 4 minerals and analytical reviews of NMI as on 1.4.1995 were prepared for 13 minerals. Besides, a Handbook of NMI as on 1.4.95 was under preparation.

Market Survey study on China clay was in progress and a bulletin of Rare alloy metals in India was under printing.

A handbook on Non-ferrous Metals in India 199596 issue was released and annual bulletin on Consumption of Non-ferrous Metals in India, copper-lead-zinc, April 1997 - March 1998 issue was under printing. Besides, 2 quarterly reports on End-use metal consumption for copper, lead and zinc for quarters ending March 98 and June 98 were prepared.

Stastical publications

IBM disseminates statistical information on mines, minerals, metals and mineral based industries through its various publications. Information on mineral production, stocks, despatches, employment, inputs in mining, mining machinery and related matters received from the mine owners on statutory basis under the MCDR, 1998 and ancillary statistics on metals production, mineral trade and market prices of minerals, revenue from the mining sector, rent, royalty and cess on minerals, etc. from other agencies is compiled regularly by IBM.

The statistical publications released during the year 1998-99 (upto Nov., 1998) include Statistical Profile of Minerals, "1997-98 issue, Indian Mineral Industry at a Glance, 1996-97 issue and 7 issues (upto June, 1998) of Monthly Statistics of Mineral Production.

Concultancy service

IBM provides technical consultancy services on prescribed charges for geological appraisals, survey of the areas, preparation of feasibility study reports, environment impact assessment and environment management plan, selection of suitable mining equipment, evaluation of feasibility reports prepared by other consultants, financial institutions, etc. The assignments completed during the year 1998-99 (upto Nov., 1998) include (i) Collection of samples for chemical analysis from Ametha Limestone Mine for M/s N.M. Dubash Stone and Lime Co. and (ii) Coal stock measurement at various collieries of Coal India Ltd.

Besides, 5 assignments on preparation of Mining scheme/Preliminary Geological Appraisal reports were in progress.

Technical publications

IBM brings out technical publications relating to mines and minerals, mineral based industries, trade, beneficiation, R&D activities, etc. During the year 1998-99 (upto Nov., 1998), Volume-II of the Indian Minerals Year Book (IMYB), 1996 issue and Volumed of the IMYB, 1997 issue were released and Volume-II of the IMYB, 1997 issue was under printing. Besides, Directory of Mineral Consumers in India a bulletin on Mineral Royalties and 2 issues of half-yearly bulletin on Mineral Information (April-Sept., 97 and Oct., 97-March, 98) were released.

10.2 Under the series 'Mineral Facts and Problems' the Monograph on copper was under printing and preparation of Monograph on clay was in progress. A bulletin on Status of the Mining Industry based on special study reports (South Zone) was released.

11. Mining Research

11.1 Applied Mining Research is carried out on various mining aspects so as to help in systematic development of mines and improvement in productivity in mines through evolution of suitable norms. Industry sponsored assignments on environment and rock mechanics aspects on charge basis are also undertaken. During the period under review,* 2 assignments on preparation of EIA/EMP of Mokhana Limestone Mine for M/s Tata Chemicals Ltd. and Geotechnical investigation of Bhotang Copper Mine for M/s Sikkim Mining Corporation Ltd. were completed and report submitted to the parties. Besides, 5 assignments sponsored by the Industry on charge basis are in progress.

Training

IBM imparts training to technical and nontechnical officials of IBM and also to persons from mineral industry and other agencies in India and abroad. During the year 1998-99 (upto Nov., 1998) 17 training programmes were conducted in which a total of 109 IBM personnel and 68 industry personnel including 2 from North-Eastern states participated. Besides, under the MoU for co-operation between India and Vietnam in the field of Geology and Mineral Resources. IBM imparted training for one month to 3 Vietnamese Mining Engineers/Geologists.

Advising central and state governments on matters connected with the mining and mineral industry

IBM continued to advise the Central and State Governments on matters concerning mines and minerals, export and import policies, mineral consumption and industrial utilisation, recovery of by products, demand and supply of minerals, renewal of mining leases. Necessary material was also furnished to the Ministry for answering Parliament Questions during its various sessions. Assistance was also rendered to private parties, institutions and foreign organisations on subjects like mineral production, consumption and other statistics.

IBM Advisory board

The 11th meeting of the IBM Advisory Board was held on 3rd April 1998 at Nagpur under the Chairmanship of Shri B.B. Tandon, the then Secretary (Mines). During the meeting following important decisions/suggestions were made:

i) IBM should reduce its role as a regulatory body and increase its role as a facilitator even though both these functions are being performed by IBM commendably

ii) IBM to ensure total transparency and promptness in discharge of its duties.

iii) IBM should try to reduce the time taken for approving the mining plans and accord priority to this work and to maintain total transparency in the process.

iv) IBM should try to reduce the time lag between the preparation and release of various technical publications and also review the cost of the publications brought out by IBM.

v) The important investigations being undertaken by OD Laboratory of IBM should be patented.

vi) IBM and National Institute of Rock Mechanics, KGF, can collaborate together undertake Various projects on geotechnical studies, slope stability, etc.

Sub-committee to make recommendations to IBM advisoryr board for more effective functioning of IBM

The sub-committee constituted by the Department of Mines, Ministry of Steel and Mines to make recommendations to the IBM Advisory Board for effective functioning of IBM, submitted its modified report after deliberations in the meetings held on 29.4.98 and 24.9.98 to the Chairperson for further consideration.

Working group meetings

Indo-french working group

Shri A.N. Bose, Controller General, IBM visited France from 3-10 Oct., 1998 as a member of the Indian delegation for the 12th meeting of the Indo-French Working Group on Mineral Exploration and Development. During 4-6 Oct., 98 he visited BRGM Laboratories and attended the Expert Group Meeting at Orleans. He also attended the 12th meeting of the Indo-French Working Group on

Mineral Exploration and Development co-chaired by Shri B.B. Tandon, the then Secretary (Mines) on the 7th and the ceremony of signing of the protocol on the 8th Oct., 98 at Paris.

Indo-South African working group

As a member of the Indian delegation led by Shri B.B. Tandon, the then Secretary (Mines), Shri K.S. Raju, Director (OD) from IBM attended the first meeting of the Indo-South African Working Group on Geology and Mineral Resources from 13-19 August, 1998. At the end of the Working Group Meeting, a protocol was signed between India and South Africa. A total of 6 projects were identified for cooperation of which one project entitled 'Characterisation and processing of gold, diamond and platinum group metal/ ores' is to be in collaboration between IBM and one of the R&D laboratories in South Africa.

IBM-BRGM projects

Assistance for setting up of a Mineral Resource and Intelligence System (MRIS) Database at IBM, Nagpur:

Under the IBM-BRGM-MRIS Project, during the year 1998-99 (upto November, 98) Mines-cum-Production and Integration outputs were modified and installed at IBM, Nagpur. With this, all the databases namely National Mineral Inventory & Beneficiation (NMI&B), Mines cum Production (MCP), World Mineral Intelligence (WMI), External Trade & Mineral Consumption (ETMC) and Mining lease, Mining Permit Geological Information System (MLMP-GIS) and their screen out-puts have been installed by BRGM experts in the VAX/VMS 3100 server in IBM. The Termination Agreement of the IBM-BRGM-MRIS Project was signed on 9.11.98 at Nagpur between IBM and BRGM, France.

Project on Development of Application Techniques in relation to Environmental Management of Mines and Waste Recoveries:

Under this project, field studies were taken up in 1997-98 by IBM teams in 3 Mines Study Sites namely in North Goa and Sukinda in Orissa State for assessing regional environment impact and for preparation of Environmental Management Plan. In Rampura Agucha lead-zinc mine in Rajasthan processing and waste recovery was continued during the period under review, Baseline data generation and processing of data in respect of air quality, water quality and quantity, collection of soil sediments and aquatic life, dust gauge samples, noise level etc. for winter and summer seasons were completed and water quality and quantity monitoring in monsoon season was completed for North Goa and Sukinda Mines Study Sites.

Five BRGM experts visited IBM from 4-18 May 1998 on a mission to observe and guide the field work of IBM teams.

BRGM experts on Rock-Mechanics Study and Rehabilitation of Waste dumps visited IBM in November, '98. After the field visits to Goa and Sukinda Mines Study Sites, the sites for drilling boreholes for installation of piezo-meters for carrying out geotechnical study and also the parameters to be analysed for soil quality testing in connection with rehabilitation of waste dumps were finalised.

Technical management information system (TMIS)

An agreement between IBM and BRGM, France on 'Setting up of Technical Management Information System (TMIS) at IBM, Nagpur' at a cost of FRIF 23.4 million was signed on 22.6.98. The kick-off meeting of the project was held on 9.11.98 between BRGM experts and IBM counterparts at Nagpur and the project formally took off. As a Phase I activity the meetings between IBM and BRGM experts were held during 10-16 November, '98 for evaluation of the database general design and the draft report was signed.

BRGM experts alongwith IBM officers visited each Regional/Zonal office of IBM and had an on-the-spot assessment for installation of Computer System and the existing system of each proposed project site.

Software Training Programme on ORACLE 8.0 in WINDOW NT operating system for 38 officers/ staff of IBM was arranged at Nagpur in 3 batches.

Golden Jubilee celebration of IBM

On 1st March, 1998, IBM completed 50 years of its dedicated service to the Nation in particular to the Mineral Industry and is celebrating the Golden Jubilee Year. Special lectures by eminent Earth Scientists and other authorities were arranged at the IBM Headquarters, Nagpur and at the Regional Offices. A 3 days function was organised at Regional Ore Dressing Laboratory, Ajmer during 11-13 August, 1998. The Ore Dressing Laboratory and Pilot Plant were kept open to the public and to the students from educational institutions and universities to acquaint themselves with IBM's activities.

Mega event to commemorate the 50th anniversary of India's independence

Department of Mines, Ministry of Steel & Mines constituted an organising Committee to celebrate the Mega Event to commemorate the 50th anniversary of India's Independence, with Shri A.N. Bose, Controller General, IBM as its Chairman and Shri Satish Chander, Director (Mines) as Co-Chairman with CMDs of Public Sector Undertakings under the Department of Mines,

Secretary General, FIMI and Chief Executives of some of the reputed Business Houses as members.

To mark the momentous milestone of 50 years of India's Independence, the 'Mega Event' was celebrated from 6-8 August, 1998 at Nagpur. It was inaugurated by Shri Naveen Patnaik, Hon'ble Minister of Steel & Mines on 6th August, 1998. During the inauguration, the Hon'ble Minister released a Souvenir which contained the brief activities and functions of the Organisations and Public Sector Units under the Department of Mines and some important mining organisations. The Hon'ble Minister presented Special Awards to 15 Geo-scientists and Technologists for their distinguished contribution to the Mining Industry. A video presentation on 'Strides of Mineral Industry since Independence' was also arranged. The inauguration was followed by a Technical Seminar with its theme as 'Indian Mining Industry : A Perspective'. The Technical Seminar was spread over 5 technical sessions on these three days. Eminent Geo-scientists and Technologists from various organisations/ mining industry of the country presented papers in these technical sessions. A compendium of all the 30 technical papers presented in the seminar was brought out on the occasion.

The valedictory function was held on 8.8.98 in which Shri Ramesh Bais, Hon'ble Minister of State for Steel & Mines was the Chief Guest and Shri Nitin Gadkari, Hon'ble Minister for Public Works and Guardian Minister for Nagpur, Government of Maharashtra was the Chairman. Shri R.K. Sharma, Secretary General, FIMI, New Delhi, gave a presentation of overview of the proceedings of the Technical Seminar. About 300 delegates from various - Organisations/Mining Industry participated in the Mega Event. An Exhibition was also arranged at Hotel Tuli International, Nagpur in which

IBM, GSI, MECL, BALCO, NALCO, HCL, HZL, BGML & JNARDDC participated.

Revenue generation in IBM

Revenue generated during 1998-99 (upto November, 1998) from the consultancy work in mining, geology, ore dressing and mining research work, training and through sale of publications etc. was Rs. 24.70 lakhs.

Foreiggn seminars/symposiums, etc.

Shri M.N. Makode, Suptdg. Officer (OD), IBM was deputed to China during 21-30 June, 1998 to witness the test work conducted by Beijing General Research Institute of Mining and Metallurgy (BGRIMM) and to study the reproducibility of the flowsheet developed by BGRIMM in connection with establishing a fluorite beneficiation plant for producing acid grade concentrates by the ESSEL Mining Industries, New Delhi.

Dr. (Mrs.) M.N. Gaikwad, Assistant Ore Dressing Officer, IBM participated in the Mineral Engineering Conference 1998 organised by Camborne School of Mines, University of Exeter (UK) during 14-16 September, 1998 at Edinburgh, Scotland and presented her research paper entitled 'Frother Blends - Effect on Flotation of Mixed Sulphide Ore of Malanjkhand Copper Project, Balaghat (India).

Computerisation

Local Area Network (LAN) has already been installed at IBM Headquarters Complex. The work on Wide Area Network (WAN) is also in progress. Regional/ Zonal Offices located at various cities are being connected with NIC district centres through dial-up modems for E-mail communications. Facility of internet surfing is also available in IBM.

Data Acquisition System (DAS) has been established and is in operation in the Pilot Plant of IBM. The DAS is used while conducting pilot plant test runs for controlling some of the circuits like pulp density in grinding circuits, pH in the flotation circuit, etc. and acquiring real time data from various field instruments like power consumption in Jaw crusher, Cone crusher, Ball mills, etc., pulp density and mass flow, water flow, pH values, temperatures etc. Off line data can also be entered in the system through manual data entry for storing and utilising in the report preparation.

Work done concerning women (perspective plan for women)

Indian Bureau of Mines has not drawn up any specific perspective plan for women, however, out of a total strength of employees, women employees constitute about 11 percent. Training was imparted to some women employees in the field of technical as well as administrative matters.

Women employees are also actively participating in various cultural and extra-curricular activities organised by IBM from time to time. The 'Women's Day' was observed during the National Integration Week.

Employment of SC/ST women as on 30.12.1998

Class	*Total No. of employees in position*	*No. of SC*	*No. of ST*	*No of Women*
Group A	245	50	19	8
Group B	88	11	5	6
Group B (NG)	55	7	6	13
Group C (Tech)	485	80	37	30
Group C (Min)	363	85	29	92
Group D	359	107	35	29
Total	1595	320	131	178

15

Mining and Processing

National aluminium company limited

National Aluminium Company Limited (NALCO) was incorporated on 7th January 1981 as a wholly owned Government company to exploit a part of the large deposits of bauxite discovered in the East Coast. Aluminium Pechiney of France, a world leader in the field, provided the technology and basic engineering for bauxite mining, alumina refinery and smelter. The project cost of Rs. 2408 crore was partly financed by Rs. 1119 crore equivalent of Euro-Dollar loans extended by a consortium of international banks and the balance Rs. 1289 crore through equity from Government of India.

Under extremely difficult logistics of implementing a multi-locational greenfield project, NALCO successfully constructed and commissioned each of its units on schedule and within estimated cost, a feat which has few parallels in the annals of Indian Public Sector history. NALCO's various production units, their locations and installed capacities are :

◆ Bauxite Mines	Panchpatmalli	22,400,000	TPY
◆ Alumina Refinery	Damanjodi	. 800,000	TPY
◆ Smkelter Plant	Angul	230,000	TPY
◆ Captive Power Plant	Angul	720	MW
◆ Port Facilities	Vizag	375,000	TPY

The Commissioning dates of the various facilities a as follows :

- Port facilities – September, 1985
- Bauxite Mines – November, 1985
- Alumina Refinery – September, 1986
- Captive Power Plant – September, 1986
- Smelter – March, 1987

.3 The systems support for the complex includes a coal mine and coal handling plant set up by the Mahanadi Coalfields Limited.

The Company is managed by a Board of Directors headed by the Chairman-cum-Managing Director and assisted by whole time functional Directors in the areas of Projects & Technical, Finance, Production and Personnel & Administration.

Physical performance

The production of NALCO during the year 1997-98 and 1998-99 are given below :

(Figure in Tonnes)

Items	*Unit*	*95-96*	*96-97*	*97-98*	*Target for 98-99 Dec./'98*	*1998-99 Actuals Upto 98-99)*	*Annual estimate (RE*
Bauxite (Crushed & Transported	'000MT	2408	2558	2662	2550	1808.69	2700
Calcined Alumina	'000MT	807	840	883	850	654.60	897.5
Aluminium	'000MT	192	204	200	218	99.52	150
Net Power Generation of CPP	MU	4147	4187	3902	4100	2590.02	3950

Financial performance

Operating results

Details	*95-96 Actuals*	*96-97 Actuals*	*97-98 Actuals*	*Annual Target 98-99 (BE)*	*Actual upto Dec '98*	*Annual esti-mates 98-99 (RE)*
Income	1813.05	1818.70	1983.71	2093.81	1194.47	1848.24
Operating cost	927.17	987.89	1052.71	1120.90	723.38	1056.99
Interest etc.	64.83	9.08	33.57	16.56	32.75	32.775
Depreciation and amortisation	285.78	265.82	272.00	281.95	205.78	278.74
Net Profit before tax and dividend	535.27	555.91	625.43	674.40	232.56	479.76

Aluminium smelter crisis

During the year 1998, NALCO had to shut down the operation of a number of pots in its Smelter plant at Angul, Orissa. In view of the gravity of the problem, Government ordered an Enquiry Committee to look into the problems affecting the smelter of NALCO and consequent loss of production. The Committee was constituted on 12.6.1998 under the chairmanship of Dr. C.G. Krishnadas Nair, Chairman , HAL.

The Enquiry Committee submitted its report on 4th August 1998. The Committee has broadly come to the conclusion that the gradual deterioration in the performance of pots over the years is mainly due to non-adherence to the standard operating practices, improper maintenance, poor work culture, improper planning and lack of team work. The Committee made several recommendations to avoid recurrence of such failure in future. The Company has taken action on the recommendations of the Enquiry Committee and the position has improved. The number of pots, which had touched the level of 239 pots on 22.7.98, has since improved to 367 pots as on 3.1.1999. The quality of the metal produced has also improved and export of metal has been resumed.

Sales performance

Items	*Unit*	*95-96*	*96-97*	*97-98*	*Annual Target 98-99 '98*	*Actuals upto Dec/ 98-99*	*Annual estimates for*
1	2	3	4	5	6	7	8
EXPORT							
Alumina/ Hydrate	'000MT	415.2	465.13	479.8	425.00	453.68	600
Aluminium	'000MT	49.13	60.36	55.48	60	18.23	30
DOMESTIC							
Aluminium	'000MT	143.09	145.52	140.66	158.00	64.75	120
Power to GRIDCO	MU	1093	903	658	800	718.51	1003

Ongoing projects

Projects under implementation:

Strip Casting Facility

Trial run has started.

Gallium Project :

A 950 Kg/annum 5 N purity Gallium Extraction Plant at Damanjodi at a cost of Rs. 12.77 crore based on indigenous technology and financial assistance to the extent of Rs. 5.54 crore coming from associated Government of India agencies e g. DSIR, DST, DRDO & NRDC is scheduled to be completed by December, 2000.

Special grade alumina

A 26,400 TPY Special Grade Alumina Plant at Damanjodi, at a cost of Rs. 56.78 crore based on technical know-how obtained from Alumina Technology Associates, USA is expected to be commissioned during the 4th Quarter of 1999.

Zeolite

A 10,000 TPY Detergent Grade Zeolite (Zeolite-A) Plant at Damanjodi at a cost of Rs. 24.10 crore with consultancy services rendered by Engineers India Ltd. is scheduled for completion during the 2nd quarter of 1999.

Aluminium Wheel Project :

The project for setting up of Aluminium Wheel Project for 4,50,000 nos. of wheels per year at Bhubaneswar and 10,000 MT per year Alloy Ingot Plant at Angul is in progress. NALCO has acquired 11.00 acres of land. M/s. MECON has been appointed as an Engineering Consultant. Finalisation of Technology supplier is in advanced stage. The total capital cost is estimated at Rs. 92.56 crores.

Expansion & diversification

Expansion

The proposal for expansion of Aluminium Smelter from 2,30,000 TPY to 3,45,000 TPY and Captive Power Plant from 6 × 120 MW to 7 × 120 MW at a cost of Rs. 2062 crores (June 1997 price level) was approved by the Government of India on 3rd February 1998. M/s Engineers India Ltd. has been appointed as the principal consultant for the expansion of Smelter Project. M/s EIL has also been entrusted with the work of Time & Cost monitoring work.

- M/s M.N. Dastur & Co. has been appointed as the Consultant for implementation of VII unit of CPP.
- An Agreement with M/s Aluminium Pechiney (AP) has been signed on 28.04.98 for supply of basic engineering for certain improvements for the Smelter. This has been approved by SIA in August '98. A team of AP experts visited Angul in June '98 to collect the basic data for preparation of basic engineering. The same has been finalised in August '98.
- The tendering procedure for award of site grading work, provision of power and water for construction are under way and are expected to be awarded shortly.
- The project is to be implemented within 51 months from the zero date viz 3rd Feb '98.

Mines & alumina refinery :

The expansion project for increasing the capacity of Bauxite Mines from 2.4 to 4.8 MTPY and that of Alumina Refinery from 0.8 to 1.575 MTPY at a cost of Rs. 1665 crores is under implementation by the Company. The project is to be implemented within 51 months from zero date i.e. 18th December 1996.

Energy conservation

NALCO has adopted modern technologies in all production units leading to optimal consumption of energy. Best efforts are being made to conserve energy to the maximum extent by constant monitoring of specific energy consumption figures, adopting energy conservation measures, getting energy audit done by in-house team and reputed external professional agencies, encouraging implementation of innovative ideas in this field, exploring possibility of utilisation of renewable energy sources and adopting other useful measures in this direction.

During the year 1997-98, M/sTata Energy Research Institute carried out an energy audit of the Smelter Plant. During the year 1998-99, they are carrying out the energy audit of the Alumina Refinery Plant and Mines.

System support (Railways)

Transportation of bulk raw materials and finished goods are highly dependant on the rail system. All the raw materials like coal, CP coke, caustic soda, furnace oil etc. were transported in sufficient quantities to match the plants requirements. Despatches of alumina for export to Vizag and for Smelter Plant at Angul made upto November '98 are as follows :

By Rail	:	5,67,290 MT
By Road	:	14,165 MT
		5,81,455 MT

The despatches of aluminium metal for the year 1998-99 upto November '98 are as under :

By Rail	:	17,209 MT
By Road	:	60,699 MT
		77,908 MT

As regards coal, a quantity of 1.67 million tonne at Angul and 0.33 million tonne at Damanjodi were handled during this year 1998-99 (upto November '98).

Computerisation

Bauxite mines :

An order placed on M/s Modular Mining System Inc., USA for Truck Despatch System to monitor and optimise utilisation of loading and hauling equipments. Order execution is in progress.

Alumina refinery : distributor control system

Distributor Control System (DCS) is being implemented along with expansion of Refinery as a part of project activity.

Smelter

Order placed on M/s Digital Equipments (India) Ltd. for implementation of Production Planning and Control System (Metal Planning System). Order execution is in progress.

Captive power plant

Tender evaluation for Plantwide Networking and Supervisory Controlled Data Acquisition System is in progress

Wide area network

To expedite project implementation activities, Wide Area Network Facility extended to M/s Engineers India Ltd. at Gurgaon and M/s Dastur & Co. at Chennai. VSAT installed and operational at EIL, Gurgaon and procurement activity is in progress for VSAT for M/s Dastur & Co.

NSDL

Hardware and software for NSDL operations have been installed. Since July '98, NALCO shares are being traded electronically through NSDL.

Pollution control & environment management efforts

During the year under review, the performance of the Company in pollution control and environmental management has been satisfactory and encouraging. NALCO's efforts have been recognised at national and state levels with Gem Granite Environment Award, 1997-98 and Sitaram Rungta Memorial Social Awareness Award, 1997-98 by FIMI, New Delhi, Pollution Control

Excellence Award, 1998 from Orissa State Pollution Control Board and Best Occupational Health Services Award for M&R complex from State Safety Award Committee, Government of Orissa. Besides NALCO has also received prize money of Rs. 50,000/- for the Indira Priyadarshini Vriskhamitra Award, 1994.

All the 4 units of the Company i.e. Mines, Alumina Refinery, CPP & Smelter have ISO-14001 environment management system certificate. The process has been initiated for implementation of ISO-14001 at Port Facilities, Visakhapatnam.

So far 53,48,150 numbers of trees have been planted at different units of the Company. Out of these 3,91,900 trees were planted during the year 1997-98. The Company has participated in the drinking water supply scheme to 11 villages around the Smelter under peripheral development.

Salient aspect of the work being done by advisory boards/ councils

There are three S&T Advisory Committees in NALCO on the following :

a) Aluminium & Allied Products Project,

b) Alumina & Allied Product Projects and

c) Raw Materials and Allied Products Projects respectively were formed by NALCO, R&D officials academia from prestigious institutions like IIT, BHU, etc., experienced heads of research laboratories and senior level officials from industry to get the best mileage out of interaction and deliberations. The meetings are also structured and planned in a way so that the time of the members are utilised to the maximum.

The committees have no executive powers and are advisory in nature. The committees help in inculcating a process of in house deliberation and problems solving and developing a learning tradition in the organisation. Till date each of the above three committees met three times in a span of two years.

The pooled knowledge of experts and deliberations held in the above committees have helped the Company to go into the nitty gritty of the process parameters alternates available, the practices being followed and optimum solutions. A time table has been drawn for implementation of some of the practical suggestions made by the committees.

Special achievement

Development of this technology has been adjudged as the Best Technology developed during the year 1998 in the chemical discipline and three NALCO's R&D technologists received "NRDC Independence Day Award 1998" for their meritorious invention titled "Process for the Preparation of Alumina Hydrate of Superior Purity and Fineness and Process Preparation of Low Soda High Alpha Pure Alumina". The invention has also been recommended for prestigious WIPO Gold Medal of 1999.

Research & development activities

NALCO's in-house R&D establishments, both at M&R Complex, Damanjodi and S&P Complex, Angul have been recognised by DSIR, Ministry of Science & Technology, Government of India upto 31.3.2000.

Keeping in view, the long term research plans and programmes, medium to short term development activities pertaining to process and product development and adoption of new technologies, revamping of in-house

R&D centres at both Damanjodi and Angul sectors have been successfully completed at a cost of Rs. 5.2 crores.

For the financial year 1997-98, total R&D expenditure as % of turnover comes to 0.367 as compared to 0.029 for the year 1996-97.

Industrial relations

The industrial relations scenario in the Company is characterised by multi-unionism and inter-union rivalry. At present a total sixteen trade unions are functioning at different units out of which five are affiliated to INTUC, four to BMS, two to HMS; the remaining five unions are not affiliated to any Central Trade Union organisation.

There was a breakdown in the Aluminium Smelter of NALCO at Angul, Orissa. NALCO had to shutdown the operation of a number of pots in its smelter plant. Government ordered an Enquiry Committee to look into the problems affecting the smelter of NALCO. The Committee in its conclusion observed poor work culture, improper planning and lack of team work as one of the reasons for the deterioration in the performance of the pots. The Committee made several recommendations to avoid its recurrence. NALCO is taking steps to improve the work culture and discipline in the organisation.

Perspective plan for women's welfare

The Company has on its roll 209 women employees including 39 executives and 170 non-executives. The Company provides equal opportunity to women in employment. However, most of the jobs are highly technical and sufficiently skilled women are often not available for the same.

Necessary amendments have been incorporated I n the Conduct, Discipline Appeal Rules of the Company to combat sexual harassment of women employees. The Company also takes active part in the improvement of quality of social life in the vicinity of its units which includes womenfolk.

Welfare of tribrals and minorities

At Damanjodi, a predominantly tribal area, 521 families who were displaced have been provided with permanent houses in the rehabilitation colony built by the Company with provisions of roads, health and educational facilities, drinking water, electricity and recreation. NALCO has also taken the following welfare measures at its two sites located at Angul and Damanjodi:

i) Direct employment of 439 persons in NALCO on the basis of one able bodied person from each displaced family.

ii) Employment of balance with contractors working in NALCO.

iii) Literacy development programmes for illiterate LDP workers.

iv) In Peripheral Development Plan, an amount of Rs. 259.66 lakhs has been earmarked during the year for development of roads, college, school, library, creation of community centres, adult education centre, renovation of village ponds and wells, development of agricultural land, etc.

A member of the minority community is associated in the Selection Committees for Group "C and D" vacancies as a part of recruitment practice.

Employment of SC/ST/EX-SM/PH/minorities as on 2331/12/1998

Group	*Total no. of employees*	*SC*	*ST*	*Ex-SM*	*PH*	*Minorities*
1	*2*	*3*	*4*	*5*	*6*	*7*
Executives	1390	162	71	09	03	62
Non-Executives	4884	900	1055	80	51	169
Trainees	186	33	64	–	01	31
Total	6460	1095	1190	89	55	262

Export/import performance

Details	*Unit*	*95-96 Actuals*	*96-97 Actuals*	*97-98 Actuals*	*Target for 98-99 Dec./'98*	*1998-99 Actuals Upto 98-99)*	*Annual estimate (RE*
Calcined Alumina Exports	'000MT	415.2	465.13	479.8	425.00	453.68	600
Aluminium Exports MT	'000MT	49.13	60.36	55.48	60	18.23	30

Mou rating achieved

The Company's performance was rated Excellent in the evaluation of the Memorandum of Understanding signed with Ministry of Steel & Mines, Government of India for last three years. The details of scoring for the last three years is as follows:

Year	*MOU Scoring*	*MOU Rating*
1995-96	1.392	Excellent
1996-97	1.220	Excellent
1997-98	1.452	Excellent

Domestic sales performance

Details	*Unit*	*95-96 Actu-als*	*96-97 Actu-als*	*97-98 Actu-als*	*Target for 98-99*	*1998-99 Actuals Upto Dec./'98*	*Annual estimate (RE 98-99)*
Aluminium	'000MT	143.09	145.52	140.66	158.00	64.75	120.00
Power to GRIDCO	MU	1093	903	658	800	718.54	1003

Progressive use oif Hindi in official work

During the year 1998-99, special efforts were continued towards achieving the targets of progressive use of Hindi in the Company. Original correspondence in Hindi, original work and noting and drafting in Hindi by the employees trained in Hindi was encouraged.

Hindi Week from 8th to 14th September '98 and Hindi Day on 14th September were celebrated with a number of programmes. During this period many Hindi competitions were organised and prizes were distributed to the winners in the closing ceremony observed on 17th September '98.

On the occasion of the Hindi Week, a special issue of the Hindi magazine 'Akshar' was published and prizes were awarded for the best compositions by the employees and officers. Many letters of commendation are received on a national level for the articles published in 'Akshar'.

Publication of Monthly Newsletter Hindi Parichaya is regular. Efforts were made for developing the design and contents of this newsletter and many letters of commendation are being received.

In the Angul sector of NALCO, meetings of the Town Official Language Implementation Committee were organised, which is working under the convenorship of

NALCO and constituted under the directions of Department of Official Language, Ministry of Home Affairs, Government of India. NALCO played a significant role in providing guidance and cooperation in promoting the progressive use of Hindi in the Central Government offices and undertakings of this area.

At Damanjodi sector of the Company, special efforts have been made for increasing the use of Hindi by the employees by organising different Hindi competitions with the assistance of Kendriya Sachivalaya Hindi Parishad.

The challenging task of computerisation originally in bilingual form of different forms used in the office has been taken up by the Hindi Cell of the corporate office. Bilingual designing of most of the forms internally "is continued successfully.

The meeting of Bhubaneswar Town Official Language Implementation Committee was organised on 19th June '98 at Nalconagar auditorium, which was hosted and co-ordinated by NALCO.

Aluminium survey

The financial crises in Asia, Russia and Latin America is expected to undermine growth in the world's developing economies in 1998 as well in 1999. The world GDP growth will be around 1.8% in 1998 down from 3.3% in 1997. The growth is estimated to be 1.7% in 1999.

World aluminium consumption fell by 0.5% in 1998 after achieving a growth of 6.1 % in 1997. The consumption growth is likely to be around 1.3% in 1999.

The Indian primary aluminium production in 1997-98 reached 5,53,000 MT (growth rate of 5.7%) as against 5,23,000 MT (growth rate of 1.5%) in 1996-97. The production in 1997-98 is around 83% of the country's installed capacity of 6,70,000 MT. Projected to grow at a rate of 8%, the aluminium industry in India recorded only around 5.7% in 1997-98 on account of general economic slow down, acute power shortage and low consumption due to financial crisis faced by most of the State Electricity Boards where expansion plans were thereby delayed.

The growth of domestic consumption of aluminium fell sharply to around 2% in 1997-98 from 7% recorded in 1996-97. The growth is expected to be around 4% during the year 1998-99.

Bharat aluminium company limited

Bharat Aluminium Company Limited (BALCO) was incorporated on 27th November, 1965 with an integrated Alumina/Aluminium Complex at Korba in Bilaspur District of Madhya Pradesh. The Aluminium Plant has 200,000 tonnes per annum (TPA) capacity and has been set up based on Soviet Technology. The downstream facilities have the capacity to produce 35,000 TPA of Properzi Rods, 40,000 TPA of Rolled Products, 7,000 TPA of Extrusions and 18,000 TPA of Billets and Slabs etc.

BALCO has a second Unit at Bidhanbag, near Asansol, in West Bengal This vested in BALCO following nationalisation in June, 1984 by the Government of the company which then owned it.

As on 1st November, 1998 the Authorised Capital of the Company stood at Rs. 500 crores and the Subscribed Capital at Rs. 488.85 crores.

Production performance

The actual production figures of Korba Complex and Bidhanbag Unit for the year 1997-98 along with the target of 1998-99 and actual production figures for April-December, 1998 are given below:

Production performance of Korba/BBU

(Figures in Tonnes)

Item	*1997-98 Actual*	*1998-99 Target*	*April-Dec. '98 Target*	*April-Dec. '98 Actual*
Properzi Rods	30588	42072	31638	26992
Extruded Products	5939	7000	5255	3208
Rolled Products	35786	36000	27135	30036
Ingots, Billets	15885	9000	6722	7456
Total	88198	94000	70750	67692

Bldhanbag unit (BBU)

(Figures in Tonnes)

Item	*1997-98 Actual*	*1998-99 Target*	*April-Dec. '98 Target*	*April-Dec. '98 Actual*
Extruded Products	1004	800	604	284
Rolled Products	954	1500	1131	945
Foils	383	600	451	203
Conductors	84	800	604	–
Others	–	200	149	190
Total	2425	3900	2939	1622

Financial performance

(Rs. in Crores)

Details	*Actual for the previous years estimates 1996-7*	*1997-98*	*Annual budget Dec. 98 Target*	*Actuals upto Actual*
1	2	3	4	5
Income	826.53	859.99	836.77	621.26
Operating Cost	647.23	670.90	646.30	490.67
Interest & Transaction Loss	7.23	6.65	12.30	5.83
Depreciation & amortisation	44.90	47.65	43.15	36.81
Net Profit Before Income Tax & Dividend	127.17	134.79	135.02	94.00

On-going projects and expansion and diversification

New cold rolling mill

The company is implementing a project of setting up a new cold rolling mill at a cost of Rs. 157.50 crores at Korba. On completion of the project, BALCO will have competitive advantage in marketing as this mill would be producing thin sheets and foils

Mainpet mine

Diversion of 376-924 hectares revenue-forest land for mining (non-forest purpose) had been approved, in principle, by Government of India, Ministry of Environment and Forests. The drilling process in these mines is already on and reserves to the extent of 20 lakh tonnes have been proved. Further results would be known after completion of the remaining drilling process of 18,000 meters.

Rajnandgaon mine

Action for land acquisition has been initiated and M/s. MECON have been appointed to prepare the report for obtaining clearance from Ministry of Environment and Forests for commencement of mining activities.

Captive power plant

Feasibility Report on proposed expansion of the capacity of the Captive Power Plant at Korba is under study in association with NTPC.

(e) The proposal for revamping and modernisation of AAA Conductor Plant, Bidhanbag is under study. Its economic and other related viability aspects have been worked out to facilitate in-depth study in association with Technical Consultants and Experts.

Conservation of energy

Energy Conservation measures taken

Alumina plant

i. improvement of insulation in order to reduce radiation losses.

ii. Descaling of Flash Tank in order to improve the heat economy.

iii. Improvement in the feeding rate of the Hydrate to the Kiln to achieve fuel conservation.

iv. Replacement of Digestor Coils to achieve improvement in heat economy.

Smelter plant

i. Use of compressed air for removal of anode effect in Cell House No. 5 &6. Similarly in Cell House No. 7 & 8.

ii. Reuse of anode paste cooling water by recirculation.

iii. Use of bar breaker for crust breaking.

Fabrication complex

i. Use of fuel oil additive is under trial for conservation of fuel oil in furnaces.

Engineering services

i. In-house efforts for reduction of fuel oil.

ii. The use of E/F grade coal in place of "B" grade coal is under study.

Computerisation

Present Computerisation activity of BALCO includes financial accounting (FA) pay-roll, long-term PF Accounting, long-term PSL Ledger, marketing and invoicing system including excise gatepass, evaluation of ore deposits, etc. Cell House monitoring is also computerised and long-term SCADA is in use.

The Company is also taking necessary steps in its Information Technology Department to develop and make use of information technology in various Departments.

Pollution control & environment protection measures

During the year, the Company planted 10,000 saplings in reclaimed mined out areas. In addition, about 40,000 saplings were also planted in and around Korba and Bidhanbag units.

The Company is making efforts to adopt environment management system to achieve Indian and international standards in environmental management.

Salient aspects of the work being done by advisory board/ Councils

BALCO is presently availing of the technical know how and other related services from Jawaharlal Nehru Aluminium Research Development & Design Centre (JNARDDC), National Environmental Engineering Research Institute (NEERI), Nagpur and Central Glass Ceramic Research Institute (CGCRI), Calcutta.

Research & development

The Company continued its in-house R&D activities in certain specific areas. As a result of such efforts, certain improvements in plant productivity, purity and quality of products have been effected. Besides, development of value added products and cost reductions have resulted from such efforts.

Industrial relations

Industrial relations in the Company remained cordial during the year under review.

Perspective plan for women

Women employees of BALCO are being given all

statutory and normal benefits, including Creche facilities for their children. Seminars and workshops are being organised specially for participation of women employees, apart from sending delegations to outside seminars, etc.

Welfare of tribals & minorities

BALCO is looking after the health and other basic amenities of the surrounding tribal population near the Plant and Mines. Five villages have been adopted by BALCO and basic civic amenities, including health-care, are being given to residents. All other Government directives regarding reservation in employment and other facilities are being followed in the case of tribal population and minorities.

Employment of SC/ST/EX--Sm/PH/LDP/minorities as on 331.12.1998

Group	*Total No. of emplo- yees*	*SC*	*ST*	*Ex Servi- ceman*	*PH*	*LDP*	*Mino- rities*
Executives	1211	78	42	11	7	–	65
Non-Executives	6074	1064	950	92	11	–	674
Management Trainees	–	–	–	–	–	–	–
Apprentice Trainees	181	41	47	–	–	–	1
Total	7466	1183	1039	103	18	–	740

Mou rating

During the last three years the Company has received MOU ratings as follows:-

Year	*MOU Rating*	
1995-96	Very Good	2.27
1996-97	Very Good	2.26
1997-98 (Provisional)	Very Good	1.59

Progressive use of Hindi in official work

The Corporate Office and Korba Complex of the Company are located in "A" Region and its Bidhanbag Unit is in "C" Region. More than 80% of the employees have working knowledge of Hindi. The Corporate and Korba Offices have been, notified under Rule 10(4) of the Official Language Act in all the Units. The percentage of originating correspondence from Corporate Office, Korba Unit to States, individuals and other Central Government Offices in "A" Region is about 85%.

Hindustan zinc limited

Hindustan Zinc Limited (HZL), one of India's leading base metal producers, was incorporated in January, 1966 as a public sector company, after the takeover of the erstwhile Metal Corporation of India Limited~, to develop mining and smelting capacities to substantially meet the domestic demand for zinc and lead metals.

Hindustan Zinc Limited is an MOU signing' Company with Ministry of Steel & Mines, Department of Mines. The performance for 1997-98 was rated as "Excellent".

At present, HZL with its Headquarters at Udaipur operates five lead-zinc mines with a total lead-zinc ore production capacity of 3.04 million tpa and four smelters with combined installed capacity of 152,000 tpa zinc and 65,000 tpa lead, besides a rock phosphate mine. The Company offers a range of zinc and lead metal grades to its customers, besides by-products like silver, cadmium, sulphuric acid etc. The following tables depict the mines and smelters of the Company with corresponding production capacity:

Mines	*ore capacity (TPD)*
Zawar Group of Mines, Distt. Udaipur (Rajasthan)	4000
Rajpura-Dariba Mine, Distt. Rajsamand (Rajasthan)	2400
Rampura-Agucha Mine, Distt. Bhilwara (Rajasthan)	3000*
Sargipali Lead Mine, Distt. Sundergarh (Orissa)	500
Agnigundala Lead Mine, Distt. Guntur (Andhra Pradesh)	240
Maton Rock Phosphate Mine, Distt. Udaipur (Rajasthan)	600

* Mechanical completion of expanded capacity to 4500 tpd.

Smel Ters	*Metal Capacity (TPA)*	
	Zinc	*Lead*
Debari Zinc Smelter, Matt. Udaipur (Rajasthan)	49,000	–
Vizag Zinc & Lead Smelter, Matt. Visakhapatnam (AP)	33,000	22,000
Chanderiya Lead-Zinc Smelter, Distt., Chittorgarh (Raj)	70,000	35,000
Tundoo Lead Smelter, Distt. Dhanbad (Bihar)	–	8,000

Physical performance

Highlights:

1998-99 (April-Dec. 1998):

- Net Profit earning (PBT) of Rs. 107 crore, compared to the budget of Rs. 77 crore.
- Sales turnover of Rs. 897.16 crore, compared to the budget of Rs. 888.25 crore.
- Lead-Zinc concentrate production at 1,03% of the target.
- Zinc metal production at 104% of the target.
- Zinc metal sale at 103% of the target.

The production of lead-zinc ore, concentrate and lead-zinc metals are given below:

(Figures in tonnes)

Product	*1995-96 Actuals*	*1996-97 Actuals*	*1997-98 Actuals 1998-99*	*Target For Upto Dec. '98*	*1998-99 Actuals*	*1998-99 estimate*
1	2	3	4	5	6	7
Lead-Zinc Ore	2398513	2271676	2467729	2620000	2006874	2620000
Lead-Zinc Conc.	350104	336793	353025	402900	312414	390000
ZincMetal	115464	110876	136271	134000	103488	134000
Lead Metal	27843	27874	35766	40500	27856	38500

The lead-zincore and concentrate production are estimated at 100% and 97% respectively of the annual targets.

Zinc and lead metal production are estimated at 100% and 95% respectively of the annual target during the current year.

Financial performance

(Rs. in crores)

Details	*Actual for the previous 3 years*			*Annual Budget Est.*	*1998-99 Actual upto 1998-99 (RE)*	*Annual Estimate 1998-99 Dec.'98 (BE)*
	1995-96	*1996-97*	*1997-98*			
Income	906.83	996.91	1282.13	1197.89	897.16	1233.87
Operating cost	736.21	842.71	996.46	1018.42	733.38	1020.94
Interest	44.05	43.21	26.74	21.06	11.50	15.50
Depreciation	53.51	54.73	57.40	62.41	45.28	61.43
Net Profit (PBT)	65.71	56.22	201.77	96.00	107.00	136.00

During the period ended December, 1998 of the current financial year, the Company had a sales turnover of Rs. 897.16 crore and the profit before tax of Rs. 107 crore compared to the budget of Rs. 888.25 crore and Rs. 77 crore respectively. In view of decline in lead-zinc sale prices, the current financial year is expected to end up with sales turnover of Rs. 1200 crore and net profit of Rs. 136 crore (PBT).

Sales performance

Zinc sales during the period April-Dec. '98 was 96,428 tonnes against a target of 95,500 tonnes. It is expected to end the year with a sale of 129,000 tonnes as per the annual target. The Company expects to export about 45,000 tonnes zinc concentrate during the current year.

Lead sales during the period April-Dec.'98 have been 18,790 tonnes as against a target of 26,000 tonnes. A sale of about 28,000 tonnes is expected during 1998-99 against the annual target of 35,500 tonnes. The shortfall in the sale of lead metal is attributed to higher imports and uncertain market condition, resulting in lower off-take.

New projects

Sindesar Khurd, Distt. Rajsamand, Rajasthan

Sindesar Khurd deposit, near Rajpura Dariba district Rajsamand, Rajasthan has been taken up for development at a cost of Rs. 92 crore as replacement to south lode of R.D. Mine. It will be a satellite mine to Rajpura Dariba Mine and all the infrastructural facilities available including beneficiation plant at RDM will be utilised. An incline is being developed for upgrading the geological results and to confirm lateral continuity of the ore body to obtain geo-technical data and to obtain ore for metallurgical tests on plant scale. The incline has been excavated upto 297.81 mRL, the surface mRL being 510. A level at 350 mRL has been partly developed to provide site for exploratory drilling. Tenders have been invited for sinking of main shaft & excavation of ramp for providing main entry to the mine.

Kayar Lead-Zinc Prospect, Distt. Ajmer

Hindustan Zinc Limited has acquired mining lease of Kayar Lead-Zinc prospect in Ajmer district. A total of 10 million tonnes of geological resource containing 2.67% Pb and 14.89% Zn in three discrete ore bodies has been indicated. In order to establish firm geological, geo-technical and metallurgical parameters and delineate the deposit with fair degree of confidence for preparation of techno-economic feasibility report, an exploration scheme comprising 16800 m of drilling at an estimated cost of Rs. 1 2 crore has been envisaged. Global tenders for executing quality drilling work have been invited and are under evaluation for award of work.

Jagpura gold prospect

As a part of its diversification strategy, HZL is continuing its exploration programme in Jagpura area, District Banswara, Rajasthan, where it holds a prospecting licence (PL) over 43.10 sq. km. Exploratory drilling in progress in the NW an NE blocks has so far outlined an ore resource of 7.99 lac tonnes with 1.91 g/t Gold in oxidized zone and 7.90 lac tonnes with 2.18 g/t Gold in sulphide zone upto a depth of approximately 50 m. The Company has planned to carry out drilling in NE, SW and SE blocks, and to continue mineralogical and metallurgical tests on oxidized/sulphide ore to establish gold recovery process/parameters. An order of magnitude techno-economic study/report is likely to be generated in 1999-2000. In the remaining area of prospecting licence it is planned to carry out ground magnetic survey to identify zones of interest for exploration planning.

Zinc smelter expansion by 10,000 TPA each at Debari and Vizag

Orders were placed for basic engineering for expansion and performance improvement of Debari and Vizag Zinc Smelters on AdZ Technologia, Spain and the draft basic engineering packages have since been submitted. MECON has been appointed for detailed engineering and as consultants for project execution.

Tenders are being issued for execution of the project as per detailed engineering of MECON for carrying out various modifications' and equipment addition for capacity expansion. Award of work and execution of the project is expected to start in the last quarter of 1998-99.

New zinc smelter expansion by 100,000 TPA

The Company's proposal for undertaking a feasibility study at a cost of Rs. 10 crores for setting up of a new Zinc Smelter with a capacity of 60,000 TPA was approved by the Government in September, 1997. The pre-feasibility study commenced in November, 1997.

Based on global tender enquiry, the Company placed an order with M/s. Kvaerner Metal, UK for preparation of the detailed feasibility report for New Zinc Smelter of 100,000 tpa capacity. M/s. EIL has also been appointed to assist the international consultant in preparation of this report. The detailed feasibility report is scheduled to be completed by December 1998/January 1999. Meanwhile the smelter site has been finalised in consultation with senior officials of Rajasthan Government. Preliminary works such as filing of applications for land acquisition under section IV have been taken up.

Nickel extraction technology proving plant

An MOU was signed between HZL and the Council of Scientific & Industrial Research (CSIR) on, the 3rd

September, 1996 for installation of Nickel Technology Proving Plant as a Joint Venture for establishing nickel extraction technology developed indigenously for low grade chromite overburden of Sukinda Valley in Orissa.

Turnkey contracts were awarded for supply and erection of the plant during August, 1998. Foundation stone was laid by the Hon'ble Union Minister of Steel & Mines in September, 1998. The contractor has mobilised at site and civil construction works are under progress. Preparation of detailed engineering drawings and procurement action are under progress, which are expected to be completed by January 1999. Manufacture/ fabrication of equipment at site, shifting of existing equipment and civil structure works are expected to be completed by March, 1999. Erection of equipment is expected to start from mid January, 1999.

International co-operation

HZL -BHPM joint centure

The HZL-BHPM Minerals joint venture for exploration of base and precious metals in Rajasthan has made considerable progress during the year.

Preliminary processing of the airborne geophysical (GEOTEM) survey data was completed and detailed processing and interpretation by BHPM is in progress. The survey has outlined 138 anomalies. Ground checking by geological mapping, geophysics and geochemistry has covered about half of the anomalies. However, on account of the soil covered nature of the terrain, presence of mineralisation can be ascertained only by test drilling.

Based on the results generated, the joint venture has identified areas warranting follow-up.

It is proposed to conduct a second GEOTEM survey over fresh PL application areas, as well as covering parts of existing PLs which could not be flown last year. The survey will involve flying approximately 17,000 line kilometers.

HZL-La source-VIGEGO joint venture

In 1994, the Company entered into a MOU with LaSource (France) and VIGEGO (Vietnam) for a joint venture project to explore and develop the Pac Lang Gold prospect in Vietnam. Approval of the Government of Vietnam, and grant of exploration and prospecting licences (EL/PL) against revised applications, submitted in line with new regulations is awaited. In the meantime, approval of the Government of India was conveyed on 28th December, 1998 to Hindustan Zinc Limited, Udaipur for undertaking the exploration of the Pac Lang Gold prospect in Vietnam in collaboration with LaSource, France. The share of HZIL in the exploration cost shall be 43% of the total cost of exploration. If the exploration work is successful, then feasibility study will be undertaken in collaboration with LaSource. HZL's share in the conduct of feasibility study will be 43%. If the feasibility study leads to setting up of the Joint Venture mining company for exploration of the gold deposit, then the share of the three participating companies will be LaSource-40%, HZL-30% and VIGEGO of Vietnam-30%.

Energy conservation

The Company has been promoting and propagating energy conservation aspects in various facets of its operation. The following measures are being continued in an effort to conserve energy in different plants/mines of the Company.

- Load and Energy management.
- Sizing of equipment.
- Use of energy efficient equipment.

- Accurate measurement and monitoring consumption of various forms of energy.
- Energy audit and survey.
- Optimisation of system power factor Process improvement/modification.

Computerisation

To be in tune with state-of-the-art technology and harness it to business advantage, HZIL has installed a number of Pentium based personal computers with latest software in various functional areas.

It has undertaken the onerous task of solving the year-2000 problem in current application software using in-house expertise and has already carried out the same successfully in a few applications.

8.2 HZL has established connections to the rest of the world electronically by acquiring internet connection at its Head Office and has established e-mail facility'

Pollution control and environment management efforts

Air and water pollution control facilities and plants at all units of the Company are operated regularly to maintain emissions within permissible limits. Regular monitoring of effluents and gaseous emissions has been carried out.

Nearly 8,000 new saplings were planted during the year in addition to the existing trees being kept well maintained at all the mining units of the Company.

Salient aspects of the work being done by advisory boards/ Councils

Joint Consultative Committees are functioning in all major units of the Company. The Committee consists of representatives from workmen and management, and the areas discussed include production and productivity improvement, reduction in cost of production, etc. The recommendations of the Committee are generally implemented.

In addition to the Joint Consultative Committees, various other bipartite committees/fora on Welfare, Safety, Canteen Management, House Allotment, etc. are functioning. The unanimous recommendations of these Committees are also generally implemented. The functioning of these bipartite fora have created a conducive climate for better production/productivity at all levels.

Research and development activities

Development of bioreactor technology

To recover the zinc metal from the Rampura Agucha tails, bioleaching technique has been explored. RRL (Bhubaneswar) was appointed in January, 1998 for developing a process technique for the same. It is proposed to set up a 1 TPD pilot plant at CRDL in which the developed process will be tested.

Manganese nodules

Ocean bed manganese nodules contain about 2% Cu+Co+Ni. Development of process for winning these metals has been in progress at some CSIR Laboratories. At CRDL a process has been developed for generation of nickel-cobalt cake and its dissolution. Further work on pressure leaching has been carried out. Also, a conceptual flowsheet has been worked out for recovering manganese from the leached residue. DOD has selected the process developed by RRL(B) for further scale up in the pilot plant (500 kg/day capacity) to be set up at CRDL.

Recovery of germanium

Various residues generated from HZL's smelters are being identified to find out potential germanium sources. Samples have been collected from the smelters for estimation of germanium. Analysis carried out by C-

MET, Hyderabad are quite encouraging. A joint venture between HZL and C-MET is being planned in this regard.

Industrial relations

The industrial relations in the Company during the period remained cordial and peaceful.

Women's welfare

The female employees of the Company are given better welfare amenities. They are also being sent for training, both in-house and outside. Participation by female employees in various national fora is also being organised.

The Company has female doctors in the hospitals/ dispensaries.

Welfare of tribals and minorities

Various welfare measures including free medical aid, drinking water, school facilities, co-operative/provision store facilities, etc. are being made available/extended to the tribals and minorities residing in the adjacent areas of the unit.

Employjment in the company

(As on 31.12.1998)

Group	*Total No. of Employees*	*SC*	*ST*	*EX-SM*	*PH*
Executives	1510	103	23	6	3
Non-Executives	10308	1718	1497	218	69
Management Trainees	69	8	2	–	–

Export/import performance

Export

The Company expects to export about 45000 tonnes zinc concentrate during the current year. Import:

(Rs. in Lakh)

Import	1997-98 (Estimated)	1998-99
Raw material	17784.36	3723.00 (Approx.)
Components, stores & spares	3720.63	1433.00
Capital goods	321.88	300
Total	5826.87	5456.06

Mou ratings

The MOU ratings achieved by the Company during the last three years are given below:

1995-96 – Very good

1996-97 – Very good

1997-98 – Excellent

Use of Hindi

Progressive use of Hindi (April-Nov., 1998)

100% compliance of Section 3(3) of the Official Language Act has been followed in all the units including the Head Office.

The situation of Hindi correspondence of the various units is as follows:

HO-32%, CRDL-39%, Debari-45.3%, Maton Mine - 65.8%, Zawar Mines-77.5%, Dariba Mine-71.8%, Chanderiya 30.5%, Agucha Mine-29.9% and Tundoo Smelter-29.6%.

Non-Hindi speaking units: Vizag - 62.1%, Agnigundala Mine - 31% and Sargipali Mine - 44.3%.

Four employees appeared in Hindi typing examination conducted under Hindi Teaching Scheme of the Government.

Twenty Hindi workshops were organized from time

to time in all the units of the Company in which 173 employees participated.

Hindi day/week has been celebrated effectively in all the units. On this occasion Rajbhasha seminars/ competitions/Hindi workshops were organized.

Active cooperation is extended to Udaipur Town Official Language Implementation Committee, constituted by Rajbhasha Vibhag (Govt. of India).

The branches of Kendriya Sachivalaya Hindi Parishad, Now Delhi are active in several units including Head Office and various competitions have been organized from time to time.

Official Language Implementation Committees have been formed in all the units of the Company and quarterly meetings are held regularly.

Following number of employees were awarded under the various incentive schemes:

(i)	Hindi Teaching Scheme (Hindi teaching)	25
(ii)	Hindi Teaching Scheme (Hindi Typing/Stenography)	6
(iii)	Hindi Cheque Incentive Scheme	6
(iv)	Monthly Allowance Scheme for Hindi typing/stenography	49
(v)	Financial Incentive Scheme for use of Hindi	4

Hindustan Copper Limited

Hindustan Copper Limited (HCL) was incorporated on 9th November, 1967, under the Companies Act, 1956. It was established as a Government of India enterprise to take over, from National Mineral Development Corporation Ltd., all plants, projects, schemes and studies pertaining to the exploration and exploitation of copper deposits, including smelting and refining, for fulfilling long-term objectives of the nation, viz. development and growth of copper mining industry on sound lines and to maximise indigenous production of copper metal. This is to be achieved by developing new copper deposits, known or to be discovered, by adopting appropriate and modern technologies.

The Government of India nationalised the only copper producing company, Indian Copper Corporation Ltd. at Ghatsila in Bihar in March 1972 and handed over i management and ownership to HCL.

In November 1982, the prestigious Malanjkhand Copp Project comprising of a large and fully mechanise open pit mine and Concentrator plant was dedicated t the nation.

The Continuous Cast Copper Rod plant at Taloja Copper Project of Hindustan Copper Ltd. was commissioned in December, 1989 with an installed capacity of 60,000 T. The Company has selected Southwire SCR-2000 technology using natural gas as fuel.

Mines

Location of Mines	*Ore Capacity (TPD)*
Khetri Copper Complex, Rajasthan	19.50 lakh tonnes per annum
Indian Copper Complex, Bihar	11.02 lakh tonnes per annum
Malanjkhand Copper Project, Madhya Pradesh	20.00 lakh tonnes per annum

Smelters

Location of mines	*Metal capacity (TPA)*
Khetri Copper Complex, Rajasthan	31000 tonnes per annum
Indian Copper Complex, Bihar	16500 tonnes per annum

Physical performance

.1 The production of ore, metal in concentrates, refined copper (cathode) and wire rod during the year 1997-98 and 1998-99 are given below:

Details	*Actual for the previous 3 years* 1995-96	1996-97	1997-98	*Annual Budget Est. 1998-99 (BE)*	*1998-99 Actual upto Dec.'98*	*Annual Estimate 1998-99 (RE)*
1	2	3	4	5	6	7
Ore Production ('000 tonnes)	4690	3893	4496	4090	3192	4090
Metal in Concentrates (T)	46563	37271	41440	37080	28875	37080
Refined Copper (Cathode) (T)	41153	38481	42374	43500	28703	35500
Wire rod (Taloja) (T)	37280	41332	31484	36600	25989	30800

Financial performance (operating results)

Details	*Actual for the previous 3 years* 1995-96	1996-97	1997-98	*Target for 1998-99*	*1998-99 Actual upto Dec.'98*	*1998-99 Estimated*
1	2	3	4	5	6	7
Income	1133.68	1001.05	807.05	890.27	545.47	741.90
Operating Cost	963.03	1037.16	849.70	870.05	625.09	790.06
Interest and Transaction loss	39.66	40.67	58.89	49.17	49.12	66.67
Depreciation and Amortisation	55.15	53.84	68.46	62.90	33.14	57.35
Net Profit before income tax & dividend	75.84	(130.62)	(169.72)	(91.85)	(161.68)	(172.18)

Capital restructuring

The Company has been incurring huge losses for the last two years mainly due to drastic fall in LME price of copper and reduction of customs duty on import of copper. To revive this important PSU, the Department has initiated a number of measures which include, inter alia, restructuring the capital base of the Company. The government has accorded approval to the proposal of capital restructuring of HCL seeking:

(i) The outstanding Government loan of Rs. 180.73 crores with M/s HCL as on 31.3.98 may be converted into 7.5% non-cumulative redeemable preference shares to be redeemed at the end of 10th year from the date of conversion and waiver of the outstanding interest as on 31.3.1998 amounting to Rs. 167.43 crores.

(ii) Raising of working capital term loans from Financial institutions/Banks by HCL to the tune of Rs. 75 crores against Government of India (GOI) guarantee for meeting its cash losses for the current financial year i.e. 1998-99.

(iii) A non-plan loan qf Rs. 414 crores be given to HCL for VRS at 14.5% rate of interest with a moratorium of 3 years on repayment of principal and interest and repayment of principal amount in subsequent twelve years for separation of 11043 employees of HCL during the years 1998-99 to 2001-2002. If, even after 2 years, the LME price of copper is less than $1850 per MT, Ministry of Finance (Department of Expenditure) will review the period of moratorium extended to HCL. The moratorium period will not be reviewed if

> HCIL faces a repayment problem due to its own inefficiency.

Action has been initiated to implement the above decision.

Sales performance

The Company achieved a total sale of 57,857 tonnes during the year 1997-98. The Company is likely to achieve a total sale of around 50,460 tonnes of copper during 1998-99.

Expansion

Expansion of Khetri Smelter and Refinery

HCL's proposal for expansion of Khetri Smelter and Refinery from 31,000 tpa to 1,00,000 tpa, which was awaiting government clearance, has been dropped owing to the financial performance of the Company. HCL has taken up technological upgradation/debottlenecking scheme of KCC Smelter and Refinery leading to enhancement of the capacity from 31000 tpa to 45000 tpa which would fit into the overall objective of raising the capacity ultimately to 1,00,000 tpa. The Government has given clearance to go ahead with the above scheme. For implementation of the above scheme, discussions have been initiated with Outokumpu Engineering Contractors Oy (OEC), Finland. Similar action has been planned for increasing the capacity of ICC Smelter from the present 16,500 to 25,000 tpa.

Energy conservation

Copper extraction is an energy intensive operation. Special attention is given in making the operation energy efficient at all stages starting from mining of ore to extraction of metal. Due to energy conservation awareness and regular monitoring on consumption of all energy inputs, HCL has been able to maintain the norms of consumption.

Constant thrust is also maintained on improvement of power factor. Improvement in power factor during last three years is tabulated below:

Units	*1996-97*	*1997-98*	*1998-99 (Upto Dec'98)*
KCC	0.92	0.93	0.94
ICC	0.89	0.90	0.915
MCP	0.97	0.98	0.993

. Computerisation

There has been further progress in computerisation in HCL during the current year 1998-99. Most of the system development work started in the year 1997-98, has been completed.

The computer resources have also been augmented in the units and offices mainly to replace the old PCs with the advanced type to take care of the increasing load of work and new jobs.

Internet uses have been initiated between Head Office and other regional offices and projects.

The computerisation effort has been strengthened by further decentralizing. Some integrated system design and development is being carried out by Systems Department with the idea of standardization among the offices.

The software packages, that had been made internally for financial, stores and commercial jobs, are being made ready for the year 2000 compliance.

Pollution control and environment management efforts

Air and water pollution control facilities and plants at all units of the Company operated regularly to maintain emissions within permissible limits. Regular monitoring of effluents and gaseous emissions has been carried out.

Salient aspects of the work being done by advisory boards/ councils

Well established system of employees participation in management in the units as well as at the corporate level are functioning. Shop Councils in each shop and joint councils at unit levels besides bipartite committees on Safety, Canteen, Grievance Handling, House allotment and Housekeeping are in existence and functioning properly. These Committees are attended by Senior Executives and union leaders and they discuss issues on production, productivity, welfare, training and other allied matters of industrial value. Meetings are held at regular intervals - every month and every three months at other committee quite often as the case may be.

At the corporate level, there are two apex committees. These are National Joint Committee for Copper (NJCC) which deals with welfare, medical and social facilities wages and service conditions etc. of workers for the Company as a whole on a national level and meet at regular intervals. The other is Joint Consultative Committee (JCC) which meets once in a quarter to discuss the issues on production and productivity, cost control, yields, safety, pollution control measures etc. These are attended by Chairman-cum-Managing Director, Directors and all the Unit Heads, Personnel Heads from the management side and very senior leaders from the workmen side.

Research and development activities

The Government of India stopped financing R&D activities of HCL from the year 1997-98 in accordance with the decision taken under financial guidelines for R&D activities of PSUs. HCL was also under acute financial crisis during the year under review. However, the Company maintained its thrust in science and technological activities also during the year 1997-98. This resulted in the following two major achievements:

Nickel electro winning

Successful development of Process Flow Sheet for extraction of associated Nickel from Copper ore and production of commercial grade electro-won Nickel cathode. A pilot plant of capacity to produce 1 tonne of Nickle cathode per month based on this process route was set up at ICC during the year. During the year under review, 3 tonnes of Nickel cathodes was produced at ICC. The plant is currently being scaled up to a production capacity of 5 tonnes per month of Nickel cathode.

Hydrometallurgical route of copper extraction

Leachability of Chalcopyrite concentrate with recovery of copper to more than 95% along with extraction of gold, silver, sulphur etc. as by - products, has been established through in-house R&D activities and also through test work carried out by Mintek, South Africa. Establishment of Flow Sheet with detailed design and development of pilot scale operating plant is currently being pursued-

Industrial relations

The industrial relations situation indifferent units of Hindustan Copper Limited was by and large peaceful. The Government order to close down the Mosaboni Mines including Badia, under Industrial Disputes Act, 1947 was challenged by the different unions operating at Mosaboni Mines in the Hon'ble High Court, Calcutta as well as at Hon'ble High Court, Patna, Ranchi Bench. After prolonged legal battle in the High Court, the judgement of the Calcutta High Court went in favour of the management. The union filed Special Writ Petition in the Hon'ble Supreme Court against the judgement of the Division Bench of Calcutta High Court which was dismissed by the Apex Court. Hon'ble High Court of Patna, Ranchi Bench had earlier modified its judgement by vacating the stay on the closure of the mines.

After dismantling and salvaging of equipment, Mosaboni Mines has been closed with effect from 28th September, 1998. Though separate groups belonging to different unions and political parties resorted to agitation for rehabilitation and redeployment of the remaining workmen of the Mosaboni Mines, now closed. The Nominee Action Committee resorted to agitation demanding and voicing their grievances for induction of the nominees of the employees who had died in harness. The casual workmen whose services were dispensed with also were involved in dharna and agitation demanding their engagement.

Mrs. Abha Mahato, Hon'ble local MP, who paid a visit to Calcutta and had detailed discussion with the management, was apprised of the problems being faced by the Company.

Perspective plan for women's welfare

Implementation of equal remuneration act

In Hindustan Copper Limited, no discrimination is made with regard to sex, caste, creed between male and female employees. Persons doing similar nature of job get equal remuneration.

Equality of opportunity in employment and recognition of the right to work as a fundamental right guaranteed by the constitution.

As per Mines Act, 1952, employment of women in underground is prohibited. In other areas, employment to women is provided. In Hindustan Copper Limited equal opportunity is provided and no discrimination is made between male and female employees. In promotion no discrimination is made and women are considered at par, subject to recruitment and promotion rules of the Company.

Application of maternity benefit act to women

Provision of Maternity Benefit Act are strictly followed in Hindustan Copper Limited.

Training facilities at the place of work on new machinery

Wherever new machineries like electronic typewriters are introduced, women employees are provided with necessary training to equip them to operate the machines.

In - company training programme

Women employees attend various in-company training programmes like adult education, workers development seminars and general development programmes organised periodically at unit training centres. Women employees were also given in service training.

Creche facilities

Creche facilities are provided to the women at the project.

Welfare of tribals and minorities

The main welfare activities in respect of Tribal and Minorities are the part of 20 point Programme of the Company. The following activities were undertaken during the period April to October, 1998:

Clean drinking water

Repair of existing tubewells at different projects and construction of 'Bandh' at KCC. 950 persons were benefitted.

Health for all

Regular multi diagnostic camp at surrounding villages. 183 children were immunised and 450 persons were medically checked up.

Expansion of education

More than 8 adult education centres run by the Company through Mahila Samaj. Relevant stationery and books are distributed to the participants free of cost 125 persons were benefited.

Employment of SC/ST/EX-servicemen/PH/LDP/minorities as on 31-12-98

Group	*Total no. of employees*	*SC*	*ST*	*Ex-service men*	*PH*	*LDP*	*Minorities*
Executives servicemen	1904	170	51	22	6	–	101
Non-Executives	16236	2367	2866	729	126	1288	1077
Trainees:							
(i) Trade Apprentices		268					
(ii) GET	–	Nil					
(iii) MT	–	1					

Mou rating of PSUs achieved

1995-96 – Very Good
1996-97 – Fair
1997-98 – Fair

Progressive use of Hindi in official work

During the period April to October, 1998, concerted efforts were made to achieve the targets fixed by the Government of India regarding progressive use of Hindi. Special emphasis was laid on employees to use their working knowledge of Hindi in day to day official work.

Check points were made more effective to ensure 100% compliance of Section 3(3) of Official Language Act.

Special Incentive Scheme for Noting and Drafting originally in Hindi continued during the period. Hindi workshops were organised and Hindi Fortnights/Weeks were celebrated in all the units including Head Office. During the year the third sub-committee of Parliamentary Committee on Official Language inspected our Head Office. The Committee expressed its satisfaction at the work being done to promote the Official Language in HCL. The 50th Anniversary of India's Independence was celebrated in all our projects and Head Office with great enthusiasm. On this occasion, various programmes/ competitions were held wherein our employees and their family members participated in large numbers. A crossword puzzle scheme has been introduced by Head Office during the period to create interest in Hindi among the employees. This has been welcomed by all the employees. During the period April to October, 1998 our Head Office was awarded with a letter of appreciation for best compliance in regard to official language policy of the Government of India by CALTOLIC.

The Official Language Implementation Committee chaired by the CMD at Head Office and the Executive Directors at units, held their meetings regularly in which constraints in implementation of Official language were discussed and measures for their removal were worked out. A new switch latest P.C. word processor was installed for Hindi Department at the Head Office for development of Official Language.

Four Manuals of the Company viz. Stores Manual, Trainer's Manual, Standing Rules for RCP and ICC have been printed on new P.C.

On the occasion of Hindi Day, the message of CMD was distributed in all the offices and units on 14th September, 1998.

Annual Hindi Programme was organised wherein prizes were distributed to the winners of various competitions held on the progressive use of Hindi. Hindi classes were conducted and employees took the Hindi statutory examination held by the Ministry of Home Affairs.

Bharat gold mines limited

Bharat Gold Mines Limited (BGML) became a Public Sector Undertaking under the Department of Mines in 1972. It is primarily engaged in mining in its captive mines in Kolar Gold Fields (KGF), Karnataka and Andhra Pradesh and production of gold in KGF. As a diversification measure, the Company also undertakes mine construction, shaft sinking, manufacture of mining machinery and other fabricated items for outside clients for which it has set up a Mine Construction and Engineering Division.

Present scenario

BGML is a sick company and is before the Board for Industrial and Financial Reconstruction (BIFR) since 1992. During June, 1997 the Government decided, inter-alia, to explore the possibility of rehabilitating BGML through joint venture route by induction of a private co-promoter(s). Accordingly, a Committee was constituted, which has since given its report. The future of BGML will be decided as per the provisions of Sick Industrial Companies (Special Provisions) Act, 1985.

Financial performance

The authorised share capital of the Company is Rs. 60 crores and paid up share capital is Rs. 51.06 crores as on 31.3.1998. The working results of the Company for the last two years and current year upto December, 1998 are as follows:-

		Loss (Rs. in lakhs)
1996-97	:	5379.94
1997-98	:	3983.40
1998-99 (upto Dec., 1998)	:	4992.74

Production performance

The quantity of ore milled, gold and silver extracted during 1997-98 and 1998-99 (April - Dec., 1998) are given below:

	Actual 97-98	*Target for 98-99 (Revised)*	*April-Dec., 98 (Actual)*	*Jan. 99 to Mar., 99 (Anticipated)*
Ore Miled (Tonnes)	151.381	174.470	115.085	59.385
Gold Extracted (Kg.)	514.17	550.00	404.1	145.90
Extraction Grade (g/t)	3.24	3.03	3.36	–
Silver Exttracted (kg.) (by-product)	43.90	–	32.10	–

Sources of funding

As the Company is continuously incurring losses and unable to generate any internal resource, the investment on the capital schemes is met by the Government as Plan loans. The Government has approved an outlay of Rs. 450.00 lakhs as Plan loan towards the capital expenditure during 1998-99. Besides, the Government has provided for non-plan loan of Rs. 16.55 crores during the current year.

Diversification

The Company is diversifying its activities in the following fields:

i) Shaft Sinking and Mine Construction.

ii) Manufacture of mining equipment and fabrication and machining of components.

Shaft sinking and mine construction

The Projects and Contracts Division established in 1973 has been taking contract jobs in shaft sinking and mine construction activities for various mining companies in both coal and metallic ore mines in the country.

The Division has so far completed 68 jobs valued at Rs. 107.74 crores for its customer companies spread all over the country. It is executing 5 contracts at present valued at Rs. 23.30 crores. In addition, contracts valued at Rs.13.00 crores are under negotiations.

This Division endeavours to maximise its revenue thereby sharing the Company's fixed costs. The company envisages undertaking contracts of high value and to execute the jobs by sub-contracting to local contractors wherever possible to cut down operating costs.

Manufacture of mining equipment and fabrication of components

As part of the diversification activity and to generate additional revenue from the workshops, engineering jobs are undertaken viz. manufacture and sale of mining machinery and equipment like winders, suspension gears, head gear, man-riding systems, skips, ore-bins, various safety gadgets, battery operated locomotives, mine car circuit systems, material handling systems, electro winning cells, "GOLD DRILL", TCT rods, etc., besides jobbing work like fabrication and machining for other major industries.

The Engineering Division has achieved a production value of Rs.220.71 lakhs during April, 98 to Dec., 98 besides catering to its captive needs of the metallurgical and mining operations at KGF and other project sites all over India. The production value for the year 1998-99 is estimated at Rs.400.00 lakhs.

The Engineering Division has secured orders worth Rs.313.64 lakhs during April 98-Nov 98. BGML has been awarded, as a result of their participation in a tender process, developmental order for 60 nos Boxn Type Wagons in February 1998 for a total value of Rs.297.79 lakhs of which three proto-type wagons have to be manufactured and approved by the RDSO, Bangalore, before executing the balance quantity. Necessary infrastructure facilities have been completed and orders for certain critical bought-out items like bogie, couplers, draftgear, braking system etc. have been placed. After approval of 3 proto-type wagons by RDSO, the balance 57 wagons would be taken up in the second phase to complete the work order in full.

Achievement during 1998-99

The sales made upto October 1998 and orders position on hand by end of Dec., 1998 are as follows-

(Rs. in lakhs)

Description No.	*Orders on hand value*	*Cumulative orders executed (April-Dec. 1998)*
T.C.T. Drill Rods	18.32	26.15
Workshop Sales	1018.83	194.56
Total	1037.15	220.71

Exploration activies

Chigargunta mine, Chittoor District, AP

The primary level development activities were continued in 4th level of IIIE & IVE Block and 5th level of South Boundary Block on E-2 lode. The ore body delineation works were continued in VE Block. In addition to the above, the stope preparatory development works were carried out in different blocks on E-2 lode.

Old bisanatham mine, Chittoor District, AP

The primary level development works were carried out in 260', 350' and 425' levels north of Downnight shaft. Stope preparatory developments i.e. finger raises and sub-level were carried out between 260' and 425' levels.

Nundydroog mine, Kolar gold fields, Karnataka

The underground developments were related to mainly slope preparatory works in the form of sub-levels and raises in G (Top), G (bottom) and J (North) sections.

Yeppamana mine, Anantapur District, AP

There was no primary level development. The underground development related to stope preparatory works in the form of sub-level, raises and orebody stripping to convert the stope block ready for production between 6th and 7th levels in BG ore shoot of the mine.

Geological services

Geological services were extended to sampling in mills, metal balance studies and updating the status of ore reserves of the mines.

Environmental protection

The Company has taken up afforestation programme on tailing dumps as a pollution control measure and on the barren lands to improve the ecology in a phased manner. Different species like Eucalyptus, Sandalwood, Accacia, Aurculiformis Sissoo, Bevu, Honge, etc., have been planted over 3230 acres of land so far at Kolar Gold Fields and Gadag in Karnataka and Ramgiri, Old Bisanatham and Chigargunta in Andhra Pradesh.

Pollution control

Domestic water treatment

The effluent after treatment is collected in the oxidation ponds constructed in Mysore Mine, Champion Reef and Nundydroog mine areas. These works have been carried out as per the recommendations of Karnataka State Pollution Control Board and National Environmental Engineering Research Institute. A Water Treatment plant has been setup at Chigargunta mine to provide potable water to the employees.

Industrial effluent treatment

Additional three bunds to prevent overflow of slurry, have been constructed over the tailing bund at Nundydroog Mill area. One earthen dam has been constructed near Mysore Mine dump area to prevent washing away of tailings due to rain.

Industrial relations

Welfare of SC/ST tribals and minorities

There are directives/guidance from the Ministry of Social Justice and Empowerment with regard to preparation of sub-component plan for Scheduled Caste and tribal sub-plan for Scheduled Tribes. This is linked with rehabilitation of tribals on account of land acquired for the project. BGML has not acquired any land causing displacement of tribals for the construction of projects and hence no plan for rehabilitation has been drawn.

Minority group members have been nominated to represent in recruitment and promotion committees to safeguard the interest of minority groups. Their grievances are promptly attended to and settled.

Recruitment of minorities and SC/STs in the PSEs

During the period, no recruitments were made.

Employment of SC/ST as on 31.12.1998

Group	*Total employee*	*SC*	*%*	*ST*	*%*
A	123	27	21.95	4	3.25
B	30	8	26.66	–	–
C	2342	920	39.28	18	0.77
D	1871	1100	58.79	23	1.26
Total	4366	2055	47.06	45	1.03

No. of employees

Technical & Non Technical as on 31.12.1998 were as follows:

Technical	—	2311
Non-Technical	—	2006
Total	—	4317

Family welfare measures

Perspective plan for women's welfare

As a part of 20 point programme, a separate cell known as Community Development Cell was formed in 1987 to encourage certain self-employment programmes. At present 40 ladies are engaged in weaving, manufacture of handgloves, helmet, liners, phenyl, etc.

Power consumption

There was an increasing trend in the consumption of power during the period April to October 1998 by 6.14% as compared to the previous year. The details of power consumption are given below:

Progress made in the use of Hindi in the enterprise

The Company has made satisfactory progress in the propagation of Hindi as per the provisions of Official

Language Act and Rules made thereunder during the year 1998-99. Incentive schemes of the Government of India have been implemented. The employees who have typed their Official Letters in Hindi were awarded special incentives under Quarterly Hindi Typewriting Incentive Scheme. To popularise Hindi among employees, competitions in Hindi Shorthand, Noting and Drafting, Letter writing and Essay were conducted. The Hindi Diwas was celebrated on 14th September, 1998.

Year	*Units consumed (in lakhs)*	*Anticipated increase during 1998-99*	*% of anticipated increase during the year (lakhs units)*
1997-98	353.24		
(April-March)		42.45**	12%
1998-99 (April-March)		*395.69	

* Actual consumption from April to October 1998 and estimate for November 1998 to March 1999.

** The increase in consumption of power was mainly due to pumping operation from mines at KGF.

Sadhbhavana day pledge

All employees of BGML collectively took the pledge at their respective working places on 31.8.1998 (Sadhbhavana Diwas) to work with dedication and desist from violence and resolved to solve all their grievances by peaceful and Constitutional means.

Sikkim mining corporation

The Sikkim Mining Corporation was established by a proclamation of the then Darbar of Sikkim in February, 1960 as a joint venture having 51% equity from Government of Sikkim and 49% equity from Government of India. After a gestation period of about 6 years, production of the complex ore from Bhotang Mine started since 1966-67 onwards. This was the only mine till recently in the country which produced three metals (copper, lead and zinc) from a polymetallic complex ore. There is also the presence of appreciable amount of silver and some amount of gold in the ore. As on 1.4.98 the mine is estimated to have (proved & probable) reserves of about 3.28 lakh tonnes and has already produced about 4.11 lakh tonnes of ore since its inception. Currently Bhotang mine is producing about 54 TPD (tonnes per day) of ore and the other exploratory mine called 'Pacheykhani', located about 15 km away from the former in the East Sikkim district, is also producing about 18 TPD. The cumulative production would be enhanced to 90-100 TPD after the major repair of the existing Cone Crusher of the Mill plant by the end of the financial year 1998-99. The copper concentrate produced by the corporation is sold of to M/s Hindustan Copper Ltd., zinc concentrate to M/s Hindustan Zinc Limited and lead consentrate is not saleable at present due to high bismuth (0.6 to 0.7%) content which contains appreciable amount of silver. The performance of the Corporation has never been good due to various reasons but recent capital re-structuring proposal already approved by the Board of Directors for enhancing the Share Capital from Rs.6.00 crores to Rs.10.00 crores is expected to result in improvement of its productivity and financial performance in near future.

Mines

Location of Mines	*Ore Capacity (TPD)*
1. Bhotang Multimetal Mine	100 TPD (Currently 54 TPD)
2. Pacheykhani Copper Mine (Both located in East Sikkim)	20 TPD (Currently 18 TPD)

Physical performance

The production of Sikkim Mining Corporation during the year 1997-98 and 1998-99 are given below :

(in Tonnes)

Product	*1995-96*	*1996-97*	*1997-98*	*1998-99 Target*	*1998-99 Actuals (Prov.)*
Ore	11026	9685	15698	20020	18000
Concentrate					
1. Copper	206	321	791	1020	1020
2. Lead	499	372	90	100	100
3. Zinc	359	337	289	20	12

On-going projects

The projects which are in progress at Bhotang Mine include :-

i) Deepening of present shaft from 3rd level to 4th level and ultimately upto 5th level under capital development along with shaft winder equipment like extension and conversion of the Air Winder to Electrical system (Approx. cost Rs. 7.00 lakhs)

ii) Owing to high cost of reliable and imported Cone Crusher, the idea of procuring a new one has been dropped and the old Cone Crusher has been given for capital repair at a cost of Rs. 11.24 lakhs and is likely to be in operation by the end of the financial year 1998-99.

iii) Capital mine development in deeper level (below 5th level) and extension in strike direction towards South, below river Tista for increasing ore reserve base is in progress. A parallel drive has also been started at 3rd level to enable exploitation of the ore available at the same level for mineral conservation.

Financial performance

Operating results

Details	*Actuals for the previous years*			*Annual Budget Estimate 1998-99*	*Actual (Prov.)*
	95-96	*96-97*	*97-98*		
Income	56.81	89.68	105.30	155.00	160.00
Operating Cost	81.70	97.83	107.29	141.00	137.00
Interest & Transaction Loss	15.76	50.52	14.00	–	9.00
Depreciation & Amortisation	13.97	13.37	13.00	14.00	14.00
Net Profit Before Income Tax & Dividend	(–)54.62	(–)72.04	(–)23.29 (Prov.)	–	–

Expansion and divesification

Expansion

In order to make the Corporation flexible and more viable another exploratory mine called "Pacheykhani" (located at about 15 km away in same East Sikkim district) has been started w.e.f. 2nd May, 1997 onwards and is producing about 18 TPD of monometal (copper) ore which is being procesed at Bhotang Mine plant. This mine is still under capital development and the production capacity is to be enhanced to about 30 TPD.

New scheme (diversification)

The organisation has applied for one Coal lease at Kamling in West Sikkim district as a part of the diversification programme. In addition to it, the organisation is likely to apply for another copper deposit (already proved) at Dikchu/upper Pacheykhani and other valuable minerals of the State.

For better conservation of minerals and enabling higher grades of concentrates as an end product, the management has planned to set up one Vertical Columner floatation process after enhancement of Share Capital.

In order to ensure safe underground working below river Tista as well as to enhance qualitative production of R.O.M. from Bhotang Mine, a stowing plant would be installed at a capital cost around Rs. 10.00 lakhs during the financial year for which necessary action has already been initiated. The system will also contribute towards environment preservation due to processing of Mill Tailing and sending it back to the underground mine for back filling at cut and fill method of stopping.

Energy conservation

The Corporation has installed one low tension (440 V) on line Voltage Stabilizer/Controller on 16th June, 1998 on capital expenditure of more than Rs. 8.00 lakhs to maintain industrial voltage level of 400+1% against fluctuating supply voltage of 300 to 460 volts. It is functioning successfully and is not only safe-guarding the electrical equipment but has also improved the power factor appreciably.

Industrial relations

Cordial, peaceful and harmonious industrial relationship prevail between the management and the workers of the Corporation.

Prospective plant for women welfare

For the welfare of women, the Corporation is running a Carpet Weaving Centre under the guidance and supervision of SMC Employees' Co-operative Society Ltd. from where many women/girls were imparted training mostly amongst the wives and dependents of the SMC employees with a view to make them self-sufficient. A number of women have taken advantage of this scheme and now some of them are doing the job independently.

Welfare of tribal and minorities

Every possible efforts has been made by the Corporation for the welfare of the tribal and minorities working in the Corporation.

Employment of SC/ST/EX-SM/PH/LPD/minorities as on 31.12.1998

Group	*Total*	*SC No. of employee*	*ST*	*EX-SM*	*PH*	*LDP*	*Minori-ties*
Executive	6	–	2	–	–	–	–
Non-Executive	234	22	62	3	–	–	–
Trainees	–	–	–	–	–	–	–
Total	240	22	64	3	–	–	–

16

Energy Development in India

Energy, an essential input for economic development, is consumed in a variety of forms in India. Fuelwood, animal waste and agricultural residues are traditional sources of energy that continue to meet the bulk of the energy requirement in the rural areas. These 'non-commercial fuels' are gradually getting replaced by 'commercial fuels' such as coal,l lignite, petroleum products, natural gas and electricity.

The Government has formulated an energy policy with the objectives of ensuring adequate energy supply at a minimum cost, achieving self-sufficiency in energy supplies and protecting environment form adverse impact of utilising energy resources in an unjudicial manner. The development and promotion of non-conventional/alternate/new and renewable sources of energy such as solar, wind and bio-energy, etc., are also getting sustained attention from the Department of Non-Conventional Energy Sources, created in september 1982. Nuclear energy to contribute significantly to the overall energy avalalbility in the country.

Coal

Coal is the main source of energy in the country and it accounts for about 60 per cent of the country's commercial energy requirement. Coal is also an essential input in steel and carbo-chemical industries.

An on 1 January 1995, the coal resources of India (upto a depth of 1,200 metre) have been estimated by the Geological Survey of India at 1,96,891.87 million tonnes.

Coal production which was around 78.71 million tonnes atthe time of nationalisation of the coal industry in 1973-74, rose to a level of 253.80 million tonnes in 1994-95. India is now the third largest coal producing country in the world. The coal production is slated to reach 300 million tonnes by 1996-97. Strategies adopted to achieve higher rate of production are: re-organising existing mines and opening up on new projects, both underground as well as opencast.

Distribution of coal is controlled statutorily under the Colliery Control Order, 1945. The distribution is to be done by the Coal Controller. However, if for any reason Coal Controller is not able to do so, coal companies have been allowed to distribute coal on the basis of linkages/ sponsorships. Short term linkages for important sectors of economy, like power and cement are decided by Standing Linkage Committee set up under the mInistry of Coal. Linkages to other consumers execpt steel are within the purview of coal companies, which allot coal to actual users as per advice receeived by them from the various sponsoring authorities New allotments by coal companies to industries are of the order of 5,000 tonnes per month. Off-take of raw coal during 1993-94 and 1994-95 to major sectors of economy is given in table 21.

Projects and planning

Under the present delegation of powers, coal projects costing upto Rs. 50 crore are sanctioned by the Board of Directors of the Coal India Limited. The subsidiary companies of Coal India Limited have powers to sanction projects upto Rs. 20 crore. Singareni Collieries Company Limited Board can also sanction coal projects upto Rs. 50

crore. Projects costing more than Rs. 50 crore are sanctioned by the Government.

After the nationalisation of the coal industry in 1973 and till December 1994, the number of projects sanctioned (each costing Rs. two crore and above) was 633. A total investment of Rs. 20,718.97 crore has been sanctioned in these projects. Og these, 419 are mining projects and remaining 214 are non-mining projects like washeries, fire control schemes, captive power plants, water supply schemes etc. Out of 633, 340 projects have been completed and 293 are at different stages of implementation. Mining projects on completion will have a capacity of 338.08 million tonnes of coal per annum.

Mining and mining technology

Even though history of Indian coal mining dates back more than two centuries, real sprut in coal production took place only after the nationalisation of the coal industry. Coal production in the country is now allmost completely in the public sector companies e.g. Coal India limited (CIL) and Singareni Collieries Company Limited (SCCL) except few captive mines of TISCO, IISCO and DVC. Coal India Limited producing over 90 per cent of the country's total coal production, has seven coal producing subsidiaries, namely, eastern Coalfields Limited (ECL), Bharat Coking Coal Limited (BCCL), Central Coalfields Limited (CCL), Northern Coalfields Limited (NCL), South Eastern Coalfields (SECL), Mahandi Coalfields Limited (MCL) and Western Coalfields Limited (WCL).

The eight subsidiary Central Mines Planning and Design Institute Limited (CMPDIL) is the planning and design institute. SCCL is a joint venture of the Centre and Government of Andhra Pradesh. About 72 per cent of the coal production is obtained through opencast mmines which are almost completely mechanised deploying dragllines, shovels, dumpers, drills, dozers, etc. Mechanisation of underground mines has also been taken up in a big way. Most of the equipment used in coal mines ae indigenously available. At present there are 19 coking coal washeries with an annual capacity of 32.56 million tonnes.

Conservation of coal is an integrated part of mine planning and operation. This is ensured by maximum recovery of *in situ* reserves of coal. Since coal deposits in India are mostly in thick seams and occur at shallow depths, special techniques for maximising recovery are being developed. Difficult geo-mining conditions prevailing in coal bearing areas like steep and irregular coal seam deposits, gassy seams contifuous and multisection seams necessitate the introduction of some suitable technology for exploitation of such deposits from coal conservation and also safety point in view. Some of the newly introduced methods of mining are: (a) to exploit seams developed in multi-sections and seams with thickness of 6 to 8 m and standing pillars, methods such as blasting gallery and sub-level caving have been adopted in Katras Project, BCCL. Blasting gallery method with sub-pannelings has been planned in Chora Colliery of ECL and GDK-10 and CDK-8 of SCCL Colliery; (b) keeping in view the limitations of conventional underground methods in terms of quantum of output as well as conservation, both Coal India Limited and Singareni Collieries Company Limited have introduced mechanised longwall technology that ensures higher extractability; (c) diversion of rivers, shifting of colonies and townships have been taken up to release sterlised coal underground; (d) adequate measures have been asopted to deal with coalfijeld fires particularly in Jhria Coalfield and latest technology like remote sensing is being applied for fire management; (e) in steep and thick seams of Margheritta Area (Assam), the system of Shield Mining has been introduced.

The extraction percentage of coal by traditional system which was 25 per cent to 35 per cent has now improved to nearly 70 per cent or even more in the system of shield mining. The flexible roofing method of mining in the thick seams of North Eastern coalfield has also been applied where the thickness of the seam exceeds 4.5 meter. The system has, however, a limited application ; and (f) since opencast working ensures better conversation, application of opencast working is now followed with much higher cut-off ratios utilising high capacity machineries. Singareni Collieries Company Limited has also made a breakthrough in a small way for extraction of developed pillars by opencast methods.The company has of late been making efforts to convert existing underground mines into high capacity mechanised Opencast projects at Ramagundam and Kothagudem areas.

The Coal mines Conservation and Development Act, 1974 provides for imposition of excise duty on coal despatches for meeting activities like conservation of coal, development/introduction of new technology in coal mines, safety in Mines and assistance in mining operation. A number of research and development activities in coal sector are carried out under overall guidance and supervision of Standing Scientific and Research Commmittee and its four sub-committees. The applied research is carried out in the fields of production, productivity, safety coal preparation, coal utilisation, environment and ecology.

Special efforts to improve lthe standard of safety in the coal industry have brought down the rate of fatalities per million tonne of output in Coal India Limited to 0.40 and in Singareni Collieries Companies Limited to 2.04 in the year 1994. A Standing Committee on Safety regularly review safety standards in coal mines.

Coal industry employs over seven lakh workers. Since nationalisation of coal mines, welfare of coal miners by way of providing facilities like housing, water supply, medical care, education, etc , is bieng given greater attention.

Lignite reserves in the country have been estimated at around 26,200 million tonnes. Out of the above, 3,300 million tonnes spread over 480 sq km is in the Neyveli Lignite fields in South Acrot Vallalar district and about 2,000 mt has been identified as minerable under the presently adopted mining parameters. Geological reserves of about 1150 mt of lignite have been identified in Jayamkondacholapuram of Trichy district of Tamil Nadu. In Mannargudi and east of Veeranam, geological reserves of around 18,200 mt and 1,340 mt of lignite respectively have been estimated. Smaller deposits exist in Rajasthan, Gujarat and J&K. Lignite reserves at Neyveli are exploited by Neyveli Lignite Corporation (NLC) Ltd. It was incorporated as a private limited company in 1956 wholly owned by Government of India. The Corporation was converted into public company w.e.f. 7 March 1986.

The main constituents of the company are lignite mines, thermal power stations, fertilizer plant and briquetting and carbonisation plant. Mine-I (6.5 million tonnes of Lignite per annum) feeds thermal Power Station-I (600 mw), Briquetting and Carbonisation Plant (2,62,000 tonnes of coke-achievable capacity) and the Process Steam Plant. Mine-II (10.5 million tonnes of lignite per annum) feeds it captive Thermal Power Station-II (7×210 mw).

The Fertilizer Plant (achievable capacity 1,29,200 tonnes of urea per annum) which initially used raw lignite as feed stock changed over to oil gasification in July 1979 on operational and technological consideration.

The power generated from Thermal Power Station-I after meeting the NLC's requirements is fed into Tamil Nadu Electricity Board grid which is the sole beneficiary.

Power generated from Thermal Power Station-II after meeting the needs of Second Mine is shared by southern states *viz.*, Tamil Nadu, Kerala, Karnataka, Andhra Pradesh and Union Territory of Pondicherry. NLC produced 154.10 lakh tonnes of lignite and generated 10,890.29 million units of power during 1994-95, registered an increase of about 23 per cent and 36 per cent respectively over 1991-92.

Raw lignite sales (12,34,001 tonnes) and power export (8916.36 million units) had registered an increase of about 61 per cent and 40 per cent respectively in 1994-95 over 1991-92. The company has been making profits since 1976-77 and its profit of Rs 171 crore (provisional) for 1994-95 is the highest profit achieved for any year since inception. In 1994-95, the sales turnover has recorded a growth of 33.23 per cent and net profit of 50 per cent over 1993-94.

Other minerals

India is richly endowed with minerals. Under the Constitution, minerals rights and the administration of mining laws are vested in the state governments. The Centre, however, regulates the development of minerals under the Mines and Minerals (Regulation and Development) Act, 1957 and the rules and regulations framed under it. This Statute empowers the Centre to formulate rules for: (i) the grant of prospecting licences and mining leases for schedule minerals, (ii) the conservation and development of minerals., and (iii) the modification of old leases. The Act, came into force on 1 June 1958. Amendments to this Act were made in 1972, 1986, and 1994.

Principal mineral found in the country along with their estimated reserves are given below.

Coal is India's largest mineral resource and presently India is the fifth largest producer of coal in the world. Vast deposits of coal of Gondwana formations occur in West Bengal, Orissa, Bihar, Madhya Pradesh, Andhra Pradesh, Uttar Pradesh and Maharashtra. It also occurs in tertiary formation in Assam, Arunachal Pradesh, Meghalaya and Nagaland. Total known reserves of all types of coals in Gondwana and tertiary coalfields estimated stands at 192 billion tonnes. Out of these, reserves of prime-coking coal have been estimated at 5.3 billion tonnes. Total reserves of lignite stands at 6.5 billion tonnes, located in Tamil Nadu, Gujarat, Rajasthan, Kerala, Pondichery and Jammu and Kashmir.

The total recoverable reserves of bauxite in the country are placed at 2,525 million tonnes while the total *in situ* reserves are 3,037 million tonnes. The conditional resources of bauxite are about five lakh tonnes. In addition, prospective resources are placed at 90 million tonnes. Orissa, Andhra Pradesh, Madhya Pradesh, Gujarat, Maharashtra and Bihar are the principal states where bauxite deposits are located. Major reserves are concentrated in the East Coast Bauxite deposits of Orissa and Andhra Pradesh.

Total recoverable reserves of chromite are estimated at 8.8 million tonnes. Deposits of economic significance occur in Andhra Pradesh, Bihar, Karnataka, Maharashtra, Manipur, Orissa and Tamil Nadu. However, refractory grade reserves of chromite are very meagre.

The total recoverable reserves of copper ore in the country are 415.86 million tonnes equivalent to 4.14 million tonnes of metal content. The all-India conditional resources of copper are 695.29 million tonnes (1.99

million tonnes of copper metal) and prospective resources are 769.9 million tonnes of copper ore. Major and important copper ore deposits are located in Singhbhum district (Bihar), Balaghat (Madhya Pradesh) and Jhunjhunu and Alwar (Rajasthan). In addition, small copper ore deposits are in Andhra Pradesh, Gujarat, Karnataka, Sikkim, Orissa, Uttar Pradesh and West Bengal.

There are three important gold fields in the country, namely, Kolar Gold Field, Kolar disrict, Hutti Gold Fields in Raichur district (both in Karnataka) and Ramgiri Gold field in Anantpur district (Andhra Pradesh). Total gold metal ore reserves are estimated at 176.9 lakh tonnes.

The total recoverable reserves of iron ore in the country are about 9,606 million tonnes of haematite and 3,143 million tonnes of magnetite. Haematite resources are located in Andhra Prades, Bihar, Goa, Karnataka, Madhya Pradesh, Maharashtra, Orissa and Rajasthan. Magnetite resources are located in Andhra Pradesh, Bihar, Goa, Karnataka and Kerala.

Lead-zinc resources are located in Rajasthan, Gujarat, West Bengal, Andhra Pradesh, Meghalaya, Orissa, Sikkim, Tamil Nadu and Uttar Pradesh. Total recoverable reserves (all grades) of lead and zinc ores are 198.5 million tonnes comprising of metal content of 2,390 thousand tonnes of lead and 9,866 thousand tonnes of zinc metal. The conditonal resources of lead-zinc are 200.29 million tonnes in the country.

The total recoverable reserves of manganese ore are 233.33 million tonnes out of which 41.05 million tonnes are proved , 142.03 million tonnes probable and 50.25 million tonnes of possible category. Main reserves are in Karnataka followed by Orissa, Madhya Pradesh, Maharashtra and Goa. Minor occurences of manganese are in Andhra Pradesh, Bihar, Gujarat, Rajasthan and West Bengal.

The total estimated conditional resource of nickel ore is 294 million tonnes located in Orissa (285 million tonnes) and Bihar (9 million tonnes). Minor occurrence of nickel in Tamil Nadu, Maharashtra and Goa are indicated.

The recoverable reserves of tungsten ore have been estimated at 25.89 million tonnes or 77.32 thousand tonnes of WO_3 content. The main reserves are at Degana, Rajasthan. It also occurs in Maharashtra, Karnataka, West Bengal and Uttar Pradesh.

The recoverable reserves of barytes are 70.15 million tonnes. The Mangampet deposit occuring in Cuddapah djistrict (Andhra Pradesh) is the single largest deposit in the world containing 67 million tonnes of recoverable reserves. Minor occurences of barytes are located in Rajasthan, Madhya Pradesh, Maharashtra, Himachal Pradesh, Tamil Nadu, Uttar Pradesh and Bihar.

Diamond deposits occur in three types of geological settings such as kimberlite pipes, conglomerate beds and alluvial gravels. The main diamond bearing areas in India are Panna belt in Madhya Pradesh, Munimadugu-Banganapalle conglomerate in Kurnool district, Wajrakarur kimberlite pipe in Anantpur district and the gravels of Krishna river basin in Andhra Pradesh. Reserves * of about a million carats, there are conditional submarginal of 265 thousand carats.

Dolomite occurrences are widespread in almost all part of the country. The total recoverable reserves of all grades of dolomite are 4,967 million tonnes. Of the total all India recoverable reserves, major share of about 92 per cent reserves is distributed in seven states– Madhya Pradesh, Orissa, Gujarat, Karnataka, West Bengal, Uttar Pradesh and Maharashtra.

Fireclay occurs as a bedded deposit, mostly associated with measures of Gondwana and Tertiary periods. Important deposits are associated with Jharia and Raniganj coalfields in Bihar and West Bengal, Korba coalfields in Madhya Pradesh and Neyveli Lignite field in Tamil Nadu. Notable occurrences of fireclay not associated with coal measures are known in Gujarat, Jabalpur region of Madhya Pradesh and Belpahar-Sundergarh areas of Orissa. The recoverable reserves of fireclay are about 697 million tonnes.

Total recoverable reserves of fluorspar in India are 2.15 million tonnes. Rajasthan and Gujarat are the only producing states in India. Fluorspar occurs in Gujarat, Madhya Pradesh, Maharashtra and Rajasthan. The recoverable reserves of gypsum are estimated at 239 million tonnes.

Out of the above, 70,000 tonnes surgical plaster grade, 39 million tonnes of fertilizer/pottery grade, 38.6 million tonnes of cement/paint grade, four million tonnes of soil reclamation grade and the rest is unclassified. The production of gypsum is confined to Rajasthan, Tamil Nadu, Jammu and Kashmir, Uttar Pradesh, Himachal Pradesh and Gujarat. Rajasthan is the main producer of gypsum followed by Tamil Nadu.

The recoverable reserves of graphite are 3.11 million tonnes. Orissa is the major producers of graphite. Almost the entire reserves under proved category are in Ramanathapuram district, Tamil Nadu. Resources of graphite are in Andhra Pradesh, Orissa, Tamil Nadu, Kerala, Bihar, Gujarat, Rajasthan, Madhya Pradesh and Maharashtra.

The recoverable reserves of ilmenite are 86.75 million tonnes. Ilmenite occurs mainly in beach sand deposits right from Ratnagiri coast in the west to Orissa coast in the east. These minerals are found in Kerala, Tamil Nadu and Orissa.

The all India recoverable reserves of kaolin, including white clay of all categories are about 986 million tonnes. Principal producing states are Bihar, Gujarat, Rajasthan and West Bengal. Kerala, Haryana, Orissa and Madhya Pradesh also produce significant quantities and ball clay is mainly produced in Rajasthan, Andhra Pradesh and Gujarat.

The total recoverable reserves of limestone of all categories and grades are placed at 76,446 million tonnes. The conditional reserves have been estimated at 360 million tonnes. Major producing states are Madhya Pradesh, tamil Nadu, Andhra Pradesh, Gujarat, Bihar, Orissa, Rajasthan and Karnataka. India is the world's leading producer of sheet mica and accounts for about 60 per cent of global mica trade.

Economic deposits of mica occur in three important belts in Bihar, Andhra Pradesh and Rajasthan. The total recoverable reserves of magnesite are about 233 million tonnes of which 41 million tonnes are in theproved category. Magnesite is found in Uttar Pradesh, Tamil Nadu and Rajasthan while minor occurrences are in Karnataka, Jammu and Kashmir and Himachal Pradesh.

The total recoverable reserves of kyanite and sillimanite in the country are 2.7 million tonnes * respectively. Besides, conditional resources of 175.84 million tonnes of kyanite are also estimated. For sillimanite conditional resources of 5.9 million tonnes and prospective resources of 0.8 million tonnes have been estimated. Kyanite deposits are located in Andhra Pradesh, Bihar, Karnataka and Maharashtra. Sillimanite resources are in Kerala, Orissa, Madhya Pradesh, tamil Nadu and minor occurrences in Andhra Pradesh, Assam, Bihar, Karnataka, Maharashtra, Meghalaya, Rajasthan and West Bengal.

Deposits of phosphorites are located in Madhya Pradesh, Rajasthan and Uttar Pradesh. Besides, apatite deposits of commercial importance are reported from Bihar, Andhra Pradesh, Rajasthan, West Bengal and Tamil Nadu. Recoverable reserves of rock-phosphate are estimated at 146.95 million tonnes of all grades and of apatite at 13 million tonnes.

Other minerals occuring in significant quantities in India are bentonite (Gujarat, Rajasthan, Bihar, Jammu and Kashmir and Tamil Nadu), corundum (Maharashtra, Madhya Pradesh, Andhra Pradesh * and Gujarat), fullers earth (Rajasthan, Karnataka and Andhra Pradesh), garnet (Tamil Nadu, Rajasthan and Andhra Pradesh Pradesh), pyrites (Bihar and Rajasthan), steatite (Rajasthan, Uttar Pradesh, Andhra Pradesh, Tamil Nadu and Bihar), wollastonite (Rajasthan and Gujarat), zircon (beach sand of Tamil Nadu, Kerala and Orissa) and quartz and silica minerals are wide spread and occur in about all states. Besides, the country has vast resources of building dimension and ornamental stones such as granite, marble and slate. Granite is mainly mined in Tamil Nadu, Karnataka, Andhra Pradesh and Rajasthan, marble in Rajasthan, Uttar Pradesh and Gujarat and slate in Madhya Pradesh, Andhra Pradesh and Haryana.

Mineral and metal production

In most states the growth rate declined during the decade. However, Andhra Pradesh, Arunachal Pradesh, Madhya Pradesh, Maharashtra, Nagaland, Tripura, West Bengal, Daman and Diu, Lakshadweep and Pondicherry which account for one third of the country's population, recorded increase in growth rate. Nagaland registered the highest growth rate of 56.08 per cent while Keral the lowest 14.32 per cent.

Unlike the Eight Five Year Plan of which the structural framework claimed more than a three-year time under the exercise of repeatedly reconstituted Planning Commission by as many as three Prime Ministers appearing in the see-saw political scene since 1989 to get itself approved in May 1992, the approach paper to the Ninth Five Year Plan has happily received approval of the National Development Council on 16 January, 1997 which still leaves two-and-half-month period to complete the tenure of the current Plan. The approach paper to the Ninth Plan, now available, will reap the benefit of being commented upon widely in various media. This is a definite advantage and, if everything goes well, the Ninth Plan comprising the period from 1 April, 1997 to 31 March, 2002 will take off in time without suffering a delay like the pre-Eighth Plan two-year plan holiday.

The approach to the Ninth Plan is undoubtedly bold and highly ambitious. The Plan envisages an annual economic growth rate of seven per cent per annum with an increase of savings and investment rates of 26.2 per cent and 28 per cent respectively, within the limit of ceiling on current account deficit at 2.4 per cent of GDP. The Prime Minister, Mr H.D. Deve Gowda had called for collective efforts to raise the huge resource quantum of Rs. 8,75,000 crore for implementing the Plan.

The approach paper to the Ninth Plan does initiate a departure from traditional lines of the past in more than one way.

First, the States are being given a wider latitude in the affairs of rural development under a basket of programmes complex with, however, an added responsibility of mobilizing additional funds.

Secondly, the role of government has been deeply examined against the backdrop of a fast-changing economic scenario and emerging dynamism in the international politico-economic horizon that is increasingly necessitating a larger role of the private sector.

Thirdly, the role of involvement of people in the process of nation building through of nation building through decentralized planning has received deeper attention than in the VIII Plan.

Fourthly, the question of growth with social justice and equity has received greater focus with stock taking of achievements in the areas of basic minimum services and a renewed emphasis on quick realization of the remaining tasks.

Fifthly, the need for an effective family welfare and population policy has been spelt out as an indispensable factor in the planning process and the employment generation target is aimed at eight million jobs per year with the emphasis on high employment-elastic activities in the agro-allied areas of animal husbandry, fishery, horticulture, dairy farming, fish preservation and the like.

The important thrust areas as highlighted in the approach paper are agriculture, infrastructure and the social sector areas which have by and large remained neglected during the VIII Plan. The Ninth Plan expects to achieve an agricultural growth rate of 4.5 per cent annually which is looked upon as a chief engine of poverty removal and rural development.

Though the output of agricultural sector during the VIII Plan grew by 3.5 per cent per annum, the approach paper expects that a higher rate of public investment in irrigation, soil conservation, flood and drought preventive measures, marketing infrastructure and in sectoral diversification to high value crops will achieve the Ninth Plan target of 4.5 per cent of annual output growth.

The loss of community reality and participation jeopardize many values of the democratic tradition. Those generous impulses that grow out of an awareness of a local common good are weakened. One is merely lost in the amorphous anonymity of a huge population.

As a consequence, the ordinary citizen becomes less and less articulate and makes fewer contributions to the decisions that shape his own destiny or the collective destiny. The democratic experience, whereby the voice of the ordinary citizens at the local grass roots has been heard in higher-level decisions, is lost. So a method of work that promises to increase the responsibility of the citizens, is pertinent to the treatment of the malaise of our time.

Much of the literature on community development is more expressive of the writer's enthusiasm to do good than of any discipline of description and evaluation. Both the enthusiasm and discipline are necessary if this field of work with people is even to approach the fulfillment of its promise,

As to values, let it be stated immediately that development is always normative. That is, it takes place in the midst of actions that serve chosen goals. No scientist (social or any other kind), when he takes part in development, can be content with description only. He must approve actions and evaluate results in the light of some scheme of values towards the attainment of which the development is directed. The paradox for the scientist is that he will never describe man as he is. He will need also to describe man in the process of becoming and this latter task requires planned development that seeks chosen goals.

In regard to community development and people's participation, the emerging consensus clusters round a concept of the improvement of people, the underprivileged, the overprivileged, and all in between. Improvement is evaluated in terms of democratic skills, responsibility to serve growing awareness of a common good, ethical sensitivity, and willingness to co-operate. All other improvements are judged good or bad by reference to what is happening to the people involved.

In the preceding paragraphs we have emphasized upon some value loaded normative ideas which may appear like Utopia but they are the sine qua non of all the development strategy. If we look into the successive Five Year Plan documents from the I Plan to the VIII Plan, it is evident that by and large they have been laudable and reflected the pious dreams of the founding fathers of the nation. However, on the performance side, we have always drawn, if not blank, at least little achievements. The Ninth Plan document emphasizes more on rural infrastructure, the social sector and equity, which are based on the Common Minimum Programme of the United Front government. No doubt, the approach is very laudable but again it is a million dollar question as to what we will achieve at the end of the Ninth Five Year Plan. Instead of lamenting over this question, in the succeeding pages the approach to Ninth Five Year Plan is being discussed in brief and finally our observations on various aspects of the approach paper are given.

The Strategy of development adopted in the Ninth Five Year Plan aims at reaching out to those regions and sections of the society which have been bypassed by the process of development. At the same time, it also has to aim at efficiency of resource use in areas and sectors which have already been developed. Supply—side efficiency and technological transformation have to be interwoven with the economic process of increasing the production potential. In order to sustain a growing and well—diversified economy in the Nith Plan, it would be necessary to evolve judicious public policies towards investment and technology, which can mobilize resources that are lying unutilized in the economy and can unleash wider processes of agricultural growth and decentralized developments linked to national and world markets.

Thrust needs to be given to develop modern communication and information system in the villages. Those could be managed and operated by community initiative or growers' association. This would enable the farming community to know about the latest trend of the prices both in the domestic and international market and also quality of food products of other countries, taste and preference of the consumers. Based on the input structure, the output pattern for major crops during the Ninth Plan has been tentatively worked out. In the output projections, adequate emphasis has been laid on relative self—sufficiency in food production, keeping in view the imperative of maintaining food security in the country. In fact, it culd be stated that the Indian economy attained high rates of growth and better economic stability and resilience during the eighties, among other factors, due to the factor of relative food self—sufficiency. It is important to constantly keep this factor in view while chalking out the broad contours of the Ninth Plan.

The State Agricultural Board should construct Haats with necessary infrastructure facilities at important areas/mandis for small and marginal farmers so as to enable them to get rid of dalall agent and sell their agricultural commodities direct to the buyers/consumers. Tis would also generate a number of employment oportunities in the process of marketing activities, besides better price to the farmers. Necessary infrastructure would need to be created in the major growing areas for encouraging the entrepreneurs to set up food processing industries. It would be more appropriate if encouragement is given to joint ventures with growers' participation as members. An agri–business corporation should be set up for marketing the agricultural produce both in the domestic as well as in international markets. The corporation would establish both forward and backward linkages with the growers and help them to improve quality and productivity. For increasing India's share in the world trade of food and food products, modernizaton of agricultural marketing system would need to be encouraged with more emphasis on quality control, sophisticated and eco—friendly packaging and consumer packs.

There is need for flow of investment in dryland agriculture, which is insufficient at present. It can be suggested that if a part of the huge funds allotted in the Ninth Plan for famine relief in the event of drought could be spent for proper nutrition of poor dry land soils and crops, the recurring problem of famines could be solved to a great extent. Given the level of food stocks of the order of 36.4 million tonnes, food avvailibility has ceased to be a constraint on economic development. Also, while due emphasis would continue to be laid on the diversified crop structure in the Ninth Plan, attention would also have to be paid to the development of dairy, poultry, fisheries, friits and vegetables, tea, coffee, rubber plantation, etc. Development of non—crop oriented agricultural activities would involve, inter alia, strengthening of the existing processing facilities for value—addition operations as also installation of new capacities in these fields. During the Ninth Plan, each village information centre will have one Biological Software Library (BSL) to take care of soil health, earthworm farming and biofertilisers production/supply. Thus, this library will provide all types of organic/biotic inputs at the doorsteps of farmers.

The special needs of water management and its integration with agricultural operations call for a selective and systematic approach to conjunctive use of water at micro and macro levels. This would help eliminate deterious effects on soil and environment and also help optimize the use of water in crop productivity. There is an urgent need to recognize water as a national asset and its proper utilization whould be a top priority area brooking no delay to increase use–efficiency. Low efficiency of irrigation use ranges from 30 to 70 per cent and there is inequality in distribution of water. Increasing problems of soil salinity, water–logging and soil degradation associated with irrigation are also to be looked into. In working out of the production potential of agriculture during the Ninth Plan, the approach to water development strategies at the subregional level is to be vigorously pursued. This approach sets specific targets for projects like tank irrigation, watershed development, modernization and completion of canal system and diversification of cropping sequences in different agro–climatic regions of India. It is also necessary to strengthen the appropriate input structure of irrigation, fertilizer consumption, crop intensity and crop diversification, etc. for building up the production potential of agriculture during the Ninth Plan.

Emphasis should continue to be laid on the Integrated Watershed Development Projects. Various soil and water conservation technologies need to be energetically pursued to raise productivity in the marginal and rainfed land holdings. As per preliminary estimates, the share of irrigated area in gross sown area is likely to be 48.4 per cent in the terminal year of the Ninth Plan diversified agriculture and crop intensification should be propagated with the crop intensity reaching the level of 1.40 by 2001—2002.

It is necessary that institutional finances as advanced by the co—operative credit system and commercial banks and regional rural banks to the agricultural sector should consistently increase during the Ninth Plan. The priority sector lending target set by government for commercial banks should be fulfilled by all the public sector banks during each year of the Ninth Plan. Such a commitment on the part of institutional financing agencies will considerably help in financing development needs in the agriculture and rural development sectors.

The sectoral allocation of the total investment has to be so designed that investment in agriculture and rural development should get a big push in the Ninth Plan. In the Ninth Plan, out of the total investment, the share of agriculture and rural development needs to be increased to about 30 per cent. This is very important, as in recent years, capital formation in the agricultural sector has tended to decline.

The agricultural sector is likely to have a bright future due to the overall expansion of the economy through liberalization, globalization and privatization. The agricultural production, productivity, export and employment is likely to pick up in the future due to its forward linkages with the economy. At the same time, the liberalized economic environment is expected to show some side—effects on crokpping pattern, income distribution and employment. In the overall context, the Ninth Plan hopes to integrate the planning process for the globalization of agriculture.

According to Prof. Madhu Dandavate, Deputy Chairman of the Planning Commission, the Ninth Plan accords "the highest priority to generating adequate productive employment, eradication of poverty, focus on agriculture and rural development with emphasis on radical land reforms".

Pointing out that the power sector constitutes the most crucial infrastructure both for agriculture and industry, he said that the problems of power must be carefully handled in a co-ordinated fashion with due attention for the proper choice of fuels, the adequacy of their availability, the need to rationalize tariff structure, and to prevent transmission and distribution losses.

In fact, the problem of power may reach crisis proportions in the next few years unless urgent action is taken by every state. The financial, managerial and administrative structue of State Electricity Boards (SEBs) and their policies must be changed dramatically and urgently so that the Electricity Boards can raise tariffs to realistic levels, improve the quality of supply, contain power theft and become financially viable. The Finance Minister, Mr. P. Chidambaram, is of the view that the Central and State laws need to be changed to allow SEBs and private electricity companies to function autonomously subject to independent regulatory authorities.

In respect of sectoral strategies, the document emphasizes that agriculture has a vital place in the economic development of the country as it contributes 29.4 per cent of GDP and employs about 64 per cent of the workforce. There has been a significant improvement in agricultural productivity which has helped in reducing rural poverty. It is noted that capital formation (at 1980-81 prices) in agriculture grew at tha rate of 6.05 per cent during 1989-90 to 1994-95. In the accelerated growth scenario for the Ninth Plan, efforts will need to be made to achieve an agricultural growth rate of 4.5 per cent per annum in contrast with 3.5 per cent growth rate during the Eighth Plan period on an average.

The role of basic inputs in agriculture cannot be underestimated. Timely and adequate availabilty of inputs for agriculture and agriculture-related infrastructure will need to receive special attention.

Therefore, regional programmes have to be formulated in such a manner as to ensure provision of inputs to the farmer, particularly in the remote, hilly, backward and tribal areas. Likewise, augmentation of irrigation facilities is necessary to increase the gross cropped areas even under rainfed vonditions and invreasing cropping intensity in agriculture areas and assinging priority ot the completion of ongoing projects—both major and minor irrigation.

Another vital input is rural credit. Greater credit flow will be ensured to meet the investment requirements of the farming community for stepping up the growth of production. The approach paper of the Plan stresses that efforts would be made to ensure timely and adequate availability of credit, particularly to small and marginal farmers and tribal farmers at reasonable rates so as to enable them to make investments necessary for higher production. More importantly, the crop insurance scheme is going to receive a big thrust for providing security to marginal and small farmers in rainfed areas during the Ninth Plan period.

Referring to the controversy over poverty estimates exercise, Prof. Dandavate points out that a group in the Plan panes has smoothed out some 'kinks' in the poverty estimate arising out of the appliation of the Lakadwala Committee methodology. He said that the group has suggested that in assessing rural poverty, the agricultural labourers' consumer price index should be used and for estimating urban poverty, the industrial workers' consumer price index should be untilized for updating the poverty line. It is hoped that the Planning Commission would finally decide on this issue during the final draft of the Plan.

A common symptom of rural poverty which India

shares along with other developing countries is the existence of underutilized resources, such as land, water and endemic underemployment of labour. Poverty itself is the lot of about 39 per cent of the population as against about 20 poer cent as per calculations of theearlier government. During the period 1983—84 to 1987—88, rural poverty fell from 45.6 per cent to 39 per cent while between 1987—88 and 93—94, it fell only by a further 1.7 per cent.

In 1987—88, unemployment inperson—years was estimated to be 12.43 million in usual principal status, 15.30 million in weekly status, and 18.95 million on daily status. Even causal labour employment is 38.4 per cent among rural males and 31.4 per cent among rural females.

The above phenomenon has been interpreted from different perspectives. It is regarded as due to the fickleness of the poor and, therefore, the total literacy campaign in India seeks to encnouraged the poor to come together and improvve their lot. It can also be seen as an inherent attribute of the socio—economic structure retarding growth and perpetuating poverty. Land reforms is the answer to this situation. A third perspective is to look at it as a potential for local resource mobilization and its concomitant local—level planning. In this context, the 73rd constitutional amendment conferring constitutional status to local bodies and for greater decentralization in the country is worth noting.

It is this point of view that the present paper has adopted. It is noted that there is an enormous potential for alleviating poverty which such underutilized resources represent. Along side with the resource augmenting aspect, the mobilization of local resources also promises the simultanneous attainment of other adjectives which are apecial to rural development like greater decentralization in planning, increasing popular paraticipation and ensuring a greater degree of self—reliance on the part of local communities. Macro planning embodied in the Ninth Plan alone cannot cope with the highly particularized and the localized problems of identifying development potentialities in the rural communities. Even though the basic criteria of rural development are participation, production, distribution and consumption, participation takes on a different meaning.

The disadvantaged people are not to be cast inthe role of the objects of participation, but they are to be integrated as the subjects of the operation. Both human resource development and human development are the objectives in rural development and a World Bank study has shown that there will not be adequate resources for human development if government funds alone are to be depended upon. It is imperative to use local resources and community resources will have to be mobilized. Also the interdependence between eduction, health, sanitation and other social development sectors has to be taken care of because all of them jointly promote rural development.

In this paper, we have discussed, the broad outlines of the Ninth Plan to show the resource constraints. Secondly, the interdependence between agriculture and rural development is noted and it is concluded that there is no alternative except to mobilize local resources. Reference in this context is not only to mobilization of financial resources through imposition of appropriate taxes in agriculture, but also more importantly to mobilize non–financial resources like labour, locally available material and technical expertise.

Resource mobilization

To achieve the ambitious objectives of the Ninth Plan (1997-2002), the government has to face hard realities in mobilizing the required amount of huge resources. The

Prime Minister and Chairman of the Planning Commission has called for collective efforts to raise resources of the order of Rs. 8,75,000 crore to finance the Plan. The approach paper urges that the country has to take 'difficult decisions' which, as Mr. H.D. Deve Gowda explained, would in include reduction of fiscal deficit, rational user charges for power and irrigation, disinvestment of public sector and transparent and focused subsidies. The Deputy Chairman of the Planning Commission, Prof Madhu Dandavate has rightly emphasized that the much needed public investment in various sectors could be available only if the required will is demonstrated in exploring new sources of revenues at all levels—the Centre, the States and local governments. He also noted that serious efforts are necessary to ensure better tax compliance and also to bring presumptive incomes computed from high expenditures of creamy layers under the tax net.

Insofar as disinvestment of public sector undertakings as a source of revenue mobilization is concerned, the earlier experience is not at all encouraging. The failure of the disinvestment programme in 1995-96 and all indications of its repetition in regard to the target of mopping up Rs. 5,000 crore in the current fiscal year amply shows that the Ninth Plan should not bank much on this source prior to restructuring of the PSUs.

It may be noted here that an important reason for the inefficiency of PSUs is the defective MOUs which fix responsibilities of the organisations but remain silent on the responsibilities of government and administrative ministries. This needs to be corrected and efficiency enhanced since the government has to justify the existence of this sector and make the enterprises commercially viable.

Need for political will: Insofar as the States' efforts are concerned, there is room fro enhancing revenue collection provided political will is mobilized, administrative machinery for taxation is properly cleaned and temptation of the government for populist spending is arrested. There is huge amount of tax arrears, under assessment of levy, tax evasion through foul means, complete absence of or unjustifiably low rates of tariffs and charges against public services rendered and inefficiently managed State PSUs running on heavy government subsidies. Bold steps to reverse the trend is urgently necessary. This also applies to the Union government by and large. The approach paper aims at an annual rate of savings at the rate of 26.2 per cent as against the peak of 24.6 per cent in 1989-90. Since the biggest source of savings in the household sector which mobilizes around one-fifth of GDP, there is ample opportunity of raising this source through tax-related saving incentives and stability of the capital market for shares and debentures. Proper incentive pattern is also necessary for saving in physical assets which alone comprise more than 55 per cent of the total household sector savings. The savings of the private corporate sector is only 2.7 per cent which may be easily raised to three per cent of GDP through incentives and better collection. The lowest is the public sector savings which are stagnating at around Id. 7 per cent. The savings from government companies and statutory corporations have started declining since 1990-91 and presently accounts for less than three per cent of GDP. Unless the negative savings on account of government administration and departmental enterprises are checked effectively, one could nolt expect larger savings from the public sector.

At the same time, the huge amount of government subsidy on account of food and fertilizers, petroleum and petroleum products, sugar and other selective items should be withdrawn from those who have the capacity to pay at the rate of open market prices. The oil pool deficit alone has reached public destribution system would claim a whopping Rs. 2,000 crore. There is no justification of suppresssing the administered prices since its substitute is only a resort to deficit financing that would come in the way of macro-economic adjustment in the country.

The system of income taxation in India has remained utterly inequitable as millions of highly rich people go untaxed due to fear of unpopularity among politicians. Thus, the much talked about unexploited source of agricultural income tax has remained a forbidden fruit. In spite of the fact that the Green Revolution and the new agricultural strategy with all kinds of agro-mechanisation subsidy together with a price support programme for farm products have placed more and more wealth in the hands of rich farmers, no political decision has yet been taken to bring the wealthy section of farmers under the income tax net. The K.N. Raj Committee recommended long ago a progressive tax structure for agricultural incomes along with the incomes from non-agricultural sources and also from allied activities of the farm sector. Some members in the NDC while approving the Ninth Plan approach paper, urged upon mobilization of black money as a revenue raising device. Since the agricultural sector offers a golden opportunity to earners of illegal incomes to conceal black money and black wealth under the veil of untaxed farm incomes and since the gap between poverty and prosperity in the farming community has greatly widened as a result of the emergence of highly rich agriculturists, the imposition of agricultural income tax along with non-agricultural income will not only fetch huge funds to the resource-starved exhequer, but will also reduce considerably the prevailing inequality of incomes in rural areas on the one hand and mop up a large part of black money on the other. The other areas of unequal treatment lies in the complete absence of income tax among Scheduled and backward classes, where, too a large section of people has become millionaires due to business activity, government contracts, construction works and heavy development expenditure incurred in backward regions by the government in course of the five year plans, These rich people also go untaxed. In order to remove such utter discrimination, it is urgently necessary that these creamy layers be invariably brought within the income tax net.

Thus, what the foregoing discussion implies is that bold decisions and hard determination are necessary to give a proper shape to the economy after the aspirations of the Ninth Plan approach paper. While political will is a pre-condition, the States' unqualified co-operation will be the most basic factor. However, the aspirations of resource-starved States will urgently need attention particularly with respect to their autonomy and larger access to Central tax sharing which has been the main irritant in the Centre-State relationship. The Centrally-sponsored schemes which have remained only half-hearted attempts for all these years should be left to the responsibility of the States with hundred per cent resource disposal to them. The declining trend of the share of the State' Plan in the total public sector plan outlay needs to be reversed in the Ninth Plan and the decentralized planning should call for strengthening of the administrative set-up of Panchayati Raj institutions at all levels. Accountability and monitoring of activity must be ensured at every step so that development plan does not degenerate into expenditure plan. If all revenue sources are properly exploited, implementation of programmes is carried out in the right perspective and utmost care is maintained in government consumption expenses, there is no reason why the aspirations of the approach paper should not come into reality.

Underutilization may be in the intensity of land use and agricultural productivity or the levels of utilisation of labour force. Measures ofunderutilization can be: (a) a straightforward measure of idle resources, of production capacity at a given level of technology and organization, eg fallow land, unemployment and underemployment according to atime measure; (b) misallocation of resources due to lack of knowledge of superior alternatives or distortion in the structure of incentives; and (c) underutilization in terms of productivity. According to Prof. Brahmananda, even though aggregate capital may be adequate potentially at the macrolevel, capital in the form of wage goods capacity may be deficient. It is in the process of production of wage goods at the local level through local planning that local resource mobilization can take place and productivity can be improved and social change brought about. At the grass roots level in the rural areas, there is urgent need for improving productivity and promoting social change with better education.

Rural development refers to a number of development programmes. Earlier it was linked only with agricultural development but on the basis of the experience during the last few decades we can speak of holistic rural development which includes agriculture, rural development, rural industries, and hollistic self—supporting development.

In order to accelerate such a holistic rural development there are three major potential areas for integration which are: (a) stepping up the existing wage employment programme in rural areas ofor capital construction in agriculture and for ecodevelopment; (b) stimulating the growth of households by intergrating them with the existing self—employment programmes like IRDP; and (c) accelerating the pace of social development.

In sum, we will emphasize that poverty alleviation programmes should be properly integratd with over—all development. No rural development is possible without wipping out p[overty or reducing it in stages. The integration of poverty alleviation objective with the over–all development strategy has to be distinguished from the issue of integrating poverty alleviation programmes with the over–all development strategy. The over—all development strategy is concerned with questions like investment priorities, choice of technique and location of projects through trickle down effects. It tries to reduce poverty. A greater and more specific role has to be given to investment in agiven resources, eg bringing down the capital output ratio to a certain level sector by sector). But integration of poverty alleviation programmes with over–all development strategy tries to ensure that poverty alleviation programmes subserve the goals of over—all development. At present, the schemes for increasing incomes and employment do not adequately take care of it. In this also there should be a greater role both for human resource development and human development.

Whether it is fully realized or not, the Ninth Plan planning represents a new age planning of an age of management culture, economic restructuring, resource scarcity, economy, value for investment, global competition, MNCs, mega investments, free trade, intellectual property rights, R & D, productivity, quality, efficiency, hardware and software of production, human capital, strategic planning, economic vision, government-private sector partnership, value by results, international capital, regional economic groupings, delicensing, decentralization, lean taxation, FDI, foreign borrowings, JVs, market pricing, opening of the economies, public-private sector parity or equality, fiscal discipline, public-orientation, deregulations, budgetary imbalances, de-nationalisation, corporate takeovers, subsidy-cuts, commercialization of agriculture and free trade in agricultural goods, non-farm enterprises in rural areas, entrepreneurship, innovations, paid lunches, cutting down free rides, user-charges gender equality and empowerment of women, and soon.

Break from the past: In spite of its not insignificant achievements, the bane of Indian planning has been poor implementation and results, viz operational shortcomings and 'targetism'. The Ninth Plan should and ought to make a break from it, to justify its nearly Rs. 1 m crore investment. It must have multiple effect, without which it is bad planning, though the plans do not work out the multipliers. The plan has to learn a leaf or two from corporate planning, particularly of MNCs which mean business of every dollar of investment. Not that the Plan should be devoid of human concerns and values, which it or for that matter any public planning anywhere should be responsive to, given the concern of planning with the have-nots. That is, the results of the planning need be measured not only, by the hard facts of growth rate but also by the light and laughter in the lives of the common people, visible to the naked eye. Otherwise, the purpose of the whole planning exercise would be much lost.

All said and done, the fact should be brought home to the planners in the Ninth Plan that it requires a lot of suffering and sacrifice to make the Plan operative with so much investment and it should yield commensurate returns in health, education, employment, social infrastructure, economic overheads, employment, enterprises, etc. for which the Plan is intended. India is one of the most poverty-ridden and low income countries. Our per capita income is not even $ 400 per annum. Millions and millions of people's daily concerns water, sanitation, medical aid, food and employment.

Accordingly, the new age planning consists of making plan investments go as far as possible or maximum yielding. Planning must make the deserts bloom, not allow the forests to vanish so to say. If not, it is not proper planning.

Whether the plan size is optimal, suboptimal or overoptimal is irrelevant in the context of the plan. From plan-to-plan, planning efforts anyhow need to be raised. Considering This the plan is not at all oversized, considering the magnitude of the problems facing the economy and the efforts needed to overcome them. It is a different thing if the nation opts for a soft and small Ninth Plan. At no time, the plans had escaped the label of being ambitious and oversized. Notwithstanding plan size, the basic economic problems remain intact, if the poverty-line population increasing recently to 37 per cent is any indication.

Only, the Ninth Plan should be a new age planning or plan of operational efficiency, economy, efficiency, discipline, human and grass roots development, competitive, forward looking, co-ordinating and comprehensive. In addition, it must be time and cost bound. No doubt, it is a tall order of things but it is unavoidable if the Ninth Plan is to spell a success and make a dent into the thousand problems of the economy and the people. We have been lethargic with planning and it is time to be strictly business and management minded about planning and plan and the Ninth Plan is the right and opportune time to commence new age planning, without which it becomes increasingly difficult to sustain planning.

That is the law of diminishing returns which appears to have set in planning, since long, needs to be reversed in the Ninth Plan, failing which zero and even negative marginal productivities may set in for plan investments. There are increasing constraints on plan resources due to which the Ninth Plan should successfully go through its arithmetic of investments and returns in different lines of production and try to realize them for the first time in planning history of the country in tune with the new age stress on returns rather than or just investments. The Ninth Plan, in other words, should incorporate into its functioning strict business principles. The Plan thus should open a new chapter in planning not only in India but also the world over. Planning should assert itself and march ahead in the so-called market ruled economy and dispense its benefits to its large multitudes standing second to none in economy, efficiency and execution. It is the mandate of the populace. There is a national consensus behind planning, particularly the Ninth Plan, which promises to be a plan of action and of the people. It promises to give thrust to the thrust areas. Economy, productivity, returns and people should be the watchwords of new planning to commence with the Ninth Plan. There is no activity commensurate in importance with the Plan that should be No. 1 programmes, as nothing involves such a massive investment and the welfare and happiness of millions and millions of people and their living and natural environment.

One has to harp at length about the need for new planning because of the debris that is being left behind by improper planning, which is downward rather than upward. Rural development, for instance, is a greatly neglected aspect of our planning and the Ninth Plan promises to remove the whole backlog of it including human resource development and women and child development. Great challenges lay ahead of the new planning process.

Sustainable planning

Sustainable development has become a key catch-phrase in eonomic planning and resource management. However, the interpretation of this concept is still obscure, and definitions of it are abundant ranging from continued economic growth to steady economics where economic growth to steady state economies where economic growth mainly serves to compensate for environmental degradation.

Sustainability, as defined by the Brundtland Commission, is essentially a holistic notion, and as such all aspects of the system need to be included in it. Now, the same may also be defined as the preservation of the production possibilities of an economy to produce useful goods and services. Such a definition could provide some guidance on the rate at which one can exploit exhaustible resources or the level of degradation of renewable resources that may be permitted. However, this raises another issue that in the production of such goods and services, man-made capital and natural resources (we can call the latter environmental capital) can substitute for each other, at least within some limits.

In this context, it is essential to evolve techniques for planning and decision-making with a view to working out a viable programme for sustainable development. The tools of benefit-costs analysis and project appraisal need to be so recast as to combine the traditional economic efficiency criterion with the criterion of sustainable development. The problem of discounting the future streams of benefits and costs and the choice of appropriate discount rate assume especial significance in this regard. The concept of benefits and costs will have to be redefined to take account of the effect of a project on environment and sustainability of development in the long-run.

Gives the levels of development of States on the basis of the following determinants: (1) Per capita net State domestic product, (2) Unemployment rate, (3) Poverty ratio, (4) Per capita education expenditure, (5) Literacy rate, (6) Infant mortality rate, (7) Annual population growth rate, etc.

Adjudged on the basis of the statistical evidence, the five most backward States in India in terms of socio-economic development are Uttar Pradesh, Orissa, Bihar, Madhya Pradesh and Rajasthan. These States are extremely backward not only in terms of economic development but also by the levels of their per capita net State domestic product. It can also be said that states with higher per capita income tend to do well in terms of overall socio-economic development as well. Kerala, however, is an exception to this rule and proves that a high success rate in social development is possible with higher levels of expenditure in the social sectors even when the levels of per capita income in a State is low.

The region's natural resources used as goods are ground-water for drinking and irrigation and timber for paper and pulp. The ecosystems provide services of outdoor recreation and nature conservation while they assimilate surplus ammonium and nitrate from nature. Land is the most important resource in the region and any model that deals with the problems of land use and changes in the quality of land is of considerable interest. Land pressure in various districts of the region is fairly high, particularly in small districts, given the available technology and the production constraints in such semi-arid parts of the region. Land pressure is particularly important in case of overstocking

The critical success factors in coping with the problems of land pressure are the following:

— Controlling population growth in the areas concerned;

— Ensuring balanced livestock development;

— Controlling land alienation, mainly in smaller districts; and

— Controlling technological developments and related policies regarding boreholes.

Ecologically sustainable economic development has become a policy issue of major significance. Conceptualizing and analyzing sustainable development is clearly important at the regional level. The openness of a spatial system evokes the question of environmental sacrifices in space and time. When the issue of the substitutability of environmental decay is at stake, the related concept of weak and strong sustainability requires further exploration on the basis of a thorough investigation of underlying welfare concepts and associated collective welfare function.

In order to obtain a homostatic balance of resources in space and time, much attention has to be given to regional resource accounting. Efficiency, equity and externality aspects of resource use can then be given due emphasis, while attempts at valuing unpriced resources may provide a sound basis for project appraisal. Geographic information systems may be helpful to visualize all relevant policy aspects. In many cases, governments in an attempt to cope with environmental deterioration, have misjudged the causes of such decay and have even aggravated the original conditions. Thus, a closer analysis of the costs and remedies regarding both signal and response failures would be desirable. In the context of sustainable regional development, critical sucess factors refer to major focal points for policy intervention. Identification of such factors may induce proactive sustainability of policies. In sustainable regional development planning, where regions are open, critical success factors may also be found outside the specific region.

Power

Electricity is the most convenient and versatile form of energy. Demand for it, therefore, has been growing at the rate faster than other forms of energy. Power industry too has recorded a phenomenal rate of growth both in terms of its volume and technological sophistication over the last few decades. Electricity plays a crucial role in both industrial and agricultural sectors and, therefore, consumption of electricity in the country is an indicator of productivity and growth. In view of this, power development has been given high priority in development programme.

Studies have shown that while the demand for electricity in the entire economy has riisen at the rate of 9.73 per cent during 1986-87, the demand in the residential and agricultural sectors has been increasing at an alarming rate of 14.03 per cent and 14.58 per cent respectively per year. Installed power generation capacity in the country has increased from a meagre 1,400 mw in 1947 to 81,164.41 mw at the end of 1994-95 comprising 20,829.04 mw hydro (25.66 per cent) and 58,110.37 mw thermal including gas, diesl and wind (71.60 per cent) and 2,225.0 mw nuclear (2.74 per cent).

Various measures being taken to improve power generation in the country include commission of new generation capacity, renovation and modernisation of old units, assistance to Electricity Boards in undertaking plant betterment programme, supply of requisite quantity and quality of coal, training of operation and maintenence personnel and strengthening of transmission and distribution system and implementation of short gestation projects, reduction in T & D losses, implementation of demand management and energy conservation measures.

The target of power generation during 1995-96 has been 377.15 billion units out of which 297 billion units are programmed for generation by thermal stations 72.3 billion units by hydro stations and 7.85 billion units by the nuclear stations. Thus an increase of about 7.4 per cent over the generation achieved during 1994-95 is envisaged.

The Plant Load Factor (PLF) has shown a steady improvement over the years. It has improved from 53.8 per cent in 1990-91 to 60 per cent in 1994-95. The following table highlights the achievement of the power sector in major areas during 1994-95.

Electricity is a concurrent subject at Entry 34 in the List III of Seventh Schedule of the Constitution of India. The responsibility of its development lies both with the Central and state governments. At the Centre, the Ministry of Power is responsible for the administration of the Electricity (Supply) Act, 1948 and the Indian Electricity Act, 1910. The Ministry is also concerned with perspective planning, policy formulation, processing of projects for investment decision, monitoring of the implementation of power projects and training and manpower development.

The Central Electricity Authority (CEA), constituted under the Electricity (Supply) Act, 1948, advises the Ministry of Power on technical and economic matters. The construction and operation of generation and transmission projects in the Central Sector are entrusted to Central sector power corporations, namely, the National Thermal Corporation (NTPC), the National Hydroelectric Power Corporation (NHPC), the North

Eastern Electric Power Corporation (NEEPCO) and the Power Grid Corporation of India Limited (POWERGRID). POWERGRID, which was incorporated on the 23 October 1989, is responsible for all the existing and future transmission projects in the Central sector and also for the formation of the National Power Grid. There are two joint ventures power corporations under the administrative control of the Ministry of Power, namely, Nathpa Jhakri Power Project and projects of the Tehri Hydro Power Complex. The Damodar Valley Corporation (DVC), constituted under the DVC Act, 1948, the Bhakra Beas Management Board (BBMB) constituted under the Punjab Act, 1966, and three autonomous bodies, namely, Central Power Research Institute (CPRI), the National Power Training Institute (NPTI) and the Energy Management Centre (EMC) are also under the administrative control ofthe Ministry. Programmes of rural electrification are within the purview of the Rural Electrification Corporation (REC). The Power Finance Corporation (PFC) provides term-finance to projects in the power sector. There is one subordinate office Badarpur Management Control Cell (BMCC), directly under this Ministry and 16 subordinate offices under the Central Electricity Authority.

Significant progress has been made in expansion of transmission and distribution facilities in the country. Total length of transmission lines of 66 kv and above voltage level increased form 10,000 ckt km in December 1950 to about 2.36 lakh ckt in March 1994. Highest transmission voltage at present is 400 kv and about 30,240 ckt km of 400 kv lines had been constructed upto March 1994. In addition, the first +500 kv HVDC bipole Rihand-Dadri transmission line of about 820 km length is also in operation. An inter-regional link (vindhyachal 2 × 250 mw HVDC back-to-back) connecting western and northern regions is also in operation.

Five regional grid systems, namely, northern, western, southern, eastern and north-eastern covering all the states of the country are already existing. All the regions except north-eastern have fairly well inter-connected systems of 220 kv voltage level with progressive overlay of 400 kv transmision systems. The Union Cabinet in 1981 approved in principle the establishment of a Centrally owned and operated National Power Grid. The National Power Grid would eventually comprise strong regional networks with suitable synchronous HVDC links between the regions. Power Grid Corporation of India Limited (*POWERGRID*), created in October 1989, has been vested with the responsibility of developing a National Power Grid. The development of National Power Grid is an evolutionary process and would be achieved over a period of time through development of the regional grid systems and further inter-connections between the regions. National Power Grid will promote integrated operation and transfer of power from one system to another with ultimate objective of ensuring optimum utilisation of available resources in the country.

In order to promote integrated operation of power systems, the country has been demarcated into five regions, namely, north, west, south, east and north-east. Regional electricity boards were set up in 1964 in each of these regions. Northern region covers Haryana, Himachal Pradesh, Jammu and Kashmir, Punjab, Rajasthan, Uttar Pradesh, Chandigarh and Delhi, western region covers Gujarat, Maharashtra, Madhya Pradesh, Goa, Daman and Diu and Dadra and Nagar Haveli; southern region covers Andhra Pradesh, Karnataka, Tamil Nadu, Kerala and Pondicherry; eastern region covers Bihar, Orissa, West Bengal and Sikkim and north-eastern region covers Assam, Manipur, Meghalaya, Nagaland, Tripura, Arunachal Pradesh and Mizoram.

To coordinate operation of the grids of the constituent power systems and to optimise utilisation of the existing generation capacity, regional load despatch centres (RLDCs) have been set up in each region. RLDCs, hitherto functioning under the Central Electricity Authority/regional electricity boards, are being transferred to *Powergrid* in phased manner. In the northern, western and eastern regions, permanent RLDCs equipped with computer based telemetry and the data acquisition system were establilshed around mid 1980s. In the southern region, RLDC equipped with analog telemetry equipment, mimic board, transducers, speech communication, telex and teleprinters facilities is working. In the north-eastern region, an interim regional load despatch centre is operating. Unfied schemes covering the long-term requirements of RLDC and constituents systems in respect of all the five regions are in different stages of formulation. The schemes in respect of southern, northern, and north-eastern regions have got technoeconomic clearance of Central Electricity Authority while the scheme pertaining tothe eastern and western regions are still under finalisation.

Efficient operation of integrated power systems through moderanised computer-based load despatch centres is vitally dependent on efficient data transfer over distance. Thus there is a need for developing a highly reliable communication network Subsequent to an in-depth analysis of requirements carried out by the Planning Commission, the Central Electricity Authority (CEA)) has developed a Master Telecom Plan for the power sector. Concrete schemes have been framed based on modern communication system. Several such schemes have been techno-economically approved by CEA and most ofthese have also cleared by DOT.

With a number of inter-regional links commissioned during the Eighth Plan period and subsequent years in form of National Grid and the five regional load despatch centres already in operation, National Electric Power System Information Centre (NEPSIC) has been set up which is equipped with PC-based data acquisition system linking all the RLDCs in the country. The data acquired from RLDC is also available at CEA headquarters for getting an overview of current power system status. Teleconferencing and FAX facilities are also provided. The system is fully functional since June 1993.

State electricity boards have been established in 18 out of 25 states. These are mainly responsible for generation and distribution of electricity in their respective states. Arunachal Pradesh, Goa, Manipur, Mizoram, Nagland, Sikkim and Tripura are yet to establish their electricity boards.

Regional co-operation

The first major step in this direction had been the setting up of 336 mw Chukha Hydroelectric Project in Bhutan at a cost of Rs. 243.71 crore with Indian technical and financial assistance under an agreement signed in March 1974. The first unit of the project was commissioned in September 1986 and all the four units of 84 mw August 1988. Since then the project has been generating power, the bulk of which has been exported to India. Bhutan has earned the entire cost of the project in about five years time by export of power to India alone besides their internal consumption.

Gratified with the success of Chukha Project the Royal Government of Bhutan are keen on development of their Hydro Resources for the mutual benefit of the two countries. To this end, India and Bhutan have signed an agreement in February 1994 for implementation of Kurichu Hydroelectric Project (3×15 mw) in western Bhutan at a cost of about Rs. 310 crore on a turn-key basis through NHPC within a period of five years. India and Bhutan have agreed to execute Tala HE Project downstream of existing Chukha Project with an installed capacity of 1,020 mw. Discussions have been held between the two countries and modalities for implementation of this mega project are being worked out.

India had constructed a number of mini/micro hydel schemes at Thimpu (360 kw), Gidakom (1000 kw), Wangdi (3000 kw), Gyesta (1500 kw), Khaling (600 kw), Chenarry (750 kw), Lhuntshi (20 kw) during 1960-80. These projects have been identified for rehabilitation in a phased manner by the Government of India. Proposals for taking up impementation of new mini/micro hydro schemes at Ungrichu, Yonglachy, Dongdichu and Chhalori are under consideration.

Energy Conservation has been identified as one of the major thrust areas in the Eighth Plan, as a part of the National Energy Efficiency Programme, with an objective of saving 5,000 mw of installed capacity by the terminal year of Eighth Plan. Apart from the awareness campaign and launching of demonstration projects in agricultural and industrial sectors for promoting energy efficiency technologies, other main activities relate to organising training programmes and studies in the field of energy conservation. A number of internationally supported projects for cooperation on energy conservation in Indian industries and other areas have also been undertaken.

Concerned with the deterioration in the performance of the thermal power stations in the country, Government of India launched a Centrallysponsored programme for renovation and modernisation (R and M) of thermal power stations to improve their performance. Likewise, a programme for renovation, modernisation and uprating (RM and U) of hydro-electric power stations was formulated by the Central Electricity Authority in 1987. R and M schemes are relevant also in the context of energy conservation and optimum energy usage.

At present, 3,544.58 mw (around 4.4 per cent of India's installed capacity) is in the private sector. The Government of India announced in September 1991 the policy to encourage private enterprises participation in the electricity sector. In pursuance of the policy announcement, the legislation governing the electricity sector was amended in October 1991 and the two part tariff notification was issued on 30 March 1992. The primary objective of the policy was to bring a additionality of resources, increase efficiency in operation and encourge commercial operations in this sector. The response has been encouraging. As on date, interest has been expressed in putting up 196 power projects for a total capacity of 77,720 mw involving an investment of Rs. 2,88,252 crore.

While exploring newer forms of renewable sources of energy is no doubt the ultimate remedy to this global malady, improving energy efficiency is the most urgent task to be addressed by our planners and administrators. Especially when it is simultaneously pursued along with substitution of scarce oil by coal by a quick shift from oil-fired power plants to coal-fired and nuclear-powered ones in a phased manner, there is a chance of making a reasonable dent on the issue of global warming.

Improved energy efficiency conserves the precious non-renewable sources of energy like coal and oils on one hand, and reduces the total carbon emissions indirectly on the other. In fact, no other approach offers as cost-effective an opportunity for limiting carbon emissions as energy efficiency does.

Shifting to more fuel-efficient transportation can sharply reduce carbon emissions, which if left untouched may double by AD 2010 capable of causing considerable rise in global temperature. In fact, the efficiency of US buildings industry and transportation had resulted in freezing the carbon emissions at 1.2 billion tonnes per year between 1973 and 1987. Taking cue from such success stories we in the less fortunate part of the globe could as well employ a combination of energy-efficient methods like improved mass transit, greater use of bicycles for short trips along with a continuous accent on fuel-efficient automobiles to keep the carbon emissions in check.

With 64 per cent of the world's electricity being produced from fossil fuels such as coal and oil contributing as much as 27 per cent of global carbon emissions, it is time we became conscious of the efficiency of motors. It is estimated that the electric motors currently in use can be made 40 per cent more effective and refrigerators 75 per cent more energy efficient without a major shift in technology. What all our technicians and technocrats have to do is to be conscious about the growing importance of preventie maintenance schedules that are often given the go-by due to callousness and abject neglect on the part of the operating staff.

Worldwide, lighting accounts for as much as 17 per cent of electricity use that is responsible for 250 million tonnes of carbon emissions in an year. With the vast scope for expansion of lighting into the rural scene in Indian villages as also the rest of the developing world, the potential hazard on this count is very high by the turn of the century. With a little concern on the part of our electrical engineers and policy-makers of public and private business, it should be possible to cut the consumption of electricity to the tune of 75 per cent even with the present level of technology, according to Hofemeister and Rosenfeld (1988).

Doubling the efficiency of lighting through the use of compact fluroscent bulbs consuming 11-18 watts of electricity to provide as much illumination as the incandescent bulbs that are mostly in use in domestic as well as public buildings that consume at least 60 watts of power is a practical solution to power shortage as well as pollution.

Non-conventional energy

The non-conventional sources of energy are capable of solving the twin problems of energy supply in a decentralised manner and helping in sustaining cleaner environment.

A new strategy and action plan for the remaining period of the Eighth Plan has been formulated. Against the original Plan target of 500-600 mw, the new action plan envisages a four-fold increase aiming at a target of 2,000 mv of renewable energy, through mobilization of institutional financing (including bilateral and multi-lateral funding) and purely private sector investments stimulated through entrepreneur development and a package of incentives. Policy changes have been made in both solar photovoltaics and solar thermal fields to encourage market development and minimize dorect subsidies. This opening up of the market especially for solar photovoltaics, has resulted in greater competition, modernization and cost reduction and in overcoming programme infirmities and encouraging genuine entrepreneurs. Rapid growth of solar photovoltaic and solar hot water industry has started as a result of introduction of incentives and soft loans against the budget-drive subsidy programme. Policies have been pursued to encourage direct foreign investment and collaborations including tapping of NRIs have shown interest and are in the process of setting up of projects such as wind farms, solar plants in the states of Andhra

Pradesh, Gujarat, Karnataka Madhya Pradesh and Kerala.

Inter-agency and inter-ministerial contacts have been pursued to bring about greater involvement of user agencies. Initiatives have been taken to promote renewable energy applications in Defence, Railways, Tele-communications and similar establishments. Initiatives have also been taken to develop joint programmes with the Rural Electrification Corporation for promotion of decentralised renewable systems in villages still remaining unelectrified.

India is today recognised as one of the pioneer country in the field of renewable sources of energy. A three-fold strategy has been pursued by the Ministry of Non-conventional Energy Sources (MNES) for the promotion of new and renewable sources of energy (NRSE). This includes: (a) providing budgetary resources of Government for demonstration projects; (b) extending institutional finance from Renewable Indian Energy Development Agency (IREDA) and other financial institutions, for commercially viable projects, with private sector participation and external assistance from multilateral agencies like World Bank, GEF, ADB etc.; and (c) promoting private investment through fiscal incentives, tax holidays, depreciation allowance, facilities for wheeling and banking power for the grid and remunerative price for the power provided for the grid. The MNES intends to promote a new community of 'energy entrepreneurs' whereas the Government will act as the 'mission leader' giving a special focus and direction to the NRSE sector.

Wind

The total potential for wind energy in the country is estimated to be 20,000 mw. The Central Government intends to create a wind energy capacity of 500 mw in the Eighth Five year Plan. With the achievement of this target India would become a major wind power producer in the world. Asia's largest wind farm cluster of 150 mw is located at Muppandal in Tamil Nadu.

A comprehensive wind mapoing programme to identify prospective sites for wind farming has been undertaken, 179 wind mapping and 83 wind monitoring stations are operational in the country. Eighty sites have so far been identified in the states of Tamil Nadu, Andhra Pradesh, Gujarat, Karnataka, Kerala, Madhya Pradesh, Maharashtra and Lakshadweep. The total capacity of wind energy to be generated is expected to be 3,000 mw in these areas. The installed capacity in the wind farm sector is 370 mw and a number of projects are under installation in tamil Nadu, Gujarat, Andhra Pradesh, Kerala, Karnataka and Madhya Pradesh. Several major developers, particularly from United States such as Cannon, Ford, Seawest, Carter Wind Turbines, Optimum Power, etc., are actively working on large proposals. So far 500 million units of energy has been generated and fed to the grids.

Hydro power

MNES is dealing with the implementation of small hydro power projects upto three mw. The new strategy and action plan aims at achieving a goal of 600 mw of energy power generation during the Eight Plan period through small hydro power projects. This is three times the target originally envisaged for the Eighth Five Year Plan.

Around 2,000 potential sites with an estimated capacity of 5,000 mw have been identified in various states including potential states of Uttar Pradesh, Arunachal Pradesh, Orissa, Andhra Pradesh, Kerala, Madhya Pradesh, Himachal Pradesh, Punjab and the target of 600 mw in the Eighth Plan is expected to cover almost 1,000 sites in different states.

To encourage exploitation of this potential, Ministry has announced a composite scheme for survey, investigation and DPR preparation under which cent per cent cost of survey and investigations and 50 per cent of the cost of DPR preparation is provided as grant, 44 projects aggregating 29 mw for survey and investigation, 36 projects aggregating 52 mw for DPR preparation and in addition 87 projects aggregating to 94.5 mw have been sanctioned under the Ministry's capital subsidy scheme for actual implementation of SHP projects.

Projects of 114 mw capacity have so far been installed and projects worth 220 mw capacity are under implementation. It is anticipated that the potential of small hydro power projects upto 15 mw per site in the country may exceed 10,000 mw. The state governments of Kerala, Karnataka and Tamil Nadu have already signed MOUs with private developers and agreed to lease out a number of sites for private investments in small hydro power projects.

In view of the remoteness and lack of infrastructure and grid in various areas, particularly in the hilly areas, an innovative scheme for providing 50 portable micro-hydel sets upto 15 kw capacity each for local communities in these areas was also launched. A UNDP/ GEF project on optimizing development of small hydel resources in the Himalayan and sub-Himalayan regions become operational with a UNDP contribution of US dollar 7.5 million and counterpart funding of Rs. 22 crore. Thirteen hilly states will participate in the project under which a Master Plan will be evolved and twenty demonstration projects will be installed.

Biomass

Bagasse based co-generation new programme, launched in January 1994, envisages creation of 300 mw power generation capacity during the Eighth Plan. The programme is targeted at around 420 existing and around

90 new sugar mills, where a potential of 3,500 mw of power generation is estimated. The thrust of the programme is towards upgradation of existing co-generation facilities of sugar mills, which basically cater to captive steam and power requirements, to ensure generation of surplus power. A salient feature of the programme is the demonstration project scheme, under which 10-12 selected state-of-the-art projects in major sugar producing states will be provided with 30 per cent subsidy by the Ministry. USAID/GEF have approved a project for alternative biomass co-generation during off-season with funding support of US dollar 12.5 million for technical assistance and to leverage financing for such projects in selected sugar mills. Programmes are also being developed for direct biomass combustion and grid-connected gasification projects using woody biomass and agricultural residues.

Solar

The solar photovoltaic systems are currently being used in the country on a commercial basis for powering a variety of lower power applications in rural, remote and un-electrified areas for lighting and water pumping, power for railway signalling, rural telephones, microwave repeater stations and TV transmissions. Under the new strategy and action plan, one lakh number of solar lanterns initiated for both socially oriented and market oriented schemes. So far, 30,000 solar lanterns have been distributed under the programme. Over 60,000 solar photovoltaic systems with total capacity of four mw have been installed in the country. The socially oriented programme specially meant for designated areas and provide subsidy of 50 per cent of the cost. Solar photovoltaic systems with total capacity of 25 mw are proposed to be installed during the Eighth Plan period.

In August 1993 the Ministry has launched a demonstration project for the deployment of 1,000 solar photovoltaic (SPV) water pumps for agriculture and related uses at a cost of about Rs. 28 crore. So far, 397 pumps have been installed and orders for 625 have been booked. Seven manufacturers have finalilsed business plans and some of them have secured loans from IREDA. The first two 100 kw partial grid interactive solar photovoltaic power projects at Kalyanpur in Aligarh district and Saraisadi in Mau district of Uttar Pradesh have been commissioned. A concept of strengthening of substations with small additions of 20 to 25 kw PV capacity to enhance grid stability is also under examination. In pursuance of the special emphasis being accorded by Government of India for generation of grid quality power from non-conventional energy sources, the Ministry has received several proposals of about 10 mw capacity from prospective promoters in the private sector for establishing grid interactive solar photovoltaic power plants which are being negotiated on build, own and operate (BOO) basis. Three preliminary proposals from American companies have already been received.

Technologies for solar water heating systems and solar cookers have been developed and are being commercialized. Solar thermal systems for various other applications like, solar air heating, crop drying, timber seasoning and water desalination have also been developed and the new action plan envisages their commercialization.

Solar thermal systems are today supplementing thermal energy requirements at various temperatures from 60-380 degree celsius for different domestic and industrial applications including process heating and power generation. One lakh LPD solar water heating system at 8 degrees celsius installed at the Hindustan

Spinning and Weaving Mill, Bombay. About three lakh sq.mt collector area has been installed in the country for various domestic and industrial applications. There are about 3.5 lakh solar cookers used in the country. Solar water heating systems have vast potential to save electricity in domestic and commercial sectors and furnace oil in industrial sector which otherwise are being used for hot water supply. A provision in municipal law is beingmade for mandatory installation of solar water heating systems in functional buildings.

All state governments have been requested to issue directives to local bodies under their control to extend this decision to buildings in private sector by making suitable provision in building bye-laws. A proposal for setting up a 35 mw size solar thermal power project at Maithania village, Jodhpur, Rajasthan based on line focussing collectors has been under the consideration of the Ministry. Detailed feasibility and project reports have been prepared which are under discussion with World Bank, GEF and Government of Germany for soft loan financing.

Rural energy

So far 21.85 lakh numbers of family type biogas plants and 196 lakh improved *chulhas* havebeen installed. Under the new strategy and action plan, it is envisaged to install 10 lakh numbers of bio-gas plants during the Eighth Plan period as against 7.5 lakh numbers envisaged earlier. The strategy for the universalisation of rural cooking energy programmes envisages covering 20-25 per cent of the potential beneficiaries by the end of Eighth Plan.

Integrated Rural Energy Programme (IREP) has been transferred to the Ministry of Non-Conventional Energy Sources from Planning Commission with effect from 1 April 1994. The IREP provides a comprehensive framework for macro level planning of energy requirements of rural areas. The programme is being implemented taking block as a unit, and has been extended in 552 blocks so far. To enhance the effectiveness of the programme at the field levels, inputs from ongoing rural energy programmes are being harmonized and increased involvement and concentration of renewable energy programmes is being planned.

Biomass occupies a predominant place as an energy source in rural India. Fuel-wood requirement has gone upto around 166 million tonnes per year, the availability has declined to about 28 million tonnes, resulting in a deficit of 138 million tonnes per annum. It has been estimated that India is having about 93.69 million hectare of waste lands out of which about 20 million hectare is productive non-forest land which would be able to produce 400 million tonnes fuel-wood per year equivalent to 60,000 mw of power.

Ministry of Non-Comvertional Energy Sources have initiated biomass programme with a view to increase bio-productivity fast-growing short rotation fuel-wood species, suitable for plantation under the given set of agro-climatic conditions through scientific input and to evolve methodologies/package of practices forincreasing the productivity to around 40 tonnes per hectare per year compared to the average forest tree production rate of 0.5 tonnes per hectare per year. Biomass yield ranging from 12 tonnes to 36.8 tonnes per hectare per year have been achieved by the established Biomass Research Centres.

Of the total energy generated in the country, the contribution of animal energy is close to 50 per cent. This is mailny for farming operations and transportation. The MNES has launched a national programme in this field in

March 1994. The programme is implemented in close coordination with the Ministry of Agriculture and involve comunity awareness campaigns about the role of animal energy, support for improvement in equipment, devices and transport vehicles which are animal driven. Under the programme, 15 models of improved bullock carts have been developed.

Energy from urban and industrial wastes

Large quantities of wastes (solids and liquids) are generated in India in urban, municipal and industrial sectors and mostly find their way into the environment with little or no treatment which results in their natural biodegradation with consequent release of methane into the atmosphere. These resources can offer viable option for energy generation with attendant benefits of reducing emission green house gases and minimising environmental pollution.

Considering the far reaching environmental benefits by proper utilisation of various wastes hitherto causing pollution problem, UNDP have agreed to provide technical grant out of GEF fund for development of high rate biomethantion process for energy recovery from all such wastes. In the first phase of the activity concerning utilisation of wastes, a national programme under the GEF assisted project for development of high rate biomethantion processes has been initiated in the Ministry. A National Energy Board has been set up as an apex body to formulate policy and over all management.

India a vast potential of renewable energy sources and a number of technologies have been developed to harness them. A sizeable industrial base has been created in the country in the various renewable energy technologies such as solar thermal, solar photovoltaics, wind, small hydro, biomass etc. An aggregate capacity of about 900 MW has been installed, based on these technologies.

The Indian Renewable Energy Development Agency Ltd. (IREDA) was established in March, 1987 as a public sector enterprise for the promotion, development and financing of New and Renewable Sources of Energy (NRSE) technologies. During 1995-96, IREDA sanctioned laon assistance of Rs. 602.22 crore in respect of 265 projects. Thus, the total number of projects financed by IREDA reached 728 with IREDA's loan commitment of Rs. 1107.48 crore and cumulative disbursement of Rs. 472.49 crore as on March, 31, 1996

National Project Biogas Development (NPBD) was taken up in the Contral Sector during 1981-82 on a country-wide basis. Against the potential of 120 lakh numbers of family tye biogas plants the installation has reached 23.59 lakh by 1995-96. Against the target of 1.60 lakh family type biogas plants during 1995-96, achievement was at 1.71 lakh plants.

Besides family size biogas plants, the Ministry of Non-Conventional Energy Sources is also promoting the setting up of community, institutional and nightsoil based biogas plants (CBP/IBP/NBP) in the country. About 1400 institutional CBP/IBP and NBP plants were installled up to 1994-95. Against annual target of 200 plants during 1995-96, completion has been reported at 228 plants at a cost of Rs. 2.48 crore.

National Programme on Improved Chulha (NPIC) was taken up as a national programme since 1985 and also included in the 20-Point Programme of the Government. Against the potential of 1200 lakh chulhas in the country, 227.35 lakh nos. of chulahs have been installed upto the end of March, 1996. Over 26 lakh improved chulhas have been installed during 1995-96 against the target of 24 lakh chulhas with budget estimates of Rs. 15 crore.

Biomass programme offer an environmental advantage over conventional fuels for various applications as they are by and large ecofriendly. A number of technologies have been commercialised such as briquetting, gastification etc. Incentive are being given for gasifier systems developed from 5 HP to 10 HP for mechanical energy, 3 KW to 5 KW for electrical applications and 7,500 k cal/hr. to 12.5 lakh k.cal/hr for thermal application. work is also in progress on 70 fast growing fuelwood tree species for raising yield and acreage in the country.

India has achieved considerable progress in the exploitation of wind energy during the last few years. A total capacity of 732 MW has been installed by the end of the year 1995-96 of which 684 MW has been installed by the private sector. It is expected to reach 1000 MW by the end of the Eighth Plan and that would place India in the second position in Wind Energy, after USA.

A total capacity of 121 MW has been constructed under the Small Hydro Power Projects (SHP) and 234 MW capacity is under construction. A numbur of financial and fiscal incentives are provided for the speedy implementation of Small Hydro Projects based on water falls, canals, small rivers and streams. Portable mini hydel sets of 10-50 KW capacity have also been introduced by the Ministry. Under the World Bank line of credit, soft loans upto 15 MW capacity are available to private developers from IREDA.

The solar Photovoltaic (SPV) programmes has now progressed from projects of a few KW to hundreds of KW installation for power generation. Two grid connected projects of 100 KW each have been installed at Kalyan Pur in Aligarh and Sarai Saadi in Mau Districts of U.P. These plants, besides meeting the requirements of concerned villages are also providing 25 KW power each to the state grid. Three solar photovoltaic projects to generate electricity of higher ratings are under consideration for the State of Rajasthan.

For accelerated development of solar photovoltaic production, Government has introduced socially oriented and market oriented schemes. The socially oriented sheme is implemented through State Nodal Agencies and involves Central subsidy. The market oriented scheme is implemented through IREDA by providing soft loan assistance. In addition. IREDA is implementing the World Bank assisted SPV Market Development Project. Under the socially oriented scheme subsidy to the extent of 50% of the cost of the system is allowed to all categories of beneficiaries. The special category covers States/UTs with desert areas, islands, hilly regions, as well as Scheduled Castes, Scheduled Tribes, Fishermen, Handloom workerts, village artisans and handicapped persons throughout the country. During tyhe year 1995-96, 680 street lighting systems, 7,470 domestic lighting systems, 44,938 solar lanterns and power plants of an aggregate capacity of 89 Kwp were unstalled.

A National programme has been launched since June 1995 for proper treatment of urban and industrial wastes and the resultant recovery of energy from these sources. In order to speed up the various programmes, a National Bioenergy Board (NEB) has been set up for evolving policy guidance and direction. A number of State Government and Nodal Agencies have initiated projects for energy recovery from industrial and municipal wastes in the country. The Integrated Rural Energy Programme (IREP) is utilising locally available energy resources at the village level which has been extended to 108 blocks, taking the total number to 660 in 1995-96.

Commercial energy

Commercial energy constitutes roughly a half of the energy utilized in India; the rest comes from a variety of non-commercial sources such as firewood, cow-dung, agricultural wastes etc. While the total commercial energy consumption has gone up from a meagre 1,400 megawatts (MW) in 1947 to 64,000 MW in 1990 the per capita consumption of commercial energy is only one-eigth of the global average. But with the growing requirements of industrialization, urbanization, the transport sector and of rural commercial energy requirements, energy is intricately linked to the development of the country.

About 60 per cent of the country's commercial energy is produced from coal and lignite. India has its own deposits of coal and produces around 200 million tonnes each year, making it the fifth largest producer of coal in the world. However, the increasing reliance on this source of energy leads to many environmental problems. Open cast mining leads to degradation of land, deforestation, soil erosion, land slips and disruption of aquifers. Many social and economic issues also need to be taken into account, such as displacement of people, their rehabilitation, and health of the workers.

India's coal is very high in ash content. Disposal of the 35 to 40 per cent ash obtained from burning it is a major problem. Thermal power stations release large quantities of particulate matter. Even the modern plants with electorstatic precipitators cannot adequately deal with the high ash content. While some of the ash is recycled, as yet it is only marginal. A survey conducted by the Central Pollution Control Board in 1984 revealed that only six out of 48 plants surveyed had adequately functioning pollution control equipment. Thirty-one plants had no anti-pollution equipment.

Singrauli in central India is called the Energy Capital of India. With giant coal fired electric power plants having an installed generating capacity of about 20,000 MW, Singrauli has the potential to produce nearly twenty times the total production capacity of the entire nation at the time of Independence.

The complex which generates billions of rupees worth of GNP and exports from India, is a classic example of the environmental impacts of increased thermal power generation and development. Just thirty years ago, Singrauli was a region of tropical forests, rich soils and self-sufficient villages. Today it is a wasteland due to polluted soil, air and water. The levels of particulate matter and oxides of sulphur and nitrogen are ten times the level deemed safe by the Government. With the damming of the Sone river 144 villages were inundated and nearly 300,000 people were displaced. Rapid industrialization of the area led to some of the oustees being uprooted as many as fice times!

About 30 per cent of electric power in India is produces by hydroelectric projects. Though hydroelectricity is a clean and renewable source of energy, these projects have raised many issues such as the submergence of forests, rehabilitation of displaced communities, problems of drainage, soil erosion and seismic impact. The silent Valley project was a significant landmark, where environmental issues played a role in determining whether a hydroelectric power project should be built or not. It was also a landmark in that citizen action finally led to the abandoning of the project. Today, several other hydroelectric projects such as the Narmada, Bedthi, Koel Karo and Vihsnuprayag, and dams at Bhopalpatnam, Inchampalli, Bodhghat etc., are the focus of debates. However, if environmental and social problems are adequately taken care of hydroelectric power generation is perhaps preferable to other sources of energy.

The other sources of commercial energy production contribute a relatively small share to the total, with natural gas acconting for 2 per cent and nuclear energy for about 2.5 per cent. However, nuclear power generation has always raised a lot of controversy because of its potential to cause extreme damage in case of accidents. Another concern is the safedisposal of high-level radioactive wastes. Though India's record in both these areas is good, the possibility of accidents can never be ruled out. In recent years there have been protests against the nuclear power plants at Narora, Kakrapar, Kaiga, Koodankulum and Nagarjunsagar, and against the possible siting of such plants in Kerala.

For domestic energy, liquified petroleum gas (LPG) is fast becoming the most popular cooking fuel, especially in urban areas, being cleaner and more efficient than traditional cooking fuels. The production of LPG shot up from 6,71,000 tonnes in 1985 to 27,64,000 tonnes in 1990.

Of 'new' energy sources, wind energy offers a tremendous potential in India. Small generating units are already producing electricity by this method and feeding it into the power grid. It is estimated that the potential for this energy is around 20,000 MW, making it an important source for the future.

The potential of energy from biomass, wind, direct solar radiation utilization and small hydroelectric power generation is immense. Technologies have been developed to a level where, with all out efforts and proper policy support, these sources can provide almost all our energy needs in the long run.

17

International Co-operation

International co-operation continued to be a thrust area in the Department of Mines during the year 1998-99. Concerted and continued efforts were made to project the mineral sector as an attractive investment destination. The International Co-operation Section of the Department played an active role in achieving this goal, the key objectives being to further strengthen areas of bilateral co-operation with countries where bilateral agreements already exist, and also to enter into fresh agreements with countries which are technologically advanced, and to offer India's assistance in developing the mineral resources of other countries. Attracting foreign direct investment and facilitating inflow of state-of-the-art technologies, was another area where emphasis was laid. During the year 1998-99, the Foreign Investment Promotion Board approved 12 proposals involving Foreign Direct Investment to the tune of Rs. 474 crores in the mining sector.

Indo-French working group on mineral exploration and development

The 12th Meeting of the Indo-French Working Group on Mineral Exploration and Development was held in Paris on 7-8 October, 1998. The meeting reviewed the progress of on-going projects, and expressed satisfaction at the pace at which the projects and programmes were moving. The meeting also discussed new project proposals and prioritised the following five projects for consideration under the Indo-French Financial Protocol: (1) Impact Assessment of Mining Activities in the Subarnarekha River Basin (Geological Survey of India); (2) Pilot Project for strengthening Natural Hazard Assessment in India (Geological Survey of India); (3) Supply of one Electron Probe Microanalyser (EPMA) to Geological Survey of India; (4) Supply of laboratory equipment to Indian Bureau of Mines; and (5) Transfer of know-how for the assessment and economic evaluation of the mineral potential of Kerala State. The estimated cost of these Projects is about FF 49 million.

The 12th Meeting of the Indo-French Working Group on Mineral Exploration and Development concluded with the signing of a Protocol between the Secretary, Department of Mines and the Director General, Energy and Raw Materials, State Secretariat of Industry, Ministry of Economy, Finance & Industry, Government of France on the 8th October, 1998.

Indo-South African co-operation

South Africa is one of the major mineral producing and exporting countries in the world, with the largest known reserves of gold, chromium, platinum and vanadium. The country also has substantial deposits of minerals like coal, uranium, diamonds, iron, zirconium, titanium, felspar, nickel, phosphates, etc. South Africa has an impressive track record of mineral development and holds great potential for meaningful and mutually beneficial cooperation in the mineral sector. Ever since diplomatic ties with South Africa have been established in November, 1993, the Department of Mines has been exploring the possibility of co-operation with South Africa as both countries have some geological similarities.

India and South Africa entered into an Agreement for co-operation in the field of Geology and Mineral Resources on the 7th October, 1997. For the implementation of this Agreement, a Joint Working Group was formed, and the First Meeting of the Working Group was held at Johannesburg, South Africa in August 1998. At the end of the Working Group Meeting, a Protocol was signed in Cape Town on the 18th August, 1998, identifying six projects for mutual cooperation. Secretary, Department of Mines signed the Protocol on behalf of the Indian side, while the Director General, Department of Minerals and Energy signed on behalf of the South African side. The six projects identified for co-operation are: (1) Establishment of a detailed correlation on a formation level between the Karoo sequences in Southern Africa and the Gondwana sequences in India; (2) Geoscience Mapping in the near-shore environment along the eastern Indian coastal margin for the purpose of identifying off-shore diamond deposits; (3) Development of a pre-Gondwana precambrian crustal evolution and metallogenic map for India and Southern Africa; (4) Evaluation of stability of underground mine workings through micro-seismic techniques; (5) Hydro-fracturing for street measurement; and (6) Characterisation and processing of gold, diamond and platinum group of metal ores and to evolve suitable beneficiation processes. With the signing of the Protocol, a beginning has been made for a long and fruitful cooperation between the two countries in the field of geology and mineral resources.

The South African Deputy Minister for Minerals & Energy, Ms Susan Shabhangu, accompanied by a seven member delegation, visited India on the invitation of the Minister of State for Steel & Mines from 27th to 31st October, 1998. The Hon'ble Minister visited the Indian Mining Machinery Exhibition (IMME) '98 at New Delhi and also addressed the Mining Summit.

Vietnam

The Department of Mines and Public Sector Undertakings participated in the 2nd 'Pride of India' Exhibition organised from 23rd to 26th, October, 1998 at Hanoi, Vietnam. The Indian delegation for the Exhibition held encouraging discussions with the Vietnamese authorities and company representatives on enhancing co-operation between the two countries in the mineral sector. Discussion was also held with the Vietnamese authorities from the Pac Lang Gold Joint Venture Project between Hindustan Zinc Limited, LaSource, France and VMC, Vietnam.

Russia

The fifth session of the Indo-Russian Working Group on Ferrous and Non-Ferrous Metallurgy was held in Moscow, Russia on 24-25 November, 1998. The meeting reviewed the progress on bilateral co-operation in the areas identified by earlier Working Group meetings such as technology transfers in copper, zinc and aluminium industries.

Myanmar

The Department of Mines was represented in the Indian delegation which visited Myanmar in October 1998, for bilateral talks for enhancing trade and economic co-operation between India and Myanmar. In the mineral sector cross border co-operation along the Manipur/ Mizoram border has been identified as an area of mutual interest.